Personal Injury Practice

JOHN HENDY QC specialises in personal injury, medical negligence, and industrial relations cases. He is Standing Counsel to the National Union of Mineworkers, the National Union of Journalists and the Prison Officers' Association. He founded and was the first Director of Newham Rights Centre. In 1987 he took silk. He is also co-author of *Redgrave's Health and Safety*, 2nd Ed, 1993, Butterworths.

MARTYN DAY is a solicitor and the joint senior partner of a London personal injury practice. He is head of the firm's environmental team, which specialises in representing plaintiffs. He is also co-author of *Toxic Torts*, 1992, Cameron May.

ANDREW BUCHAN is a barrister whose practice is predominantly personal injury and medical negligence claims. He has written for the *New Law Journal* and lectured on the conduct of personal injury litigation.

JENNY KENNEDY is a Fellow of the Institute of Legal Executives and specialises in personal injury actions.

Personal Injury Practice

The guide to litigation in the county court and the High Court

SECOND EDITION

John Hendy QC

Martyn Day

Andrew Buchan

(with assistance from Jenny Kennedy)

Legal Action Group
1994

First edition published in Great Britain 1992
Second edition 1994
by LAG Education and Service Trust Limited
242 Pentonville Road, London N1 9UN

British Library Cataloguing in Publication Data
A CIP catalogue record for this book is available from the British Library.

ISBN 0 905099 48 6

Phototypeset by Kerrypress Ltd, Luton
Printed in Great Britain by BPC Wheatons Ltd, Exeter

Foreword to the first edition

By the Hon J Melville Williams QC, President of the Association of Personal Injury Lawyers, 1990 to 1994.

Personal injury accidents potentially concern everyone in society. Individually or through family and friends any one of us is vulnerable to the kind of personal tragedy that an accident can bring. Accidents can strike at any time, on the way to work, on holiday, in hospital, as well as on the road or at work. It is vital, therefore, that society should have a system of redress which can deal efficiently, quickly and fairly with the problems created. For such a system to work as it should, it must be administered by well-informed and competent people, in particular the lawyers who operate the legal process.

Twenty years ago, personal injury litigation arose almost exclusively as a result of road traffic accidents or accidents at work; it was relatively simple and was treated by the legal world as neither very important nor very interesting. Although I am afraid that that attitude lingers on, it is disappearing. The press and the public know that this is a subject of vital concern to individuals involved and, largely I think as a result of public pressure, the legal system and the legal process are responding to criticism, much of it fully justified and much based on our own failings. Reforms are being introduced to improve the service to litigants. In particular, the increase in the jurisdiction of the county court, the proposed introduction of personal injury and medical negligence specialist panels and the debate on no-fault liability, if it results in a scheme, will lead to radical changes in the way in which personal injury claims are handled.

In this climate of change and increasing complexity in personal injury cases, it is vital that all those who offer their services to litigants should be fully competent to advise properly and handle a case expeditiously and efficiently. That is why I welcome this handbook, written as it is by three very experienced practitioners, who between them cover the whole range of practice from the moment that the victim comes through the door to the final appeal in the House of Lords and beyond. It has a refreshingly practical approach and will answer all those nagging questions which so often can be solved only by those who have done it all before. The authors have done it all before and in the book they share their experience with the reader, who can use it either as a guide to the whole process or to dip into to solve those awkward and pressing problems that arise in any case, usually at the most troublesome time.

I believe that this book will make a significant contribution to raising the standards of those who practise in personal injury work. Perhaps it can help particularly those whose main practice is in other fields, but who from time to time are pressed by faithful clients to act when there has been an accident, to understand what they should do or to recognise when they need help.

J Melville Williams QC

Foreword to the second edition

By the Hon J Melville Williams QC, President of the Association of Personal Injury Lawyers, 1990 to 1994.

Even in the comparatively short time since the first edition of this very useful handbook was published there have been many important developments in the field of personal injury law. Indeed it sometimes seems as though we are under siege from changes and new regulations. It is all the more important therefore that practitioners have available in a convenient and reliable form a guide to help them achieve justice for their clients. This guide continues to fill that need.

John Melville Williams QC

Preface

This book is intended for solicitors, legal executives and barristers who handle personal injury work. The authors hope that it will be useful to specialists, to those who handle the occasional personal injury case, and to trainees and advanced students alike. It is intended to be comprehensive – covering every aspect of practice from the first interview through to appeal. The text is written to enable the reader to 'dip in' to the book to answer specific problems, as well as to guide the reader through the case, stage by stage.

We have written this book primarily for practitioners who act for plaintiffs. This has been done for two reasons. First of all, because the expertise of the three authors is in plaintiffs' work. Secondly, because the spread of solicitors who handle personal injury claims for plaintiffs is much greater than the relatively small number of firms who do the bulk of insurers' work. This means that many plaintiffs' lawyers are not specialists in this field, though they will usually be pitted against highly experienced defendants' lawyers. This problem was recognised by the 1988 Civil Justice Review.

Between 1990 and 1994 there has been a revolution in personal injury litigation, the key element of which has been the transfer of most work from the High Court to the county court. One of our main objectives has been to explain and clarify the new regime. In addition, the legal aid scheme has been transformed. These radical changes have given rise to some serious procedural problems and it may be a long time before they are properly resolved. As a consequence, in some areas, we have been able only to highlight the difficulties and not to provide solutions.

We have sought not only to write about law and procedures, but rather to focus on the strategies and tactics of the personal injury lawyer. To give these considerations more space, we have not dealt with the substantive law on liability or quantum of damages, nor with the highly specialised areas of practice of medical negligence and environmental law.

The authors would like to express their thanks to Paul Crane, their original editor at Legal Action Group, for his care, patience and inspiration. We would also like to thank his more than capable successor, James Lamb. Jenny Kennedy gave us enormous assistance in the writing of this second edition, as did Helen Curtis, who checked the references, and Carol Ellison, who helped with the chapter on structured settlements. We are indebted to them all. For any errors or omissions that are in the book, we remain responsible.

The law in England and Wales is stated as on 1 May 1994.

John Hendy QC
Martyn Day
Andrew Buchan

Contents

PART V PRECEDENTS

Table of cases

Table of statutes

Table of statutory instruments

Introduction

A lawyer's determination and dedication are as important as skill and experience in conducting a successful personal injury case. The solicitor who starts a case with the objective of avoiding a trial by reaching a settlement is playing into the insurance companies' hands. The solicitor who starts off a case unsure of his strategy and how to pursue it is putting the client's interests at risk. The solicitor who is not prepared to pursue the case relentlessly, with energy and enthusiasm from beginning to end, will fail to achieve the maximum for the client. The catchword of the personal injury lawyer is speed: drive the case towards court as hard and as fast as possible. This strategy, rather than one which has settlement as the objective, is far more likely to result in a satisfactory settlement.

It is, on the other hand, in the interests of defendants to prolong proceedings for as long as possible. Their catchword is delay. The longer they are able to put off paying damages and costs to plaintiffs, the longer they earn interest on that money, and the greater the chance of plaintiffs giving up, disappearing or dying. For insurers handling hundreds or thousands of claims a year, these possibilities are statistically significant.

As Lord Diplock said:[1]

'Where the delay is on the part of the plaintiff, there are some steps, such as obtaining an order for directions or setting down the action for trial, which the defendant may take himself; but it is seldom in the defendant's interest to press on with the trial of the action, whichever view he takes of the plaintiff's chances of success. He has in any event the use during the period of delay of any money which he might ultimately have to pay in damages. Where the plaintiff's chances of success seem good, there is the possibility that he himself will grow impatient of the law's delay and be willing to settle for a lesser sum than he would be likely to recover if the matter were treated expeditiously. Although delay may make a fair trial of the issues more difficult and no one can be certain who will be the loser by

1 *Allen v Sir Alfred McAlpine & Sons* [1968] 2 QB 229.

this, it is likely at first to operate more to the prejudice of the plaintiff on whom the onus of proof lies than to that of the defendants.'

Corporate and institutional defendants, insurance companies and their lawyers have a whole host of stratagems – discussed in the course of this book – to delay the case. By far the best and quickest way of countering these is by pushing the case through the court as speedily as possible. The machinery of the courts, generally speaking, favours the injured plaintiff, and the skilful lawyer can exploit the procedural advantages to the full. When the trial is reached, judges are usually sympathetic to the victim of accident or disease.

Furthermore, as the case nears trial, costs swiftly escalate, interest accumulates and the pressure on the defendants to settle the case increases. It used to be the plaintiff's solicitor's practice to commence proceedings as soon as possible after taking over a 'runnable' case. This approach has had to be modified as a result of the recent procedural changes (discussed in full in the main text) such as disclosure of the medical report and schedule of special damages with the particulars or statement of claim, and the enforced timetable in the county court by which a case will be automatically struck out if not set down within 15 months (or such time as ordered by the court). It is now no longer appropriate to issue proceedings and prepare the case as it proceeds. Much of the preparatory work must now be done before the case is issued. This is called 'front-loading'. In consequence the issue of proceedings must be delayed for the medical report and the schedule of damages to be prepared. These steps should nonetheless be pursued with vigour and when complete and the case is commenced, there is even less reason for delay on the plaintiff's part.

The plaintiff's solicitor must remain 'in the driving seat' throughout, controlling the pace and direction of the case. Waiting for the defendant to do something is to be avoided at all costs. So, also, is merely reacting to the steps the defendant takes. The initiative must be seized at the outset of the case and not relinquished at any stage.

These general principles must guide personal injury lawyers in their use of the strategies, tactics and procedures which are laid out in this book.

Part I

Preparation

CHAPTER 1

Case management

For those practitioners who are intent upon gaining entry to the Law Society's personal injury panel or who are intending to apply for or have gained a franchise for personal injury work from the Legal Aid Board, to devise procedures and ensure compliance with the strict criteria laid down for the administration of cases is obligatory. The requirements of the two structures are onerous and it is not the purpose of this book to replicate what is set out in great detail in the documents provided to applicant solicitors.

In order to keep the initiative, to remain on top of the case, and to run it hard and fast, all lawyers must have in place efficient administrative systems. Such systems differ from solicitor to solicitor and it is not within the scope of this book to indicate a 'best buy'. The best systems will be those with which the solicitor feels comfortable and which work effectively and quickly. The size of the firm is a major determinant of the resources available. What is vital is that each file must be maintained at all times in good order. The test is 'could a colleague who knows nothing of the case pick it up and continue it without difficulty if I dropped dead tomorrow?'.

Files should be returned to the filing cabinet when not in use, rather than piled on the floor in random order; documents and letters must be filed *daily*. All this is commonplace for any branch of solicitors' work. The successful personal injury lawyer, in particular, needs this discipline because of the high number of ongoing cases that must be handled at any one time. An expert personal injury practitioner with an effective staff and the full range of efficient administrative systems often handles 350 cases at any one time; some handle up to 500. Dealing with a smaller number does not excuse using all the administrative systems available; they are as effective and as useful for five cases as for 500.

Also crucial to success is a faultless system of keeping future dates recorded. Such a system may be computerised, or in the form of a diary, or on a wall chart. It is vital that the date recording system is kept outside the file and is checked and updated daily. Most, if not all, specialist personal injury firms use two different systems simultaneously in order to ensure that dates are not missed.

One systematic aspect of personal injury practice which must become habitual is periodic review of each and every file. This is obligatory for franchised solicitors, but is vital for all PI lawyers. Indeed the authors consider, in addition, that, whenever a client's file is considered for whatever reason, important or trivial, the practitioner should mentally review all aspects of the case to ensure that every possible step is being taken and that no time limit is approaching.

A further practice required of franchised solicitors which should be universal is audit of the files of one fee-earner by another. A small but fixed percentage of files is sufficient but the audit should be applied to the files of all fee-earners including the senior partner.

File management

In all types of legal work a practitioner should keep well-ordered files, but for the personal injury lawyer it is particularly important. For the great majority of personal injury cases, little more than 20 hours' work will be spent over what can be a three or four-year period. Cases often have many similarities, and the more cases there are, the more difficult it becomes to remember the stage which each has reached. It is, therefore, important that files are kept in a logical order so that the current position can be quickly assessed. The guiding principle is to keep each category of document on a separate tag and, usually, in reverse chronological order (so as to add to the top of each pile).

The correspondence between the plaintiff's and defendant's representatives ('party and party' correspondence) must be kept separate from the rest. The current state of the proceedings is quickly revealed by the progress of party and party correspondence. The franchised lawyer is required to keep legal aid correspondence and documents on a separate tag or file within a file. Pleadings, medical reports, statements, special damage documents and other expert evidence should each be kept separately. Large cases may warrant keeping each category of document in a separate ring binder or lever arch file. This also facilitates copying to counsel preparing court bundles. All surplus copies of documents, together with papers that are no longer relevant to the current running of the case, should be held together at the back of the file and kept out of the way.

Important dates

For any lawyer handling a heavy caseload, it is impossible to remember every crucial date in all the cases. No deadline is as important as the date on which the statutory limitation period expires (see p281). The Limitation Act 1980 provides that personal injury actions must be commenced no later than three years from the date of the accident or the date when the plaintiff first knew, or ought to have known, the facts which could give rise to a claim, or, if the plaintiff is a minor, three years from his or her 18th birthday. If the action is commenced after that period, the defendant can apply to have it struck out. Unless the court can be persuaded to exercise its discretion – usually if the defendant is not prejudiced – this is very likely to succeed. One of the most common negligence claims against solicitors is for failing to issue proceedings in this limitation period.

The basic principle for statutory limitation periods should be: when in doubt issue a county court summons. There will be times when the expiry of the three-year period is approaching and it appears that there is little chance of the case succeeding. If there are still enquiries being made, it is far better to issue proceedings than to face the possibility of a negligence action. Another vital deadline is the requirement to request a county court hearing date within 15 months of close of pleadings or be automatically struck out (see pp164–7).

There will be many important dates in every personal injury case to be kept in the recording systems: dates for steps in the proceedings, summonses, hearing dates, applications to fix, dates to serve and receive documents. There will be dates for checking replies to queries that have been received and for reminder letters to be sent, dates on which time is to be set aside for special damage calculations, dates for inspections, dates for conferences with counsel, and so on.

A check list on the inside of each file with the standard steps of an action set out against which the practitioner can insert the dates when each task is completed is also of great assistance as a quick reminder of the stage the case has reached.

File reviews

There will be times when, for a period, nothing further can be done to progress a case. A doctor's report, for example, or an extension of legal aid might be awaited. Without a regular review a case may lie dormant for months. Consequently, each file should be checked regularly. Consideration should be given to see if any step can be taken to push the case forward and to ensure that no dates have been, or are about to be, missed. The file review should take place at least once every 6 weeks. Time to carry out file reviews must be set aside and noted in the diary without fail.

File review is time-consuming and contrasts with the speed and efficiency which marks all the personal injury practitioner's other work. It is, however, an essential tool.

Standard paperwork

A significant proportion of a personal injury solicitor's correspondence is repetitious. By keeping standard letters and documents on computer disc – inserting information specific to each where needed – a great deal of time and money can be saved. Documents that can be drawn up on a standard basis include: lists of documents, writs, acknowledgments of service, and summonses. Part V (pp471 et seq) of this book contains a set of standard form documents, the use of which is referred to in each relevant chapter.

Time recording

In litigation, time is money. It is a matter of the greatest importance to the financial viability of personal injury litigation to ensure the development of a good costs-recording system. Making a note of every telephone call and every attendance on the case, with time spent, must become a matter of habit if a solicitor wishes to stay in business. Attendances on clients, witnesses and experts, conferences with counsel, perusing and preparing documents should all be rigorously timed and recorded. As a general principle, because of the standard nature of a lot of personal injury work, there is a rough kind of tariff of charges, depending on the size and complexity of the case; neither the taxing master nor the insurance companies will be impressed by, or pay for, a lot of needless work. The question of whether a particular piece of work will be paid for should never be far from the practitioner's mind.

More and more firms are purchasing off-file time computer recording systems. Amongst the benefits of this are that the practice obtains an estimate of work in progress and the practitioner gains an overview of his or her efficiency in respect of fee-earning hours. Such a system is also a franchising requirement. It is a supplement but never a substitute for the diligent recording of time against each piece of work on the file.

A system which gives a warning as accumulated costs on a case near any limit imposed by a legal aid certificate is a necessity for those doing legal aid work.

Costs in personal injury cases are described in detail in chapter 19 (pp250 et seq).

Communicating with clients

A client who is regularly kept informed and who has confidence that the case is being vigorously pursued will be more likely to accept unpalatable advice than one whose faith in the solicitor has ebbed away with the passing of time. Clients should be systematically informed of significant steps in the case. If no step is being taken for some reason, they should be told at least every couple of months that the case is under review and the reason for any lack of progress.

Legal aid cases require that the client's written authority is obtained for particular steps such as instructing leading counsel. It is wise to obtain written authority for all steps involving significant outlay since the client may have to pay in the end. So written authority to issue proceedings or to obtain a specialist's report should normally be sought. Such practice also makes the client feel he is taking the important decisions and is being kept in touch.

Many clients have an impression of what their cases are worth, based on stories from the press or friends with a 'similar' injury. In many instances, that opinion is totally wrong. Hence, the lawyer must not only explain the true position and the strengths and weaknesses at the outset, but also communicate all developments which may affect the amount of damages recoverable. Then, when discussions about a settlement eventually take place, the client is more likely to understand the true value of the claim.

The complexity of legal issues and jargon places an obligation on all lawyers to communicate clearly, without being pompous or patronising. A significant number of people have difficulty reading and writing, and few will have any familiarity with lawyers or litigation. Plain simple English, short sentences and no legal jargon without explanation are vital rules.

The franchise rules put special emphasis on letters to clients and make specific requirements of the initial letter to the client.

Remuneration

A key part of a profitable law practice is to ensure that there is a good system of billing, obtaining payments on account and paying disbursements promptly. As mentioned above, accurate time recording is essential. Modern technology facilitates all these tasks.

In a private case, the client should receive regular invoices for work done and disbursements paid. Payments on account should be regularly requested, so that the solicitor maintains a proper cash flow.

In a legally aided case, payment for disbursements can be sought either when the invoice is received or when it is quantified but not yet received. There is a standard Legal Aid form (CLA 28) by which applications for payment can be made.

Solicitors may apply for the interim payment of costs in legal aid cases. For those lawyers without a legal aid franchise, applications may be made 12 months after the issue of the certificate and then after 24 and then 36 months. The application is made to the Legal Aid Board on their form CC1/Feb 90. In a system that defies understanding, solicitors will be paid a maximum of 62% of their profit costs for the financial year 1993/4; 70% for 1994/5 and 75% for 1995/6. For those who have a franchise, as a part of the sweetening of the pill, it is possible to claim nine months after the granting of the certificates and to claim, immediately, 75% of the costs.

Except in legal aid cases, counsel's fees must be paid within three months of the delivery of the fee note to the solicitor, unless otherwise agreed in writing. Counsel is under a professional duty to write to the solicitor, and thereafter to report the facts to the chairman of the Bar Council, if the fees are not paid within three months and no satisfactory explanation is received. Therefore, solicitors must ensure that they have money on account in privately funded cases. In legally aided cases, counsel should apply for interim payments to the Legal Aid Board. Counsel must have a record of the legal aid number and date of issue of the certificate for the case. There is a strict period of time during which applications can be made.[1]

The solicitor must have a system that keeps a continuous check on costs incurred, paid out and received, to ensure that s/he is not out of pocket and that experts and counsel are being properly dealt with. There are a number of excellent accounts packages available for word processors. An efficient payments system helps ensure that the various people who are assisting on the case will themselves act in an efficient manner.

1 Civil Legal Aid (General) Regs 1989 reg 100. See, further, reg 101(1)(b) in cases of hardship, and reg 101(2) for payments outstanding for at least six months after an event giving rise to a right of taxation.

CHAPTER 2

Case funding

The first interview

The first full interview with the client forms the bedrock of the case, in terms of both the information given by and to, and the relationship developed with, the client. It is, therefore, a meeting to which time should be given and which should not be squeezed in between other important events. It is important that the person handling the case is introduced at this meeting, if the interviewer will not be the person in day-to-day charge. There are many matters that need to be sorted out at this first meeting, as well as much information that must be understood and assessed. In some cases, a preliminary interview may be necessary before the first full interview, just to consider whether the case is worth proceeding with or not. A precedent telling a client she has no prospect of success is at B7 p334.

For most clients, the whole issue of the funding of a case weighs very heavily at the first meeting. It is, therefore, important that the client goes away fully understanding how the case will be funded and the extent of the financial commitment to it. Whether that discussion takes place at the beginning or end of the interview is a question of style, but time must be spent on this subject before the client leaves the office. The position should be set out clearly in a letter immediately after the interview.

Even if a client is eligible for a legal aid certificate, the cost of an initial interview and any connected work may not be recoverable. Applications for a certificate will take time to be processed and it is not possible to backdate it to incorporate the work done prior to grant. The lawyer usually has to accept that the work will go unremunerated if the case is lost.

Free initial interview schemes

For some lawyers, the prospect of giving a free interview is anathema. In personal injury cases, such a view may well be being 'penny wise and pound foolish'. Free initial interviews are often appropriate in privately funded cases and even more common in cases likely to be funded by legal aid.

It is known that a large percentage of those who are injured in accidents never seek advice on making a claim. Part of the reason for solicitors in this field giving free advice at an initial stage is to give the public the confidence to take that first step. By doing this, solicitors not only provide a service to the community but also enhance their reputations and hence increase their volume of this sort of work. Some solicitors may wish to limit initial free interviews to, say, 30 minutes. If their advice is that the case should proceed, then a longer interview can take place later to discuss matters in greater depth.

The Law Society formalised the principle of unpaid first interviews into a system known as ALAS (Accident Legal Advice Service). From 30 June 1994 this service is replaced by an 'Accident Line'. Members of the public can call the Law Society's Freephone number 0500 192939 and are given details of a nearby solicitor on the Personal Injury Panel (see p77) who will give a free first interview.[1]

The Law Society has also reached an agreement with the key trade unions known as 'Union Law', whereby trade union members are referred to a local solicitor who is a part of the scheme. That solicitor will then give the member free, initial 'diagnostic' legal advice on any matter which is not covered by the union's own scheme.

Green form

Up to two hours of work can be remunerated by the Legal Aid Board if a client is eligible under the legal advice and assistance ('green form') scheme. The only criterion for eligibility is the client's financial position. The merits of the case are irrelevant. The financial limits are rather lower than for full legal aid and the client cannot deduct any items from his/her income other than tax, national insurance and an allowance for each dependant.

There are two financial aspects to consider: capital and income.[2] If the client's capital, less allowances for dependants, is above the capital limit, s/he is not eligible for green form. Net income is assessed by deducting

1 For further information, contact the Law Society on 071–320 5764.

2 For limits, allowances and contribution scales, see Legal Advice and Assistance Regs 1989, as amended each April and published by the Legal Aid Board in the current edition of *Legal Aid Handbook*. Revised figures are given annually in *Legal Action* and the *Law Society's Gazette*.

dependants' allowances from the client's weekly income. Where the net income is below the limit, the client is entitled to green form advice without having to make a contribution. Above that limit, the client is now disqualified from green form assistance.

It is possible to apply for an extension of the green form limit, but this is rarely worthwhile. It is lik to be appropriate only where further initial work is necessary to decide whether the claim has the reasonable chance of ultimate success which is necessary for the full certificate application. For example, if the client does not have a very clear recollection of how a road accident has happened, it may be necessary to apply for an extension of the green form to obtain the police report, in order to reach a conclusion as to whether there is the basis for a full certificate application.

Franchised solicitors are empowered to extend the green form themselves though the board can subsequently disallow the extension (subject to appeal) – see p77.

The legal aid area office staff, who deal with applications for such extensions, are usually reluctant to extend the green form and often suggest that a full certificate application be made instead. They have the power to extend it in appropriate cases to pay for reports from 'costly' experts.[3]

The case

There are a number of ways in which the case can be funded and it is the practitioner's job to consider with the client at the initial interview how this will be done.

Civil legal aid

The principal advantage of having a client with a legal aid certificate is obvious. The claim proceeds with the client secure in the knowledge that, whatever the outcome, his/her maximum liability for his/her own costs is finite, and with the solicitor knowing that whatever happens s/he will be paid for the work done. Legal aid is dealt with more fully in chapter 7 p71 which also deals with franchising (p76).

A second benefit is that a legally aided plaintiff puts the defendant at a distinct disadvantage. Even if the defendant wins, the costs are likely to be limited to the client's maximum contribution. For the plaintiff this means

3 *R v Legal Aid Board ex p Higgins* (1993) *Times*, 19 November.

that, even if it becomes clear during the course of the case that the case is not as strong as it appeared at the beginning, it is often possible to negotiate a settlement simply because economically it may be cheaper for the defendant to settle than to fight and win.

The disadvantages of obtaining legal aid are that the initial application and subsequent requests for authority can add three to four months to the length of the case. It also means that the client/solicitor relationship is diluted by the duty on the solicitor to report to the Legal Aid Board.

In most cases, the benefits easily outweigh the problems, but there are cases where that may not be so. In particular, where liability appears certain, it may be in the client's better interests to pursue the claim without recourse to legal aid. These risks and benefits need to be discussed between the solicitor and client carefully.

The process of obtaining legal aid is relatively straightforward, provided that the solicitor is aware of the Legal Aid Board's two criteria: finance and merits.

Financial criteria

The financial criteria change every year, usually in April.[4] The changed criteria are notified to legal aid practitioners by the Legal Aid Board and are set out in all the main lawyers' journals (such as the *Law Society's Gazette* and *Legal Action*)[5] shortly afterwards. Although the figures change, the formulae remain broadly the same. Officers of the Benefits Agency carry out the assessment of means. Their decisions are subject to judicial review.

In the evaluation of capital, the following are taken into account: bank and building society deposits, all other assets readily convertible into cash (such as shares), the sale value of sizeable capital items (such as boats and caravans), insurance policies which can be cashed in, some items of jewellery and sums that could be borrowed against the client's business interests. The value of the client's home, household furniture, tools and clothing is not included.

Clients with more disposable capital than the upper limit are not entitled to legal aid. The upper capital limit is higher for personal injury cases than for other cases. Those with less than the lower limit are eligible with a nil contribution. Those with disposable capital between the two limits are eligible, but have to make a contribution. The maximum

4 See Civil Legal Aid (Assessment of Resources) Regs 1989, as amended, and current *Legal Aid Handbook*.

5 See for example April 1994 *Legal Action* 21 for 1994/5 rates.

contribution is equal to the difference between the client's disposable capital (which must, of course, be below the upper limit) and the lower limit.

Disposable income is assessed by taking into account the weekly household income, less tax and national insurance but including child benefit. Reasonable costs of the household, such as housing costs (rent or mortgage repayments), council tax payments, costs connected with the client's employment, trade union subscriptions, and travelling expenses, are deducted. A further deduction of a set amount for each dependant is also made.

Where disposable income is below the upper limit, the client receives legal aid. The upper income limit also is higher for personal injury cases. Where income is less than the lower limit, the client receives full legal aid without a contribution. Between the two limits, the client is eligible for legal aid with a maximum contribution of a quarter of the difference between the disposable income figure and the lower limit. Ineligibility on either one of the financial criteria debars the client from legal aid.

Children under 18 are now eligible for legal aid without reference to their parents' resources (see chapter 28). Only the minor's own income and capital are assessed.

Merits of the claim

The criterion of the claim's merits involves an assessment of the chances of success, the likely costs of the case and the likely value of a successful claim.

The Legal Aid Board makes its own assessment of the claim, based on the papers, taking into account the solicitor's opinion. The main question is whether a person 'has reasonable grounds for taking . . . proceedings'[6] ie, a greater than 50 per cent chance of success. Whether a client of moderate means would pursue the claim is sometimes used as the test.

A degree of latitude is given by the regulations to the board's officers in the exercise of their discretion. They must weigh up the three elements: prospects, costs and value. For example, unless a claim were almost certain to succeed, the board would not grant a certificate in a complex case which was worth only a few hundred pounds but where the costs were likely to be many thousands of pounds.[7]

Application forms

Two forms must be completed in every case: CLA 1 and CLA 4 (4A where

6 Legal Aid Act 1988 s15(2).
7 Civil Legal Aid (General) Regs 1989 reg 29.

the client does not receive income support, 4B where she does, and 4F where the client is a child under 16); a third form, L 17, is also needed where the client is employed.

Among other information to be included on form CLA 1 – 'Application for Legal Aid' – are: details about the client and the claim, the proposed defendant, the defendant's likely ability to pay any judgment debt and the prospects, costs and value of the claim. Rather than fill in the details of the claim on the form, it is better to send the client's proof of evidence together with an explanatory letter. On page 4 questions are raised in relation to the outline of the claim that need to be answered. Page 7 is a blank sheet where details of the case are to be inserted. It is sensible to draft a proper statement and enclose that rather than completing the empty sheets. Page 8 has to be signed by both applicant and solicitor and should be read carefully by the client.

Ten pages of detailed questions make up the 'Financial application form' – CLA 4A. Clients in receipt of income support need only complete the one-page form CLA 4B. Form 4A is quite complex and the solicitor should usually go through it with the client. The five or ten minutes that this will take is time well spent if it ensures that the form is completed properly. The client must be warned of what happens when the Board receives the application (see p71).

The 'statement of earnings by present employer' (form L 17) must be completed by the client's employer. The client should, therefore, be asked to take the form to his/her employer to complete immediately. The form asks the employer to state details of the client's current and likely future earnings, details of absences and deductions from earnings. The completed L 17 must be sent with the legal aid application, so the solicitor should keep a diary check to prevent undue delay in its completion.

Making an application

The solicitor should send to the Legal Aid Board the required forms, the client's statement, any correspondence with the proposed defendants (often there will be only the letter before action), the names of their solicitors or insurers, and any other relevant documents or correspondence – whether or not they support the claim.

A letter should accompany the application (see precedent B22 p342). In short, the letter should, in the opening paragraph, confirm that it accompanies an application for legal aid (to ensure that it is immediately passed to the appropriate person in the local area office) and outline the case. It should provide details of the client, how the accident happened, the parties involved and the injuries sustained. The solicitor's view on liability and quantum must be outlined.

It is often useful to suggest the appropriate limitation on the certificate or, where appropriate, to suggest that there should be no limitation at all. The most common limitation imposed is: 'to the close of pleadings, (but excluding setting the action down), discovery and the obtaining of counsel's view on the merits, evidence and quantum.' Other common limitations are: 'investigation and report by the solicitor on the merits and quantum'; 'obtaining counsel's advice on the merits and quantum (and to include the issuing of a protective writ, if necessary)'; 'all unaccepted offers of settlement and payments into court to be referred on to the Legal Aid Board'.

The Board now inserts a standard limitation on certificates restricting the amount of costs than can be incurred without further authority. An application can be made to extend the amount, but it ensures the Board has a closer control than in the past over the scale of the costs it may have to meet if the claim is unsuccessful. The Board normally limits the costs to £2,500 but in more complex cases it can be as hight as £7,500. Whatever the limit it is vital for the solicitor to have systems in place which warn when the impending limit is being approached since expenditure over the limit is irrecoverable.[8]

If the Board has less confidence in the case than the plaintiff's solicitor, counsel's opinion will be requested at the outset. That is sometimes appropriate, but it can also reflect an unduly cautious attitude. Where liability is relatively clear, such a condition should be challenged to avoid delay waiting for counsel before any other steps can be undertaken. (See precedent B23 p343). While it is usual to obtain counsel's opinion before setting the case down for trial, at that stage little time is wasted, since other work can be done simultaneously. Solicitors who do a substantial amount of personal injury work and are successful at obtaining damages – and so avoid calling on the legal aid fund for costs – are more likely to have their opinion accepted by the board. Since 1 April 1990, the board requires a progress report on all cases where the certificate has been in effect for more than 12 months.[9]

Client's contribution

Contributions towards the legal aid fund from the client's income are usually paid by instalments. Contributions from the client's capital are usually paid in a single lump sum. The contribution is then used to pay any costs to be offset against the fund. Where the solicitor is able to agree costs at the end of a successful claim, the client will get back all the

8 *Drummond & Co v Lamb* [1992] 1 WLR 163, HL.
9 Civil Legal Aid (General) Regulations 1989, reg 70; LAB Form CC3/Feb 1990.

contribution and all the damages awarded. If costs are to come out of the contribution and there is a taxation of the costs, the client is entitled to attend the taxation hearing to protect his/her interests. The client will not usually have to pay any more in costs than the amount of his/her contribution, even if the claim is lost.[10]

Franchised solicitors must set out in writing the estimated costs of the case and estimated client contribution. The letter to the client on contribution will also deal with the statutory charge. An example is at Part V B4 p331.

Statutory charge

The statutory charge refers to the claim that the Legal Aid Board has against any damages that are awarded to the plaintiff. Damages must all be paid into the legal aid fund. Costs that are not recoverable from the defendant will then be deducted from those damages before the balance is paid to the client.

This must be explained at the initial interview (with the help of the 'Note' on the back of form CLA 1) and should be confirmed in a letter, either straight after the interview or when the certificate is granted.

Franchised solicitors must set out in writing the effect of the statutory charge on the costs of the case. The letter to the client concerning the statutory charge will also deal with the client's contribution. An example is at Part V B4 p331.

Capped fees

Solicitors must bear in mind that the rate of remuneration for legal aid in payments on account and for unsuccessful cases is subject to a limit imposed on all certificates on or after 25 February 1994 (see further p75).

Emergency certificates

Where an aspect of the case requires urgent action, an emergency certificate may be sought.[11] This may arise, for example, where a

10 Legal Aid Act 1988 s17. This applies only for costs incurred when the legal aid certificate is in force: *Dugon v Williamson* [1964] Ch 59. The costs awarded are not usually higher than the amount of contribution payable under the legal aid certificate: *Barling v British Transport Commission and Woodall* [1955] 2 Lloyd's Rep 393. If there is any doubt about the legally aided plaintiff's means, the court can adjourn the decision on costs, order the plaintiff to swear an affidavit of means, carry out an oral examination of the plaintiff and hear other evidence. The decision can be varied within six years of the order: Civil Legal Aid (General) Regs 1989 Pt XIII.

11 Civil Legal Aid (General) Regs 1989 reg 19.

protective writ must be issued because the limitation period is about to expire, or where a witness needs to be interviewed before s/he emigrates, or where the defendants are about to dispose of a crucial piece of evidence.

In these circumstances, form CLA 3 should be completed and sent with the full application, together with a letter explaining why an emergency certificate is needed. The board will usually make a decision on this part of the application within three to four days. Where necessary, a decision can usually be obtained even more quickly. In matters of extreme urgency, an emergency certificate may be granted by the legal aid board office over the telephone.

Franchised solicitors may carry out emergency work and then seek (within seven days) an emergency certificate (see p77).

It should be made clear to the client that, if the board grants the emergency application but subsequently does not grant the full certificate, it will require the client to pay the costs of the work done under the emergency certificate.

Private funding

From the solicitor's point of view, the easiest way for a case to be funded is for the client to pay personally. Private funding will be necessary where the client does not come within the financial limits of the legal aid scheme, or where legal aid is refused on the merits of the case. There are also cases which could be funded by legal aid but where liability is so clear-cut that the client decides that the backing of a legal aid certificate is not necessary.

A number of plaintiffs' personal injury firms have run their entire caseload without legal aid and without charging their clients.[12] This means that the 70 percent or so of chargeable costs recoverable from defendants on winning cases must cover 100 percent of their actual costs plus the costs of the occasional lost case! A very high degree of efficiency is required for such an operation.

Cases that are directly funded by the client are easiest, in the sense that decisions on the case are made by the client and the solicitor without the involvement of a third party. The need to refer matters to funding bodies always involves delay in running a case.

Where there is a choice, the benefits of private funding must be weighed against the security of knowing that, with the legal aid certificate, a client is very unlikely to have to pay a legal bill if the case is lost.

Where the funding is to come from the client's own pocket, the

12 This practice is now inhibited by *British Waterways Board v Norman* (below).

delicate matter of the timing and method of payment must be raised immediately. The system of charging, including hourly rates, should be explained at the first interview and that should be followed up with a letter explaining the solicitor's charging rates, when these rates change or are reviewed and how 'time' spent on a file is calculated in costing terms. This letter should be a standard letter and include an explanation of the clients' rights to challenge the costs at the conclusion of the case. Two copies of the solicitor's costs letter should be sent to the client, with a request that the client agrees the level of costs by signing and returning one copy. It is often convenient to set out the detailed terms in one document and send it under a covering letter; see precedents B3A and 3B p327. The client must be given a clear estimate of the likely overall costs if s/he wins and if s/he loses, at what stages payments will be required, and how much each is likely to be. The efficient solicitor should ask for payment on account, particularly for disbursements such as experts' reports and counsel's fees, which are payable within three months.

The solicitor must beware of making a contingency funding arrangement which is not yet permissible.[13] It is prudent therefore in a privately funded case to make clear that the plaintiff is liable for the solicitor's costs, win or lose. If after the conclusion of the case the solicitor decides to waive part or all of the costs, that is entirely permissible. See also p22 below.

Trade union funding

Most trade unions offer free legal advice and representation to members who are injured at work. Sometimes accidents on the way to and from work are also covered. Some extend the service to other legal problems. Many have a scheme for paying for a member to have a half-hour consultation with a solicitor on any matter. Unions appoint firms of solicitors and it is almost invariably a requirement of the union's support that the member obtains legal advice from a nominated firm. About 8 million people are trade union members entitled to this form of help. They include retired and unemployed members who may have claims in respect of injury or ill health sustained while at work.

The role of the union is rather similar to the role played by the Legal Aid Board. The union has the right to refuse to support a case if it is not

13 In *British Waterways Board v Norman* (1993) *Times*, 11 November, DC it was held that where there was an express or implied agreement between solicitor and client that the solicitor would look to the client for costs only if the case was won, then the solicitor was prohibited from obtaining an order that the other (losing) party paid the costs, since that would be a contingency fee arrangement and currently unlawful.

satisfied that there is a reasonable chance of success. If that happens, solicitors acting for unions usually advise the client to go elsewhere if s/he wishes to continue the case privately. It is essential to couple that advice with a warning about the limitation period. This should always be given in writing in case of any future dispute.

The advantage to the plaintiff of a union-backed case is that there are no financial eligibility criteria, apart from the requirement of keeping union subscriptions up-to-date. The member does not have to worry about the costs of the case under any circumstances. There is no deduction from the damages, as there is with the legal aid charge; the union will pay all costs shortfalls so that the member receives every penny of the damages. Union cases give the opportunity for the nominated solicitors to build up a body of expertise round the particular kinds of work and workplaces and the particular kinds of accident and ill health with which they frequently deal. They also get to know relevant experts and particular defendants and their tactics.

Insurance company funding

There has been an increase, in recent years, in the number of insurance policies that include financial support for taking legal action in personal injury claims. The policies are usually an extension of household policies and cover the legal costs for the members of the family of the homeowner. Membership of sporting bodies often automatically includes insurance to pursue third party claims in relation to accidents whilst involved in the sport (eg, cycling). Some leisure activities are insurable (eg, sailing) and the client should be asked about these possibilities in relation to a relevant accident. Some motor insurances now provide as standard on comprehensive policies cover for third party claims arising from accidents which occur even when not driving the car. Some credit cards include a measure of cover for claims. These possibilities should not be forgotten when taking instructions and discussing funding.

Unlike the unions, the insurance companies are increasingly willing to allow the insured to choose the solicitor. Like the other funding sources mentioned, insurance companies also reserve the right to withdraw if their solicitors advise that there is no reasonable chance of success.

All these sources of funding require reports to be given at particular stages of the case and invariably when any financial offer has been made. If they consider that the client has unreasonably refused an offer, they reserve the right to withdraw funding. It is the solicitor's job to advise on whether the offer is reasonably or unreasonably refused.

Contingency funding

Contingency fee agreements will, in the future, be possible for both barristers and solicitors.[14] If a case is taken on this basis, the lawyer will be allowed to charge if the case is successful, but not if it is lost. The present proposal is that plaintiff's solicitors will be able to charge an uplift of up to 100% of normal rates (including on the disbursement of counsel's fees). The proposals for barristers were still under debate at the time of writing. The client, therefore, knows that, if the case is won, the damages may be reduced to pay the fees. If the case is lost, the plaintiff remains liable to pay the defendant's costs. It will be possible to insure against defendants' costs and the premium (under current discussions with insurers) is likely to be about £100. This will therefore represent the plaintiff's maximum liability if the case is lost. This standard insurance policy will not be available in medical negligence and other more complex cases (yet to be defined).

The system is substantially different from the American system, where the lawyer receives a proportion of the damages if the case is won, and nothing if it is lost. This is because in the USA neither side pays the other's costs. The stated intention in Britain is to enable litigation, particularly in personal injury cases, by those who are above legal aid limits but who are not wealthy enough to pay in the usual way. The prime concern about the present proposal is that once in place it may be used as a device to restrict legal aid, with the Board declining to fund a case on the ground that the prospects of success are not sufficiently high because the solicitor has not agreed to run it on a contingency basis.

14 When the Courts and Legal Services Act 1990 s58 comes into force. The Legal Aid Board is expressly prohibited from taking into account the fact that the applicant could or ought to have entered into a conditional fee agreement: Legal Aid Act 1988 s15(4A) as amended.

CHAPTER 3

The plaintiff's proof

The plaintiff's proof of evidence is the core of the case. It should, therefore, be well ordered, concise, clear and accurate. Getting it right from the start will save time and effort (often unrecoverable in costs) later. A '**proof**' should be distinguished from a 'witness statement'. The proof of evidence should contain all the relevant evidence of the plaintiff or witness. This might include hearsay, gossip about other witnesses and a whole variety of matters that are relevant because they relate to the issues in the case but are not necessarily for disclosure to the defendants. The 'witness statement', on the other hand, now has a strict legal format and is for disclosure to the defendants. It should therefore contain only that information which is necessary to prove the plaintiff's case and not contain any information that is likely to harm the plaintiff (unless essential) if disclosed (see also p179 below). This chapter looks at the three main problems dealt with in the proof: the description and cause of the accident or ill health; the nature of the injuries or illness; and financial losses.

The client may wish to recount details which are more extensive than the essential information required for the case. However, it is often counterproductive to try to control the client's telling of the story. Letting the client tell the story in his/her own way often provides an opportunity to evaluate the client as a witness, as well as getting the 'feel' of the case. Pertinent questions will need to be asked and the story may be differently expressed by the solicitor in the plaintiff's eventual proof of evidence.

It can be useful to dictate the proof in the client's presence. Mistakes and misunderstandings can then be corrected as the solicitor goes along. When an account is particularly long and rambling, it may be better to take notes during the interview and later dictate the proof in an ordered form.

In some discreet way, the solicitor should endeavour to discover the client's level of literacy. Knowing this will affect communication with the client, and may require more meetings in the solicitor's office than correspondence to the client's home, where an intermediary of unknown skill may be interpreting request and answer. This knowledge will also be relevant to counsel at trial, if the client is asked to read a document in the witness box.

While every case is unique and requires different details to be noted, the nature of the information required is fairly common to each case. A standard format for the proof of evidence should be used to ensure that all basic matters are covered. Always presenting information in the same way saves valuable time when looking in the proof for particular details. The required basics are: the client's full name, date of birth, address, telephone number, national insurance number, hospital reference number, marital status, children, employer's name and address, client's occupation and position. Every proof should bear the solicitor's name and case reference. A guide to the substantive information required in the plaintiff's proof of evidence is outlined below. A specimen proof is set out in Part V A1 p322.

The plaintiff's 'witness statement' for exchange under RSC Order 38 2A and CCR Order 20 r12A is, as mentioned, a different document from the 'proof of evidence' taken initially by the solicitor and described here. Witness statements are dealt with in detail in chapter 13 at pp178–81.

The accident or ill health

The date, time and place of the accident are the starting point. Then will follow the explanation of the accident and why the defendant was at fault. Last of all are the details of injuries. The most common types of accident have similarities from which some basic lines of guidance can be drawn. (Statements/particulars of claim arising out of the kinds of accidents dealt with below will be found in Part V section C.)

Road accidents

The basic question is – how did the accident happen? The answer must be set out fully and clearly, without ambiguity.

A road map should be available to pinpoint the accident spot. Model cars and lorries are also helpful. The directions of the vehicles and/or pedestrians should be clarified – so draft out a sketch plan with the client indicating the route of all relevant participants. Traffic signals and signs should be noted, as well as the width of the road, the lighting, parked cars, and other relevant features in the area.

Photographs should be taken as soon as possible of all relevant aspects of the scene. This can be done by the client, by a friend, or by someone from the solicitor's practice. A professional photographer is not usually necessary at this stage. A useful dating technique is to place the day's newspaper in a corner of the frame of at least the first photograph of the series.

Registration numbers of vehicles should be recorded, as should names and addresses of all the parties and witnesses involved. Scraps of paper on which numbers and names were originally noted must be saved. If the client has taken down details of the insurers of the likely defendant, this may save some time in the earlier stages of the case.

The solicitor should next try to ascertain, from all the information, who was legally liable for the accident and the basis of that liability. Blame in a road accident case is generally a matter of common sense. However, compared with a lay person, the courts look more critically at the standard of care exercised by a car driver.

The client should be asked whether anything was said about blame by the proposed defendant or any of the witnesses at the time of the accident.

The solicitor will always be alive to the possibility of a conflict of interest; one such situation calling for alertness is where driver and passenger wish to instruct the same solicitor. There will be a conflict unless the solicitor is sure the driver cannot realistically be held liable to any extent for the passenger's injuries.

Courts are keen to do justice to injured parties in road accident cases, since it is recognised that insurance companies, rather than the defendant in person, will be footing the bill. Road cases should, therefore, be approached with a certain robustness. Plaintiffs' solicitors should not be too put off if it appears that the client contributed to, or was even the major cause, of the accident. Damages are still recoverable, even if there is a degree of contributory negligence.

As a part of taking the initial statement, the sources of corroborative evidence for the client's story should immediately be sought. These may include witnesses' names and addresses and, more likely, the police who attended the scene of the accident. All road accidents involving personal injury should have been reported to the police, so their official report can be obtained, and the outcome of any prosecution can be ascertained.

The exact nature of the weather can be important in a road accident case. The police report usually notes it but the accuracy must be checked with the client. Where the client is unable to recollect, or if the issue is likely to be contested, the Meteorological Office should be asked for a weather report on the precise area at the particular time. The office will make a charge for giving the information but is usually able to give accurate information in writing relatively speedily. A precedent for such a request is at B42 p355.

Tripping

With the local government expenditure cuts of recent years, the poor condition of many pavements and roads has given rise to an increasing number of accidents. The great majority of clients are elderly people who, having lost the agility of youth, trip over uneven pavements or roadworks. Their claim is usually against the highway authority under the Highways Act 1980 s41,[1] although many claims are made against a utility company or sub-contractor which created the danger.

The courts have held that members of the public must accept that pavements will not be perfectly level.[2] People should, therefore, keep a look out and must accept some risks. By and large, claims where the difference in levels is less than one inch are unlikely to succeed, whereas claims where the difference in levels is greater than one inch are likely to do so. Claims depend on the nature and position of the defect and on surrounding conditions including lighting.[3] The best defence for the local authority is that it regularly checked the particular street and that the defect had arisen only shortly before the accident took place.

Proof of the defect is a crucial part of winning tripping cases. This is all the more important since authorities are often remarkably fast in repairing defects following notification of an accident. A camera and measuring tape should always be available at the office so that, if necessary, a clerk can be sent out with the client to the locus in quo immediately after the interview to take photographs. It is crucial to identify the actual paving stone or obstruction that caused the accident. The exact nature of the defect and, most particularly, the depth or height of the defect must be measured and photographed. Prior to taking the photographs, a ruler or coin should be placed in the hole or against the obstruction, so that the dimensions of the defect are quite clear. Including the day's newspaper in one shot is a convenient way of showing the date of the photographs.

1 The highway authority, usually the district council or metropolitan borough, is under a duty to maintain the highway. The plaintiff has to show that the highway was not reasonably safe and that it caused the accident. The burden then shifts to the defendant authority to satisfy the statutory defence, ie, that it had 'taken such care as in all the circumstances was reasonably required to secure that the part of the highway to which the action relates was not dangerous'. If the highway authority arranges for a competent person to maintain the highway, it must show that proper instructions were given and that the person carried out those instructions: Highways Act s58(1) and (2). See also *Pridham v Hemel Hempstead Corpn* (1970) 114 SJ 884, CA.

2 *Littler v Liverpool Corpn* [1968] 2 All ER 343.

3 *Griffiths v Liverpool Corpn* [1967] 1 QB 374; *Meggs v Liverpool Corpn* [1968] 1 WLR 689; *Mills V Barnsley MBC* (1992) PIQR 291.

As before, the possibilities of corroborative evidence from witnesses should be pursued.

A useful source of information is the Health and Safety Executive's booklet *Watch Your Step* (see bibliography p474).

Work

Many areas of employment are closely regulated by statute. This high degree of statutory protection together with the very developed law of negligence at work put the plaintiff in a strong position in relation to illness or accident at work. These factors, and the court's natural sympathy for the injured, allow the solicitor to take a robust attitude to these cases.

In cases of accidents and ill health arising at work, it is particularly important to understand the nature of the tasks carried out by the client. First, a feel for the workplace should be obtained by asking questions about its size and location, the nature of the work carried out, the number of employees, the nature of the tasks undertaken by the client and the process which gave rise to the accident.

Once a picture of the working environment has emerged, details need to be obtained of the accident itself. If the accident involves machinery, the client might draw the relevant piece. The sketch is only for the plaintiff's advisers and should not be released to the defendants. This is because a machine can often be misrepresented, albeit sincerely, in the client's mind. Only when the workplace and equipment are fully comprehended can the solicitor ask the questions which will give a clear picture of how the accident or ill health occurred and what or who caused it.

It is far more likely in a work case than any other that there will have been witnesses to the accident, witnesses who are traceable and who are happy to help with the case. Their names and home addresses should be obtained. Because of the fear of being penalised by the employer for giving evidence against them, the best way to approach work colleagues should be discussed with the client. It may be best if the client makes the initial approach.

The client should be asked whether there is a shop steward or safety representative and, if so, statements must be obtained from them, even if they did not witness the actual accident. They often have useful information, particularly about the system of work, previous accidents and previous complaints. If the accident occurred because of defective equipment, it should be ascertained whether there is a witness, shop steward or safety representative in the maintenance section who can say something about the piece of equipment, its maintenance, previous similar occurrences, or repairs after the accident.

For many work cases, a sure understanding of the accident is really only possible from photographs or even from a visit (lay inspection). Often an expert engineer needs to be instructed (see chapter 6) and the photographs can be left to him/her. It is usually helpful to attend the inspection with the engineer and the client. Arrangements are made with defendants or the defence solicitors and may be several months away. Check with the client whether the machinery or the workplace is likely to be changed or moved in the meantime. If there are any doubts, the client and/or workmates should attempt to get photographs at once. The solicitor should seek from the defendant's insurers, facilities for immediate inspection and photographs (by the solicitor, if an engineer cannot be instructed in time) and an undertaking to preserve any piece of equipment pending the trial. If the other side refuses to co-operate, the court can be requested to order inspection, photography, preservation, custody and detention of property which may become the subject matter of subsequent proceedings.[4]

The client must be asked whether details of the accident were entered in the firm's accident book. This document is required to be kept in premises to which the Factories Act 1961 applies, in mines or quarries, and in premises where 10 or more persons are employed in a trade or business.[5]

The client should be asked whether any other evidence relating to the accident may be available from the employer, such as an investigation carried out by the employer or the safety committee, or a report in a complaints book or at the first aid centre.

The client may be entitled to disablement benefit, if the accident occurred at work and if national insurance has been paid. The benefit may be claimed up to six months from the date of the accident. If a claim has been made, copies of the application forms, which are partly completed by

4 Supreme Court Act 1981 s33(1)(a); County Courts Act 1984 s52(1)(a) and RSC Ord 29 r7A(1); CCR Ord 13 r7(1)(g).

5 Social Security (Claims and Payments) Regs 1979 reg 25. Also, under Reporting of Injuries, Diseases and Dangerous Occurrences Regs 1985 regs 3 and 5 and Sch 3, employers must keep the following records: a) For accidents: the date and time of the accident or dangerous occurrence; the full name and occupation of the person affected; the nature of the injury or condition; the place where the accident or dangerous occurrence happened; and a brief description of the circumstances. This applies to all accidents requiring admission to hospital for more than 24 hours or incapacity from work for more than three consecutive days. b) In disease cases: the date and diagnosis of the disease; the occupation of the person affected; and the name or nature of the disease. Diagnosis of the disease must be made by a GP.

the employers and contain a description of the accident (possibly with useful statements or information relevant to liability) should be requested from the DSS.

Injuries and illness

The client should be asked to describe the circumstances immediately after the accident, including what happened and who was involved by way of rescue and treatment.

A clear description of the injuries should be obtained, together with details of the treating hospital(s), general practitioner, and any other treatment or therapy (eg, osteopathy or acupuncture) received. The hospital number is also needed, to facilitate correspondence with hospital medical records officers.

Brief information is also needed about the number of hospital visits, operations performed, time spent in the hospital, physiotherapy sessions, time at home convalescing, and, most importantly, time off work. The client should also be asked for details of all current symptoms and any long-term prognosis given by the client's medical advisers. The client should be asked for any personal records of the effects of the accident, for example, in the form of a diary or notes. If symptoms continue, the client should be asked to keep a diary as a nearly contemporaneous record of the impact on daily life.

The client should be asked carefully and sympathetically what effect the accident has had on his/her life. This includes details of social life, sex life, sporting activities, hobbies, housework, DIY and so on. Questions should be asked about relevant pre-existing injuries (if any) and whether any symptoms were persisting at the time of the accident.

Finally, the client should be asked to sign a consent form for disclosure of his/her medical records. The solicitor will usually prepare a consent form seeking disclosure of medical records in relation to the accident injuries and treatment. Sometimes the consent will need to be wider, for example, if there is a suspicion that some pre-existing condition has been exacerbated.

Financial losses

For the great majority of cases, the most important potential area of loss is that of earnings. For those who were in work at the time of the accident, details should be obtained of the type of work, the gross and net earnings, overtime, bonuses, the name and address of the employer, any sick pay received during the period of absence, DSS benefits paid, details of the DSS office and reference number and national insurance number. Any contractual liability to repay amounts received while sick needs to be verified with the client and employer. Further details of the client's tax office should be obtained, including the client's reference number, if known. If not, the NI number will suffice. The client should be asked at this time to sign a consent to disclosure of earnings details. The defendants are entitled to employment and earnings details if loss of earnings is claimed, so it is inefficient not to put them on file at the earliest opportunity.

If the client was in long-term employment before the accident and the period of absence was relatively short, the above information will probably be sufficient. Where the client is unable to return to work on a longer-term basis, a fuller work history needs to be established, with the names and addresses of previous employers, job details and wages earned. If there is any hint that loss of earnings may be difficult to calculate (because not on a fixed and ascertainable salary, for instance), then details of comparable earners should be taken forthwith in case they subsequently move away or lose track of their earnings. If, in the first interview, there is a suggestion that there may be a sizeable future loss claim, it is generally worth obtaining a brief outline of the client's career, but a more detailed discussion can usually be left until later.

All other expenses incurred by the client should be recorded, including travelling expenses to and from hospitals, doctors and so on. Damage to clothing, with an estimate of its value, should be noted. For some cases, there will also be the cost of health care. A client is not under any obligation to use the National Health Service and, if treatment obtained under the private health system can be justified, the defendant has to pay the costs. The solicitor should make sure that the client is aware that costs of private treatment are borne personally (unless there is also private medical insurance) in the event of either the case failing or the court not accepting that it was reasonable to seek private treatment.

An increasing nuimber of people are covered by private health care insurance. It is usual for the policy to include a contractual obligation to repay the insurance company in the event of a successful claim by the client in respect of treatment for which the insurance company has paid.

The courts attempt to place plaintiffs in the same financial position that they held prior to the accident. However, the law requires plaintiffs to mitigate their losses. If the client loses employment, it is imperative that all reasonable efforts are made to find alternative work. All job adverts, all letters seeking work and rejection letters must be retained. A note of all visits to job centres and other employment agencies and all telephone calls in connection with the search for work should be kept.

A major area of financial loss to be considered is that of care and treatment. Many people who are injured may not need professional nursing care but may well require a relative to carry out a caring role during the period of recuperation or rehabilitation. That assistance, even if gratuitous, should be noted and added to the claim. Any payments or gifts made by the client must be noted, as should the nature, times and duration of the carer's work, so that a commercial valuation can be made later. Any loss of wages the client thinks the carer may have incurred should be noted for later confirmation with the carer and the carer's employer.[6]

The client should also be told to make a note of all further expenses incurred during the course of the case and, where possible, to back up expense claims with documentary proof (ie, receipts for taxis, bus tickets etc). It is an unusual case where every part of the financial loss claim can be substantiated by documentary evidence but, the smaller the unsubstantiated aspects of the claim, the greater the chance the client will be fully compensated for all the losses incurred.

Conclusion

The plaintiff's proof and subsequently her/his witness statement should bring out points which will enhance the plaintiff's standing in the judge's eyes: military or community service, sporting achievements and the like – even if not directly relevant (see p236).

The proof should bear the date when it was taken by the solicitor, with provision for the plaintiff's signature and date of signing when s/he comes to read and agrees the typescript. It is remarkable how frequently these dates are omitted from proofs. Such omissions, coupled with use of the client's age rather than date of birth or with phrases such as 'up until six months ago', can render the proof frustratingly defective in the months or years ahead.

The need for the client to state the exact date when the proof of evidence was dictated and when it was subsequently signed can be important if the plaintiff dies during the action and the statement is required to be put in evidence under the Civil Evidence Act 1968. If the

6 *George v Pinnock* [1973] 1 WLR 118; *Donnelly v Joyce* [1974] QB 454. The commercial valuation of care provided by a relative as an item of allowable special damages was confirmed in *Roberts v Johnstone* [1989] QB 878. This applies even if the services are provided by the tortfeasor: *Hunt v Severs* [1993] QB 815.

date of the statement is not apparent from its face, the solicitor will have to refer to attendance notes to establish when it was made in order to complete the notice under RSC Order 38 r22(2).

By the time the proof of evidence is completed, the solicitor must be satisfied that the whole case is understood. The advantage of dictating the proof in the client's presence is that fewer errors and misunderstandings are likely. After the proof has been dictated, the client must be told in the firmest way that any part of the typescript that is unsatisfactory must be corrected and amended. This must be repeated in writing when the typed proof is sent out (see precedent B5 p333). Reticent clients often feel that it is an impertinence to correct the solicitor's draft, especially if it is in formal language with which the client is not familiar. An error arising perhaps from phraseology might thus be perpetuated, with dangers for the future of the case.

Preliminary medical assessment

After the proof has been taken, it is worth discussing with the client the nature of the medical evidence needed, since a medical report will be needed to issue proceedings. Usually an orthopaedic consultant will be required but the client should be told about other specialties (see p57) which the solicitor feels may be necessary, even if not initially. Most people are upset at the suggestion that they might need to see a psychiatrist, neurologist or clinical psychologist and need reassurance that such skills are essential if there is to be any recovery of damages in respect of emotional upheaval or personality change. In fact a psychiatric or psychological opinion ought always to be sought where the solicitor suspects any emotional or mental consequences of the accident and these should be probed, particularly if there has been a head injury. Even if there has not, it may still be worthwhile, since treating hospitals often overlook such subjective symptoms as headache, dizziness, anxiety, sleep disorder, depression, phobias, lack of concentration, irritability or loss of memory. The client should be warned about the nature of the (many) medical examinations likely during the course of the proceedings.

Initial assessment of case

At the end of the initial interview, it should be possible to give an initial assessment of whether the case is winnable, where its weaknesses lie, the possibilities of the client being found partly to blame for the accident and the consequences for damages if this happens. Requirements for further evidence will have to be discussed. The factors which go to make up the award of damages need explanation, though it is unlikely that anything but the broadest assessment of the range of likely damages is possible, or even desirable, at this stage. Finally, the client should be told in outline how the case will proceed, what work needs to be done and how long the whole process will take. This summary of the legal process of the case should be repeated in a letter and is required to be repeated by legal aid franchise firms. A specimen letter is in precedent B6 p333.

At this stage, the solicitor should emphasise that most contact in the future will be by correspondence. Speedy and legible responses by the client are required, as delay in responding to queries from the solicitor may be damaging to the case. Many solicitors supply a sheet of paper and a prepaid envelope when writing to clients or witnesses. If the client has difficulty reading or writing, arrangements must be made for a reader/writer to be quickly available. Further meetings to discuss matters of importance may be arranged but telephone calls, except on matters of real urgency, are unhelpful. While the solicitor can give a considered response to a letter, when there is time to think, a telephone call is likely to find her busy with other cases and without the facts to hand.

Clients need to feel committed to their case and it is, therefore, important that they fully understand the process and can properly weigh up the pros and cons of proceeding. Properly explaining procedures at the beginning helps to gain clients' confidence and also helps to avoid telephone calls from them demanding to know why the case has not yet been settled. Where a client is applying for a full legal aid certificate, the implications must be discussed (see chapter 7).

If the client decides to go ahead with the case, the first job is to list the tasks requiring immediate attention. It is good for 'customer relations' to dictate the letters to the various people described in the next chapter while the client remains in the office. This ensures that the client is confident that the case is already under way, and will help the client to develop a greater understanding of the direction which the case is taking. The client also hears, and can correct, the way that the case is being put at this early and critical stage.

CHAPTER 4

Preliminary correspondence

Letter before action

Contact should be established with the proposed defendant as early as possible after the first interview (subject to having first obtained the evidence in a tripping case, as discussed at p26). This provides the maximum amount of time to resolve any of many potential problems with the defendant, while the rest of the case is being put together. The questions of whether the defendant is insured, whether some other party is blamed for the accident, whether the defendant is still traceable, or indeed still exists, and whether more than one defendant should be joined, are all matters which need to be faced and resolved quickly. In the majority of cases, the letter from the plaintiff's solicitor will be passed on to the defendant's insurers. An early response from them will confirm their interest and answer the above questions (or most of them). It is the cases where no response is received that should particularly put the solicitor for the plaintiff on guard.

Letters before action must contain certain basic elements so that defendants recognise the case that they are facing. Without this information, there can be no prompt settlement, nor can defendants comply with their duty to complete form CRU 1 (see p64) relating to social security benefits.

The letter before action should contain:

- confirmation of the client for whom the solicitor is acting, including the client's name, address and, preferably, date of birth and national insurance number; together with the solicitor's reference
- brief details of the accident and a short description of the role alleged to have been played by the defendant
- an outline of the injuries suffered
- a concise statement explaining why the defendant is liable

- the name and address of the plaintiff's employer (if there is a loss of earnings)
- the suggestion that the letter should be passed on to the defendant's insurers.

The description of the accident, outline of the injuries and statement of liability should be brief and general, even if the solicitor feels sure of the detail of the case. (Standard letters of claim, illustrating these guidelines, are set out in precedents B.12–14 pp337–8). B15 is a tough letter if there is no reply to the initial letter.

Sending a letter before action may cause the client some embarrassment, for example, where it is received by the employer if the latter is small, or by a member of the client's family blamed in a road accident case. In such a case the letter should be written, if possible, to the insurer directly. In most cases the letter will be passed on to the insurers as a matter of routine without difficulty but this is not always the case. The solicitor needs to be sensitive and to talk through any such potential problems with the client.

The letter before action is one of the most important letters in a personal injury action. It is, therefore, useful to dictate it in the client's presence and it is also good practice to send a copy to the client for information.

Key letters

Most of the conduct of a personal injury case is by correspondence. In the main, the correspondence will be with lawyers and institutions familiar with the language and procedure of litigation. Clients and lay witnesses will not usually have the same familiarity with legal language and it is very important in writing to them that clear, straightforward English is used, free from legal jargon.

The first letter to the client after the interview is, as has been stressed, of importance. In it the solicitor will repeat the solicitor's view of the prospects and the basis on which the court will value the claim if successful. The letter will indicate who will be dealing with the client and who is in charge of the case ultimately (and to whom any complaints should be made). Costs rates and the way they are calculated will be provided for clients funding the action themselves, and the statutory charge will be explained to legally aided clients. Franchised solicitors will, in addition, need to set out the estimated costs of the case. The draft proof will be enclosed with instructions repeated to correct and return, signed. The correspondence will list the tasks the client undertook (obtain witnesses' details etc) and will contain a resumé of the solicitor's plan of action.

This initial correspondence with the client may be in one or several letters. Precedents B1–6 cover these points. The letter before action is dealt with above. Below, other standard letters are considered.

Legal Aid Board

The essential letter here is the request for legal aid funding (see chapter 2 pp13–19 and precedent B.22 p342). The Legal Aid Board insists that letters to it start by setting out exactly that which is being requested. The first letter to the board will accompany the application for legal aid (see p16); this should be followed by a resumé of the case, the reasons why the defendant is liable, a short note of the injuries and a rough valuation of the case. It is also useful to state whether the request is for a limited or unlimited certificate.

In cases which are at all complex or where liability is clearly in doubt, the certificate is likely to be limited to obtaining counsel's opinion on the merits, evidence and quantum before grant (or refusal) of the certificate. As mentioned on p17, this takes up time and should be challenged if the solicitor thinks it is unnecessary (see precedent B.23 p343). If the damages claim is very substantial but not particularly complex, the limitation on the certificate is likely to run to close of pleadings and completion of discovery before counsel's opinion is required. For simpler cases, where the damages are unlikely to be large, no limitation at all is usual and the case can be taken through to trial without the need to refer back to the Legal Aid Board.

A standard limitation imposed is that, if any offer of settlement or payment into court is made but not accepted by the client, the case must be referred to the board.

The forms and documents referred to in chapter 2 (pp13–19) must be attached to the letter of application.

Medical practitioners

As soon as the funding of the case is secure, it is usually advisable to apply for a medical report which will substantiate the personal injuries alleged. An early report is almost invariably helpful in maximising damages. Since medical reports usually take months to obtain, a late request for one may significantly delay a settlement of the case. Furthermore, in both the High

Court[1] and the county court,[2] a plaintiff has to serve with the particulars/statement of claim a copy of a medical report, substantiating all the personal injuries, unless the court specifies the period of time within which it is to be provided or makes such other order as it thinks fit, including dispensing with such service or a stay of proceedings. It is possible to rely on later medical reports to cover the client's subsequent progress and treatment, or to introduce a further condition not known at the time of the original medical report. Nonetheless the medical report served with the particulars/statement of claim should, so far as possible, cover all aspects of the client's medical condition, treatment and progress.

It is better that any medical report disclosed under these rules should not contain reference to privileged information – such as the plaintiff's proof. However, if such reference is made the Court will not order disclosure of the document without an unequivocal act of waiver of privilege.[3]

In any event, it is wise to ensure that the nominated doctor has sight of all relevant medical records at the time of reporting, as it is not uncommon for an accident to exacerbate pre-existing medical problems – and sometimes clients attribute pre-existing problems to the accident in question. A comprehensive medical report in the early stages can save embarrassing revisions later on.

The most common injuries in accidents are bruising, damaged ligaments and broken bones, so an orthopaedic report is generally required. Such reports also deal with the usual restrictions on activity which are caused by accidents. Other injuries require other specialties. Some cases require several medical experts (see p57). Whatever the specialty, the choice is either to apply to the hospital where the client received treatment or to appoint an independent specialist. The choice requires some thought and the considerations are dealt with in chapter 6 (pp54 et seq).

If the treating hospital is chosen, it is important to give written details of the client and his/her hospital number (if known), the accident, the injuries suffered and the date and time of admission. The medical records officer should be asked to arrange an appointment for the client to be seen by one of the orthopaedic staff and for the provision of a medical report. Hospitals have their own systems of determining who will write the report, unless a particular person is specified. Usually, cases are dealt with

1 RSC Ord 18 r12(1A).
2 CCR Ord 6 r1(5)–(7).
3 *Booth v Warrington Health Authority* (1992) PIQR 137 and also *AB and others v Wyeth and Roche* (1992) PIQR 437.

by senior registrars. Only in more complex cases is the report written by a consultant. It is good practice therefore to request specifically that the report is prepared by the consultant. It is certain that the defendants will instruct a consultant.

The letter must contain an undertaking to pay the expert's fee. The cost of a first orthopaedic report is usually between £100 and £200. An authority to release the report to the firm of solicitors is also required by many hospitals and, therefore, the client should be asked to sign one to be enclosed with the letter.

If an independent specialist is instructed, a letter must be sent, giving similar details to those provided to the hospital (see B.28 p345). In addition, a letter must be sent to the treating hospital, asking the medical records officer to send a copy of the hospital records to the independent medical expert (see B29 p346). Again, an authority should be signed by the client and sent with this letter (see precedent B.30 p346).

The client should be told to keep a note of any expenses incurred (and receipts) in attending the appointment, as these can be recovered.

Where the case is legally aided, the letter to the medical expert should not be sent until the legal aid certificate has actually been granted. If the case is privately funded, the solicitor should be sure of the funding of the report, since there is a commitment to paying the expert's fee once the letter commissioning the report has been sent.

The letter instructing the medical expert, besides identifying the client, describing the accident and what is known of the injuries, should also point to any specific matters the solicitor thinks should be investigated, for example, an estimate of the costs of treatment likely to be needed now or in the future (as in precedent B.31 p347).

DSS Compensation Recovery Unit

Where the client has been absent from work and/or has been claiming benefits, it is necessary to write to the Compensation Recovery Unit (CRU) of the DSS, asking for details of the amounts paid (see precedent B.37 p352). If the period of sick leave is continuing but the client is likely to return to work within a reasonable time, it is usually easier to wait until s/he goes back to work before writing to the CRU. This avoids having to obtain a second letter updating the first.

Most employees are entitled (under the Social Security and Housing Benefits Act 1982) to statutory sick pay (SSP) from their employers while they are off work. Since April 1986, SSP is payable by the employer for the first 28 weeks off work. Between 1983 and April 1986, it was payable for only the first eight weeks. It is, therefore, usually wise to check with the DSS whether any state benefits have been paid after the expiry of SSP.

An important part of the solicitor's job is to ensure that the client receives full DSS benefits. Clients will then receive the regular income to which they are entitled while off work. This is especially important, as it may be a couple of years before the case is concluded. For those firms with a personal injury franchise, the Legal Aid Board has deemed this point to be of such importance that it insists that at least one member of the firm has to be suitably qualified in welfare benefits and that all the firm's lawyers are able to recognise the need to be able to refer people to the appropriate sources of advice. In the authors' opinion firms of solicitors not similarly equipped will be at risk of negligence suits if state benefits are consequently lost. But if the plaintiff fails to claim state benefits, no deduction from damages is made for failure to mitigate the loss.[4]

Employees who are injured at work are entitled to industrial disablement benefit, provided that sufficient national insurance contributions have been paid prior to the period of absence from work. Those who are injured permanently will be entitled to industrial disablement gratuity, assessed according to the client's level of disability. This assessment is useful evidence in itself. Clients who are injured outside work and who pay the national insurance contribution will be entitled to sickness benefit. For those who do not pay the contribution to the national insurance scheme, there will be an entitlement to income support only.

Police

Usually, the police will become involved in a road accident case if a person has been injured. The officers who attend the scene of an accident make notes of various matters, such as names and addresses of the parties to the accident and the witnesses, car and insurance details, any witness interviews and interviews with the parties themselves. Where the accident is particularly serious, the police will send out one of their technical officers, who will measure skid marks, note the position of blood and debris, take photographs and make a sketch plan. The police often do an on the scene assessment of the vehicles involved in the accident, noting the location of dents and other damage. Sometimes, the vehicle will be taken to a police garage for examination by a technical officer, who will report on every significant aspect of the vehicle and its performance in terms of its potential contribution to the accident.

The police report will contain all this useful information, including

4 *Eley v Bedford* [1972] 1 QB 155.

statements and diagrams, and should be sought (see B.19 p341). The police will not release their full report on an accident until the Crown Prosecution Service has made a decision on whether to prosecute anybody in connection with the accident. This decision must usually be made within six months of the accident. In the meantime, for a reduced fee, an abstract of the accident report may be provided by the police together with police notebooks made up at the time. The police normally destroy their reports three years after the accident; the initial letter to them ought therefore to request that the report is not destroyed until the conclusion of the claim.

If a client is eligible, the report can be obtained under the green form scheme, though an extension will be needed to authorise payment for the report. Alternatively, the report can be obtained under the full legal aid certificate, in which case no extension is needed. By and large, as already stated, it is better to apply straight away for the full certificate and wait until it is granted before seeking the report. Where there are serious doubts about the merits of the case, the report may be needed first to support the application for legal aid. In that case, authority to obtain the police report should be sought under the green form scheme.

Lay witnesses

The first interview will identify potential witnesses other than the plaintiff. Where the client has their names and addresses, it is best to write to them straight away, while the accident remains fresh in their minds. If the client does not know the names or addresses of witnesses, s/he should be asked to obtain them immediately. Any delay runs the risk of losing touch by the witness moving away. An indirect approach (through the client or someone else) may be necessary where a witness fears for his job or was herself severely injured.

Though witness evidence is useful, as a general rule, time should not be wasted waiting for witnesses to respond before taking the next steps in the case. Sometimes, however, witnesses do need to be interviewed before proceeding. This may be the situation where the client has no recollection of the accident.

A letter from the witness is usually sufficient at the initial stage of the claim. Consideration of the letter on its receipt, and subsequently when reviewing the case as it proceeds and the issues become clearer, will dictate whether the witness should be asked for further comments or to attend for interview so that a full proof of evidence can be taken. If the case proceeds to trial, unless the lay witness's evidence appears to be irrelevant, then a witness statement (see pp178 et seq) in accordance with RSC order 38 r2A and CCR Order 20 r12A must be prepared from the proof in order that it can be disclosed. A witness statement should not be prepared for disclosure on the basis of letters: in the authors' view a witness must be seen and interviewed before a witness statement is prepared and subsequently released into the defendant's hands.

The letter to the witness should state the name of the client and give the date, time, place and a brief outline of the accident. There should be a questionnaire with space for the witness's answers. Standardisation of the questionnaire is possible to some extent, but each needs to be adapted to the requirements of the particular case (see precedent B.38 p352).

The essential information to be ascertained (except from witnesses who are only providing evidence of loss, eg comparable earners) is, of course, what the witness saw and heard and who, in the view of the witness, was to blame for the accident and why. The witness should be asked to draw a diagram (which should at no stage be disclosed to the defendant), if that helps define the accident. If an authoritative plan is to hand, include a copy with the letter. Enclosed should be a blank sheet of notepaper, which, like the questionnaire, should have the witness's name, address and the reference number typed in the corner so that it is readily recognisable when it comes back. A stamped addressed envelope must be provided.

If an apparently valuable witness has disappeared, enquiries should be made as soon as possible before the trail goes cold. Competent and sensitive private investigators are available and very effective. In a substantial case the investment can be well worth it.

Employers

Where there is a loss of earnings claim, details must be obtained from the client's employer. Often in work accidents, the employer will also be the defendant. In other cases, the employer will be simply another witness. Consideration needs to be given to the most appropriate time to obtain this information. Where the client has already returned to work and no long-term loss of earnings appears likely, it may well be appropriate to obtain the earnings details immediately. In other cases, it may be worth waiting to see how the client's recovery proceeds before seeking information which will probably need to be updated later.

The nature of the information required should be set out comprehensively and precisely in the letter (see precedent B.41 p354). Follow-up letters to request information omitted or to clarify items is a waste of the solicitor's time and unwelcome to the employer who has to draw up the earnings schedules. The letter should explain why the information is needed and should enclose, if it is known that the employer requires it, an authority from the client to release the information. The letter will then seek the client's gross and net weekly earnings for a period (usually 13 weeks – though this should be extended if any of the weeks were untypical) before the accident. It is useful to ask for a few – say six – weeks' figures after the return to work, to ensure that a change in pay rates has not taken place while the client has been off sick. The employer should be asked for details of all changes in rates and the dates and amounts produced thereby during the period of absence.

The employer should also be asked to confirm the precise dates of absence and to quantify any monies paid out by way of statutory sick pay (SSP) while the client was unwell. Overtime earnings, bonus and pension entitlements should be specifically requested. If there is anything unusual about the pay, such as commission, or where it is difficult to understand the earnings loss, the employer should be asked to explain the position. Confirmation of the client's job title should be considered, in case this is questioned later. The employer must be asked whether the plaintiff is obliged to repay any earnings received during absence and should also be asked to supply a copy of the employment contract or other agreement establishing this.

Most large employers now include a contractual provision to recover payments made to an employee whilst they were off sick as a result of a third party's negligence when the employee recovers money from that party and they will readily respond to a request for details of their continuing outlay. The solicitor ought to discuss with the client who, at the end of the day, should repay the money to the employer – ie, the client direct or the solicitor from the client's damages. The advantage of repayment by the client is that usually the sickness is struck from his or her employment records. If the payment of sick pay is a conditional loan, it should not be deducted from the plaintiff's damages.[5]

Where the client's earnings vary from week to week, comparative earnings figures should be sought for other employees identified by the client as those whose earnings s/he believes are most comparable. Where the client has had a number of short jobs, each of the employers in the period leading up the accident should be contacted.

It is useful to obtain from the client details of the appropriate person to write to within the employing organisation. Some employers are good at responding but many are not. Extracting information from large organisations like local authorities and government departments can be

5 *IRC v Hambrook* [1956] 2 QB 641 at 656-7.

very time-consuming and it helps enormously to write directly to the appropriate person.

Proceedings should not be delayed because of difficulties in obtaining earnings information. Unknown losses of wages can be claimed in the schedule to accompany the statement/particulars of claim by inserting: 'details to be supplied in due course' or 'full particulars will be provided after discovery' (where the defendant is the employer) in which case the schedule should be marked 'provisional'.

Where the employer is also a proposed defendant it is unusual to seek even preliminary discovery of documents relating to liability at this stage, though the possibility is worth considering. Discovery of documents of liability in work accident or ill health cases is dealt with later (chapter 14, p188).

Health and Safety Executive

In all accidents at work, it is worth writing to the Health and Safety Executive (HSE) at the outset to ask whether it has investigated the circumstances of the accident and taken photographs and, if not, whether it has visited the work premises prior to the accident and made any recommendations (see precedent B.43 p356). Because of serious understaffing, investigations are unusual, reports are short and bland, prohibition and improvement notices extremely rare and prosecutions rarer still. Employers are required to report to the HSE accidents to employees involving more than three days off work or longer than 24 hours' hospitalisation.[6]

If the HSE has become involved, it will usually provide form F2508 (the employer's report of a dangerous occurrence to the HSE), a statement of bare factual findings and any photographs it has taken. The HSE does not usually release its formal reports containing opinions, facts and statements until served with an order for 'non-party' discovery, which can usually be made only after proceedings are commenced[7] (see pp46–47). Documents that may be disclosed by the HSE are: form F155 – the factory inspector's report; form F142 – the health and safety inspector's report; correspondence between the HSE and the employer; and form F2508.

6 Reporting of Injuries, Diseases and Dangerous Occurrences Regs 1985 reg 3.

7 Supreme Court Act 1981 s34(2) and (3) and RSC Ord 24 r7A; County Courts Act 1984 s53(2) and (3) and CCR Ord 13 r7(1)(g).

CHAPTER 5

Urgent action

At the first interview, the solicitor must identify any step needing urgent or immediate attention. Some examples are given below.

Protective writs and summonses

Where the limitation date (see chapter 22 p281) is fast approaching, a decision has to be made speedily about whether a 'protective writ' should be issued. A protective writ is the same as any other writ in personal injury litigation. The adjective 'protective' describes the purpose of issuing it at that stage, ie, to protect the client from falling foul of the limitation period. A protective writ can be used in the High Court only, where of course, the solicitor must be able to certify that the case is worth more than £50,000 (see pp95–6).

There is no equivalent procedure in the county court. So, if the limitation period is about to expire while the plaintiff's solicitor does not have full information, eg, a medical report, the best course is to use whatever is available and draft brief particulars of claim (see chapter 10 pp109 et seq). A request should be made in person to the county court to issue proceedings in this form. A fuller amended particulars of claim would then be drafted as soon as possible. This situation is unsatisfactory but currently under review.[1] Alternatively some county courts are amenable to an ex parte default summons seeking extension of time by up to 90 days in which to serve particulars of claim, medical report and schedule of damages.

The solicitor must be alert to the expiry date of the three-year limitation period for commencing proceedings from the very first contact with the client. A surprising number of clients have an unhappy knack of turning up at the office with only days to go before the limitation period

1 See C Harmer *APIL Newsletter* Vol 1 no 5 p7.

expires. The subject of limitation in a personal injury action is complex and the essential questions are dealt with in chapter 22 pp281 et seq. Basically, proceedings must be issued within three years of the cause of action or, if later, the 'date of knowledge', though this may, in some circumstances, be extended.

The maximum period allowed for service is four months.[2] The court has power, upon application, to extend that period up to 12 months, if satisfied that, despite all reasonable efforts, it may not be possible to effect service within the stipulated period.[3] If the validity of the writ or summons has been renewed ex parte without good cause, the defendant has the draconian remedy of being able to apply for discharge of the order for renewal and set aside service. This can result in the plaintiff's claim being statute-barred. Therefore an extension should only be sought in the clearest of cases, eg, where the defendant cannot be traced, or by consent.

If defendants realise that a writ has been issued, they can give 14 days' notice requiring the plaintiff to serve it or discontinue the action.[4]

The deadline for service needs to be entered in the solicitor's diary and filing systems. Quick work is required to consider whether the claim is worth pursuing, and, if so, to obtain all the necessary information to formulate a statement or particulars of claim. To avoid expiry of the limitation period, the writ or summons (unless renewed) must be served at least the day prior to the due time elapsing. In the county court, the particulars of claim is endorsed on the summons.

Where the expiry of the limitation period is about to occur, the client should be advised whether there appears, from the evidence, to be a sufficient prospect of a reasonably strong case. If so, and with the client's authority, protective proceedings should be commenced. When there is insufficient evidence, the question is whether further information could be obtained before deciding whether to continue. A protective writ or summons should be issued where such further investigation is necessary.

The client must be advised against issuing proceedings only if there is no reasonable prospect of success on the information available, and either an attempt to find further information is clearly unlikely to be successful, or such information as may reasonably be found is unlikely to have a material impact on the chance of success. In these circumstances, oral advice should be given clearly and plainly, and reiterated in writing, specifying the time limit within which the proceedings have to be issued or served.

2 RSC Ord 6 r8(1); CCR Ord 7 r20(1). Some county courts seem to allow less time.
3 RSC Ord 6 r8(2A); CCR Ord 7 r20(3).
4 RSC Ord 12 r8A.

Preserving evidence

There will be times when it is imperative that the solicitor acts immediately to ensure that a piece of evidence is available at trial. For example, in 'tripping' accidents, it is important for photographs to be taken before the relevant road or pavement is repaired. There are other cases where vital evidence may also disappear very quickly. Preservation of the evidence, whether by photograph, authoritative report or retention of the object, should be in the forefront of the solicitor's mind from the initial interview.

Crucial witnesses who it is thought may die, emigrate, disappear or change their evidence, may need to be interviewed. The statements of such witnesses, when written, should be signed, dated and preferably witnessed.

With an accident at work, it may take too long for consent to be obtained for a site inspection by the solicitor – let alone an engineer – in order for photographs to be taken. The client, or a colleague or shop steward, may need to take photographs at the work place. Occasionally, the client may feel it will be impossible to do this, other than surreptitiously. The solicitor should not encourage any conduct contrary to any express or implied term in the contract of employment.

While scaffolding structures or buildings cannot be preserved until the trial, the defendant can be asked for an undertaking to preserve such things, or a vehicle, machinery or documents, pending an inspection. An order for such inspection may be obtained.[5] In exceptional circumstances, where there is strong prima facie evidence that the defendants will destroy or materially alter relevant evidence if put on notice of a claim for inspection, consideration should be given to an Anton Piller order to preserve machinery, equipment, documents and other tangible items.[6]

It may be necessary to obtain an expert's report urgently where there is concern that the relevant equipment or building may be altered, removed or demolished. This will require telephoning around the lawyer's own list of experts to find one with time available.

5 Supreme Court Act 1981 s33(1) and RSC Ord 29 r7A(1); County Courts Act 1984 s52(1) and CCR Ord 13 r7(1)(g).

6 RSC Ord 29, 29/2–3/6. The county court does not usually have the power to make an Anton Piller order. An application addressed to the High Court will be deemed to include an application for transfer of county court proceedings to the High Court. After the application has been dealt with, the proceedings will be transferred back to the county court. See County Court Remedies Regs 1991 regs 4 and 5.

Discovery

Sometimes, proceedings cannot be commenced until further documentary evidence is obtained. Where the documents are in the hands of a potential defendant, this evidence may be obtained by pre-action discovery.[7] The defendant must first be asked to provide the documents voluntarily, usually in the initial letter of claim. If the documents are not forthcoming within a reasonable time – usually four to six weeks, depending on the number and complexity of the documents – an originating summons should be taken out and served (see precedent D.16 p451).

The court will order the production of the documents only where it is satisfied that: the defendant possesses the documents or they are in his/her custody or control; disclosure of the documents is necessary prior to proceedings being issued; and the two parties are likely to become protagonists in the action.

The affidavit supporting the application should go into some detail about the reasons for anticipating that there is likely to be a claim, why the documentation is necessary to assist making the decision whether to claim, and why it is believed that the defendants have the documents in their power, possession or control. There is no need to disclose more of the plaintiff's case than is necessary at this early stage.

Where the documents are in the hands of a 'non-party' (ie, a party who is not a potential defendant), there is usually no way of enforcing the production of the evidence prior to the issue of the writ or summons. Exceptionally, if the non-party though innocent, has in some way facilitated the wrong in question, the court can order pre-action disclosure[8]. Once a writ or summons has been issued, a non-party application for specific discovery may be made[9] (see p189). The plaintiff's solicitor should first write to the non-party to request the evidence without having to use legal proceedings.

The plaintiff usually has to pay the costs of non-party or pre-action discovery.

7 Supreme Court Act 1981 s33(2) and RSC Ord 24 r7A(1); County Courts Act 1984 s52(2) and CCR Ord 13 r7(1)(g). For an example of the need for pre-action discovery of the medical records in a personal injury case, see *Seecharran v Streets of London Ltd*, Kemp Vol 2 C4 – O17. The defendants can be ordered to verify their list of documents by affidavit if there are grounds for believing that inadequate disclosure has been given: *M v Plymouth Health Authority* (1993) PIQR 223.

8 *Norwich Pharmacal Co v Customs and Excise Cmrs* [1974] AC 133, HL.

9 RSC Ord 24 r7A(2); CCR Ord 13 r7(1)(g).

Inquests

Where there is an inquest pending in a fatal case, it is almost always desirable to have the client represented by counsel or a solicitor. This will ensure that as much information as possible emerges from the hearing.

The legal aid scheme does not extend to inquests, so any representation has to be privately funded. Work preparatory to representation at an inquest may be undertaken under the green form scheme or under a full certificate granted for a PI claim. If a case for damages is subsequently successful, representation at the inquest should be allowable on taxation. If an inquest is to be held, the coroner should be contacted and told that the client will be represented. This can be done through the coroner's officer whose telephone number is that listed for the coroner's court.

It is occasionally useful to obtain a second opinion on the cause of death recorded in the post mortem report prepared for the inquest. For example, it might be thought that the pathologist is in error (perhaps if death by a rare industrial disease is recorded as death from some more innocent cause). More commonly, a second opinion is a useful step if the pathologist's report is correct, but the cause of death (eg, mesothelioma) may be disputed in the civil proceedings. An independent pathologist should be instructed to make an immediate second post mortem and will supply a report which may be fuller than the original. Legal aid can be made available for this. Usually, it is necessary to apply for an emergency certificate to pay for the pathology report. The Legal Aid Board must be satisfied, however, that there is a reasonable chance of the second opinion uncovering evidence that could be used in a subsequent action.

The law on inquests is developing fast but is beyond the bounds of this book. It is worth noting that pre-action discovery is available prior to, and for use in, an inquest.[10]

10 *Stobart v Nottingham HA* (1993) PIQR 259. There is a useful charity for those needing help, 'Inquest', tel. 081-802 7430.

CHAPTER 6

Collecting evidence

The process of collecting the evidence in a personal injury case continues from the first interview with the client right up to the court hearing itself, during which last-minute instructions will inevitably be needed from experts and other witnesses. This chapter looks at gathering evidence in two parts: liability and damages.[1]

Evidence on liability

Lay witnesses

First of all, there are the people who actually saw or heard the accident, or witnessed the scene soon after or just before it took place. Second, the lawyer must determine whether there are witnesses who can testify about the circumstances prior to the accident, remedial changes (or lack of them) since the accident, previous complaints about the situation and previous similar accidents or 'near misses'. Any evidence which will help to establish that the accident was reasonably foreseeable should also be gathered.

In work accidents, witnesses are usually needed about the system of work and the usual precautions taken for the relevant operation. Safety representatives and shop stewards, in particular, should always be asked for their views and suggestions for further leads and documents. They may have access to – or knowledge about the existence of – memos, letters, reports and minutes of meetings, including health and safety committee meetings. They may be able to supply copies, or provide the basis of an application for specific discovery. Witnesses from the maintenance

1 In the discussion which follows, the possibility of videoconferencing potential witnesses should not be overlooked. Facilities are available from the General Council of the Bar (studio manager, 071–242 1289) in London, Manchester, Birmingham and Wakefield.

section or engineer's department should be sought if equipment may be at fault. Managerial witnesses are worth seeking since their evidence is likely to be authoritative. However, experience shows that they are often unwilling to assist those working under them.[2] The solicitor and plaintiff should jointly decide whether the plaintiff or other colleagues should warn a potential witness that s/he should expect a solicitor's letter and the reasons for it, since many people are frightened by such things. Particular tact may be required for the family of someone killed or an employee fearful of giving evidence against an employer.

Occasionally, it may be worth advertising for witnesses in the local media, at the roadside or through a union or other journal.

It is usually sufficient to obtain the evidence of lay witnesses by means of a questionnaire or letter, at least at the initial stages of a case (see precedent B38 p352). However, if the case is not settled at an early stage, then the witnesses must be interviewed and proofed in the usual way (see precedent B39 p353). From the proof the witness statement will need to be drafted if the witness is to be called, and this will have to be exchanged.

Engineers and other experts

The judgment of whether and when to instruct an independent engineer comes only with experience.[3] (A precedent for instructing an engineer is at B33 p348.) It is common to instruct an engineer in work accidents. There are a number of independent firms of consultant engineers who do nothing but write reports for the purposes of litigation on accidents and injury to health. Their experience of writing reports and giving evidence makes them highly respected by judges. They can usefully explain and illustrate how the accident happened and how it could and should have been avoided.

While most cases can be dealt with by the general consulting engineer, there are cases which require an expert specialising in a specific field of work, such as mining engineering or the ergonomics of work stations. Broadly speaking, it is usually worth having an engineer if machinery or equipment is involved, even for the simplest and most straightforward

2 If a statement is obtained, the court can allow it to be given in evidence (even if a Civil Evidence Act notice has not been served nor a counter notice received) if otherwise it would require the witness to be called to give evidence against his/her employer: RSC Ord 38 r29; CCR Ord 20 r20. The rule does not apply to an ex-employee: *Greenaway v Homelea Fittings Ltd* [1985] 1 WLR 234.

3 The court has an inherent jurisdiction to refuse leave to adduce expert evidence (though it is almost unheard of to do so): *Winchester Cigarette Machinery Ltd v Payne* (1993) *Times*, 19 October.

accident. The criteria applied by some plaintiffs' lawyers when deciding whether to instruct an expert engineer are: if the machinery, equipment or safety precautions require explanation, plans or detailed photographs; if the system of work is challenged; or if the safety of plant or materials is challenged. 'Where it is necessary to show that a prudent employer should have taken precautions not taken by the defendants, there should normally be expert evidence'.[4] The Association of Personal Injury Lawyers (see p473 for address) has a list of engineers. An engineer is the best choice to take the necessary photographs and prepare plans. Engineers are often useful in slipping cases for analysing flooring materials and co-efficients of friction.[5] They are invaluable where dangerous substances are involved.

The plaintiff and lay witnesses should not usually be relied on to explain cause and prevention convincingly to the judge. This is because there is usually an imbalance of expertise. The defendant employer will often have 'in-house' experts, who may be senior operating personnel or engineers familiar with the relevant materials, machines and equipment to give evidence. Expert senior employees often have a tendency to defend 'their' equipment and systems of work against criticism. If the defendants instruct an independent engineer, then the plaintiff should almost always do so too.

Whilst it may be the usual course, it should not be the invariable rule for the plaintiff's lawyer to engage an engineer in work accident cases. There are many accidents which are obviously so simple that the judge may be irritated by the calling of an engineer and may disallow the engineer's costs.

In road traffic accidents, the use of experts is less frequent, since usually the scope of dispute about cause and prevention is straight-forward. However, specialist road traffic accident experts are useful where the accident needs to be reconstructed or its cause established by calculations from the length of skid marks, or the location of accident debris or blood. Lines of sight can be plotted and the speed of the vehicles calculated – this is particularly useful to calculate whether speed limits were being exceeded. The recorded damage to the vehicle and to the body of a pedestrian may provide the evidence for the expert to calculate bodily position and direction at the moment of impact. Ergonomics experts can provide calculations of length of stride to help determine whether a

4 Per Stuart Smith LJ in *Dale v British Coal Corporation (No. 2)* (1992) 136 SJ (LB) 199.

5 See also *Watch Your Step* Health and Safety Executive, HMSO, 1985. This contains measurements of slip resistance for different floor coverings and the relevant legislation.

pedestrian stepped, or ran, into the road. A precedent for instructing a road traffic engineer is at B35 p350.

Specialist experts are sometimes required in other types of accident. An architect or surveyor may be called on where building design or maintenance is at fault. Aircraft, lift, or marine engineers may be needed in relevant cases. The bio-engineering or ergonomics expert is useful in relation to work stations which are often the cause of chronic disability, such as repetitive strain injury (RSI). Academics may be useful in areas of esoteric knowledge, such as highly specialised processes or substances. Handwriting experts are sometimes useful in investigating authenticity of documents.[6] Experts should refer to the recommendations of the British Standards Institution (BSI) where they are applicable. The Court of Appeal has held that BSI recommendations represent the consensus of professional opinion and practical experience on sensible safety precautions. Though not legally binding, they are strong evidence of good practice at the date of issue.[7]

Experts' reports[8] to be relied upon must be disclosed. This is provided for in the automatic directions or may be the result of an order. Disclosure is almost invariably by mutual exchange after setting down. Occassionally for the purposes of an interim payment, for example, an expert report may be disclosed unilaterally by the plaintiff's solicitor. Disclosed experts' reports will in due course need to be included in the court bundle and lodged with the court. Every lodged report must state:[9] the name of the party to whom the expert has given the report (ie, the plaintiff); the date on which it was given; and whether or not it has been agreed.

Police

Whether the police have had any involvement always needs to be considered.[10] If they have, their evidence is likely to be regarded as authoritative by the court and must be obtained in advance. Where the police have investigated an occurrence – which is rare in workplace

6 In a criminal case it has been held that a judge cannot assume the role of a handwriting expert: *R v Simbodyal* (1991) *Times*, 10 October. More flexibility might be allowed to a civil judge.

7 *Ward v Ritz Hotel (London) Ltd* (1992) PIQR 315 CA.

8 For the duties of expert witnesses, see *National Justice Compania Naviera SA v Prudential Assurance Company Ltd* (1993) *Times* 5 March; [1993] 2 Lloyds Rep 68.

9 *Practice Direction (Personal Injuries Action: experts' reports)* [1990] 1 WLR 93.

10 For the principles applicable to bringing civil proceedings when a criminal prosecution is pending, see *Jefferson Ltd v Bhetcha* [1979] 1 WLR 898 at 904–5.

accidents, other than fatalities, but common in road traffic accidents – they will release copies of their notebooks and witness statements on payment of a standard fee. These should always be obtained when available (see pp39–40 and precedent B.19 p341). If there is a full report it is likely to be withheld by the police for up to the 6 months allowed the Crown Prosecution Service to decide whether to prosecute. Reports are normally destroyed after three years unless otherwise requested.

If it appears that an officer might be called to give evidence on behalf of either party, the plaintiff's solicitor should always seek to interview the officer. A more detailed statement than the official one supplied should be taken, in order to assess the strength of the officer's evidence. The police usually make good witnesses in civil cases. They will always require a subpoena.

Documentary evidence

There is an infinite variety of documents which may have some relevance to liability in the client's case. There are, however, classes of documents that are common to most personal injury cases. They are dealt with in chapter 14 pp188–9.

Much evidence will be in the form of documents. Many of these are likely to be agreed by both sides and, therefore, will not require the author to prove the document. As soon as possible, all documents needed for the plaintiff's case which are not agreed by the defendant's solicitor should be ready to be proved by calling the appropriate witnesses. Refusal to agree a non-contentious document – necessitating the author's presence in court – will, of course, be penalised in costs. Service of a notice to admit should be considered, to encourage the other side to heed the costs point (see precedent E.4 p459).

The basis of agreeing documents must be made clear. The agreement may be merely that the document is what it purports to be, or that it is written by whoever purported to write it. Agreement in these terms is insufficient if it is intended to rely on the document as proof of the truth of its contents. Take, for example, agreement about a copy of a police officer's notebook supplied by the chief constable to both sides in a road traffic accident. It may be agreed (i) that the photocopy is merely a true copy of the original; or (ii) that it represents what the officer wrote at the time; or (iii) that what is written is the truth about what happened. Both sides need to be clear what is or is not agreed, so as to have the relevant witnesses available at trial to prove whatever is not agreed.

Many documents are almost invariably agreed as the truth, eg, reports from the Meteorological Office and lists of benefits paid by the Benefits Agency.

Where the author of a document is unavailable, the document may be put into evidence by means of the Civil Evidence Act 1968.[11] A frequent example is the statement of a witness (including the victim of the accident, the original plaintiff) who has died, disappeared, emigrated or is otherwise unavailable. This possibility emphasises the importance of getting proofs signed and dated (see pp31–2). Even where the witness is available, the proof can be served under the Civil Evidence Act and will be admissible if the defendant does not object within 28 days. The weight to be attached to such a proof is, of course, a matter for submissions by both parties to the judge at the hearing.[12]

Photographs, videos, plans, models

Photographs are invaluable. Solicitors, clerks, clients and their relatives and colleagues should all be considered as potential photographers to take pictures of equipment, defective paving stones, skid marks, or scenes of accident, as soon as possible. The date of the photograph, as already stressed, must be recorded. At a later stage, these pictures can be supplemented by more professional photographs by the expert engineer or by a photographer.

Videos are increasingly common to demonstrate injury but are seldom useful on liability unless to illustrate a complex industrial process.[13] Filmed reconstructions of accidents can be considered, but the camera distorts reality and judges are not very amenable to this form of evidence.

Plans and maps are useful, however, and should always be considered. Models are expensive and very rarely justified on questions of liability.

Evidence on damages

Medical evidence

Principally given by doctors, medical evidence is also provided by the plaintiff who will describe the injuries, their treatment and effects in the proof of evidence. In addition, if the plaintiff's injuries are visible at the

11 RSC Ord 38 r29; CCR Ord 20 r20; *Minnesota Mining and Manufacturing Co v Johnson and Johnson Ltd* [1976] RPC 671.

12 Civil Evidence Act 1968 s6(3).

13 In *Ash v Buxted Poultry Ltd* (1989) *Times* 29 November, the court ordered the defendants to permit the plaintiff to make a video film of poultry processing in a repetitive strain injury case.

time of interview, photographs should be taken immediately, before the bruises disappear, scars fade, or plaster casts are removed. Bruising is difficult to photograph and usually justifies a professional photographer, though for more visible injuries 'home snapshots' may be sufficient. The medical report may ultimately render these photographs inessential, but often they will remain a useful supplement.

A medical report is always required, even where the injury appears simple and straightforward, or where all the injuries seem to have healed with no apparent after-effects. This is because a doctor's evidence is the best and most persuasive form of evidence on physical and mental injury. Also, a medical report guards against the danger that both client and solicitor are unaware of some underlying damage or future possibility of symptoms or treatment that only a medical expert could identify.

The first question is whether the medical report should be obtained from the hospital which gave the treatment (the treating hospital) or from an independent expert (see precedent B.28 p345). The advantage of the treating hospital is that the report may be quicker and less expensive, and written with immediate access to all the hospital records, usually by the doctor who treated the plaintiff and saw the injuries on admission. The disadvantages of a report from the treating hospital are that it is usually written by a senior registrar rather than a consultant. Although senior registrars are immediately junior to consultants, their evidence is less likely to persuade a judge if disputed.

Furthermore, a report from a treating hospital will often be short and ill-designed to maximise the client's compensation, which requires reviewing every facet of the way in which the injury affects, has affected and will in the future affect, the client and his/her life. This is because most doctors, including consultants, are not greatly experienced in the process and requirements of personal injury litigation.

There is almost no occasion on which a report from a GP will be adequate. They do not have the status, nor the experience, nor often the time to write an effective report or become an authoritative witness. The defendants will instruct a consultant and, sometimes, a professor of the relevant specialty.

All doctors will require to see the client for an up-to-date medical examination solely for the purposes of their reports, even if the client has only just been seen for treatment. The treating hospital may take a couple of months to send out the appointment to the client and, by the time the report has been written and despatched, four or five months may have elapsed.

If the case is at all complex, it is likely that an expert, who has not treated the client, will be required. It is therefore usually preferable, especially in more serious cases, to go straight to an independent medical expert. One advantage for the client in adopting this procedure as a standard practice is that the solicitor may have built a relationship with a particular consultant, which can be very useful when urgent reports and consultations are needed.

The most appropriate consultants (or in some cases professors) are usually those who do a great deal of 'medico-legal' work. Their knowledge of writing medical reports for court, and giving evidence to judges, means that their evidence is much fuller than that of doctors with little experience of litigation. The need for follow-up letters – asking the doctor to comment on matters missed out, such as future likelihood of returning to the particular physical demands of the plaintiff's work, or the future risk of epilepsy, osteoarthritis or any loss of expectation of life – is often avoided by instructing experienced experts. Since such possibilities will be considered as a matter of course by a medical expert experienced in litigation the solicitor can usually rely on an omission to mention them in the report as indicating that there has been no change in the plaintiff's pre-accident condition. Failure to mention these details by the inexperienced doctor may simply mean that it was not realised that such matters needed consideration.

Plaintiffs' solicitors will quickly get to know those doctors whose reports tend to be sympathetic to plaintiffs and those who tend to accuse plaintiffs of malingering in every case (often expressed in euphemisms such as 'functional overlay', 'compensationitis' etc). Most usefully, practitioners (and judges) get to know those whose reports are fair, balanced and usually unassailable under cross-examination. Some doctors write good reports but tend to try and compromise to a position agreeable to the defendant's expert when at the door of the court. Some tend to write reports of unattractive brevity but can be counted on to stand by their report, and more important, to persuade the judge, in court. Others, who provide both a full report and a firm performance in court, tend to be so overworked that it takes many months to get an appointment.

Building up the necessary knowledge about medical experts will be helped by membership of the Association of Personal Injury Lawyers (see p473 for address). APIL provides names of experts, information and avenues of communication with other lawyers.

The solicitor should note on the file why she chose the particular expert and whether the expert has been used in the past. Not only will this assist the taxing master when the case is costed, but it is essential for the franchised solicitor operating under a legal aid certificate. The expert needs to be on or added to the list of experts which a franchise-holder is required to maintain.

Inevitably, good independent consultants are in great demand and it can often take three or four months to obtain an appointment for the client. They also usually charge more than hospital doctors. Many of the medico-legal experts rely largely on this work for their income, whereas for hospital doctors, fees for reports are a supplement to their NHS salaries.

The independent medical expert is usually a consultant. In very complex cases, or in cases where the injury could be diagnosed in more than one way (such as pulmonary fibrosis), or in esoteric branches of medicine, it may be necessary to seek the opinion of a professor of the relevant specialty. If in doubt, this is a matter to be discussed with counsel.

The expert most commonly sought is an orthopaedic consultant, because most cases involve injury to soft tissue and broken bones. However, other injuries and diseases may require attention from different specialties. The choice of specialist is usually obvious, but it is worth mentioning three particular areas of medicine.

Neurology

Neurologists are, of course, appropriate for lesions of the nerves and brain. In addition, there are those difficult, but all too common cases, where symptoms of pain or loss of power in the back, legs or arms, are said by the plaintiff's orthopaedic doctor to be 'difficult to explain', or said by the defendant's expert to be simply 'compensationitis'. Damage to the nerves, particularly in an injury involving the back, may cause symptoms in the extremities. Usually, a neurologist is appointed by the lawyer as a second consultant and is sometimes able to explain the mechanism by which symptoms, inexplicable by orthopaedic consultants, may have been caused by the client's injury.

Psychiatry

It should be explained to the client that a psychiatrist is invariably instructed by the lawyer where there is some mental, emotional or personality disturbance as a result of the accident or because of the injuries. This will plainly be necessary where there has been a severe reaction. However, lesser symptoms also require full investigation. These include depression, difficulty in sleeping, irritability, swings of mood, depression, headaches, loss of concentration, loss of memory, loss of libido, lethargy, unsociability or fear of using road transport after a traffic accident. Instructing such an expert does not imply doubts as to the plaintiff's sanity. On the advice of the psychiatrist, other associated experts may also need to be instructed, such as clinical psychologists, psychometrists, behaviour therapists and so on.

Sometimes, the psychiatrist will say that treatment such as counselling would help. If so, the costs of this can be claimed on a private patient basis and the psychiatrist must be asked to give an estimate of the likely cost per session and duration of treatment.

Plastic surgery

Where there is scarring, a plastic surgeon may be instructed to consider the prognosis for natural or artificial improvement. If the latter, an estimate of the cost of treatment should be given, which may be claimed as an item of future loss. Consideration can be given to having the improvement carried out prior to trial; it may then be claimed as an item of special damage.

Continuing disability

Where the client may have a provisional damages claim, the medical expert should be asked to give an opinion on whether, at some definite or uncertain time in the future, the plaintiff will, as a result of the injuries, develop a serious disease or suffer a serious deterioration in his/her physical or mental condition. The expert should be asked to predict – even if reluctant to do so – the percentage chance of such worsening and the time span during which it could occur. Common examples of cases which sometimes involve provisional damage awards include: epilepsy, eye injuries, cancer, chest conditions, deafness, spinal injury, and blood diseases. Every case should be considered with this possibility in mind.

As the case develops, the other medical evidence obtained on behalf of the plaintiff, the views of counsel, the experts appointed by the defendants and their reports will all guide the choice of medical expert(s) to be instructed, the final choice of report(s) to be relied on and expert(s) to be called. Automatic directions[14] permit only two medical experts. If more are needed, an application for directions will be required (see pp173 et seq).

Usually, and almost always in cases of continuing disability, defendants will wish to have the plaintiff medically examined and a reasonable opportunity for this medical examination should be given. If it is not, the defendant may apply for a stay of proceedings.[15] It is a

14 RSC Ord 25 r8(1)(c); CCR Ord 17 r11(7)(a).

15 The High Court has an inherent power: *Edmeades v Thames Board Mills Ltd* [1969] 2 QB 67. The county court has a statutory power: County Courts Act 1984 s38; CCR Ord 13 rr2 and 3.

reasonable requirement to stipulate that the plaintiff be accompanied during the examination by a friend or other third party, if the plaintiff is nervous or the defendant's doctor has a reputation for roughness and hostility.[16] The client should be told that the defendants are entitled to have their own medical evidence. The client should be reassured that this is not only normal, but a good sign that the defendant is taking the case seriously!

Defendants can, and usually do, ask for the plaintiff to be examined by a particular doctor. The plaintiff's solicitor can object if there are substantial grounds for refusal. Such a ground may be that the particular doctor is not suitably qualified, or is likely to conduct the examination in an unpleasant manner, or to make a biased report.[17] Also good grounds are that the doctor is too far away or that the examination is not reasonably necessary. Where the defendant's doctor wants to carry out incursive tests or further exploratory operations, going beyond the usual physical examination, objection should be made. The chances of an objection being upheld if the defendants make an application will depend on the court's view of the balance of interests between the parties.[18]

In appropriate circumstances the plaintiff can request a medical examination of the defendant on pain of being struck out.[19] Such an occasion might arise where an allegation is that the defendant was unfit to drive through an infirmity which would have caused a reasonable person not to do so.

Unless the defendant decides to rely on a medical report, there is of course no obligation to disclose it. However, the plaintiff's solicitor should seek the defendant's undertaking to disclose the report before agreeing a medical examination. If necessary, this can be achieved by a court direction.[20] It is possible that, since the plaintiff is now required to disclose a medical report with the statement/particulars of claim, the courts will take a tougher line in requiring disclosure of defendants' medical reports. Accordingly, the plaintiff's solicitor should take a firm stand in insisting on disclosure, usually seeking the defendant's agreement to the following conditions:

16 *Hall v Avon Area Health Authority* [1980] 1 WLR 481.

17 *Starr v National Coal Board* [1977] 1 WLR 63.

18 In *Aspinall v Sterling Mansell Ltd* [1981] 3 All ER 866, the court would not allow examinations involving the use of a hypodermic syringe, the administration of a drug, or exploratory operations. But in *Prescott v Bulldog Tools Ltd* [1981] 3 All ER 869, the court was prepared to allow examinations involving short-term injury, provided that the plaintiff was compensated accordingly.

19 *Lacey v Harrison* (1992) *Times* 22 April.

20 *Jones v Griffith* [1969] 1 WLR 795.

- disclosure of the report as soon as available (or by mutual exchange, if before the service of proceedings or where the plaintiff has a further report)
- no payment in to court to be made pending the defendant's disclosure of the report
- the defendant to pay the plaintiff's reasonable travelling expenses, subsistence and loss of earnings in attending the examination
- an assurance that the medical expert nominated has not previously treated or examined the plaintiff.

Experienced defendant's solicitors are likely to agree only to the third and fourth conditions (although in fact the plaintiff can really only insist on a different expert if the proposed defendant's expert can be shown to be likely to be unkind or unfair). The decision whether to attempt to insist on the first and second will depend upon the circumstances of the case.

Often medical evidence can be agreed prior to the trial and this will save costs and uncertainties. The decision to agree the defendant's report and not to call a doctor requires much attention. It is necessary to ensure that no point in the defendant's favour has been conceded by oversight, and also that the judge is not faced with an irreconcilable difference in the written reports on some aspect. The Court of Appeal has many times deprecated this latter situation.

Agreement of a medical report implies not calling the author, otherwise there is likely to be a costs penalty. Ultimately it must be decided whether these costs might be worth risking. By calling the plaintiff's expert, notwithstanding that the report is agreed, the damages awarded may more closely reflect the full flavour and intensity of the plaintiff's medical expert's view, aspects which might be lost in confining the evidence to the expert's written report.[21] It is important, as ever, to include the client in the decision-making process; he or she may feel very aggrieved to turn up to trial to find his or her own expert doctor not there with no prior explanation. The client's instructions must be obtained before a defendant's medical report is agreed.

The trial judge is entitled, having heard all the evidence, to reject an expression of opinion in an agreed medical report.[22] This is very unlikely to happen, but the possibility should be borne in mind before standing down a medical expert whose evidence has been agreed.

21 In *Dimmock v Miles*, Kemp Vol 2, D4–103, the Court of Appeal held that the judge can insist on oral evidence to supplement the agreed medical evidence.

22 *Stevens v Simons* (1987) *Times* 20 November.

Lay witnesses

The plaintiff is usually the leading lay witness on the question of damages. Testimony will be needed about how s/he was before the injury, the pain and horror of the accident (and treatment), and the subsequent effects on health, happiness, employment, social and domestic life.

These matters should be investigated very closely and not simply left to doctors. Loss of amenity should be a matter for the plaintiff, supported by medical evidence. For example, a cut tendon on the second finger of the dominant hand might not materially interfere with the client's work, social or domestic life. It may, however, end his career as a top amateur darts player, his sole sport and hobby. An elbow injury to the non-dominant arm may impose little limitation on most activities and no pain except when pressed. The injury may, nevertheless, severely disrupt a plaintiff's sex life. A fear of travel in cars and buses as a result of the accident could radically upset the plaintiff's working and social life.

Evidence on these matters may be brought in various ways. Interference with sports and hobbies that were an important part of the plaintiff's life may be graphically demonstrated by the production of medals, cups, photographs and certificates. The effect of an accident can be supported by the plaintiff's spouse, parents, siblings and close friends. The need for this evidence should not be overlooked. Work colleagues, especially managers above the plaintiff, trade union officials, fellow sportsmen and women, school teachers, scout leaders, military officers, holders of religious office and the like should all be considered as potential witnesses.

Such evidence, if likely to be needed at trial, must be taken in the form of a proof and then carefully reduced to a witness statement for exchange prior to trial in accordance with the automatic or other directions.

Care and treatment

Where the plaintiff faces the need (or possible need) for treatment and care in the future – whether an occasional prescription for pain killers or constant nursing care and physiotherapy for life – expert evidence must be produced about those requirements and their cost. The first step is medical evidence about the plaintiff's need for care and treatment. Evidence on costs may be supplied by doctors, but is often best given by experts in the provision of care and treatment. They know precisely what will be provided and at what capital and annual costs. There are nursing experts specialising in this kind of evidence and also physiotherapists, speech therapists, occupational therapists and the like, to deal with particular aspects of treatment. There are architects specialising in accommodation for the disabled, who can deal with costs of new and adapted housing to cater for disabilities. APIL (see p473 for address) can suggest names. A precedent for instructing a care expert is at B34 p349.

The medical and the other evidence must be both comprehensive and consistent. A court will not award damages for 24-hour nursing attendance recommended by a nursing expert, if the doctor says that only an unskilled helper is necessary for three hours a day, five days a week. Even if the care has ceased by trial, and was never provided commercially but by a devoted spouse or neighbour, the cost may be recoverable at a commercial level.[23] Likewise, the commercial cost is recoverable for the future, even if the care is likely to be provided free of charge by a friend or relative.

The cost of future operations or treatment which may be necessary, such as the replacement of an arthritic joint or counselling, should always be claimed. Though most people will be treated by the NHS, the cost of private care is recoverable if reasonable. The court is obliged to disregard the possibility of avoiding this expense by taking advantage of the NHS.[24] Provided that the medical treatment is reasonably incurred, it does not matter if the particular treatment transpires to be unnecessary or more expensive than other alternatives.[25]

Loss of earnings

The primary evidence will be from the plaintiff's employer (or last employer, if the plaintiff has lost or left the job). Usually this evidence is set out in a letter or schedule and agreed by the defendant. If not agreed, an appropriate witness, with all the relevant knowledge, documents and authority, must be called at trial.

All lost earnings from the date of accident to the date of trial must be specified, both gross and net. Only the net loss is recoverable. The losses should be set out week by week, in case there is a challenge on whether specific periods are attributable to the accident and in order to allow the losses to be checked. This will also show changes in the rate of earnings. Usually, the last 13 weeks prior to the accident are taken to produce an average weekly rate of loss as at the date of accident. There is no magic about 13 weeks and a shorter or longer period can be taken if more

23 *Donnelly v Joyce* [1974] QB 454, reaffirmed in *Hunt v Severs* [1993] 3 WLR 558.
24 Law Reform (Personal Injuries) Act 1948 s2(4).
25 *Clippens Oil Co Ltd v Edinburgh and District Water Trustees* (1907) SC HL 9; *Rialas v Mitchell* (1984) 128 SJ 704; Kemp & Kemp, *The Quantum of Damages*, 5–019.

convenient. If the period taken includes non-typical weeks, it is best to ignore such weeks and go back over a longer period so as to obtain a sufficient number of typical weeks from which an average pre-accident week can be calculated.[26]

Increases in earnings after the date of trial are not recoverable where their cause is, in effect, inflation or the change in the value of money.[27] Increases in earnings not the product of inflation, eg, promotion or merit increase, which would have occurred but for the accident, are recoverable. The solicitor should ascertain these possibilities from the plaintiff and get confirmation from higher managers, colleagues and trade union officers. For potential promotions the following must be established: the likelihood, but for the accident; the position and salary of each level of likely promotion; and the likely timespan of the plaintiff achieving each level. Documentary evidence in the form of academic and trade qualifications, assessments, personnel files and reports are relevant and should be sought on discovery. They will certainly be sought by the defendant if such a claim is made. Wage rises prior to trial are likely to be less contentious and the employers' wages department may confirm the increases without the need for seeking evidence from work colleagues.

For the self-employed, the plaintiff's accountant is a necessary witness to show actual earnings and losses. The plaintiff's prospects but for the accident, may require expert evidence from comparable or leading figures in the field of the plaintiff's work and from an employment consultant who will carry out much useful research – even into highly specialised occupations.

The plaintiff who was unemployed at the time of the accident, and remains so, requires evidence from the last employer and possibly from other less recent employers. Evidence of the plaintiff's records from the Inland Revenue may also need to be produced. The number of years to go back will depend on the size of the loss, the length of absence from work following the accident and the period of unemployment. The evidence of an employment consultant will be needed, as well as from comparators, if there is to be any chance of showing that the plaintiff would, in spite of being unemployed at the time of the accident, have obtained work but for it – unless s/he can prove a concrete job offer.

Inland Revenue records and employment consultant evidence is also needed for casual, seasonal, temporary and other 'atypical' workers. Such

26 Loss of earnings, like any other item of special damage, must be particularised and proved: *Hayward v Pullinger and Partners Ltd* [1950] WN 135; *Bonham-Carter v Hyde Park Hotel Ltd* (1948) 64 TLR 177.

27 *Mallet v McMonagle* [1970] AC 166, per Lord Diplock at 176.

plaintiffs may well require evidence from potential employers, trade union officials, colleagues in the same line of business or other experts who can vouch for the availability of work, and the level of earnings which the plaintiff might have achieved.

Employment consultants, who specialise in providing evidence of earnings and job availability in whatever locality and trade the plaintiff may be in, are extremely useful in many situations beyond those referred to specifically above. Their reports are the product of skilled knowledge, research in the particular case, and their courtroom experience. A precedent for instructing an employment expert is at B36 p351.

An employment consultant is classified, in relation to automatic directions, as a non-medical expert so the solicitor should ensure that there is sufficient provision made to call the employment consultant. Again, as when a medical expert is chosen, the solicitor should note on the file why that particular employment expert has been chosen.

If the defendants allege that the plaintiff can obtain better-paid employment, any request by them to have the plaintiff interviewed by their employment consultant should be refused. The expert can only give evidence on the present and future state of the job market and there is no need for an interview.[28]

Much of the evidence mentioned above will also be needed for a claim for loss of earning capacity (ie, handicap on the labour market) – see pp214–5.

Clawback of social security benefits

It is necessary to know the amount of benefits that the plaintiff has received in order that statutory deductions from compensation ('clawback') can be calculated for the schedule of damages.[29] All enquiries about benefits, including small payments, are dealt with by the Compensation Recovery Unit (CRU) (see p473 for address). Information from the CRU should be carefully checked.[30]

The plaintiff's letter before action to the defendant should specify the following information: the plaintiff's name, address, date of birth, national insurance number (wherever possible), and a brief description of the injuries, as in precedents B12–14 pp337–8. (The more precise the description, the easier it will be for the DSS to eliminate unrelated benefit

28 *Larby v Thurgood* (1993) PIQR 218.

29 An agreement that the statutory deduction from damages is not to be made must be express: *Rees v West Glamorgan CC* (1994) PIQR 37.

30 See the useful article by D Roberts, 'A Simple Case of Writing to the CRU?', *PMILL* Vol 10, No 1.

claims). If the claim does not involve the employer as defendant, the name and address of the plaintiff's employer (if any) should be given. If the plaintiff was already receiving a benefit before the accident it is prudent to ask the defendant to include this information in form CRU1 so that it can be discounted as a relevant benefit from the start.

The defendant is under a duty to notify the information to the CRU by completing form CRU1, unless the compensation payment is an exempt payment – see below. The CRU will acknowledge the notification by returning form CRU4 to the defendant's solicitor, and the plaintiff's solicitor is given confirmation of the benefits paid as a result of the injury or disease.

The plaintiff's solicitor may apply to the CRU for benefit information at any time (see precedent B.36 p351). That information will not be copied to the defendant. If negotiations are in progress and the defendant has not yet obtained details of benefits paid, it will be a useful piece of information for the plaintiff's lawyer to have in reserve. It will give the sum that should be deducted by the defendant before making any payment and therefore enable the plaintiff to evaluate correctly any settlement offer.

The rules for deduction have been changed for accidents which occured after January 1989.[31] In respect of those which took place before that date, the plaintiff must give credit against the recovered damages of 50% of all benefits specified in the Law Reform (Personal Injuries) Act 1948 and 100% in respect of certain other benefits. This applies to benefits that have accrued or are likely to accrue as a result of the injuries for five years from the cause of action. Benefits received after five years are not deducted. These deductions are taken into account in the assessment of damages in respect of past and future loss of earnings or profits, but are not deducted from general damages, except for loss of earning capacity (ie, handicap on the labour market).

For accidents occurring after 1 January 1989, the Social Security Act 1989 applies. The rules are, briefly, as follows. No compensation payment (with the exception of an exempt payment – see below), whether voluntary or in pursuance of a court order, should be made until the CRU has furnished the defendant with a certificate of total benefit (s22(1)). The defendant deducts from the payment of compensation to the plaintiff the gross amount of relevant benefits received in respect of the injury or

31 Law Reform (Personal Injuries) Act 1948; Social Security Act 1989 s22; Social Security (Recoupment) Regs 1990; Social Security (Recoupment) Amendment Regs 1990. The CRU guide *Deductions from Compensation* can be obtained from: Leaflets Unit, PO Box 21, Stanmore, Middlesex, HA7 1AY. See also Paul White, 'Social Security Act 1989' *APIL Newsletter* Vol 1 no 5.

disease from the date of injury, or for a disease, the date of the first claim based on that disease, to the date of settlement or for five years, whichever is less (s22(3)). The defendant then pays the deducted sum to the CRU and gives the plaintiff a certificate of deduction.

Relevant benefits for these purposes are the following:[32]

Attendance allowance	Reduced earnings allowance
Constant attendance allowance	Retirement allowance
Disablement benefit	Severe disablement allowance
Family credit	Sickness benefit
Income support	Statutory sick pay
Invalidity benefit	Unemployment benefit
Mobility allowance	Dependency increase payable with
Old Cases Act benefits	any of those above.

These benefits are deductible in full for the period between accident and payment of compensation (or 5 years after the accident, if shorter). The deduction will be made, irrespective of any percentage deduction for contributory negligence. The deduction should be made from special damages first, then if necessary, general damages other than damage to property. If the benefits exceed the damages, the plaintiff will get nothing.[33] Costs are not taken into account in assessing the compensation payment.

Certain compensatory payments are '**exempt payments**' and are not subject to deduction of benefit.[34] Small payments (set at £2,500 by paragraph 3 of the Social Security (Recoupment) Regulations 1990) are the most important 'exempt payments'. The phrase is misleading, however, since the payment is not wholly exempt: 50 per cent of benefits are deducted nonetheless. The period of deduction is the period between accident and cessation of payment of benefit (or 5 years after the accident, if shorter).

The solicitor should give special consideration to claims worth around £2,500 since it may be worthwhile to the plaintiff to settle at or below £2,500 and have only half benefits taken into account, than to recover more and find that the effect of taking into account full benefits leaves him or her with less in the end.

The defendant must obtain a certificate of total benefit from the CRU before making any non-exempt payment to the plaintiff or into court. The CRU issues an acknowledgment to the defendant quoting the date by

32 See Social Security (Recoupment) Regs 1990 reg 2 and *Deductions from Compensation*, 1990, DSS.

33 *R v CICB ex parte Lazzari* (1993) PIQR 421.

34 Social Security (Recoupment) Regs reg 4.

which a certificate of total benefit will be issued. If no certificate is issued by the date quoted, the compensation payment can be made without the deduction of total benefit as the debt due to the DSS is unenforceable. The CRU usually issues a certificate within four weeks of receipt of a properly completed application. A copy of the certificate is sent simultaneously to the plaintiff's solicitor and is valid for eight weeks from the date of issue. This should put the plaintiff's lawyers on notice of an imminent offer or payment into court.

On receipt of a certificate of benefit, the plaintiff's solicitor should consult the plaintiff, to ensure that it is correct. If there is any doubt, a request can be made for the certificate to be reviewed. The request should be sent to the CRU, outlining which aspect is being queried and why. Most commonly, if there is no link between the injury and the payment, the benefit should not be deducted.[35] A reviewed certificate cannot be increased. If, on review, the CRU concedes that the certificate is incorrect, a fresh certificate is issued. If the payment has already been made, the excess is paid to the plaintiff. There is also a formal appeals procedure against the amounts of benefits in the certificate. This must be exercised within three months from the date of payment to the DSS.[36] However, by then the case will have been settled and legal aid will not be available.

At trial, an order for the payment of damages will involve the defendant in paying the amount of benefit specified in the certificate to the CRU within 14 days. The same applies to any offer made and accepted: the benefits specified in the certificate must be paid to the CRU in 14 days, the balance being paid to the plaintiff.

If the defendant wishes to make an interim payment, the application for the certificate should be marked 'interim payment'. This will ensure it receives priority.

Where the defendant wishes to make a payment into court, the full amount, less the deductions in the certificate, should be paid in. If the payment in is accepted within 21 days, the defendant must account to the CRU within 14 days of acceptance. Where the plaintiff accepts the payment in, an order for costs is deemed to have been made for the purposes of the Judgments Act 1838 s17, and thereafter interest will accrue on the costs.[37]

If the plaintiff does not accept within 21 days, the defendant can agree

35 *Phillips v Salford Health Authority* PMILL vol 7 no 4 p31.

36 DSS leaflet NI 246. The Medical Appeal Tribunal must when giving its decision, follow the criteria set out in *Evans v Secretary of State for Social Services* (1993) PIQR p370.

37 *Hunt v RM Douglas (Roofing) Ltd* [1990] 1 AC 398. RSC Ord 62 r5(1); CCR Ord 38 r1(3).

to late acceptance of the payment in. However, if the plaintiff has received relevant benefits since the date of the payment in, the defendant may well be reluctant to allow late acceptance since a fresh certificate must be obtained and the amount of additional benefits received by the plaintiff paid to the CRU by the defendant.

In both the county court and the High Court, the plaintiff must apply for an order for payment out of court if the defendant objects to late acceptance. The court may, in these circumstances, reduce the money paid out by an amount equivalent to relevant benefits paid to the plaintiff since the date of the payment in.[38]

Defendants who have applied for but not yet received a certificate of total benefit are entitled to make a *Calderbank* offer (see pp147–8) indicating the size of their total offer which is subject to deductions in accordance with the yet to be received certificate of benefits. This is permissible and thus may affect the plaintiff's entitlement to costs just as a *Calderbank* offer would in any action without the complication of benefits.

A certificate should be applied for when the total amount of compensation is agreed in a structured settlement. The defendant then pays the CRU the amount on the certificate. No further deduction is made from future periodical payments.

Other losses

Small items, like the loss of clothing and jewellery, will usually be agreed without the need for strict proof. The loss of a no-claims bonus on the insurance of a written-off car will invariably need only a letter of confirmation to be agreed. Other costs, such as additional trousers required because of wear from a calliper, or gloves for turning the wheels of a wheelchair, will probably need to be supported at trial only by the plaintiff's say-so. The onus of proof is on the plaintiff to prove the loss s/he has suffered. But the court may well be satisfied with oral evidence that the damaged property would be or had been repaired without the need for the plaintiff to produce a receipt for the repairs.[39] So also, with additional heating or laundry or the costs of more frequent visits to the baths for therapeutic swims. In general, the rule applies that only reasonable expenses may be recovered and this is a question of fact in every case.

The additional costs of home decorating, perhaps because the plaintiff

38 RSC Ord 22 r5; CCR Ord 11 r5(3) and (4).
39 *Jones v Stroud DC* [1986] 1 WLR 1141.

can no longer raise his/her arm above shoulder height nor mount a ladder, require preferably two estimates from local decorators, builders or estate agents. They should state how frequently both the interior and the exterior will require redecoration, so that an annualised cost can be calculated. Only the labour cost is recoverable, because the materials would have been needed whether or not the accident had occurred. The estimates must therefore separate the labour costs from the materials cost.

Maintenance of the home (ie, repairs, renewals etc) which can no longer be performed because of the accident are dealt with in the same way by similar potential witnesses. Inability to maintain the family car (assuming it was maintained before the accident by the plaintiff's labour) requires estimates from garages.

Recovery of damages can be made for post-accident inability to tend the garden, do heavy digging or prune fruit trees, on the basis of estimates by gardening firms. If the client has had to give up an allotment or vegetable patch, the solicitor must calculate the annual purchase of lost fruit and vegetables. The cost of other handicaps may be met in similar ways, for example, additional taxi costs can be estimated on a periodic basis by local taxi firms. Additional car costs can be calculated on the basis of estimates of the cost of owning and running a particular vehicle. These estimates are provided by the AA and RAC at a reasonable charge and are accepted by the courts.

Estimates of the kind listed above are usually agreed, subject to liability, or to proof of causation, or proof of medical incapacity. Every aspect of the plaintiff's life should be discussed, to see what additional, and possibly hidden, costs the accident or ill-health has brought or may bring – work, travel, sports, hobbies, holidays, domestic and other relationships, ability to play with the children, domestic tasks, shopping and so forth. With experience and imagination the solicitor can investigate these matters with the plaintiff. With serious disability however, it is worth instructing an expert who will often turn up many aspects of loss of which the plaintiff was barely conscious.

A checklist of losses is to be found at pp206–8.

Catastrophic injuries

The same principles apply as before, but more aspects of the plaintiff's life are affected to a greater extent and all need consideration. Three or four different medical specialists may be required. Damage to brain or psyche may require reports from a neurologist, psychiatrist, psychologist, psychotherapist and psychometrist. The nature of nursing and therapy needs and costs will require detailed investigation. The additional costs of provision, while carers are on holiday or sick, or to cover between the resignation of one carer and the appointment of another, must be taken into account. So must the additional costs of a severely incapacitated plaintiff going on holiday, or requiring additional care if s/he falls ill, the likelihood of which may be increased by disability.

The huge range of additional costs incurred by the severely injured are admirably dealt with in *Special Damages for Disability* by Noble and others (see bibliography p474) which specialises in providing detailed damages reports and evidence in disastrous injury cases.

There are too many possible items to allow discussion here (but see pp206–8 and precedents C.22–24 p425). Without a report it is virtually impossible to be sure that all the matters which may need evaluation and costing have been covered. There are a small number of specialist accountants who will provide detailed schedules of damages. Although they are generally very expensive they may prove a worthwhile investment. The plaintiff's solicitor should, however, be wary of the possibility of such accountants' costs not being recovered on taxation. Special reasons for employing an accountant for this purpose, such as financial complexity, will need to be demonstrated. If the schedule is calculated by solicitor and counsel on the basis of expert evidence from the appropriate witnesses, the costs will be recoverable on taxation.

Housing needs invariably arise in catastrophic cases and adaptations will be necessary or a new home may need to be purchased or even built. Specialist architects are available for costings and advisability of adaption, purchase or building. The proper calculation of recoverable housing costs in the claim has been radically reduced from former practice by the ruling in *Roberts v Johnstone*.[40]

Finally, the additional costs of entertaining a plaintiff, whose life has been tragically limited and whose former pastimes and work are curtailed, should never be overlooked. The claim could include the cost of a raised garden at wheelchair height, a computer and associated equipment, more videos, a car for visiting places, cinemas and friends, and so on.

40 [1989] QB 878.

CHAPTER 7

Legal aid

Legal aid considerations at the first interview with the client have already been dealt with in chapter 2 pp13–19.

It usually takes six to eight weeks for the Legal Aid Board to process an application (see p16). The board forwards instructions to the Benefits Agency, which acts on behalf of the board in obtaining details about the client's financial circumstances. The agency then sends a questionnaire to the client. If this is not returned within about a fortnight, the agency will report to the board that the client has failed to co-operate. The application may then be refused. The client should, therefore, be warned, in the first interview, of the need to deal with the form promptly.

Once the questionnaire is completed, it will be passed to the Board for its financial assessment. The Board will decide whether the client comes within the legal aid financial limits, whether a contribution will have to be paid and, if so, at what level (see chapter 2).

The board will also consider the merits of the client's case and determine whether it has a 'reasonable prospect of success'. This usually means an assessment that the case has more chance of succeeding than of failing, ie, a 50% plus chance of success. This is despite the fact that a paying client of moderate means might, in some circumstances, be advised to begin proceedings – at least until discovery, if not to trial – with a slightly less than even chance of success. Nevertheless, the Board can take account of unusual circumstances, such as a test case, which may justify support of a case. In assessing the merits, the board takes into account not just the prospects of success but also the potential value of the claim and the potential costs. It remains to be seen whether contingency fee arrangements will increase legal aid refusals (see p22).

Prior to making a decision, the board often writes to the solicitor, asking questions to assist its deliberations. Thus, the more information that can be provided on the initial application, the less likely is delay at this stage. Common questions are whether there has been correspondence with the defendants and, if so, whether there is any chance of a negotiated settlement. These details should, therefore, always be provided in the initial application.

Where the board questions whether or not a negotiated settlement is possible, it should be told that negotiating without the authority to commence and pursue legal proceedings is bad practice which wastes time and money, with little prospect of achieving a proper result. Experience suggests that such a challenge will bring about a shift in attitude in the particular officer at the board.

Refusals

If it refuses legal aid, the board will set out the reasons for so doing in a notice supplied to both plaintiff and solicitor.

If the application for legal aid is turned down because the client has not co-operated, the reason for such apparent non co-operation should be ascertained from the client. Sometimes, it will be found that the client was simply unable to cope with the complicated form sent by the Benefits Agency. If this is the case, the solicitor should see the client and assist with filling in the form. Another common cause is delay in the completion of the employer's form, which is particularly common where the employer is also the defendant in the action. Here, the solicitor can write to the defendant or his/her solicitors. In either case, the solicitor should write to the board explaining the reason for the delay. Usually, the board will agree to revive the application, provided that the delay is not excessive. If it refuses to reconsider the application, a fresh one should be made.

Where the client has been refused legal aid on financial grounds, the board can be asked to provide its assessment so that the solicitor can check the information and the calculations.

Another reason for refusal is that the case is not worth pursuing. The only way of challenging such a decision is by formally appealing to the area committee of the Legal Aid Board. The decision to appeal must be sent to the board within 14 days of the notice of refusal reaching the client and solicitor.[1] If there are difficulties communicating with the client, it is usually best to appeal first and then consider with the client whether to pursue the appeal later. The appeal may then be withdrawn if the client decides not to proceed with it or it was, on reflection, not warranted.

The decision to refuse or grant legal aid is actually taken by employed officers of the board who are engaged full-time to make these decisions. The area committee consists of experienced solicitors and barristers

1 Civil Legal Aid (General) Regs 1989 reg 36.

practising in the area, each of whom will probably sit on the committee every six weeks or so. The area committee considers the application afresh, taking into account the officer's reasons for refusal and the grounds of appeal. Clients have a much better chance of succeeding in their appeals if they attend the area committee. It is likely to help if the solicitor accompanies the client to deal with the committee's questions, although legal aid is not available for such attendance.[2]

If the area committee dismisses the appeal, there is no further right of appeal,[3] although the applicant is free to make a fresh application, or even successive applications.[4] Alternatively, it is possible to apply for judicial review of the board's decision.[5] Legal aid can be granted for such an application. Nevertheless, it may be worthwhile applying for leave for judicial review (if there are strong enough grounds), since the board is not usually represented and is unlikely to incur costs. If leave is granted, it adds weight to a fresh application for legal aid on the merits.

Granted applications

Where legal aid without contribution is granted, the certificate is sent to both solicitor and client. Where a contribution is required, the offer of legal aid – also sent to both – is conditional on accepting the contribution requirement. In cases involving persons under a legal disability (including minors), the offer is made to the 'next friend' (ie, the person appointed to take responsibility for giving instructions in the case). If the offer is acceptable, the client signs the acceptance section of the form and sends it back to the board, with the first instalment. The board will then issue the certificate.

The details of the certificate and any limitation imposed should be checked. If the limitation is unduly restrictive, for example, requiring counsel's opinion on a straightforward case, the board should be asked to reconsider the limitation while the case is pursued (see precedent B23 p343). If the information on the certificate is not correct, for example, if the wrong defendant is named, the solicitor must apply to have the

2 Ibid reg 38.

3 Ibid reg 39(2).

4 But if more than three applications are made and the board considers that the applicant is abusing the facilities of the Legal Aid Act, a prohibitory direction may be made: ibid regs 40 and 41.

5 When deciding applications for legal aid, legal aid committees are acting judicially and can therefore be judicially reviewed: *R v Manchester Legal Aid Committee ex p R A Brand & Co Ltd* [1952] 1 All ER 480.

certificate amended or it may be ineffective to protect the costs of the litigation.

There are a variety of limitations which the board can impose on the certificate. The most common are to limit the certificate to obtaining counsel's advice; to authorise proceeding only up to close of pleadings and discovery and then to obtain counsel's opinion on the merits; to require that any offers of settlement or payments into court be referred to the board, if not accepted within the appropriate time. Nowadays an overall financial limitation including all solicitors' costs, disbursements (including to counsel and experts) as well as VAT, is usual. An accurate costing system giving adequate warning as any financial limit is reached is therefore an imperative for the legal aid solicitor.

Where the board imposes a limitation which authorises no more than the obtaining of counsel's opinion on the merits, counsel should be instructed forthwith. Sometimes counsel will want to meet the client before giving an opinion. It is likely that the costs of such a conference will be allowed on taxation but to be certain approval should first be obtained from the board. Sometimes, counsel will be able to give only an interim advice, saying that further work needs to be done before a proper assessment can be made – for example, an expert's report is required or witness statements are needed. This, when reported to the board, will usually result in the extension of the certificate to authorise that work to be done.

Usually, however, counsel will have sufficient information to come to a view. In the instructions to counsel it is helpful for the solicitor to give either a reasoned opinion about the merits or state that no conclusion has been reached. Counsel might be asked to telephone the solicitor before committing to paper an adverse view, contrary to that expressed by the solicitor in the instructions.

Where the certificate is either unlimited, or the limitation allows all steps up to close of pleadings, the solicitor must assess the work that needs to be done so that proceedings may be issued and served. The solicitor can then pursue the case almost as if it were privately funded.

The major difference between legally aided and privately funded cases is the obligation to comply with any limitations on the legal aid certificate. A second difference is that, in legally aided cases, certain work always needs to have prior approval from the board to ensure payment – for example, any unusual step such as pre-action discovery, commissioning a professional photographer, or commissioning plans to be drawn professionally. Approval is required before instructing experts to report,[6] and failure to obtain such approval may result in the cost not being met by the legal aid fund. This may occur either if the plaintiff ultimately loses the case, or if s/he wins but the report is deemed unnecessary on taxation or by the judge hearing the case.[7] In most cases, the need for such a report is not open to doubt on taxation. Since costs are usually agreed between parties at the end of the case, the cost of reports is almost invariably covered. Nevertheless, approval for reports should be sought as a matter of routine, where the solicitor has any doubts. A precedent is at B25 p344.

The main problem with obtaining the Legal Aid Board's approval for experts is delay. The board will usually want to know not only the name of the expert, his/her area of expertise and the reasons for wanting to instruct the expert, but also the amount of the fee and often confirmation that another expert cannot be obtained at a cheaper price. This can take a considerable amount of time and, if there are three or four experts to be approved, it can appreciably increase the length of the case.

The authority of the board must always be obtained before instructing leading counsel. A precedent is at B26 p344. Failure to do so will mean that the costs of the QC will not be met by the legal aid fund if they are not recovered from the other side.[8] Any failure to get Legal Aid Board approval for a step which requires such approval may mean that the step will fall to be paid for by the client. If the board does approve the step, it adds to the costs which may be sought by way of statutory charge against the client. Either way, therefore, the client's instructions on steps to which s/he did not agree at the outset must be obtained.

The plaintiff's solicitor must remember that since 1 April 1990, the Legal Aid Board requires a report on all civil legal aid cases where the certificate has been in force for more than 12 months. The report form is sent out automatically by the board after 12, 24 and 36 months and requires a series of questions to be answered, failing which the certificate may be suspended.[9]

Capped legal aid hourly rates

There are now (for certificates issued on and after 25 February 1994)

6 Civil Legal Aid (General) Regs 1989 reg 60.
7 Ibid reg 63. To avoid the problem of having expert reports and attendance disallowed on taxation, the advocate should ask the trial judge, where there is some doubt, to indicate that such evidence was reasonably brought.
8 Civil Legal Aid (General) Regs 1989 regs 59 and 63.
9 Ibid reg 70.

prescribed maximum hourly rates for legal aid for certain purposes. All legal aid payments on account are to be made on the basis of these rates, which may cause cash-flow problems for firms dependent on a significant flow of legal aid turnover.

If a case is unsuccessful, the solicitor's claim for costs from the Legal Aid Board will no longer be reimbursed at the rates which would be claimed (and would be allowed by a taxing master) from the defendants on a successful case. Instead, no more than the fixed fee rates are recoverable.

The rate for 1994–5 is, for solicitors outside London, £65 per hour for county court work and £74 per hour for High Court work. For solicitors inside London the rates are £69 per hour for county court work and £78.50 for High Court work.

These rates are without regard to the level of fee-earner doing the work. A partner and a junior clerk will be able to charge the same fee rate. Consequently on the small number of high-risk cases which come into the office, the financial incentive is to devolve work to the most junior fee-earner. However, for cases of great complexity or where there has been great efficiency, the lawyer may claim an uplift of 100%, and in cases of the most extreme complexity an uplift of 200% is possible.

Standard fees

Fixed fees to cover the various stages of the run-of-the-mill PI action are proposed by the Lord Chancellor to be phased in during 1995. At the time of writing, the details and implications were unclear.

Legal aid franchises

Since October 1993 firms of solicitors have been able to apply for legal aid franchises. Any solicitor carrying a reasonable personal injury caseload should consider obtaining such a franchise. The ostensible purpose of the scheme is to develop a more efficient service with improved quality. It is to be anticipated that eventually it will only be franchised solicitors who will be entitled to undertake personal injury work under the legal aid scheme. At the time of writing the Law Society was advising solicitors not to sign franchise contracts without a firm commitment from the Lord Chancellor that the terms of the franchise would not be subsequently detrimentally altered.

For a firm to set up the administation and to put together the paperwork necessary for the franchise application is extremely onerous. A preliminary audit is followed by pre-contract monitoring for 4–6 months, followed by an in-depth pre-contract audit, during which conformity with the Legal Aid Board's transaction criteria is assessed. There will be monitoring of bills, costs, grants and refusals of legal aid applications. Many of the aspects of good practice, client communication, file review, costs control and analysis advocated in this book are requirements of the franchise scheme, though the latter is far more detailed. However there is a degree of inflexibility and loss of what the authors consider to be important discretion on the part of the solicitor.[10] In particular, some requirements appear to be more appropriate for large firms supervising lots of clerks than for a small firm where the senior lawyers undertake most of the work personally.

The effect of obtaining a franchise is that it devolves to the franchised solicitor much of the authority for the expenditure of funds recoverable from the legal aid scheme.

Green form financial limits may be extended by the franchisee. This requires a record to be made of the date of the extension, the extent of it, the reasons for it, and the identity of the person making the decision to extend. When the work under the green form is completed, it is sent in for payment. If the extension authorising the additional work done is queried and refused, the solicitor can appeal to the Area Committee.

A franchised solicitor can take action under an emergency legal aid certificate without obtaining prior authority form the Legal Aid Board. Within seven days, however, the solicitor has to submit a formal application for an emergency certificate together with an application for the full certificate. In these circumstances the solicitor can also claim £250 on account. If the board subsequently refuses the full legal aid certificate, it will nevertheless normally allow the emergency certificate.

The financial benefit of holding a franchise is that the solicitor can claim 75% of the profit costs (subject to the capped fee limit – see p75) incurred on a case, nine months after the issuing of the legal aid certificate and after every further nine-month period. After becoming a franchisee, the solicitor will be able to claim on certificates issued up to six months before that time.

Personal injury panel

Many of the requirements of the Legal Aid Board's franchising scheme are

10 See S Harman 'Franchising: the preliminary audit experience' January 1994 *Legal Action* 9 and C Piggott, 'Franchising: audit pains, problems and predictions' February 1994 *Legal Action* 21.

necessities in order to be accepted onto the Law Society's personal injury panel. Apart from the prestige of having the cachet of specialist, the benefits of being on the panel are that potential personal injury litigants who make first contact with the Law Society and other referral agencies will only be referred to solicitors on the panel.

To become a member the lawyer has to have been responsible for at least 60 personal injury cases over the last five years or 36 over the last three years. Out of those, at least ten need to have been set down. The lawyer needs to be a qualified solicitor or a member of the Institute of Legal Executives (ILEX) with the appropriate qualification in civil litigation.

A questionnaire of over a hundred questions needs to be completed, the answers to which are considered by the Law Society's adjudicators. If they deem it necessary, the applicant will be asked to attend for an interview. The questions are intended to elicit expertise in the personal injury field but some appear to favour applicants from large specialist personal injury firms. It is to be hoped that candidates who are perhaps the sole personal injury practitioner in their firm are not thereby excluded from the panel.

CHAPTER 8

Negotiations

Nearly all negotiations leading to settlement are conducted on a 'without prejudice' basis, meaning that they cannot be revealed to the court, because of privilege. One of the remarkable aspects of personal injury cases is the disparity between awards in apparently similar cases. This disparity means that, in negotiations, estimating the worth of each case is more an art than a science.

Defendants and insurance companies

Insurers will be acting for most defendants, whether the case is a road accident, an injury at work or a tripping case. If a case is to be contested, insurance companies usually appoint from their retained firms of solicitors. Solicitors specialising in work for plaintiffs will face the same solicitors for defendants time and again.

While there are advantages in getting to know the opposition, there are also dangers. A principal benefit is that defence lawyers' tactics and style become predictable. Where the opponent is known, serious negotiations can often be commenced earlier. It may be possible to obtain an offer to settle a near-hopeless case during discussions of several cases, where a number are being dealt with by the same firm. While a tough approach to litigation – complying with every deadline and issuing a summons every time the opponent fails to comply with one – is usually the best policy, a bit of give-and-take with familiar opponents may pay dividends. Letting the insurer's solicitors have more time for the service of a defence, or waiting an additional couple of days before issuing judgment in default, may, for example, produce assistance from the defendant's solicitors when a hearing date can be put back only by consent and the plaintiff's case depends on an expert who cannot attend on the fixed date. The reverse side of this familiarity is that it is more difficult to hide the fact that a plaintiff may have 'a difficult case' from an insurance representative or solicitor who knows the plaintiff's solicitor well. It also becomes easier to surrender, perhaps subconsciously, to the temptation of settling cases that ought to be fought.

There is a balance to be struck. On the one hand, it is undesirable to become too cosy with the insurers and their solicitors to the detriment of the client's interest[1]. On the other hand, to become so hard with them that they are looking for opportunities to take every point and use every stratagem against the plaintiff's solicitor is also contrary to the client's interest.

Some insurance companies retain the control of negotiations once proceedings have begun; others hand over control to their solicitors. Where the negotiations are handled by solicitors, the insurers remain behind the scenes and the defendant's solicitor usually has to obtain instructions from them before any deal can be struck. At times, the negotiations are complicated by the presence of re-insurers. Insurance companies often arrange for the re-insurance of large risks. Where this happens, the plaintiff's solicitor still has the first insurer's solicitors to deal with. However, the latter have to obtain authority both from their insurance clients and the re-insurers, where a case is to be settled at or beyond the financial level at which the re-insurers assume all or part of the risk.

Some large defendants carry their own risks without insurance. The government, health authorities and some public transport undertakings are examples. Such organisations have such a huge financial base that they can cover all potential liabilities, without fear of being unable to meet damages claims. These bodies usually have their own in-house solicitors as well. They separate the solicitor from the rest of the organisation so that the formal relationship of solicitor and client within the organisation is preserved. The drawback for the plaintiff may be that decisions in settlement negotiations often have to be decided by a committee within the organisation which meets infrequently, thus causing delay. The only way to deal with this is to keep pressing the case forward towards trial. The organisation's solicitor will be able to tell the decision-making body that delay in giving sufficient authority to settle is costing the organisation more money.

In general terms, the plaintiff's solicitor should avoid becoming involved in the bureaucratic procedures of the defendant's financial backers. This is best done by not allowing delays by the defendant in

1 The court warned against solicitors striking up cosy relationships (in the context of vacating fixed dates) in *Boyle v Ford Motor Co Ltd* [1992] 1 WLR 476.

deciding to make settlement offers to delay the plaintiff's solicitor in proceeding to trial.

Unless a clear and unambiguous intention to settle the case is shown by the defendant's insurers, proceedings should be issued as soon as the plaintiff's solicitor is satisfied on the following points. These are that:

- funding has been secured;
- the case has a reasonable prospect of success;
- there is, or will be, a medical report to serve with the statement/particulars of claim (see p128); and
- there is a schedule of damages (see p129).

Negotiations can proceed as the court action proceeds. As costs mount, the prospect of the case getting quickly to court is by far the most powerful inducement to bring about an early and satisfactory settlement. The solicitor who pursues a negotiated settlement instead of getting on with the case is doing the client a grave disservice.

Often the first response to the initial letter of claim is a pro forma letter from the defendant's insurers notifying their interest in the matter, saying that they are investigating the case, that they will come back on the issue of liability, and asking, in the meanwhile, for a full description of the accident and, on a without prejudice basis, to be provided with a copy of the medical report, police report and financial loss details. The implication is that, if the information is supplied, then fruitful negotiations will commence. This should not be accepted at face value. A precedent for a response is at B17 p339.

The insurer's initial response often has three underlying motives: to delay the action; to save the cost of obtaining their own reports; and to get the plaintiff's medical evidence so that it can be more easily attacked. The request for a 'full description of the accident' is partly intended to test the mettle of the plaintiff's solicitor. The competent solicitor will have provided a sufficient description in the letter before action. Any fuller statement at this stage will give the insurers greater opportunity to know and subsequently attack the plaintiff's case. More information may convey an exploitable keenness to settle, and may demonstrate a lack of familiarity with personal injury work. This may encourage insurers to make an early payment into court which will impose pressure on the solicitor and plaintiff. The payment in is likely to be low but the decision to reject it creates a nagging doubt in the client's mind and may well undermine his/her expectations so as to make him/her more susceptible to a low offer later on (on payments in see p144; on *Calderbank* offers see p147).

The defendant's insurers often say that it is not their policy to admit liability but are prepared to negotiate on a 'without prejudice' basis. This attitude does not warrant co-operation and the case should proceed relentlessly unless and until an admission of liability or an acceptable offer is received. Any other response will invariably lead to the insurers doing what they can to delay the progress of the negotiations.

It cannot be overstressed that delay for the defendants is an economic imperative (see p1). Not only will a significant number of plaintiffs die or become dispirited and give up their claim, but also unpaid damages remain part of the insurer's investments earning interest daily, forming a significant proportion of the insurer's profits. While it is true that, if the plaintiff receives compensation, interest is payable on special damages at (usually) half the 'special account' rate, this is a future cost, which is significantly less than the actual rate of return received by the insurers while that money is invested. General damages attract interest only at the meagre rate of 2% per annum and then only from the date of service of the writ or summons. This rate is a mere fraction of the investment value to the insurer of retaining that money. Delay means profit and is, therefore, a proper business objective for the insurer.

Tactics

There is an obvious exception to the general rule that negotiations should not hold up litigation. That is where the solicitor forms the view that the claim is unlikely to succeed. Before abandoning such a case, no matter when that view is formed, it is almost certainly worthwhile for the solicitor to apply some pressure on the defendant, if only to seek to achieve a 'nuisance value' settlement (ie, a nominal payment by the defendant to settle, in preference to taking the case all the way through to trial to defeat the plaintiff, with the risk of not recovering all actual costs). Of course, the solicitor's doubts should not be communicated to the other side, nor should the solicitor be seen to be looking for a nuisance value offer. On the other hand the solicitor must not intentionally mislead the defendant. In legally aided cases, defendants know that, whatever happens at trial, it is highly likely that they will end up paying their own costs. There is no doubt that this acts as an inducement to settle cases, even those which are weak from the plaintiff's point of view.

When negotiating with defendants, the cardinal rule is *never* to put forward the first figure. The person who puts forward the initial figure is, in effect, setting the upper (or lower) limit for negotiations. It is, therefore, bad practice for the plaintiff's solicitor to initiate the bidding. There may be exceptions to this rule. For example, where there are fundamental weaknesses in the plaintiff's case which are unlikely to emerge before trial, it may be advantageous for the plaintiff's lawyer to force the pace of negotiations. The convention that defendants' representatives make the first offer, either in discussion or in a meeting, should otherwise be insisted on, since it is quite remarkable how often the defendant's opening bid is a figure as high, or even higher, than the plaintiff's solicitors' valuation.

It is almost a truism that defendants' first offers are below the figures at which they are prepared to settle. So, a second general rule of negotiating is that the opening offer should not be accepted. (An exception to this is where it is absolutely clear not only that the offer is an extremely good one, but also that the continuation of negotiations may jeopardise the offer, which might be withdrawn.) The response should almost always be to make a higher counter-offer, even if the original offer seems to be above the real value of the case. The solicitor's duty is to obtain the best settlement for the client. Furthermore, if the defendant sees the claim as being more valuable than the plaintiff's solicitor, it is foolish to assume that the former is wrong and the latter right. There is nothing improper in seeking a higher settlement than that which it is thought a court might award. While there is a duty not to put forward untruthful or misleading matters in negotiating, or at court, there is no duty to draw defendants' attention to errors or misunderstandings in their assessments while negotiating. There is a duty to ensure that the court is not misled.

Solicitors need not worry that the insurers will withdraw the offer if it is not accepted. This never happens, except in the most extraordinary circumstances. Neither solicitor nor client should feel harassed or panicked by the imposition of a deadline for acceptance of an offer. The insurer will not usually refuse to renew an offer where acceptance is late, unless some previously hidden weakness in the plaintiff's (or strength in the defendant's) case has been discovered between the expiry of the deadline and the acceptance by the plaintiff. In every other instance, the insurer will be delighted to be rid of the case, at that figure, without incurring extra costs.

A deadline needs to be taken more seriously, however, if further significant expenditure will be incurred by the defendant after the deadline. Often, the defendant makes an offer before the trial brief is sent to counsel. But even if the brief has been delivered, costs are not likely to be so large in proportion to the settlement figure that the defendant will prefer to fight rather than reinstate an offer which s/he knows the plaintiff will now accept.

It is bad practice to let a deadline expire so as to pressure the defendant to increase the offer. It would, in any event, be a high risk strategy both for the particular client and for the solicitor's future clients. Likewise, it is not the practice of defendants to substitute a lower offer for no other reason than that the deadline has expired. This, too, would be a high risk strategy, when facing a tough plaintiff and solicitor.

Less experienced defence negotiators will sometimes make a ridiculously low first offer. This should be treated with contempt and it is unwise to be lured into going back with an alternative figure. By refusing to respond to unrealistic offers, the pressure is on the defendant to put forward an improved offer without the plaintiff's side giving away anything.

Every offer, even if it is absurdly low, must, of course, be conveyed to the client, preferably in writing or confirmed in writing, with clear advice on its acceptability. An example is at B10 p335.

The solicitor must have a feel for the likely parameters of the value of the claim before negotiations commence. This involves not merely the valuation of each element in the claim, but also the risks of winning and losing. These will already have been explained to the client. Some solicitors like to fix a 'bottom line' with the plaintiff, which is the lowest acceptable figure. It is wise not to be too dogmatic, however, since factors can arise in preparation of the case, and indeed in the course of negotiation, which were previously unforeseen or perhaps overlooked. Furthermore, fixing a bottom line may induce, subconsciously, an inertia about extracting a higher amount, once the defendant has made an offer at, or above, the minimum.

The techniques of negotiation are beyond the scope of this book. It is foolish to imagine that the books and courses available for the business skills of negotiation are of no value to the personal injury lawyer. American personal injury practitioners have given much study to these techniques.[2]

It is wise to develop more than one approach and to bear in mind not only that every negotiator has his/her own style(s) but that every case requires a style appropriate to it. In one case, it may be appropriate to take an unwavering stand on a particular figure, making it clear from the start that the client will accept only that figure, or fight. In another case, it may be wiser to indicate flexibility and exchange offer for counter-offer time and again, until compromise is reached.

Sometimes, it may be best to make it clear that the solicitor is running the negotiation and that the client will accept whatever is advised. At

2 See the many articles and reviews of other material in the magazine *Trial Lawyer* published monthly by the Association of Trial Lawyers of America (see p473 for address).

other times, it may be wise to convey – as long as it is not untrue or misleading – that, though the solicitor sees the reasonableness of the defendant's proposal, the client is determined and will not budge.

Solicitors will occasionally feel that it is best to argue the minutiae of the issues, heads of claim and calculations, but in other cases, it will be appropriate not to condescend to detail at all.

One technique of negotiation is to establish such a relationship that the opponent feels embarrassed to put forward an offer too far away from that proposed by the other. Solicitors should be aware of this, but while trying to impose this relationship on the defendant's representative, should never themselves feel embarrassed or intimidated about asking for a high settlement.

Negotiations may take place by letter, but this is not very effective for either side in 'getting the feel' of the opponent and the opponent's case. Such letters should be marked 'without prejudice'.[3] Negotiations can take place by telephone, and this has its attractions. A telephone discussion can be broken off easily to get time to consider the situation and think out the next tactic, and then resumed easily. A telephone discussion removes all eye contact and body language. This may be advantageous or disadvantageous, according to the personality and skill of the solicitor and the opponent. The plaintiff's solicitor must consider in each case the comparative advantages of methods.

Insurers often suggest meeting to discuss cases. This can be useful, but it is obviously necessary to be on top of every aspect of the case and its calculations. A convention which should always be insisted on is that such

3 Documents marked 'without prejudice' which form part of negotiations are prima facie privileged from disclosure at the trial, even if they do not contain an offer. Discussions and/or documents passing between the parties with the purpose of resolving a dispute are privileged, even if the express words 'without privilege' are not used: *Chocoladefabriken Lindt & Sprungli AG v Nestlé Co Ltd* [1978] RPC 287. Conversely, the words 'without prejudice' do not by themselves render privileged a document so marked: *South Shropshire DC v Amos* [1986] 1WLR 1271. 'Without prejudice' in a letter means without prejudice to the position of the writer of it, if the terms proposed therein are not accepted. If the terms (or some of them, if severable) are accepted, an enforceable contract may be established. The court can look at the correspondence to decide if this is so: *Tomlin v Standard Telephones and Cables Ltd* [1969] 1 WLR 1378. The parties can use a form of words that enables the without prejudice correspondence to be referred to, even though no concluded agreement is reached. Conversely, the parties may exclude reference to such correspondence, even where an agreement is reached. The privilege does not depend on the existence of proceedings: *Rush and Tompkins v GLC* [1989] AC 1280. If one party switches from 'without prejudice' to open negotiations, s/he must make the change clear to the other side. It might not be enough to use the word 'open': *Cheddar Valley Engineering Ltd v Chaddlewood Homes Ltd* [1992] 1 WLR 820.

a meeting should take place in the plaintiff's solicitor's own office. This has the benefit that she is on home territory and can control the layout, environment and timing so as to have maximum psychological advantage.

At whatever stage negotiations occur, the solicitor should try not to be caught off guard by the defendant's representative. If the latter telephones unexpectedly to talk about a settlement, the plaintiff's solicitor should call back later, after the file has been re-read, or should simply listen to the proposal and refuse to react in any way, saying that instructions need to be taken before any response is made. Time can thus be taken for a considered response. The plaintiff's solicitor should not be harassed into putting forward a figure that might be regretted on due reflection with all the papers available. The solicitor must resist any temptation to advise settlement of a case either to reduce workloads or to ensure that costs are paid more quickly.

It is the solicitor's job to conduct the negotiations right up to delivery of the brief. Counsel should be kept abreast of events, especially in the months leading up to the trial. On the eve of trial, counsel will usually take over any negotiating, but the team work developed prior to the hearing should continue. (See also pp239 and 242–4.)

In some cases, it is an effective technique to hand over negotiations to counsel, perhaps in the fortnight to so before trial (see p231) or on an appropriate interlocutory hearing, to deal with the opposing barrister. If counsel is delegated to negotiate, it is, of course, vital that the solicitor refuses to discuss anything with the defendant's solicitor which may affect those negotiations. There can only ever be one negotiator at any time, otherwise one will undermine the other.

It is probably wise to remind counsel of the need to obtain instructions from the client before agreeing any settlement. This is counsel's duty, but it is possible for counsel to assume authority to reach a settlement within a certain bracket although such authority has not in fact been given. Counsel should always seek the views of the instructing solicitor and the client whilst negotiating. Three heads are better than one both as to the advisability of settlement at a particular figure and on the tactics to adopt.

Part II

Proceedings up to close of pleadings and discovery

CHAPTER 9

Issue and service

Before the issue of proceedings, the solicitor must be satisfied that: there is a reasonable prospect of success; a settlement is not imminent; funding is secure; a medical report is to hand; and that there is sufficient information to draft a schedule of damages. If in doubt about the prospects of a negotiated settlement, the rule is to issue, because the threat of proceedings is always the best inducement to settlement.[1] The client must authorise issue of proceedings. See precedent B9 p336.

In some privately funded cases, the client will insist on the issue of proceedings, even if the solicitor advises against it. In such circumstances, the solicitor should record the advice and the client's instructions in a letter to the client. Where the case is legally aided, funded by a trade union or by an insurance policy, the appropriate body must immediately be notified of the disagreement, before issue. There is nothing unethical about the solicitor continuing to act in such cases. The letter to the client should explain the reasons for the advice. The client should be required to write, acknowledging receipt of the letter and confirming the instruction to proceed. These steps are an essential protection against any subsequent allegation of negligence.

Before issue and service of proceedings, it is essential to have thoroughly investigated and formed a view on the case and on the defendant, on liability and on loss and damage. The recent procedural changes such as disclosure of the medical report and schedule of damages with the particulars or statement of claim, and the enforced timetable in the county court, by which a case will be automatically struck out if not set down within 15 months (or such time as ordered by the court), have meant that it is no longer appropriate to issue proceedings and then prepare the case as the matter proceeds. Most of the preparatory work should be done before the case is issued. This is called 'front loading'. It means that when proceedings are issued the plaintiff will be in a very

1 See generally chapter 8 p79.

strong position to prosecute the case at speed and thus put maximum pressure on the defendants.

Defendants

It is crucial to ensure that the defendant will be able to meet a judgment debt, or that there is a corporation or institution behind the defendant, such as insurers or employers, who will foot the bill. In most cases, there will be a response from the defendant or the insurers within a few days of the initial letter being sent, but if there is no response, care should be taken to assess the position of the defendant.

Where there is evidence that the defendant is likely to dissipate assets out of the jurisdiction, an application for a Mareva injunction in the High Court[2] should be considered (and, of course, recorded on the file). If granted, the defendant's assets may be seized and preserved pending trial. The county court does not have jurisdiction to grant a Mareva injunction in a personal injury case unless a Lord Justice of Appeal or High Court judge is sitting. The application should be addressed to the High Court and will be deemed to include an application for transfer of the proceedings to the High Court.[3] After the application has been dealt with, the proceedings will be transferred back to the county court.[4]

An order for security for costs is available against a defendant outside the jurisdiction, and within the jurisdiction only if the defendant is a company without assets which makes a counterclaim (not merely allegations of contributory negligence).[5]

If the case is a road traffic accident, where the defendant was driving a vehicle and where no insurers have confirmed that they will cover the defendant's liability, the Motor Insurers Bureau should be notified formally before or within seven days of the issue of proceedings (see p301).

Identity of the defendant

It is important to select the right defendant. Usually, this presents no problem, but where there are several potential defendants, it is generally wisest to sue those against whom liability is clearest. This then places the

2 *Allen v Jambo Holdings Ltd* [1980] 1 WLR 1252.
3 County Court Remedies Regs 1991 reg 4.
4 Ibid reg 5.
5 CCR Ord 13 r8(1); RSC Ord 23 r1(1).

onus on them, as primary defendants, to decide whether others should be brought in as third parties to the action.

The court has to be satisfied that the plaintiff was reasonable in joining more than one defendant. A reasonable doubt concerning which defendant may be liable is sufficient for the court to make either a Sanderson or Bullock order for costs at trial, ordering the unsuccessful defendant to pay the costs of the successful defendant either directly[6] or indirectly.[7]

Where the primary defendant adds third parties to the action, the plaintiff's lawyers may add those parties as further defendants if the allegations made against them by the primary defendant are sufficiently strong. The plaintiff may avoid that burden if s/he joined that person as a defendant only because the primary defendant had first brought in the innocent defendant as a third party. The risk to avoid, in taking this course of action, is that the statutory limitation period expires before the potential third party is joined as a defendant, assuming that the latter's identity is known to the plaintiff. A defendant who is found at trial to have no liability is entitled to costs.

If the defendant dies intestate before the commencement of the proceedings, the plaintiff's solicitor should obtain a copy of the letters of administration and commence the proceedings against the named administrator. Alternatively the solicitor should apply for an order that a person be appointed to represent the defendant's estate and thereafter commence proceedings against that person.[8]

If protective proceedings to avoid limitation problems (see p44) are issued, it is wisest to sue *all* potential defendants, irrespective of probable blame, so as to protect the plaintiff's position.

In road accident cases caused by drivers of commercial vehicles, it is usually sufficient to sue the employer or vehicle operator on the basis of their vicarious liability. If, however, there is any doubt about whether the driver was acting in the course of his/her employment so as to establish vicarious liability, the best policy is to sue both. The court will look at the reality of the relationship between the parties as found in express or implied terms of the contract.[9]

In 'tripping' cases the local authority should be sued first. If it is absolutely clear which contractors are responsible, they should also be

6 *Sanderson v Blyth Theatre Co* [1903] 2 KB 533.
7 *Bullock v London General Omnibus Co* [1907] 1 KB 264. For the principles of applying these orders see *Mayer v Harte* [1960] 1 WLR 770.
8 RSC Ord 15 r6A(4)(a); CCR Ord 5 r8(4); *Foster v Turnbull and Others* (1990) *Times* 22 May.
9 *Ferguson v John Dawson & Partners (Contractors) Ltd* [1976] 1 WLR 1213.

joined. If not, it should be left to the local authority to identify the appropriate defendants.

In work cases, the usual practice is to sue the employer as well as any other party obviously at fault. So, for example, where an accident has happened while the client is on another contractor's premises, both the employer and other contractor should be sued.[10] The employer's responsibility to ensure that the employee has a safe place of work and a safe system of work does not end at the factory gates.[11]

The Consumer Protection Act 1987 established new liability for defective products from 1 March 1988. The producer (or anybody that can be identified from the product or its wrapping to be the producer) or the importer may be sued. Suppliers may be sued if they fail to identify the producer within a reasonable time of being so requested (see p296).

It is important to use the correct address for service on the defendant. It is good practice to do a company search on a corporate defendant to establish the address of the registered office. This becomes essential if expiry of the limitation period is nearing. Where the defendant is not domiciled in England and Wales, application must usually be made for service out of the jurisdiction.[12]

Insolvency of an insured defendant

Where a defendant was insured but becomes insolvent, the plaintiff's ability to enforce a successful claim against the insurers is protected by the Third Parties (Rights against Insurers) Act 1930. This statute enables the injured person to stand in the shoes of the insured. In these circumstances, the solicitor should write to the insured party and ask for copies of the contract of insurance, receipts and other relevant documents. These may also be obtained from the insured's insurance company, if known. The plaintiff has a right to demand, and the liquidator of a company has a duty to provide, details of a company's employers' liability insurance.[13] The solicitor should notify the insurance company, by recorded delivery letter, of proceedings to be brought against the insured, if this is an express

10 *Dexter v Tenby Electrical Accessories Ltd* [1991] COD 288; [1991] Crim LR 839; (1991) *Times* 11 March; see also *Alcock v Wraith* [1991] EGCS 137; [1991] NPC 135; (1991) *Times* 23 December.

11 *Smith v Cammell Laird* [1940] 2 AC 242; *McDermid v Nash Dredging* [1987] AC 906; *Morris v Breaveglen Ltd* (1993) PIQR 294. But see *Cook v Square D Ltd and others* (1992) PIQR P33. For the application of statutory duties to different parties, see Redgrave's *Health and Safety* 1993, Butterworths.

12 RSC Ord 11; CCR Ord 8.

13 Third Parties (Rights against Insurers) Act 1930 s2(1).

stipulation in the policy.[14] Judgment should then be obtained against the insured in the usual way.[15] Subsequently, if necessary, proceedings can be commenced directly against the insurance company for the judgment order.

Bankruptcy, liquidation and dissolution of a defendant

Corporations in compulsory liquidation have a winding up order issued by the Companies Court. After the winding up order is made, but before the defendant company is dissolved, proceedings are commenced or continued by an application to the Companies Court for leave.[16] This is usually a formality. If a company has already been dissolved an application (usually by originating summons) to the Companies Court is necessary to restore the company to the register.[17] A company is dissolved automatically three months after the date of the final return lodged by the liquidator with the registrar of companies. Companies in voluntary liquidation have no order from the Companies Court and leave to commence proceedings is not required.

No application to commence or continue proceedings can be made later than 12 years after the dissolution of the company.[18] Once the company is dissolved, time for the purposes of the Limitation Act 1980 ceases to run, as there is no one in whose favour it can run.[19] Companies struck off the companies register can be restored within 20 years under Companies Act 1985 s653 and, if struck off after 16 November 1989, at any time under Companies Act 1989 s141. It is arguable but not yet clear that claims outside the limitation period should not be statute-barred and the discretion under the Limitation Act 1980 s33 should be exercised because a company so resurrected could not be prejudiced.[20]

If a company has gone into liquidation and the details of the employers' liability or other insurance are not known, consideration ought to be given to joining the directors of the company personally, if it

14 *Pioneer Concrete (UK) Ltd v National Employers Mutual General Insurance Association Ltd* [1985] 1 All ER 395.
15 *Bradley v Eagle Star Insurance Co Ltd* [1989] AC 957.
16 Insolvency Act 1986 s130(3).
17 Companies Act 1985 s651.
18 *Bradley v Eagle Star Insurance Co Ltd* [1989] AC 957.
19 *In re BBH (Middletons) Ltd* (1970) 114 SJ 431.
20 The court should consider Limitation Act 1980 s33 when deciding whether or not to restore a company to the register: *Re Workvale Ltd (in dissolution)* [1991] 1 WLR 294.

can be shown that one or more of them might personally be liable in tort.[21]

After a bankruptcy order has been made against an individual debtor, no action may be commenced without the leave of the court having bankruptcy jurisdiction.[22] Any action commenced without such leave will be stayed.

Liability

It is not within the scope of this book to consider the law on liability, though some aspects are dealt with in chapter 10 and in Part IV.

When preparing to issue and serve proceedings, the strength of the case must be reassessed. Once proceedings are issued and served, the defendant will start incurring significant costs, which may include instructing counsel to settle the defence, a request for further and better particulars, interviewing witnesses and commissioning experts. Therefore, the plaintiff and his or her solicitor need to be convinced that the case has a reasonable chance of succeeding. There is a balance to be struck here, between on the one hand excessive caution, in unduly delaying the case to complete investigations and exhausting the prospects of an early negotiated settlement, and, on the other hand, excessive zeal in commencing proceedings which may turn out to be hopeless. In either of these instances, a client is likely to resent greatly being kept from receiving compensation for years by fruitless negotiations, or having to pay both sets of costs if the case should never have been started.

Injury, loss and damage

Full details of financial losses are unlikely to be complete at the stage of issuing proceedings and may be very vague. Nevertheless a schedule of damages is required (see p129). Where detail is lacking, at least the heads should be set out. The medical position should be clearer and a medical report is required at this stage to accompany the statement or particulars of claim (see p128). The problem is that it can sometimes take months to obtain a medical report, which can greatly delay the case. It is important, therefore, to do everything possible to speed up this process, for example, by regularly instructing a selected number of specialists who will feel obliged to give some priority to regular clients.

21 See *Ambler v Hepworth* PMILL Vol 9 No 1 p4.
22 Insolvency Act 1986 s285(3).

High Court or county court

One of the decisions to be taken at this stage is in which court to issue proceedings. For most personal injury solicitors, until recently the High Court was the natural home of PI litigation. However, since July 1991, most personal injury cases have been tried in the county court.[23] The jurisdiction provisions of the High Court and county court are contained in the High Court and County Court Jurisdiction Order 1991.[24]

Since January 1992 all actions concerning personal injuries with a 'value' of less than £50,000 must be commenced in the county court.[25] The value is that which the plaintiff reasonably expects to recover.[26] An action with a value of less than £25,000 will be tried in the county court unless, having regard to:

- the financial substance of the action, including any counterclaim
- whether the action is otherwise important and whether it raises questions of importance to persons who are not parties, or questions of general public interest
- the complexity of the facts, legal issues, remedies or procedures involved, and
- whether the transfer is likely to result in a speedier trial of the action (but not on this ground alone),

the county court or High Court consider that the action ought to be transferred. At any such application a 'statement of value', must be completed by the plaintiff's solicitor (see precedent C2 p364). Alternatively, if such an action is commenced in the High Court, the High Court may, having regard to the above criteria, consider that it ought to try the action. Cases involving professional negligence; fatal accidents; fraud or undue influence; defamation; malicious prosecution or false imprisonment; and claims against the police are likely to be considered suitable for the High Court.

If the action has a value of £50,000 or more it must be tried in the High Court unless, having regard to the above criteria, the county court considers that the action should not be transferred or alternatively the

23 The High Court is reserved for public law and other specialist cases and for general cases of unusual importance, substance and complexity: Courts and Legal Services Act 1990 s1.

24 Reproduced in the Green Book 1994 p19.

25 High Court and County Courts Jurisdiction Order 1991 art 5(1).

26 Ibid art 9(1)(a).

High Court considers, having regard to the above criteria, that the case should be transferred to the county court.[27]

If the action is worth between £25,000 and £50,000, it is open to either party to apply to have the case transferred to the High Court for any of the reasons given above.

Where proceedings are commenced in the High Court but should, in the opinion of that court, have been commenced in the county court, the action will not normally be struck out[28] unless the court is satisfied that the plaintiff knew or ought to have known that the case should have started in the county court, but the trial judge will have regard to the error when determining costs. The reduction in costs should not exceed 25%.[29] The court also has the power to make a 'wasted costs' order against legal representatives.[30]

The plaintiff's solicitors must decide in which court the claim should be commenced. If proceedings are started in the High Court, the solicitor must certify that the claim is worth more than £50,000. This is known as the 'certificate of value' and its form is to be found in C4 at p367.

Transfer from High Court to county court

If the High Court is not satisfied that the action is worth £50,000 or more or that otherwise the action does not meet the criteria set out above (financial substance, interest to non-parties, public interest, complexity, and speed of trial), it can order the proceedings to be transferred to the county court.[31]

Proceedings which must be commenced in a county court

If at any stage of the proceedings it appears to a judge, master or district judge that the case should be transferred to the county court, then, unless all the parties are before the court, a notice (form PF 200, see precedent E6 p461) will be sent to all parties, stating that the court is proposing to transfer the case to a particular county court. Any party wishing to object to either the transfer or the court proposed, must complete form PF 201

27 Ibid art 7(3)–(5). In a case brought in the county court when the limit was £5,000 a jury award of £15,000 was set aside by the Court of Appeal and £5,000 substituted on the grounds that the defendant had conducted his case on the basis of exposure to a risk of a maximum of £5000: *Gilsenan v Commissioner for Metropolitan Police* (1994) PIQR 65, CA. The same principle might apply in relation to the new limits.

28 *Rastick v Crickmore* [1994] 1 WLR 420, CA.

29 Supreme Court Act 1981 s51(8), as amended.

30 Ibid s51(6).

31 County Courts Act 1984 s40(1); CCR Ord 16 r6.

(see precedent E7 p462). This form must be filed at either the central office or the appropriate district registry within 14 days of receipt of form PF 200. If no notice is filed within the time limit, the master or district judge either transfers the case to the proposed county court or, if appropriate, strikes out the action. If a notice is filed, the court fixes an appointment and sends the date to the parties.

Proceedings which might be transferred to a county court

A case can at any stage be transferred to the county court if, having regard to the criteria above, the court considers it suitable for transfer[32]. The High Court can, of its own motion or on application by any party, transfer the case to the county court.[33] This usually happens at a directions hearing or on setting down.

A party wishing to apply should do so by means of an inter partes summons. Where it appears to the judge, master or district judge that the case ought to be transferred, the court must, unless all the parties are before the court, give notice using form PF 202 (see precedent E8 p463). The court will consider the need for transfer within seven days of setting down. If any party objects to the transfer or to the particular court, they must file form PF 203 (see precedent E9 p463) at the central office or appropriate district registry, within 14 days of receipt of the notice. If no notice is received, the court will order the transfer. If notice is received, a date is fixed and sent to all the parties within 14 days. In deciding to which county court to transfer the case, the High Court should take account of the convenience of the parties and other persons likely to be affected and the state of business of the courts concerned.

Appeals from an order of transfer can be made to the judge in charge of the non-jury list (in London) or to the presiding judge, or as directed. Cases transferred to the county court should be heard by a circuit judge, with prior approval of the presiding judge or of a recorder or assistant recorder.[34]

For proceedings commenced after 1 July 1991 and all proceedings after 1 January 1992, where an order is made transferring proceedings to a county court, all pleadings, affidavits and other documents filed in the High Court relating to the proceedings, including a copy of the order for

32 For an example of the exercise of discretion see *McLaughlin v British Coal Corp.* (1992) *Times* 16 December.

33 County Courts Act 1984 s40(3).

34 *Practice Direction (Queen's Bench Division: transfer of proceedings to county court)* [1991] 1 WLR 643, which applies equally to proceedings transferred from county court to High Court.

transfer,[35] will be sent to the county court. Automatic directions apply to proceedings transferred from the High Court.[36]

Transfer from county court to High Court

If the county court is satisfied that the action should be heard in the High Court, it will order that the proceedings be transferred.[37]

Effect of the 1991 changes

While it is not one of the aims of this book to take part in the debate about the changes that have taken place, it is relevant to mention some of the concerns felt by many plaintiffs' personal injury lawyers at those changes. This relates to the different ways in which the two courts operate.

In the High Court, virtually all the running of the case is left in the hands of the solicitor. However, county courts intervene to a far greater extent in the conduct of the case. While the latter system may have advantages for the unrepresented party or to the generalist solicitor, the change is a significant disadvantage to the specialist personal injury lawyer. It removes control and is most likely to cause delay. Most county courts are understaffed, both administratively and judicially, and there are often long delays in obtaining a summons or hearing date.

In the High Court, the solicitor is responsible for serving all documents. The county court serves certain documents itself. Solicitors are therefore unable to time service to suit their requirements and must often wait until staff are ready to serve documents by post. This difficulty is to some extent ameliorated by CCR Order 7 r10A, which now enables plaintiffs' solicitors to serve summonses by post and CCR Order 50 r4A, which permits preparation (not service) of any document by the plaintiff's solicitor if allowed by a proper officer. Nevertheless, the norm is that phone calls and letters are necessary in order to check whether steps, which would be taken by the solicitor personally in the High Court, have been taken by the county court staff. Simply getting through on the telephone to many county courts is a major problem in itself.

Hearings that overrun the number of days allocated to them run on to the next day in the High Court. This is unusual in the county court and cases are often adjourned part-heard for weeks or months. At present, the expertise and experience of county court and district judges in personal

35 RSC Ord 107 r2(1A).
36 CCR Ord 17 r11(1A).
37 County Courts Act 1984 s42(1); CCR Ord 16 rr9 and 10; Green Book 1994 pp271–2.

injury cases is often less than that of High Court judges. This may improve as more personal injury cases are heard in the county court. On the whole, county court and district judges award lower damages than High Court judges for cases of equivalent value. Their horizons seem to be lower, perhaps because they customarily deal with cases (of every kind) of much lower value than High Court judges.

Another problem arises in relation to smaller claims. On issue of a default summons in the county court the plaintiff now must specify whether the case is 'worth' over £5,000 and, if not, the trial will automatically be heard by a district judge.[38] There must be a large question-mark over whether a busy district judge, hearing maybe 30 to 40 applications each day, has time or ought to be expected to set days aside to hear trials. Because a case is worth (say) £4,000 does not mean that medical evidence is easier to agree than in a claim worth (say) £7,000.

It used to be the case that obtaining a fixed date for a county court trial could be achieved far more quickly than in the High Court. This is no longer so,[39] as the county courts take the weight of personal injury litigation and the High Court speeds up its procedures.

The most difficult aspect of having cases heard in the county court is obtaining a trial date that is convenient to all parties. A system that asks parties to lodge available dates and then leaves it for six weeks or so before actually providing the parties with the trial date is of no use to busy counsel and experts whose diaries alter on a daily basis.

The writ or summons

Writs and summonses are simple documents and there are few details to insert.[40] It is important that the information included is accurate, especially the description of the parties.

The first matter is the heading of the action. What is required is the full name of the plaintiff (ie, the client) and the full name of the defendants, if necessary giving their description and capacity. The crucial point is to have the proper name of defendants. It is sufficient to have the initials of defendants' first names, provided that the surname of the individual is clear. A list of common titles of parties is given in C1 p362.

If the defendant is a limited company, the full registered name should

38 CCR Ord 21 r5(1)(b).

39 *Listing Statement (Queen's Bench judge in chambers and non-jury lists)* (1990) *Times* 17 March.

40 The writ must be in the form as set out in White Book, prescribed form 1. Standard forms can be purchased from law stationers.

be used. Usually, the company will have responded to the letter before action, even if only to confirm that the letter has been passed on to insurers. That acknowledgment should set out the full name and registered address of the company in the letterhead. If the company's name is not clear, it is usually possible to obtain confirmation from the insurers or, if necessary, by a company search. The description 'limited company' or 'PLC' must be included.[41] Where the defendant is a partnership, the claim should be in the name of the partners of the firm or in the name of the firm. If the partners are personally named, the firm's name and the words 'trading as a firm' should be added.

Actions against local authorities are brought against the full title of the authority, eg, 'The London Borough of Tower Hamlets'. Actions against the police are brought against the chief constable, or, in London, 'the Commissioner of the Metropolitan Police'.

The address of the defendant must be set out. This need be only the last known address. This may be difficult in road accident cases, either where the police were not called or where there is no address for the defendant, or where it is clear that the defendant has disappeared. It can also be difficult in cases where there are no insurers involved. Where there are difficulties in establishing the defendant's address, an enquiry agent might be instructed. A company is sued at the address of its registered office.

If there are insurers, an order for substituted service on them will be required in the last resort, although they will almost invariably provide the proper address of the defendant.

Issuing in the High Court

A High Court writ is issued either by taking the original and one copy (together with a copy for each defendant) personally, or by posting them, to the writ room at the High Court in London or the district registry most convenient to the plaintiff.[42] The cost in 1993 was £70.

The High Court writ requires only an endorsement, although a full statement of claim may be added. It is usual to serve a writ bearing only a brief endorsement. The statement of claim should follow within the 14-day period after receipt of the notice of intention to defend (acknowledgment of service).[43]

The endorsement on a writ sets out the outline of the case. It should be brief – three or four lines at most. It is a concise statement of the claim

41 *Practice Direction* [1969] 1 WLR 1259.
42 White Book Vol 2 para 707.
43 RSC Ord 18 r1.

made or the relief or remedy required.[44] It must state: that the claim is for damages for injuries suffered, loss and damage; the date of the occurrence or dates between which the occurrences or exposure causing injury occurred; the place(s) of the accident, occurrence or exposure; the essence of the relationship between the plaintiff and defendant(s) (eg, employee, lawful visitor, pedestrian etc); that the claim results from the defendant's negligence and/or breach of statutory duty (an explanation that the accident occurred 'by reason of the defendant's negligent driving' covers both this and the previous point); that damages and interest[45] are claimed; that the action is not one which must be commenced in the county court.[46] Examples of writ endorsements are given at C3 p365.

Issuing in the county court

Unlike the High Court, where the writ requires only a short endorsement in order to be issued, the county court default summons[47] cannot be issued without there being full particulars of claim (unless the court orders otherwise). The particulars must specify the cause of action, the relief or remedy sought and a brief statement of the material facts.

If commencement is urgent because of the limitation date, it may not be possible to issue full particulars of claim. There is no county court equivalent of the 'general endorsement'. However, provided the particulars of claim also include material facts such as the date, time and place of the accident, the parties and their capacity, and a brief explanation of why the defendants are to blame, that will often be sufficient to escape the time bar until the particulars can be amended by the inclusion of more detail.

As for a writ, a medical report and a statement of the special damages claimed must also be filed. If the plaintiff's solicitor is not able to provide these documents with the particulars of claim, the court should still enter the plaint but may stipulate the time within which they are to be provided or make such order as it thinks fit, which may include an order dispensing with the requirement or even a stay of proceedings.

The plaintiff's solicitor may prepare the default summons if allowed

44 RSC Ord 6 r2.

45 There is no requirement for a generally indorsed writ claiming damages to include a claim for interest: *Edward Butler Vintners Ltd v Grange Seymour Internationale Ltd* (1987) 131 SJ 1188, CA.

46 RSC Ord 6 r2(1)(f).

47 CCR Ord 6 r1. For a request for a default summons, see Green Book form N201. For a default summons, see ibid form N2.

by the proper officer and must then file (either by post or by attendance at the court) with the court:

- a copy of the default summons if the plaintiff is to effect service by post, or, if service is to be by the court, a request for issue of the default summons
- a copy of the particulars of claim together with sufficient copies for each defendant
- a medical report, if available, together with sufficient copies for each defendant
- a schedule of special damages, if available, together with sufficient copies for each defendant.
- the plaint fee[48]
- if the plaintiff is legally aided, a notice of issue of legal aid and appropriate copy certificate
- if the summons is to be served by the bailiffs, their fee or if by post, a stamped addressed envelope
- in an infant claim, the next friend's undertakings.[49]

The court will enter the plaint in the records. This is the moment when the action has been commenced or 'brought' for the purposes of the Limitation Act 1980 11(3). If the plaintiff sends the prepared summons or request to the court by post, it may take a considerable, or at least an uncertain, time for the action to be commenced. Therefore, if limitation is a problem, attendance at the court is essential.

The plaintiff can commence proceedings in any county court.[50] It is no longer necessary in personal injury actions to issue a county court summons in the district registry nearest to the place of accident or residence of the defendant, although of course it is always open to the defendant to have the matter transferred to his or her local district registry.

The court will deliver or hand over to the plaintiff's solicitor a plaint note and (if the solicitor is to serve the summons by post or personally) the summons, together with supporting documents. These include all the documents listed above and a form of admission, defence and counterclaim for each defendant.

48 At the time of writing – £60 for cases worth between £300 and £1,000; £65 for cases between £1,000 and £5,000; and £70 for cases over £5,000: County Court Fees Order 1982; Green Book 1994 p1712.

49 Ibid p1920 form N235.

50 CCR Ord 4 r2(1)(c).

Between issue and service

In the High Court, the writ must be served within four months of issue.[51] This period may be useful to protect against expiry of limitation while continuing to investigate. If the four-month period is about to expire and more time is required, the best course is to serve the writ and apply for an extension to serve the statement of claim. Alternatively an application to the court for an extension of the period may be made.[52] This is an ex parte application to the master, supported by an affidavit[53] made by the plaintiff's solicitor.[54] The danger of this course is that the defendant may apply to set aside the extension and may well succeed. The deadline has then passed, leaving the solicitor open to a negligence claim.

If service is not made within four months plus the maximum one-year renewal period, subsequent service is irregular but the writ remains valid. In the event of no application being made to set aside the service, the defendant may be held to have waived such irregularity.[55]

The same principles apply to the county court, although it is rare not to serve immediately after issue. Service there must also be within four months.[56]

Service of High Court proceedings

In the High Court, service is effected by the plaintiff or his/her solicitor and the writ need not be accompanied by a statement of claim.[57] The writ must be served personally on the defendant, unless solicitors representing the defendant have given notice that they have instructions to accept

51 RSC Ord 6 r8(1).

52 RSC Ord 6 r8(2). Applications will not be allowed after the period permitted for service has expired, if to do so would deprive the defendant of a limitation defence: *Chappell v Cooper* [1980] 1 WLR 958. Where the action is struck out, any subsequent proceedings relying on the Limitation Act 1980 are unlikely to succeed: *Walkley v Precision Forgings Ltd* [1979] 1 WLR 606. See also *Singh v Duport Harper Foundries Ltd* (1994) PIQR 87.

53 The plaintiff has to show a good reason for the extension and a satisfactory explanation for the failure to apply for the extension before the validity of the writ expired: *Kleinwort Benson v Barbrak Ltd* [1987] 1 AC 597, per Lord Brandon at 623B. White Book para 6/8/3. For recent cases on these principles, see *Harris v Lopen Group Ltd* (1993) PIQR 1 and *Singh (Joginder) v Duport Harper Foundries Ltd* (1994) PIQR 87.

54 White Book paras 6/8/3–6/8/6.

55 RSC Ord 12 rr7 and 8; *Sheldon v Brown Bayley's Steelworks* [1953] 2 QB 393, CA, at 400.

56 CCR Ord 7 r20(1)(b). See also *Barr v Barr* (1994) PIQR 45.

57 RSC Ord 18 r1.

proceedings on their client's behalf. In practice, most writs are served by post,[58] by sending the writ to the last known address of the defendant[59] or the registered office, if a company. Unless the contrary is shown, it is deemed to be served on the second working day after posting in the case of first class post, and on the fourth working day after posting in the case of second class post.[60]. However, if the defendant refuses to accept the letter, some other form of service is required. Personal service is usually tried next,[61] followed, in exceptional cases, by some other method such as substituted service.[62]

If the defendant lives outside the jurisdiction, attempts should first be made to get the insurance company to agree to nominate solicitors within the jurisdiction to accept proceedings. If the insurers refuse, then leave of the court will have to be obtained to serve outside the jurisdiction.[63]

Service of county court proceedings

In the county court, the plaintiff's solicitor now has a choice in the procedure for service. It can either be done by post, through the court or by personal service.

By post

The summons and particulars of claim, together with copies for each defendant, should first be filed with the court.

The plaintiff's solicitor must then serve the summons by sending it first class post to the defendant at the address stated on the summons. Thereupon, the summons is treated as if it were served by an officer of the court.[64] The date of service, unless the contrary is shown, is seven days after the date on which the summons was sent.[65]

Where the summons is not served as above and the defendant delivers a defence, admission or counterclaim, the summons is deemed, unless the

58 RSC Ord 10 r1(2).

59 The address must be one at which the defendant is to be found from time to time: see *Willowgreen Ltd v Smithers* (1993) *Times* 14 December.

60 'Working day' means Monday to Friday excluding bank holidays; on this see *Practice Direction (Central Office: First and Second Class Mail)* [1968] 1 WLR 1489.

61 RSC Ord 65 r2.

62 White Book 1993 para 10/1/5; RSC Ord 65 r4.

63 RSC Ord 11 r5.

64 CCR Ord 7 r10A.

65 CCR Ord 7 r10(3).

contrary is shown, to have been served on the date when the defence, admission or counterclaim is delivered.[66]

By the court

An officer of the court sends the default summons, together with supporting documents, by first class post to the defendant at the address stated in the request. Service is deemed to have been completed, unless the contrary is shown, on the seventh day after the summons was sent to the defendant.[67] To avoid giving defendants an excuse for delay in preparing the acknowledgment and defence, it is wise to serve them informally with a copy of the particulars of claim at the same time as issuing a request for service by the court.

By personal service

Service will be effective if the default summons is handed to the person to be served,[68] or left at the registered office of a company registered in England and Wales, or at any place of business of the company which has some real connection with the case.[69] In exceptional cases another form of service will be ordered, such as substituted service.[70]

Service via the Document Exchange

Service by Document Exchange (DX) is permissible in the High Court and county court for documents other than writs or summonses where the other party or solicitor has displayed a DX number on the notepaper unless a letter is written indicating unwillingness to accept service in this way. Service is deemed to be effected on the second working day following the day on which the document was left at the DX addressed to the recipient's box number.[71]

66 CCR Ord 7 r12.
67 CCR Ord 7 r10(3).
68 Or if s/he will not accept it, left with or near the person: CCR Ord 7 r2. Consensual service can be valid: *Kenneth Allison Ltd v AE Limehouse & Co* [1992] 2 AC 105.
69 CCR Ord 7 r14(2).
70 CCR Ord 7 r8.
71 RSC Order 65 r5(2A), para 65/5/8.

Service of documents by fax

Though neither a writ nor a summons can be served by fax, all other documents may be in the High Court and county court. The fax must be followed by dispatch of the original as soon as practicable thereafter. Service is deemed to be the same day provided the fax is sent before 4.00 pm (so every solicitor must ensure the clock setting is accurate). Service by fax is only permissible between solicitors and so long as the receiving solicitor has indicated consent to service by this means: display of a fax number on notepaper presumes consent.[72]

Service of legal aid documents

Where the action is legally aided, a notice of issue of legal aid must be served on the defendant with the other proceedings.[73] If a legal aid certificate is granted after proceedings are issued, the notice must be served immediately on the defendant. If the notice is not served, it will be open to defendants, if they win the case, to apply for the plaintiff's solicitor to pay the costs up to the time the notice was served.[74] Although it is imperative to serve the notice, the question as to whether the defendants need to be told of any limitation in the certificate is a matter of unresolved debate.[75]

As well as serving the notice on the defendant, it is also the plaintiff's solicitor's job to serve a copy of the legal aid certificate on the court. Any amendments to the certificate must also be filed as and when they are notified to the solicitor.[76]

Service of other documents

The plaintiff has two principal choices for effecting service on an individual. The first, which is the easiest and cheapest, is simply to send a letter by ordinary first class post[77] to the defendant's address in the acknowledgement of service or, in the county court, the last known address, or, if a proprietor of a business, sending it by first class post to the last known place of business.

The second method is to effect personal service. This method of service

72 RSC Ord 65 r5(2B), para 65/5/9.

73 Civil Legal Aid (General) Regs 1989 reg 50(1).

74 *Mauroux v Pereira* [1972] 1 WLR 962 at 969; *Sinclair-Jones v Kay* [1989] 1 WLR 114, CA.

75 White Book 1993 Vol 2 para 4096/1; *Scarth v Jacobs-Paton* (1978) *Times* 2 November, CA.

76 Civil Legal Aid (General) Regs 1989 reg 50(4).

77 RSC Ord 65 r5; CCR Ord 7 r1(1).

is usually adopted only where there is real doubt about the defendant's true address or where any delay might result in a time-limit being exceeded. Where there is personal service of the pleadings, they are deemed to have been served on that same day, provided that it is within business hours.

If the defendant is a limited company, the documents should be served either personally or by first class post on the registered office.

Documents can also be served by document exchange and by fax (see above) or by any method which the court may direct.[78]

Acknowledgment of service

High Court

It has already been stated that on serving a High Court writ it is also necessary to serve the defendant with an acknowledgement of service form.[79] This is a standard form and the only information that needs to be inserted by the plaintiff's solicitor is the full title and number of the action.

The defendant has 14 days, including the date of service of the writ, to lodge the completed acknowledgment of service with the High Court.[80] Once lodged, the High Court forwards a sealed copy to the plaintiff's solicitor. The importance of this process is that, if the acknowledgment is filed, it will confirm whether the details given on the writ about the defendant are correct, and, if they are not, an application to amend may have to be made. The acknowledgment also confirms whether the defendant is represented by solicitors or acting in person.

County court

There is a standard form of admission, defence and/or counterclaim for the defendant to complete. The defendant must either return this

78 RSC Ord 65 r5(1)(c), (ca) and 2(B); CCR Ord 7 r1(1); *Hastie and Jenkerson v McMahon* (1990) 134 SJ 725.

79 Failure to do so may result in the writ being set aside if the defendant is prejudiced: *Bondy and Another v Lloyds Bank plc and Another* (1991) 135 SJ 412. If the defendant wishes to challenge the validity of the writ, s/he should acknowledge service, issue a summons to set aside the writ then sit tight until the summons has been heard: *Sage v Double A Hydraulics Ltd* (1992) *Times* 2 April; otherwise s/he might waive any right of challenge.

80 RSC Ord 12 r5. Defendants can apply to be struck out of the proceedings if they consider they should never have been joined: RSC Ord 15 r6(2)(a); CCR Ord 5 r4; *Littrell v USA* (1993) *Times* 24 November, CA.

document duly completed or serve a defence within 14 days of the date of service of the summons.[81]

Judgment in default of acknowledgement of service

If the acknowledgment of service is not filed within 14 days of service of the writ, the plaintiff's solicitors may apply for judgment in default. This applies to both the High Court and county court.[82] Where provisional damages are claimed as part of the relief, judgment in default is not permissible.[83]

Leave to issue an application is not required, except in proceedings against the Crown and proceedings served out of the jurisdiction without leave (and in some rarer circumstances). Judgment can be given against any one of several defendants.

Obtaining judgment in default of acknowledgment of service is a straightforward procedure and is granted if there is no acknowledgment. However, defendants are likely to apply for judgment to be set aside as soon as their predicament is realised. They will almost certainly succeed if they have some excuse for their failure to lodge the acknowledgment in time.[84] Furthermore, because it usually takes a few weeks, if not months, for the application to be heard, it may slow down proceedings, since it effectively prevents the plaintiff from doing anything to advance the case. Judgment in default is thus usually more effective in the threat than in the execution.

If judgment is obtained in default of acknowledgment, the next step, since damages are unliquidated, is to seek a hearing for the assessment of damages. This is done by applying first to the master or district judge for a summons or hearing for directions, at which the direction can be made for a hearing for assessment of damages.[85]

81 CCR Ord 9 r2(6).

82 RSC Ord 13 r2 and Ord 19 r3; CCR Ord 9 r6.

83 *Practice Direction (Provisional Damages)* [1988] 1 WLR 654.

84 RSC Ord 13 r9 and Ord 19 r3; CCR Ord 37 r4. If the judgment is regular, the court will consider whether the defendant has a defence on the merits, the explanation of the defendant and the prejudice involved to the plaintiff: *Ladup Ltd v Siu* (1984) 81 LS Gaz Pt I 283, CA.

85 RSC Ord 13 r2, Ord 19 r3 and Ord 37 r1; CCR Ord 9 r6(2).

CHAPTER 10

Statements of claim/particulars of claim

The statement/particulars of claim should be served within fourteen days of receipt of the acknowledgement of service. Unless an extension of time can be agreed or is ordered, the defendants can apply to the court to dismiss the action. If such an application is made, a cross-summons (precedent at D5 p440) should be issued immediately under RSC Order 3 r5 to extend time for service of the statement/particulars of claim. Save in the most exceptional circumstances, it is not appropriate to deny the plaintiff an extension (where the denial would stifle the action) because of a procedural default which, even if justifiable, has caused the defendant no prejudice for which s/he cannot be compensated by an award of costs. In short, an application under Order 3 r5 will ordinarily be granted where the overall justice of the case requires that the action be allowed to proceed.[1]

Instructing counsel

It has been usual to instruct counsel to 'settle' the statement or particulars of claim. Except in rare cases – for example, where pre-action discovery has been sought or where counsel's opinion has been obtained at the outset – this is the first time that a barrister comes into the litigation. Some PI solicitors undertake pleadings themselves, but this is not advised save for the experienced specialist.

Whether counsel is instructed to settle the statement or particulars of claim, or is brought in at a later stage, it is important to ensure that the instructions are appropriate. What counsel is required to do should be made explicit and precise. The right balance should be sought between ensuring that counsel has all the relevant documents and not sending down the solicitor's entire file on the case.

1 See *Erskine Commissioners Ltd v Worthington* (1991) *Times* 8 July, CA; *Costellow v Somerset County Council* (1993) PIQR 147, CA.

Both in London and elsewhere, there are a substantial number of good, efficient and effective barristers, sympathetic to plaintiffs, who specialise in personal injury work. Most are members of the Association of Personal Injury Lawyers (APIL) and, with experience, the solicitor will build up a list of barristers that can be relied on. Expertise is not enough. One of the qualities a solicitor is entitled to demand – the lack of which should result in a barrister being taken off the solicitor's list – is speed in returning drafting and advice. A statement or particulars of claim in a straightforward case with competent instructions, without any computation of special damage, should take an experienced counsel no more than 30–45 minutes to draft. Solicitors are entitled to expect that a statement or particulars of claim will be returned within three to four weeks of delivery, excluding holidays. If the papers are likely to take longer than this, the barrister should make sure that the solicitor is given the reason for the delay. The solicitor (upon whom the responsibility for time limits ultimately rests) should not have to worry that the barrister's delay in dealing with straightforward papers will jeopardise the case.

It is a general principle of giving instructions – whether to draft a statement or particulars of claim, an interlocutory application or an advice on some aspect of the case, or to prepare for trial – not to repeat what is in the documents, but to give an overview, so that counsel knows what to look for when reading the documents. Thus, the brief should, after listing the documents contained in it, begin with a short summary of the facts of the case. In legally aided cases, the documents must include a copy of the legal aid certificate.[2] A rambling repetition of the plaintiff's proof of evidence is a waste of time, since the barrister must read the original. In addition, the solicitor's own ideas on the case should be added and any particular aspects that need consideration at that stage. The purpose of the instructions is to obtain the benefits of the barrister's skill and experience, but these benefits will be enriched by the sharing of the solicitor's skill and experience.

Caveats

The purpose of the statement or particulars of claim is to put the client's case as succinctly as possible. All reasonably plausible allegations should be stated, bearing in mind that the case will have been only partly investigated by the time the pleading is drafted. It is, of course, not

2 Civil Legal Aid (General) Regs 1989 reg 59(2)(a).

permissible to put forward a case for which there is no supporting evidence.

The pleader must allow for the possibility that the plaintiff's proof of evidence has not been prepared as well as it might have been. It is common for failures of communication or errors to creep into the proof of evidence so that it does not, in some vital respect, reflect the reality of the client's experience. For example, the solicitor may not have fully understood the situation described by the plaintiff, the latter may still be in shock or confused, or there may be uncorrected typographical errors. If the pleading perpetuates an error, at trial there will be a danger of perceptive cross-examination exploiting some discrepancy between the pleading based on the proof of evidence and the plaintiff's own testimony in the witness box.

With this in mind, the pleader should be cautious about revealing too much of the plaintiff's proof of evidence. The pleader should opt for broad, rather than detailed, assertions. Sketch plans drawn by a client – no matter how skilfully – should not be relied on. Nor should the accuracy of any measurements taken by the plaintiff be assumed, except in the broadest way. Further detail may be required later by the defendant in a request for further and better particulars. If so, more precise information may have to be given.

Essentials

In order to begin drafting a statement or particulars, a minimum number of essential facts are required. Here are checklists of the information that is necessary in three common situations.

Road traffic accidents

- The identity of the parties.
- The make and registration number (and any other means of identification, such as colour, bicycle, moped, motorcycle, car, van or lorry) of any vehicle involved in the collision.
- The location of the accident.
- The directions in which the plaintiff and the defendant were travelling, defined in any appropriate way: by compass bearing, destination, road name, carriageway etc.
- The date and, preferably, the time of the accident.
- A description of how the accident happened.

- Whether any prosecution ensued and, if so, for what offences, in which court, when and the result.
- The plaintiff's date of birth.
- A medical report.
- A description of loss of amenities.
- A statement of damages.

Accidents at work

- The identity of the parties and their work relationships.
- The plaintiff's job description.
- The plaintiff's place of work.
- The nature of the work or processes carried out at the place of work, so as to determine whether the Factories Act 1961 or some other statute or regulations apply.
- The location of the accident.
- The date and preferably the time of the accident.
- A description of how the accident happened.
- The plaintiff's date of birth.
- A medical report.
- A description of loss of amenities.
- A statement of damages.

Fatal accidents

In addition to the above, the following should be included:

- The date when letters of administration were taken out, or grant of probate made, and where.
- Brief details of any claim for loss of dependency and its basis.
- Particulars relating to the plaintiff and the defendant, together with all the information referred to above in relation to the road traffic accident or the work accident. The distinction must be maintained between 'the deceased' and 'the plaintiff'.

Format

The statement or particulars of claim in personal injury litigation follows a format common to virtually every case. The order is: identify the parties;

set out the date, time and description of the accident; plead legal failings which make the defendant liable; allege that injury, loss and damage flow from liability for the accident; briefly describe the injuries and the losses (or merely refer to the medical report and schedule of damages appended); and, finally, claim damages and interest.

In the county court, the particulars of claim should state that the claim exceeds £5,000. In the absence of such a statement, the claim will be treated as limited to this sum, unless the court orders otherwise.[3] If the value of the claim subsequently drops to £5,000 or less, the particulars should be amended.[4] Where proceedings are commenced on or after 1 July 1991 and a statement of the value of the claim has not been given, the case is listed for trial before a district judge. If the trial is then unable to proceed because the claim is worth in excess of £5,000, so exceeding the district judge's jurisdiction, an order may be made against the legal or other representative concerned in respect of the wasted costs.[5]

The allegations of negligence and breach of statutory duty made by the plaintiff should start with specific allegations that arise out of the particular circumstances of the accident and then be bolstered by more general allegations. Any relevant conviction must be pleaded.[6] So should exemplary and provisional damages.[7]

If a barrister settles the statement or particulars of claim, it should bear his/her name and, below that, the document will conclude:

(In the High Court)

SERVED this day of 19

by (name and address of solicitor),

solicitor for the plaintiff.

(In the County Court)

DATED the day of 19

by (name and address of solicitor)

Solicitor for the plaintiff who will accept service of all proceedings on his/her behalf at the above address.

To: The district judge of the court and to the defendants.

3 CCR Ord 6 r1A and Ord 21 r5(1)(b).
4 CCR Ord 6 r1A.
5 Supreme Court Act 1981 s51(6) as amended. RSC Ord 62 r11; CCR Ord 38 r1(3).
6 RSC Ord 18 r7A.
7 RSC Ord 18 r8(3).

Road traffic accidents

The first paragraph of the standard traffic injury pleading describes the accident. It usually starts '*On or about the* [date], *the plaintiff was [walking, cycling, driving] along* [name of road] *at or near* [some identifiable point: junction, bus-stop, public house etc] *when the defendant drove a [car, van etc] . . .*'. This last phrase should describe in a few words how the accident happened. It may be that the defendant drove his car '*around a bend and collided head on with the plaintiff*' or '*crossed the central white line and drove into the plaintiff's carriageway so forcing the plaintiff to swerve and collide with a lamp-post*'. Or it may be simply that the defendant drove his lorry '*into the plaintiff*'. All that is necessary is to give sufficient words to identify the place and date of the accident and how it occured. The second paragraph of the road traffic accident statement or particulars begins: '*The said accident was caused by the defendant's negligence*'.

Under the heading '*Particulars of negligence*' there are then set out the allegations of negligence which are levelled at the defendant. The full range of the allegations possible in road accident cases is so limited that they are set out here, and will cover all but the most exceptional case. *The defendant:*

a) *drove [or cycled or walked] when it was unsafe to do so* (this is appropriate when the activity which caused the accident was lawful and proper but for the fact that the defendant did it in circumstances where it caused the accident);
b) *drove [or cycled or walked] . . .* (this is the appropriate place to make the allegation that simply doing what the defendant did was negligent because it was unlawful or inherently dangerous, eg, *driving on the wrong side of the road, driving without lights, driving through a red traffic light*);
c) *failed to accord precedence to the plaintiff*;
d) *drove into [the path of] the plaintiff*;
e) *drove too fast*;
f) *failed to keep any or any proper lookout and/or failed to observe or heed in time, adequately or at all:*
    i) *the presence, position and direction of travel of the plaintiff and his [vehicle] and/or*
    ii) [*stop, warning or other signs or signals, or the presence of a road junction, bus coming the other way, black ice on the road,* or

whatever other visible or audible things there were which should have caused the defendant to do things differently];

g) *failed to warn the plaintiff in time, adequately or at all of the movement of the defendant's [vehicle];*
h) *drove into the plaintiff and/or failed to stop, slow down, [accelerate], swerve, or so to control or manage the defendant's [vehicle] as to avoid the accident;*
i) *failed to steer a safe course;*
j) *failed to maintain proper control of the [motor vehicle] that s/he was driving; [or lost control of the defendant's vehicle].*
k) *The plaintiff will further rely on the conviction of the defendant for the offence of . . . at the . . . Magistrates' Court on* [date] *as evidence of the negligence of the defendant, the said conviction having arisen out of the matters referred to in paragraph 1 herein and being relevant to the issues in this action.*
l) *The plaintiff will further rely on the happening of the said accident as evidence in itself of the negligence of the defendant.* (Res ipsa loquitur.)

Before a conviction can be proved, the conviction, date, court and relevance must be pleaded.[8] This shifts the burden of proof onto the defendant.[9]

The pleading then goes on to deal with injury, loss and damage, which is dealt with later in this chapter. Specimen road accident pleadings are given at C10 and 11, p392. See chapter 26 p300 for liability of drivers etc.

Pedestrian tripping cases

The statement or particulars of claim in this frequent source of litigation also follows the usual pattern. Examples of pleadings are at C12 and 13, p397. The first paragraph gives the date and place[10] of the accident and describes what the plaintiff was doing when s/he tripped or fell on the highway or pavement. Either as part of the first paragraph or in a separate second paragraph, the link with the defendant must be made, stating in what capacity the defendant caused the hole or obstruction. If the defendant is being sued as the highway authority, then this paragraph should say so.

The allegations of liability will primarily be made on the ground of

8 RSC Ord 18 r7A.
9 Civil Evidence Act 1968 s11.
10 Some precision is required: *James v Preseli Pembrokeshire DC* (1993) PIQR 114.

negligence. However, where a highway authority is being sued, there will be an allegation of breach of statutory duty, for example:

In breach of section 41 of the Highways Act 1980 and/or negligently, the defendants failed to repair and/or maintain the said highway properly or at all in that . . . [eg, a paving stone had been removed leaving a hole approximately three inches deep].

There is also the possibility of suing in nuisance in such cases, for example:

Further or in the alternative, by reason of the matters aforesaid, the defendants their servants or agents were guilty of nuisance in that they rendered the use of the said highway dangerous.

The principal allegations of negligence are obvious: creating the hazard; failing to remove it (in whatever ways are appropriate); failing to inspect and/or heed it; failing to fence, light or mark it; failing to ensure that the road was safe. So, for example, in a hole-in-the-pavement case it is pleaded that the defendant:

a) *caused or permitted the hole in the pavement;*
b) *failed to fill, level, or cover the hole so as to ensure that the same was even and level with the surrounding pavement surface;*
c) *failed to inspect regularly, sufficiently often or at all and/or heed the presence of the hole in the pavement;*
d) *failed to fence or guard the hole and/or pavement;*
e) *failed adequately or at all to light, mark or warn of the presence of the hole in the pavement;*
f) *failed to ensure that the pavement was safe for pedestrians.*

Animal injuries

Injuries caused by animals to humans are not a common source of litigation but are sufficiently frequent to require mention here.[11] The Animals Act 1971 s2(2) provides that where an animal does not belong to a dangerous species, the keeper of the animal is liable for the injury if s/he knew that (a) the injury was of a kind which the animal, unless restrained, was likely to cause, or which, if caused, was likely to be severe; and (b) the likelihood of the injury was due to the animal's particular characteristics, not normally found in animals of the same species.

11 Liability under the Animals Act 1971 s2(2) has been discussed in the Court of Appeal in: *Cummings v Granger* [1977] QB 397; *Curtis v Betts* [1990] 1 WLR 459; *Smith v Ainger and Another* (1990) *Times* 5 June. A claim to the Criminal Injuries Compensation Authority should also be considered (see p315).

The statement of claim should identify the defendant as the keeper of the animal. The incident should be described in a separate paragraph, followed by a paragraph setting out the violent propensity of the animal. For example:

The said [type of animal] *was/is of a fierce and mischievous nature and accustomed to attack and bite people, and the defendants wrongfully kept the said* [type of animal] *well knowing that it was of such a fierce and mischievous nature and so accustomed.*

PARTICULARS

[Here, state the facts and matters relied upon. Police stations keep a dog register containing complaints about particular dogs. There may be a relevant conviction which should also be pleaded. An example pleading is at C14, p402.]

Accidents at work

The statement/particulars of claim in an accident at work case has become a very formalised document.

The first paragraph describes the relationship between the plaintiff and the defendant and brings in any statutory provisions which relate to the place of work, though the latter are sometimes put in a separate paragraph. Thus, a typical example would be:

At all material times the plaintiff was employed as a lathe operator by the defendants at their premises at The Works, Railway Cuttings, East Cheam, Surrey, a factory within the meaning of the Factories Act 1961. The lathe came into use after 1st January 1993 and the Provision and Use of Work Equipment Regulations 1992 (the "Equipment Regs.") applied to it. That part of the factory wherein the plaintiff operated the lathe was modified after 1st January 1993 and the Workplace (Health, Safety and Welfare) Regulations (the "Workplace Regs.") applied to it.

Second or third defendants, having some relationship with the plaintiff other than a contract of employment, usually have a separate paragraph each.

With only one defendant, the second paragraph gives the date and place of the accident and a short description of how it happened. The description should be prefixed by the words '*in the course of employment*' so as to put beyond doubt the allegation that the plaintiff's accident was sustained while working for the employer.[12] The description of the accident should be short and in broad terms. The pleader's duty is to plead

12 For a case on employees travelling to and from work, see *Smith v Stages* [1989] AC 928, HL. The court is prepared to look at the reality of the relationship: *Ferguson v John Dawson and Partners (Contractors) Ltd* [1976] 1 WLR 1213.

material facts and not evidence. As has been mentioned earlier, the pleader must bear in mind that the explanation of the accident which s/he reads in the instructions and plaintiff's statement may not be wholly accurate, for a whole range of reasons. Where significant discrepancies are apparent, the pleader should, of course, contact the solicitor to try to ascertain the true position before drafting.

Two typical examples of a concise but clear second paragraph in a work accident case might be as follows:

On or about 18 August 1993, the plaintiff in the course of his said employment took a pace into the battery room in order to get cleaning materials when he slipped on liquid detergent on the floor which had leaked from a plastic container. The slip caused the plaintiff to fall to the ground striking his knee on a battery.

On or about 27 March 1994, the plaintiff in the course of his said employment had switched off the robot machine and lifted the guard in order to remove a broken robot within the said machine when the machine operated and the blade amputated the plaintiff's left index finger.

Often the accident will have been caused by a fellow employee. The second paragraph should name the employee (where the name is known), make clear that s/he, too, was an employee of the defendant and that s/he was acting '*in the course of his/her employment*'.

The third paragraph of the statement of claim sets out the breach of duty to which the accident is attributed. In every case, allegations of negligence will be made, but it is worth remembering that the duty in tort reflects a parallel duty arising under the contract of employment, so the action may occasionally be brought in contract as well as tort.[13]

Breach of statutory duty

In addition, there will often be breaches of statutory duty. These may be pleaded in a separate paragraph or as part of the same paragraph as the allegations of negligence. The statutory breach may depend on the nature of the premises. For example, under the Factories Act 1961, the Offices, Shops and Railway Premises Act 1963, the Mines and Quarries Act 1954 and the Agriculture (Safety, Health and Welfare Provisions) Act 1956, there are a large number of regulations dealing with particular

13 *Matthews v Kuwait Bechtel Corporation* [1959] 2 QB 57. Where the defendant's liability in contract is the same as his/her liability in tort or negligence, the court may reduce or apportion the damages claimed in contract, in accordance with the Law Reform (Contributory Negligence) Act 1945: *Forsikrings-aktieselskapet Vesta v Butcher and Others* [1988] 3 WLR 565.

workplaces, particular processes and particular substances. Examples are the Construction (Working Places) Regulations 1966, the Abrasive Wheels Regulations 1970, the Protection of Eyes Regulations 1974 and the Asbestos Regulations 1969. In addition, the 'six pack' of regulations[14] introduced in 1992 to give effect to European directives place duties on all employers. The pleader who is not familiar with them and how to plead them should not be undertaking PI work. Examples of pleadings are at C5–9 and 15, pp367 and 404. In general, all potential breaches of statutory duty should be included.

Pleading should be approached creatively. For example, a kitchen producing food for sale appears to be a factory within the definition given in the Factories Act 1961 s175. Breach of statutory duty should always be pleaded in an accident occurring in such a kitchen, even though the authority of *Wood v London County Council*[15] holds to the contrary. In the present judicial climate, the authority could be distinguished or overruled on appeal. Moreover, the insurers may wish to settle a case on the basis that a commercial kitchen is a factory rather than have a precedent established to that effect in the Court of Appeal or House of Lords.

By the same token, the principal statutes have many, less familiar sections which may be pertinent. It is therefore necessary to be familiar with and regularly to reinforce knowledge with the intricate maze of health and safety legislation. The 1992 regulations come into effect in stages and it is also necessary to consider any potential breach of statutory duty in relation to the 1992 regulations. The date of construction or modification of the workplace and the date of coming into use of equipment is relevant in order to see whether the pre-existing statutory provision has been superseded or not.

There is some debate about the extent to which the 1992 regulations fulfill the obligations under the European directives from which they were derived, so that consideration must also be given by the pleader to whether the directive should be relied on directly (against a state employer) or indirectly for the purposes of construction of the relevant regulation. It is suggested that the former would need to be pleaded, the latter would be

14 The six regulations are: Management of Health and Safety at Work Regs. 1992 SI No 2051 (which do not give rise to civil liability); Workplace (Health, Safety and Welfare) Regs. 1992 SI No 3004; Provision and Use of Work Equipment Regs. 1992 SI No 2932; Personal Protective Equipment at Work Regs 1992 SI No 2966; Manual Handling Operations Regs. 1992 SI No 2793; Health and Safety (Display Screen Equipment) Regs 1992 SI No 2792. For detail see Redgrave's *Health and Safety*, 2nd Ed, 1993, Butterworths.

15 [1941] 2 KB 232.

for argument.[16] It is also worth bearing in mind that statutory requirements may, in appropriate cases, affect the duty in negligence. In *Butt v Inner London Education Authority*,[17] it was held that a machine which injured a printing apprentice in a college of further education should have been fenced, under a duty in negligence which was analogous to Factories Act 1961 s14. The Management of Health and Safety at Work Regulations 1992 impose only criminal and not civil liability. It is arguable, however, that the standards they set may be determinative or at least persuasive of the standard of care in negligence. An example of such a pleading is in precedent C5 para 4(m) p370.

As well as the principal statutes relating to workplace safety, there are the more general statutory duties under the Occupier's Liability Act 1957 and the Defective Premises Act 1972 (see p298). These statutes appear not to require specific pleading, but it is necessary to plead the facts which give rise to the duties under them. The Consumer Protection Act 1987 also needs to be considered, but it is probably wisest to plead it explicitly (see p295).

A large number of statutory duties are qualified by the phrase 'so far as is reasonably practicable'. The plaintiff should never plead these words. It is for defendants to establish on the evidence not only that they could not do whatever was necessary 'so far as was reasonably practicable', but also to plead that defence if they intend to rely on it.[18]

As a general rule, the plaintiff should avoid pleading the Employer's Liability (Defective Equipment) Act 1969 in the statement or particulars of claim. The facts giving rise to liability under this Act have to be pleaded. However, pleading the Act specifically may alert an unskilled defendant's pleader to the danger of making admissions in the defence which would allow the plaintiff to enter judgment. Alerted, the pleader is likely to make denials or non-admissions simply in order to keep the case alive on liability. The Act must be pleaded eventually and the time to do it is by way of a reply (see p137) or by an amendment to the statement/ particulars of claim after the defence has been received.

Some lawyers tend to plead the breaches of statutory duty separately from the negligence. Specialist pleaders are divided on this issue. The advantage of dealing with breaches of statutory duty and negligence separately is that it makes clear that an allegation of negligence is not intended to be coterminous with the parallel allegation of breach of

16 On the impact of the European legislation, see Redgrave's *Health and Safety*, 2nd Ed, 1993, Butterworths, pplviii–lxxiv, and the introductions in Redgrave to each of the 'six pack' Regulations.

17 (1968) 66 LGR 379.

18 *Bowes v Sedgefield DC* [1981] ICR 234.

statutory duty. The advantage of pleading parallel duties together is that it is much shorter and less repetitious to do so. That practice, however, requires that any allegation of negligence which the pleader considers goes beyond the scope of a parallel breach of statutory duty must be pleaded separately. Examples of both kinds of pleading are to be found in precedents C5–9 and 15, pp367–92 and 404.

Negligence

The principal allegations of negligence in an accident at work are usually obvious. Examples of pleading are given in precedents C5–9 and 15, pp367–92 and 404. A checklist is needed to ensure that all appropriate allegations have been made. The starting point of such a checklist is *Wilsons Clyde Coal Co Ltd v English*,[19] where the House of Lords laid down the principal health and safety duties in negligence owed by an employer to an employee. This list can be expanded to a series of allegations which seem to cover all the usual cases. The list below has been adapted to cover the basic principles of the 1992 Regulations.[20] A form of words has been used below that will require greater or lesser adaptation to the circumstances of the particular case. Some will be completely inappropriate for some cases. The personal injury pleader will be familiar with the substantive law which is reflected in the following checklist. It is intended merely to provide lawyers with an aide-memoire, to ensure that all lines of attack in relation to accident or ill health at work have been covered.

The defendant:

a) *failed to provide and/or maintain safe, appropriate and adequate equipment, appliances, machinery, plant, or works*;
b) *caused, permitted or failed to prevent [the event, escape, spillage, hole, explosion, etc etc] happening*;
c) *failed to provide and/or maintain [the means of containing the danger: extractor hoods, guards, marked alleys for forklifts etc etc]*;
d) *failed to provide to and/or maintain for the plaintiff any or any adequate safe personal protective equipment, in particular [helmet, goggles, toetector boots, etc etc]*;
e) *caused or permitted the plaintiff to take the avoidable risk of . . .*;
f) *failed to combat the risk of . . . at source*;
g) *failed to make any or any sufficient suitable provision to avoid the risk of . . .*;

19 [1938] AC 57.
20 The allegations need modification to suit disease claims. See p119 on 1992 regs.

h) *failed to adapt the work and/or the workplace to the plaintiff*;
i) *failed to make any or any suitable and sufficient assessment or evaluation of the risk of . . . and/or keep the same under review*;
j) *failed to develop and/or implement a coherent and overall risk prevention policy*;

Allegations (h) to (j) are derived from the 1992 Regulations but it is submitted that notwithstanding their statutory force, they now set a strongly arguable standard for negligence.[21]

k) *failed to provide and/or maintain a competent staff*;

This is a difficult allegation to prove, since it is necessary to show that the employer knew or ought to have known that the relevant member(s) of staff were incompetent.

l) *failed to provide and/or maintain effective training and instruction; failed to provide and/or maintain effective supervision*;

This allegation is particularly relevant for new starters, young people and those with some physical or mental disability.

m) *failed to provide and/or maintain a safe place of work and/or access thereto and egress therefrom*;

Failure to maintain a safe place of work should invariably be pleaded. There is always the possibility that something about the place in which the accident occurred caused or contributed to it. The pleader will probably not have seen the engineer's report by the time of drafting.

n) *failed to provide and/or maintain a safe system of work*;

Pleaded in this general form, this applies both to the particular means of performing the task delegated to the employee and to the broader means by which the employer carried out the operations which involved the plaintiff in performing that task. It is an allegation which should always be pleaded.

o) *failed to inspect adequately, regularly, sufficiently often or at all; failed to heed the report of inspections carried out by . . . on . . .; failed to institute and/or maintain a system of inspection*;

This is a useful line of attack when there have been previous occurrences of some failure of equipment or structure.[22]

p) *failed to warn and/or inform the plaintiff of the risk of . . .*;

21 See Redgrave's *Health and Safety*, 2nd Ed, 1993, Butterworths, p lxvii.
22 This line of attack derives from *Barkway v South Wales Transport* [1950] AC 185, supported by *Northwestern Utilities Ltd v London Guarantee and Accident Co* [1936] AC 108.

q) *failed to fence, cover, mark off, illuminate, place hazard warning signs upon;*

r) *failed to heed the previous similar accident; failed to heed previous oral/written complaints of . . . on . . . and of . . . on . . . to the effect that . . . to . . . on . . . and to . . .; failed to institute and maintain a system of recording and investigating previous accidents and/or complaints;*

Previous accidents and complaints should be particularised as far as possible, though it is often useful to say that '*further particulars will be given after discovery*'.

s) *The plaintiff will further rely on the happening of the accident in itself as evidence of the breach of statutory duty and/or negligence of the defendants, their servants or agents;*

The allegation of res ipsa loquitur may be made[23] in a separate paragraph. Alternatively, it is often convenient to put the point towards the end of the allegations of negligence and breach of statutory duty.

t) *The plaintiff will further rely on the conviction of the defendants for the offence of . . . contrary to section . . . of the Health and Safety at Work Act 1974 at the . . . Magistrates' Court on the . . ., as evidence of the breach of statutory duty and/or negligence of the defendants, their servants or agents; the said conviction having arisen out of and being relevant to the matters referred to in paragraph 2 herein.*

Reliance on previous convictions may be put in a separate paragraph but it is most conveniently added at the end of the allegations of breach of statutory duty and negligence. Previous convictions are rare in accidents at work, but the Health and Safety Executive does prosecute and such convictions are relevant.

By way of example this checklist can now be applied to a hypothetical lifting case, where the plaintiff's back has been injured by carrying a heavy box. Such an accident is now specifically covered by the Manual Handling Operations Regulations 1992, breach of which will need to be specifically pleaded. Against a state employer consideration will have to be given also to the Manual Handling Directive (90/269/EEC) to see whether there are not additional breaches of the Directive which may not be breaches of the Regulations.[24]

In this example the pleader will wish to consider alleging the following. The employer failed to avoid the need to lift or handle the

23 Though it is not necessary to plead res ipsa loquitur expressly: *Bennett v Chemical Construction (GB) Ltd* [1971] 1 WLR 1571.

24 See Redgrave's *Health and Safety*, 2nd Ed, 1993, Butterworths, p584–5.

boxes manually. There was no or inadequate assessment of the risk if there was no alternative to manual handling. The contents of the box were not made easier and safer to handle (by for example being put in a different container, or by the provision of handles on the box). The employer caused or permitted the plaintiff to do the job when there were stronger workers available, or when the employer knew or ought to have known through proper health surveillance that the plaintiff was weak or had a bad back. No lifting equipment was provided. The plaintiff and his/her workmate were not properly trained or instructed how to lift and carry the weight. The weight of the box and its heaviest side were not marked. They were not properly supervised. The workmate might be said to be incompetent. The system of work was at fault in general and in particular in the layout of the work, which required the plaintiff to lift these boxes from ground level, rather than their being stored on benches at waist level. The place of work was not kept safe (even though there were no new facts contained in this allegation). The defendant employers failed to inspect and heed the system of work being employed. They failed to warn the plaintiff of the dangers of lifting heavy weights at all, or of lifting heavy weights in the manner utilised by the plaintiff. There were previous accidents and complaints. Res ipsa loquitur would be pleaded as a matter of course, as would any conviction of the defendants for this accident.

As a final check, the lawyer should consider the underlying essentials of health and safety at work cases, to see whether every allegation emanating from them has been made. Did the employer:

- Assess the risk;
- Use the safest means possible to achieve the employer's objective (not just the safest means of performing the allotted task);
- Adapt the work to the worker;
- Provide medical surveillance, information and training for the worker;
- Contain the danger;
- Protect the worker from the danger?

These last two principles can be applied to any accident or industrial disease case. For example, if the plaintiff has slipped on some oil, application of the first principle provides the initial allegation, viz, that the machine from which it leaked should have been properly maintained so that it did not leak.[25] Another allegation would be that there was a failure to provide a trough or barrier to prevent foreseeable accidental

25 Therefore, the duty under Factories Act 1961 s28(1) is not only to clean the floor but to prevent substances from getting there: *Johnston v Caddies Wainwright* [1983] ICR 407.

leaks. Yet another allegation would be that the oil, having got on to the floor, should have been cleaned away, covered over (by duckboards or the like), or had sand, sawdust or fuller's earth applied to it. Application of the last principle gives rise to the allegation that the spillage, floor or gangway should have been fenced off or properly illuminated, or that warning of the danger should have been given or, perhaps, that non-slip boots should have been provided.

In a noxious fumes case, the penultimate principle gives rise to the allegation that the process should have been carried out with substances which did not give off noxious fumes or by a technology which prevented noxious fumes being given off. It gives rise also to the allegation that exhaust equipment should have been provided to extract the noxious fumes before they got into breathable atmosphere. The last principle gives rise to the allegation that the plaintiff should have been provided with a respirator.

Often allegations will be made against a fellow employee. The fellow employee should be identified in the second paragraph of the statement/particulars of claim. That paragraph should also set out the facts giving rise to the vicarious liability relied on. The allegations against the fellow employee will always be in addition to broad allegations against the employer for failing to provide a safe system and place of work, safe equipment, risk assessment, safest means of achieving the objective, and the like. The allegations against the fellow employee will usually be far more limited and specific. For example, '*John Smith lowered the fork lift forks when it was unsafe to do so*' etc.

Finally, it is worth emphasising that allegations should almost invariably be made in the negative, as failures by defendants to carry out their duties. Occasionally, a positive allegation that the defendant did something is appropriate, but the plaintiff should never plead that the defendant should have done something. It is not the plaintiff's obligation to plead what the defendant should or could have done, although many of the allegations will contain implicit statements to this effect, and at trial the plaintiff may rely on evidence of what a reasonable employer would have done. That is a matter of evidence – usually provided by experts – and not a matter of fact to be pleaded. The duty is to plead negatively only.[26] Furthermore, a plaintiff who pleads positively may be asked for further and better particulars. If defendants deny negative allegations,

26 *Manchester Corporation v Markland* [1936] AC 360; *Harnett v Associated Octel* [1987] CLY 3072.

they may be asserting a positive case for which the plaintiff is entitled to particulars.[27]

Occupational diseases

Disease cases (see chapter 24 p291) follow the same format as accidents at work. The only significant difference is that diseases are usually contracted over a period of time rather than in a single incident. The second paragraph of the statement or particulars of claim should attempt to specify the beginning and the end of a period during which the disease was caught. When alleging breach of statutory duty, it must be considered whether this period is covered by statutory provisions different from those currently in force. Some diseases, like asbestosis, may take decades to manifest themselves. It is often necessary to plead breaches of long-superseded statutory provisions, such as the Asbestos Regulations 1931 and the Factories Act 1937, since they were in force at the time of the exposure.

Examples of a statement of claim in occupational disease cases can be found in precedents C9 and 15 at pp388 and 404.

Where the client has been suffering from an industrial disease for some time there could be difficulties in establishing when, for the purposes of the Limitation Act, the date of knowledge arose. In these circumstances it is better to let the defendant take the point on whether an action is time barred. For this reason it is better not to refer to the Limitation Act in the initial pleading but to plead it by way of reply or to amend the particulars/statement of claim subsequently if the limitation point is raised. An example is at C18 p417.

Provisional damage cases

Both the High Court and the county court have the power to award provisional damages.[28] If provisional damages are claimed, the facts on which the claim is based must be pleaded.[29] A precedent is at C11 p394.

A provisional damage claim may be appropriate where there is a chance that, in the future, the plaintiff will, as result of the defendant's negligence, develop some serious disease or suffer some serious

27 *Pinson v Lloyds and National Provincial Foreign Bank Ltd* [1941] 2 All ER 636, per Stable J at 644.
28 RSC Ord 37 rr7–10; CCR Ord 22 r6A.
29 RSC Ord 18 r8(3); CCR Ord 6 r1B.

deterioration in his/her physical or mental condition.[30] Provisional damages are assessed on the assumption that the plaintiff will *not* develop the disease or suffer a serious deterioration. However, as a part of the settlement or judgment, the plaintiff is entitled to apply for further damages in the future if the disease develops or the deterioration specified occurs.

There are cases where serious deterioration, when it does occur – eg, mesothelioma – is so fast that the plaintiff may die before a claim can be brought for further damages.[31] Unfortunately, an attempt to circumvent this possible injustice, by declaring that the conditional right of the plaintiff to apply for further damages was not a judgment or satisfaction which precluded a claim by surviving dependants under the Fatal Accidents Act 1976, was reversed in 1990 by the Court of Appeal.[32]

Some personal injury practitioners are against making claims for provisional damages, though the authors consider it a useful addition to the plaintiff's armoury. It is argued that, except in unusual cases, the plaintiff is generally better off receiving damages immediately, not only for his/her present condition but also for the foreseeable risk of deterioration, in spite of the fact that provisional damages, plus a further award if and when then deterioration occurs, appear to reflect better the justice of the case. Deterioration may be a long time coming and the plaintiff may have lost touch with his/her solicitors. The future condition may be overlaid by some other medical condition and sometimes the plaintiff may not want the possibility of further litigation. Defendants tend not to like provisional damages claims either. Expensive provision may be required against a possible future claim of substantial proportions. The file cannot be closed. Defendants may therefore be prepared to buy off a provisional award by paying considerably more than they otherwise would.

The rules governing orders for, or agreement to submit to, provisional damages claims are in RSC Order 37 rr7–10, and CCR Order 22 r6A.[33]

Particulars of injury

The third paragraph in a road accident case and the fourth paragraph in an accident or disease at work case should begin:

30 For a discussion on serious deterioration, in contrast to mere deterioration, see *Wilson v Ministry of Defence* [1991] 1 All ER 638.

31 RSC Ord 37 r10.

32 *Middleton v Elliott Turbomachinery Ltd* (1990) *Times* 29 October.

33 See also V Gay, *AVMA Legal and Medical Journal* No 2 p8.

By reason of the facts and matters aforesaid the plaintiff has suffered personal injury, loss and damage.

Then follows the heading 'particulars of injury'. First of all, the plaintiff's date of birth must be stated.[34] Stating his or her age is only likely to cause confusion. Then, the nature of the injury, the medical treatment received, the continuing effect of the injury, and any disability for work or handicap on the labour market, may be addressed. Although the plaintiff's solicitors must serve a medical report with the statement or particulars of claim in proceedings issued after 4 June 1990,[35] it is nevertheless occasionally useful to summarise these four aspects of the injury in the statement/particulars of claim. The medical report may not, for example, cover the indirect effects of the injury or indirect disability for parts of the work or handicap on a particular labour market.

At this stage a short summary report may simply say that the plaintiff has a fractured tibia and remains in plaster and on crutches but can carry out sedentary work. The particulars of injury may elaborate that terse statement by pointing out that the plaintiff, though attending work daily, can perform only part of his/her normal tasks and can no longer work overtime because of the injury. It may also point out that, for example, a particular plaintiff has lost a season playing semi-professional rugby league and is unable to have sexual intercourse in the position preferred by himself and his wife to such an extent that the marriage has been adversely affected. The effect of the injury on the plaintiff's pastimes, domestic, social, sexual and sporting life can be set out.

It is not, in theory, necessary to plead handicap on the labour market (or loss of earning capacity, as it is perhaps better described), since it is an item of general damages. However, it is good practice to do so[36] and the appropriate place is under the heading 'Particulars of Injury'. The failure to plead it invites arguments about whether it should be permitted as a head of recoverable damages at trial.

The following standard sentence or a variant is usually inserted at the end of the particulars of injury. This is useful to ensure that the immediate suffering of the plaintiff is not overlooked in the pleading:

The plaintiff experienced pain, shock and suffering and continues to suffer in his domestic, social and working lives.

The statement/particulars of claim has to be accompanied by a medical report and schedule of damages.

The accompanying medical report should, so far as possible,

34 *Practice Direction (Personal Injuries: Pleading)* [1974] 1 WLR 1427.

35 RSC Ord 18 r12(1A); CCR Ord 6 r1(5)(a).

36 *Chan Wai Tong v Li Ping Sum* [1985] AC 446, PC.

substantiate all the personal injuries which the plaintiff proposes to adduce in evidence as part of his/her case. However, the plaintiff is entitled to serve a further medical report.[37]

Particulars of damages and schedule of financial loss

The rules specifically require a schedule of special damages (in reality a schedule of financial loss) to accompany the claim[38] but if the specials are short, then it will suffice for them to be pleaded under the heading 'Particulars of Special Damage'.

The reason for this rule is to enable defendants to assess their liability at an early stage so that they can make a realistic payment into court. Thus any schedule that accompanies the claim must, in so far as it is possible on the evidence available, put the defendants on notice of any claim for financial loss by the plaintiff. Failure to do so may result in the defendants making a payment into court based upon the schedule served but which is too low for the plaintiff to accept because the schedule was incomplete. This could give rise to complicated arguments on costs.[39] The schedule must cover any claimed future losses and expenses (including earnings and pension); see p231.

Again, this is another reason why the case should be 'front loaded', ie, most of the work done before the issue of proceedings (see p89).

To avoid any complications, in cases where service is urgent, the schedule should contain the head of damage claimed but indicate that '*further detailed particulars are to be provided*'. If service of the claim is so urgent that it is not possible to draft even a skeleton schedule, application should be made to the court for an extension of time to serve the schedule.[40]

In many cases where losses and expenses are complicated the initial schedule will be less detailed than the final schedule. This is quite acceptable provided the basis of the claim is made clear from the start.

The schedule is an important document because it determines whether the case is for the High Court or county court and, if in the county court, the level of judge hearing the case and whether it is to be subject to the arbitration procedure. Furthermore, the schedule will indicate to the

37 RSC Ord 25 r8(1A); CCR Ord 18 r11(7)(b). It is not always necessary to amend the pleadings each time fresh medical reports lead to developments in any case: *Owen v Grimsby and Cleethorpes Transport* (1991) *Times* 14 February.

38 RSC Ord 25 r8(1A); CCR Ord 6 r1(5)(b).

39 *Cheeseman v Bowaters United Kingdom Paper Mills Ltd* [1971] 1 WLR 1773.

40 Under RSC Ord 18 r12(1A), CCR Ord 6 r1(6)(b).

defendant's lawyers the level of experience of the plaintiff's lawyers. This may well affect the conduct of the case, negotiation and offers by the defendants. The schedule ranks as a pleading which cannot be departed from without leave, but the authors believe that an updated schedule should be regarded as voluntary particulars.

Defendants used to be obliged to serve a counter-schedule, but the rules amendment requiring the plaintiff to serve the schedule with the statement of claim omitted to provide for a counter-schedule. It may therefore be necessary to serve interrogatories or requests for further and better particulars or threaten to strike out the defendant's denial of loss and damage on the ground that it may prejudice, embarrass or delay the trial (under RSC Ord 18 r19, CCR Ord 13 r2(2)) unless a counter-schedule is served making clear the case the plaintiff has to meet.

The structure of the plaintiff's schedule depends on the complexity of the claim. In a more complicated or less obvious claim the schedule should contain a narrative for the court explaining the reason for the expenditure or loss and why it is alleged to be recoverable. Past losses or expenses must be separated from future losses.[41] This is because interest can be claimed for past losses but not future losses. If interest is claimed at the full rate on some items (see p211), these should be separated from those items where interest is claimed at half the special investment account rate. Multipliers are generally not included, though they should be calculated at this stage. The claim for general damages for pain, suffering and loss of amenity should not be included. This is not special damage and interest is calculated differently:[42] at 2% pa flat rate. In what is expected to be the final schedule, it is convenient if the defendants are left a column for their figures.

Specimen schedules are set out in C21–24 pp423–35. At this stage it is necessary only to mention a checklist for the particulars of special damage. Main headings are usually:

- loss of wages, overtime, bonus, commission etc
- costs of treatment
- costs of travel for treatment
- costs of care
- additional costs directly attributable to the accident (eg, taxi fares)
- damage to clothing, equipment (eg, motorcycle, loss of no claims bonus), and personal possessions.

41 See *Jefford v Gee* [1970] 2 QB 130.
42 *Pickett v British Rail Engineering Ltd* [1980] AC 136.

The particulars should conclude by stating that 'credit will be given for ministry benefits in accordance with section 23 of the Social Security Act 1989' (see clawback of benefits pp64–8).

A fuller discussion of damages and a checklist of claimable items is to be found in chapter 15 pp206–8.

It is now practically impossible to claim for exemplary or aggravated damages, for which the facts giving rise to the claim need to be specifically pleaded, even where there is evidence that the employer has cynically calculated that the cost of allowing employees to be injured is less than the cost of preventing the injuries and has opted not to take a precaution in the certain knowledge that injuries may follow.[43]

The prayer

The statement or particulars of claim usually concludes:

And the plaintiff claims damages in excess of £5,000 [or whatever jurisdictional limit is appropriate] *and interest (pursuant to section 35A of the Supreme Court Act 1981 or section 69 of the County Courts Act 1984).*

In the county court the claim will be treated as a claim for £5,000 or less, unless it is stated in the particulars of claim or by some other method, eg, by letter, or the court orders otherwise.[44] However, it may be desirable to limit the value of the claim to £3,000 to take account of the lower scale for costs.[45] There is no longer any requirement to limit the value of the claim in the county court because the financial jurisdiction of the court has been abolished for actions founded in tort and contract.[46]

The claim for interest must be pleaded.[47] The following should be

43 RSC Ord 18 r8(3); CCR Ord 6 r1B. It is not appropriate to award either exemplary or aggravated damages in negligence, or public nuisance, involving allegedly high-handed and obstructive conduct on the part of a public utility company: *Gibbons v South West Water* (1992) *Times* 26 November; (1992) NPC 146.

44 CCR Ord 6 r1(1A). For cases of between £1,000 and £5,000 the case will be listed before either a district or a circuit judge according to the availability of judicial time: *Practice Direction (County Courts Listings)* (1991) *Times* 10 July.

45 CCR Ord 38 r3(3).

46 County Courts Act 1984 s15(1) as amended by County Court (Amendment No 2) Rules 1991 r3. But damages will not be awarded in excess of any limitation pleaded: *Gilsenan v Metropolitan Police Commissioner* (1994) PIQR 65, CA.

47 *Practice Notes* [1982] 1 WLR 1448; [1983] 1 WLR 377. It is sufficient if the claim for interest is made in the prayer and not in the body of the pleading: *McDonald's Hamburgers v Burger King (UK) Ltd* [1987] FSR 112.

added to this, to strengthen a claim for interest on special damages at the full special account rate:[48]

including interest at the full rate on the plaintiff's special damages in the particular circumstances that the plaintiff has lost earnings and has incurred expenses which will be irrecoverable from the defendants until the trial herein.

The conclusion of the statement or particulars of claim bears the name of the barrister who settled it (if that is the case) and the name and address of the solicitor in the format shown in the precedents at C5 p367 onwards.

Fatal accidents

The format for a fatal accident statement or particulars of claim is as stylised as the previous examples. An example is to be found at C15 p404. The description of the plaintiff is as given in the writ and includes, if appropriate, after the plaintiff's name that s/he is the widow/widower and administratrix/administrator or executrix/executor of the estate of the named deceased person. Letters of administration are taken out when the person dies intestate; the claimant is referred to as the administrator/ administratrix of the estate. Probate is granted in respect of the estate of a person who dies having made a will. The claimant is the executor/ executrix of the estate.

The first paragraph of the statement or particulars of claim sets out this information slightly more fully and states that the action is brought for the benefit of the dependants of the deceased under the Fatal Accidents Act 1976 and for the benefit of the deceased's estate under the Law Reform (Miscellaneous Provisions) Act 1934. It concludes by stating that probate or letters of administration were granted to the plaintiff by the (named) probate registry on a particular date.

The statement or particulars of claim follows the format previously given for road traffic accidents, accidents at work and occupational diseases, except that 'the deceased' is substituted for 'the plaintiff'. The paragraphs describe the relationship between the deceased and the defendant, and the circumstances of the accident; state the allegations against the defendant, and that, as a result, the deceased sustained injury and died, and conclude (in this part) with particulars of personal injury. This latter information is important, since damages may be claimed for pain and suffering and loss of amenity sustained between the accident and the deceased's death. Paragraphs which are particular to a fatal accident case then follow:

48 Based on *Prokop v DHSS* [1985] CLY 1037, CA.

The particulars pursuant to statute are as follows:

a) *The names of the persons for whose benefit this action is brought are:*
The plaintiff, the widow(er) of the deceased born on . . .
Mary Smith, daughter of the deceased born on . . .

b) *The nature of the claim in respect of which damages are sought is that, at the time of his death, the deceased was a healthy and happy man, aged 42, earning, at the date of his death, £200 per week net and the said dependants were wholly dependent for support on the deceased's said earnings and on the services provided by him. By his death the dependants have lost the said means of support and services and have thereby suffered loss and damage.*

c) *The plaintiff has suffered bereavement.*

Further by reason of the facts and matters aforesaid the deceased's estate has suffered loss and damage.

PARTICULARS OF DAMAGE

Funeral expenses

Loss of earnings between 15 August and 12 October 1993 £
Damages in respect of pain, suffering and loss of amenity between 15 August and 12 October 1993 £
Travel and accomodation expenses for the plaintiff in attendance at hospital on the deceased between 16 August and 12 October 1993 £

The conclusion of the statement/particulars of claim in a fatal accident case is as for the other statements or particulars of claim.

CHAPTER 11

The defence and other steps

Judgement in default of defence

High Court

Having acknowledged service of the proceedings, the defendant must file a defence. In the High Court, if the writ and statement of claim are served together, the defendant has 28 days to serve the defence. If the statement of claim is served after the service of the writ and receipt of the acknowledgment of service, the defendant has 14 days to serve the defence.[1] It is usual to allow the defendant at least one extension of 14 days, if requested, and, on more complicated cases, a further extension of the same period. If defendants want further time after that, it is appropriate to insist that they take out a time summons to apply to the court for an extension.[2] This makes clear that the plaintiff's solicitor is in control and will not brook unnecessary delay. However, from this point on, the plaintiff's solicitor should be aware that the defendant may, by way of retaliation, show little latitude to the plaintiff seeking subsequent flexibility of time limits!

The time summons will almost certainly be granted, but a 'final' or 'unless order', debarring the defendant from any further order and requiring the defendant to pay the costs, should be sought (see p157). Though a letter can be written by the plaintiff's solicitors, apologising for non-attendance, explaining the two extensions already given voluntarily and asking that any extension granted be a final order, experience shows that a final order will usually be granted only if the solicitor or a clerk attends to argue for it.[3]

1 RSC Ord 18 r2(2).
2 RSC Ord 3 r5.
3 The court will rarely make a peremptory 'unless' order on the first application: *Siebe Gorman & Co Ltd v Pneupac Ltd* [1982] 1 WLR 185.

An application for judgment in default of defence [4] is likely to succeed only on the basis of breach of a final order. There may nevertheless be tactical reasons for making it as soon as the time limit has expired (see chapter 12 p158).

The procedure for obtaining judgment in default of defence is straightforward. The original writ, two copies of the form of judgment, and an affidavit of service are lodged with the court office. The stamped judgment can later be collected. A form of summons for interlocutory judgment is shown at D7 on p440.

County court

With certain exceptions, no leave of the court is necessary to apply for judgment in default of defence. If the defendant has not served a defence or admitted the claim within 14 days of being served with the default summons and particulars of claim, judgment can be entered.[5]

The procedure is to send a form applying for interlocutory judgment with damages to be assessed (see precedent D8 p441) to the court. No affidavit is necessary. This is endorsed by the court with a hearing date, if requested, and served on the parties. The district judge's jurisdiction is £5,000, so it is important to let the court know whether the assessment of damages should be before the district judge or the circuit judge, and to give an indication of the length of hearing required. If no date is requested – perhaps because further medical evidence is required – the date will be fixed later and the plaintiff must give at least seven days' notice.[6]

General

Defendants sometimes ask for a general extension of time for serving the defence, on the pretext that they are intending to negotiate a settlement. Almost invariably, this is part of an overall strategy to delay matters. Except in quite exceptional circumstances, such a request should not be granted. This imposes a sense of urgency on the defendant who must also incur the (small) costs of the defence. The defendant will be aware that the court will not grant an extension of time on the ground that the defendant intends to negotiate.

4 RSC Ord 19(3).
5 CCR Ord 9 r6(1)(c).
6 CCR Ord 22 r6(1).

In the event of judgement in default of defence, the next step will be to seek assessment of damages.[7]

Defences

The defence[8] should be served within 14 days of service of the statement/particulars of claim or 28 days in the High Court if the statement of claim was served with the writ.[9] Defendants in personal injury cases are generally represented by skilled and experienced lawyers and the usual strategy adopted in drafting a defence to a personal injury claim is to be brief. Everything that can be legitimately denied on instructions is denied, the minimum admissions are made and, where there is any doubt on any factual allegation – as opposed to an allegation of liability – the matter is not admitted. There is often a claim that the plaintiff was guilty of contributory negligence.

The defence should be studied to see whether some fresh matter has been raised. For example some novel factual allegation may be made which requires further investigation. If a third party has been blamed, consideration will have to be given to joining him/her as second defendant.

Where the defence served discloses no real defence on liability, an application for summary judgement under RSC Ord 14 r1 or CCR Ord 9 r14 should be considered. Judgement should be given in straightforward cases where there is clearly no defence.[10]

Where the document purporting to be a defence is not such in reality (eg, '*liability is denied, a full defence will follow*'), or if it is frivolous or vexatious, application should be made to strike it out under CCR Order 13 r5(1)(a) at the earliest opportunity.[11] Failure by the plaintiff's solicitor to do so will allow the 15 month 'strike' clock to start running against the plaintiff from 14 days after close of pleadings, and it will be most unlikely that the court staff will reject the so-called defence, if they read it at all.

Where a defence is struck out or judgement entered in default, the next step is to apply for assessment of damages.[12]

7 RSC Order 13 r2 and Order 37 r1; CCR Order 9 r6(2).

8 On amendment of the defence, see the useful speech of Lord Griffiths in *Ketteman v Hansel Properties Ltd* [1987] 1 AC 189 at 220.

9 RSC Ord 18 r2; CCR Ord 9 r2(1).

10 *Drummer v Brown* [1953] 1 QB 701; *Rankine v Garton* [1979] 2 All ER 1185.

11 *Halliday v Shoesmith* [1993] 1 WLR 1.

12 RSC Ord 13 r2 and Ord 37 r1; CCR Ord 9 r6(2).

If any document is referred to in the defence, a copy should be requested. Otherwise formal notice must be served requiring inspection.[13] Having considered whether any further steps need to be taken in relation to the defence, the next step is to write to the plaintiff.

The plaintiff should have been provided with a copy of the statement or particulars of claim and must now be sent a copy of the defence. The covering letter to the plaintiff must explain in clear English the nature of the defence being put forward and any allegations of contributory negligence and that these are being made by the defendant and not by the plaintiff's solicitor. It is important to reassure the plaintiff that the defence and allegations are as expected and are usual in this sort of litigation. In any event, a plaintiff is likely to be angry and insulted at allegations of contributory negligence and the consequent threat of reduction of damages. It is usually sufficient to communicate by letter, to seek the plaintiff's comments on the defence and on every aspect of the allegations of contributory negligence. In difficult cases, it may be necessary to interview the plaintiff. Whether any of the plaintiff's other witnesses need to be questioned about any matters raised in the defence should also be considered.

Replies

It is unusual for a reply to be necessary in personal injury litigation. There is an implied 'joinder of issue',[14] ie, the issues raised in the defence do not have to be fully responded to. Where a reply is necessary, it should be served within 14 days of receipt of the defence,[15] or within an agreed extension of time. A reply is appropriate in three particular cases.

First, there should be a reply where, in a defective equipment case, the statement or particulars has not mentioned the Employer's Liability (Defective Equipment) Act 1969, in the hope of inducing the defendant to make sufficient admissions to enable judgment to be entered and an enquiry as to damages ordered (see p120). If insufficient admissions by the defence have been made to allow this, or if the defence changes the shape of the case, it will be necessary to enter a reply (or alternatively to amend the statement or particulars of claim), so as to plead the Act specifically. An alternative is to amend the statement/particulars of

13 RSC Ord 24 r10; CCR Ord 14 r4.
14 RSC Ord 18 r14(1).
15 RSC Ord 18 r3(4).

claim but this has the disadvantage of requiring leave. An example of the Act pleaded as an amendment (on joining the supplier) is given in C16 at p411.

Second, the defence may contain an allegation that the Limitation Act 1980 bars the plaintiff's claim. This will require a reply setting out in detail why the claim is not statute barred and if the claim would otherwise be out of time, why the plaintiff seeks the exercise of the court's discretion under s33 of the Limitation Act 1980. An example of such a reply is to be found in C18 at p417.

Third, a reply may be necessary where the defence contains some form of counterclaim. The latter is uncommon in personal injury litigation but would be responded to in the usual way.

If the statement or particulars of claim contains allegations under the Factories Act 1961 or other statutory provisions involving duties requiring the employer to do things 'so far as is reasonably practicable', it is worth checking to see whether the defence raises the argument that it was not reasonably practicable. Failure to plead such a defence is fatal to reliance on it at trial.[16] The onus of calling evidence that no safety measures were reasonably practicable is on the defendant.[17]

If the defence to allegations made under the 1992 health and safety at work regulations, the 'six pack', (see p119) alleges compliance 'so far as is reasonably practicable', consideration will need to be given to see whether the European health and safety directives on which those regulations were based can be relied upon directly or indirectly (if such consideration has not been given already; see pp119–24).

The defence should also be considered in the light of the requirement[18] to set out facts on which the defendants intend to rely in mitigation of, or otherwise in relation to, the amount of damages.

The defence may be in the form of an express or implied admission of liability. If so, the plaintiff's solicitor is in the happy position of being able to enter judgment on the admissions[19] with damages to be assessed. If the defence fails to deny or not admit allegations in the statement or particulars of claim, or there is no defence or a defence is struck out, the allegations are deemed to be admitted.[20]

16 *Bowes v Sedgefield DC* [1981] ICR 234; *Johnston v Caddies Wainwright Ltd* [1983] ICR 407.

17 *Nimmo v Cowan (Alexander) & Sons Ltd* [1968] AC 107.

18 RSC Ord 18 r12(1)(c).

19 RSC Ord 27 r3; CCR Ord 9 r6(1)(b).

20 RSC Ord 18 r13(1).

The defence will, in many cases. be accompanied by a request for further and better particulars of the statement or particulars of claim. These too must be paraphrased into plain English and put into the form of a questionnaire to obtain the plaintiff's response. Also, other witnesses may need to be questioned.

Receipt of the defence and request needs to be acknowledged. If there is a request, the defendant's solicitors must be told that '*such particulars will be provided as counsel considers appropriate*' – assuming that counsel is to draft the further and better particulars. Any agreed order to supply further and better particulars should also contain this qualification. Failure to do so will be taken as a waiver of the objection to any request, whether or not it would have been ordered as a matter of law or practice.[21]

Requests for further and better particulars

Of the statement/particulars of claim

It has been usual to instruct counsel to draft the further and better particulars of the statement or particulars of claim sought by the defendant. Like much personal injury work, in future this is likely to be done increasingly by solicitors. Whoever does the job, however, ought to be asked simultaneously to consider both the defence and whether a request for further and better particulars needs be drafted in relation to it. An example of further and better particulars is at C17 p415.

To deal with the request for further and better particulars, it is essential to have: all the papers that were previously used for the statement or particulars of claim; the plaintiff's answers to the request for further and better particulars; and any further evidence which has come to hand since the instructions were given to settle the statement or particulars of claim. The instructions to counsel should make clear the three categories of paperwork.

Skilled counsel for the defence probes only those vague assertions in the statement or particulars of claim which may contain some hidden trap for the defendants at trial, and those assertions which might give room for the plaintiff's case to be stretched to fit the facts as they emerge at trial. Quite rightly, the defendant's counsel wants to pin down the plaintiff's case precisely. Less talented pleaders may ask for particulars of matters to which they arc not entitled, often at tedious length.

21 *Fearis v Davies* (1986) *Times* 5 June.

On the plaintiff's side, while it is necessary fully to particularise the case, the plaintiff may be vague and a poor communicator, particularly in writing. Without a conference and a visit to the site – both of which are most unusual at this stage – a pleader should be alert to the possibility that s/he has not fully understood the case. So, if the request is 'specify which rung of the ladder broke' and the plaintiff says that it was the third rung from the bottom, there will be no problem. However, if the plaintiff's response is much vaguer or, worse, ambiguous, then it requires skill to be as specific as possible, while avoiding committing the plaintiff to an inconsistent statement.

Defendants often seek a sketch plan of the 'locus in quo'. This should be refused. The plaintiff may have provided a sketch plan but the relationship of the various parts should be described in words rather than by means of the sketch. This is because the plaintiff will almost invariably have sketched the plan from memory while sitting at home. Experience teaches that this sketch plan, no matter how proficient the plaintiff may be in technical drawing, often has material differences from the actual layout.

The duty of someone who drafts pleadings is to put forward 'material facts', as opposed to evidence.[22] A useful guide is to think that the facts constitute the essential story, whereas the evidence is the means of showing that story to be true. Admittedly, this distinction is a difficult one but it is beyond the scope of the book to investigate it in detail.

Where actual or constructive knowledge on the part of someone else is an element in the plaintiff's case, the defendant is entitled to the facts on which the plaintiff's knowledge depends.[23]

Since the statement or particulars of claim makes allegations against the defendant which are in the negative ('*failing to . . .*'), the less experienced counsel for the defence often attempts to lure the plaintiff into stating what steps the defendants should have taken or '*what a safe system of work would have been*'. These requests should be refused, because a plaintiff need not give particulars of matters on which the defendant has the burden of proof; the plaintiff's only duty is to plead negatively.[24]

In some cases, however, it may be tactically advantageous to put a positive case. This may arise where the plaintiff's expert states

22 RSC Ord 18 r7(1).

23 *Fox v H Wood (Harrow) Ltd* [1963] 2 QB 601.

24 *Manchester Corporation v Markland* [1936] AC 360; *Harnett v Associated Octel* [1987] CLY 3072.

unequivocally that all reasonable employers utilise a particular safety device which the defendant did not use. Another situation is where the defendant has taken a safety precaution after the accident which could and should have been taken before. The disadvantage of pleading positively in this way is that it ties the plaintiff to one safety precaution alone at a time when the case is not fully investigated and when further ways may emerge in which a safe system of work, and safe plant and equipment could have been provided. The best policy is to leave all options open, as the plaintiff is entitled to do.

Rather than simply deny entitlement to a request for a positive case, some pleaders take pleasure in the circular reply, for example, '*a safe system of work would have been one which did not expose the plaintiff to the danger of* [whatever happened to him/her]'.

Of the defence

A well drafted defence from a specialist practitioner usually does not call for a request for further and better particulars. Nitpicking requests and attempts to see whether the defendant's counsel will reveal some evidence are a waste of time. Further and better particulars cannot be required of a bare denial or non-admission unless it implies a positive case.[25] It is only substantive and specific factual allegations that are worth probing, and then only if it appears that there is some hidden ambiguity, or the allegation is open-ended, or more information is required to identify a piece of machinery or the like. Commonly, therefore, the request is directed to the allegations of contributory negligence and to allegations relied on to reduce damages.

A defence may allege that some safety or protective equipment was available to the plaintiff. Such an allegation should be fully probed. Is it being said that the plaintiff was actually provided with the safety goggles or could have obtained them on request, and, if the latter, where, from whom, when, by what means, and so on?[26]

The amended rules require the defence to plead 'particulars of any facts on which [the defendant] relies in mitigation of or otherwise in relation to, the amount of damages'. The defendant is further required to not admit or to deny specifically any allegation in the statement or particulars

25 *Chapple v Electrical Trade Union* [1961] 1 WLR 1290; White Book 1993 para 18/12/35.

26 See *Norris v Syndic Manufacturing* [1952] 2 QB 135.

of claim as to the amount of damages.[27] The defence should be considered in the light of this requirement.

It is important to consider whether the defence contains any 'pregnant negatives' or implied positive allegations. The defendant is entitled simply to deny allegations made in the statement or particulars of claim and will then not be entitled to advance an affirmative case at trial. Nevertheless, there are circumstances where a negative allegation by the plaintiff (eg, that the defendant failed to . . .) is met by a denial in the defence which implies not merely that the plaintiff will be put to proof but that the defendant will construct at trial a case on that point. A request for further and better particulars should be made of anything that appears to be such a 'pregnant negative'. The request might read as follows:

Of: the general denial.

Give full particulars of any positive case on which the defendants intend to rely at trial, save as is otherwise specifically pleaded.

Interrogatories

Interrogatories should be considered at the same time as a request for further and better particulars of the defence, but they are more often likely to be useful at a later stage in the litigation, particularly after discovery and exchange of witness statements. Interrogatories go beyond the material facts which must be pleaded in the statement or particulars of claim and in the defence and which are subject to requests for further and better particulars. So long as an interrogatory is not simply 'fishing', it can probe the existence or non-existence of any fact which, though not directly in issue, is relevant to the existence or non-existence of facts which *are* directly in issue.[28] The interrogatory can relate to any matter which is necessary either for the saving of costs or disposing fairly of the cause or matter.[29] If the interrogatory could have been asked by way of a request for further and better particulars, it will not be 'necessary' for the saving of costs. Even if the interrogatories are procedurally defective (eg, by not complying with CCR Order 14 r11) the district judge still has a wide discretion to order such interrogatories as s/he thinks proper.[30]

Generally speaking, masters and district judges do not look favourably on interrogatories, in spite of the support of judicial authority over the

27 RSC Ord 18 rr12(1)(c) and 13(4) and see White Book para 18/13/7.
28 *Marriott v Chamberlain* (1886) 17 QBD 154 at 163.
29 RSC Order 26 r1.
30 CCR Order 13 r2 and see *Maxiplus Ltd v Lunn* (1992) *Times* 28 February.

years. It is, therefore, necessary to formulate the questions in such a way that the court will order their answer. Thus, the questions should be short, concern only one fact and usually require a 'yes' or 'no' answer. The situations where interrogatories are most likely to help the plaintiff are, for example, where the plaintiff has lost his/her memory;[31] where the plaintiff is suing for a fatal accident at which s/he was not present; where a system of work needs to be explored; or where the defence makes some curious denial that the relevant statute applies to the premises without specifying on what ground the premises were not, for example, a factory within the meaning of the Factories Act 1961.

The High Court and county court rules facilitate interrogatories being served without an order of the court.[32] A precedent is at C20 p420. The applicant is allowed without order to serve two requests. At least 28 days must be allowed for an answer and, if necessary, the officer or member of the company or organisation who is required to answer must be specified. A party served may, within 14 days, apply to the court for the interrogatories to be varied or withdrawn.[33] Interrogatories must be answered on affidavit unless the Court directs otherwise.[34]

Interrogatories may be served by order of the court. The solicitor should send a copy of the proposed interrogatories with the summons. An affidavit is not necessary. The defendant may, of course, answer voluntarily before the summons is heard. If the answers to interrogatories, served with or without an order, are insufficient, the court may require a further answer either by affidavit or oral examination. Alternatively, further and better particulars of the answer may be requested and ordered.[35] An example of an application for interrogatories is given in C19 at p419.

Notice to admit facts

If it is necessary to prove the truth of the contents of a document or any other fact, then, particularly if there is unlikely to be a dispute, a notice to admit facts should be served.[36] This is a useful tool not used enough, in the

31 *Griebart v Morris* [1920] 1 KB 659.
32 RSC Ord 26 r3; CCR Ord 14 r11.
33 The court can still refuse to order interrogatories even where a party has failed to apply for variation or withdrawal: *Maxiplus Ltd v Lunn* (1992) *Times* 28 February.
34 RSC Order 26 r2(2).
35 RSC Ord 26 r5(3).
36 RSC Ord 27 r2; CCR Ord 20 r2.

authors' experience. The notice must be served within 21 days of setting down in the High Court or not later than 14 days before the trial in the county court. A defendant who fails to admit the fact within 14 days in the High Court or seven days in the county court[37] may be penalised with the costs of having to prove the fact at trial if the fact is in reality non-contentious. The question for the court is whether, in the circumstances, the facts ought to have been admitted. Such an order may be made payable forthwith, before taxation. An example of a notice to admit is at E3 p459. Notices to admit facts are distinct from Civil Evidence Act notices to admit statements. These are dealt with at pp195 et seq.

Payments in

There is nothing to stop a defendant making a payment into court as soon as the existence of proceedings is known, even before service,[38] but it is, in fact, unusual to have a payment in at an early stage of the case. Insurers do not like to tie up funds at the relatively low-paying investment rate provided by the court. Furthermore, insurers do not usually seek early settlement (for the reasons discussed at p282), unless such settlement is likely to be significantly lower than the true value of the case. Since the well-advised plaintiff is unlikely to accept a low settlement, there is, in the general run of cases, no point in making a low payment in. Nevertheless, the payment in is one of the defendant's most powerful weapons and the highly experienced defence solicitor and insurers will keep it under review at all stages and use it at the optimum moment to try to achieve a 'cheap' settlement for the insurers.

The payment into court is a formalised offer of settlement. The defendant's solicitor pays into the court the amount decided on and, in the High Court, must notify the plaintiff's solicitor on a standard form which must be acknowledged within 3 days.[39] In the county court, the court sends out the notification of payment in if time permits. There is no need to acknowledge receipt. The plaintiff has 21 days from receiving the notice of payment in, in both the county court and the High Court, to

37 RSC Ord 62 r6(7); CCR Ord 20 r2(2).
38 *Towers v Morley* [1992] 1 WLR 511.
39 White Book Vol 2, prescribed form no 23, RSC Ord 22 r1(2).

accept the payment without penalty.[40] If the plaintiff accepts a payment in, the solicitor must give notice and send a copy of the notice to the officer who keeps the lists.[41] Failure to do so may mean that the solicitor has to bear personally any costs thrown away.

It is vital to take into account social security benefits received by the client when considering a payment into court. (The relationship between payments into court and certificates of benefit is dealt with at pp67–8.) If the payment in is not accepted and the client is, at trial, awarded a sum, including interest, the same as or lower than that paid in (or is awarded nothing), the client usually has to meet both parties' costs from the date of payment in. This is equally true in legally aided cases. The costs are, of course, taken out of any damages recovered. Since the costs of trial are likely to run into thousands of pounds, this is a formidable weapon and one which can cause sleepless nights for even the strongest willed client. This graphically illustrates how the question of costs is used to put pressure on the parties.

If the case is conducted at a leisurely pace, the defendant's lawyers have more time to review the case carefully and then make a telling payment in. If the case is pursued vigorously, it is surprising how often slow-acting defendants find that the trial is only days away by the time that they get round to making a payment in. This is partly through the inertia of the general policy of delay, though it may also be because of overwork or oversight. It is exacerbated by the need to consult insurers and re-insurers. A further frequent cause is the defendant's general policy of saving costs, which discourages taking reviews of cases or taking counsel's advice until the last possible moment.

Where payments in, or offers, are made before the immediate run up to the trial, they are often well below the real value of the claim. The insurers are hoping that the plaintiff, and perhaps his/her solicitor, will prefer to accept the offer rather than face the work, worry and stress of taking the case through to trial. Obviously, at such a time, it is important that the client is given clear and concise advice about whether to accept the offer.

40 RSC Ord 22 r3(1); CCR Ord 11 r3(1). If the defendant makes a payment in less than 21 days before the date fixed for trial, the court can still take it into account in the assessment of costs: *King v Weston-Howell* [1989] 1 WLR 579. The court can ignore the late payment in: *Bowen v Mills and Knight Ltd* [1973] Lloyds Rep 580. If the defendant establishes that, as a result of the plaintiff's fault, the defendant was unable to make an earlier payment in, the court can make an order for costs in the defendant's favour from that earlier date.

An action should not normally be struck out for want of prosecution during the 21 days after payment in: *Draper v Ferrymasters Ltd* (1993) PIQR 356.

41 RSC Ord 34 r8(3).

An example is at B10 p335. The client needs a firm appraisal of the upper and lower limits of what would be achievable at trial and the risks involved. The advice is often that the payment in or the offer should be rejected. If so, the client needs support, since the prospect of both having to give evidence and also taking the risk of recovering less than the payment in, or even losing, at court is very daunting.

If the client wishes the take the payment in, normally no order is needed and the case settles with the defendant paying the plaintiff's costs. The rules are more complicated if there is more than one defendant but where not all make the payment in. If there are several plaintiffs the payment in can be apportioned or if it is not and the plaintiffs cannot agree on a division, the court will apportion it.[42]

Where there are two or more defendants sued in the same action and one makes a payment into court that the plaintiff wishes to accept, three situations may arise. The procedure is clear in the High Court and equally applicable, it is believed, in the county court.[43]

1) *Where the claims are joint or alternative*, the matter is governed by RSC Order 22 r3(4) and 4. The plaintiff can accept the payment in from the one defendant and the action will be stayed or discontinued against the other defendants. If the plaintiff wishes nevertheless to proceed against them, leave must be obtained. In any event the plaintiff needs an order for payment out of the money in court under r4(1) and the court has to deal with the question of costs and make an order, since the case does not fall within r4(2).

   Where discontinuance occurs without leave, the discontinued defendant is entitled to his or her taxed costs under RSC Order 62 r3(4), and the plaintiff to his or her taxed costs under Order 62 r5(4), provided notice was given that the plaintiff has abandoned any other causes of action not covered by the payment in. If the plaintiff has to get leave or the defendants did not give written consent as required by Order 22 r4(2), the court must make an order as to costs both of the plaintiff and the defendants against whom the action was discontinued.
2) *Where the claims against the defendants alleges several liability only*, that is, not within Order 22 r3(4) or r4, the plaintiff does not need an order for payment out and may tax costs against the paying-in defendant under Order 62 r5(4). The action against the other defendants is not stayed and can proceed. If the plaintiff wishes to

42 *Walker v Turpin* (1993) *Times* 2 November.
43 County Courts Act 1984 s76.

discontinue against the other defendants, this can be done with or without leave as the case might be.

3) *If the plaintiff's claims include both joint or alternative claims and several claims*, the procedure outlined in (1) above is applicable to the joint or alternative claims and that in (2) to the several claims.[44]

In a legally aided case, notification of a rejected payment in or offer must be made with reasons to the board, who may decide to discharge the certificate.[45] This obligation is nowadays frequently made as an explicit limitation on the certificate. The solicitor should explain why the payment in or offer has been made and why it has been quantified at that amount. Reasons for the rejection must be given and a copy of counsel's advice, if any, should be included. Where the board is not satisfied with the reasons for the failure to accept the offer or payment in, and where the client refuses to change his/her mind the board can discharge the certificate. Where a payment into court is accepted, the defendant is liable to the CRU for benefits paid to the plaintiff up until the date of the payment in. If the payment in is accepted late (ie, after the 21-day period), the defendant is liable to compensate the CRU for benefits paid up until the date when the defendant was notified of the acceptance of a payment out of court. Thus, in cases where the benefits paid after the 21-day period are a large amount of money, defendants are less likely to agree to acceptance of late payments in.

Calderbank offers

A Calderbank letter – so named after the case of *Calderbank v Calderbank*[46] – is a letter making an offer of settlement 'without prejudice save as to costs'. It cannot therefore be brought to the court's attention during the proceedings until the question of costs arises (ie, after all other matters are dealt with). At that stage, if the offer amounts to more than or the same as the award, the letter can be produced to sustain an argument that the plaintiff should not receive costs from receipt of the letter onwards.

There is no obligation to respond to a Calderbank offer (though the usual etiquette demands an acknowledgement).[47]

The use of Calderbank letters in personal injury cases is, in fact,

44 *Scania (GB) Ltd v Andrews* [1992] 1 WLR 578; see also *Magee v Armstrong Engineering Services (London) Ltd and Others* (1994) *Times* 10 February.

45 Civil Legal Aid (General) Regs 1989 regs 70(1)(a) and 77(a).

46 [1976] Fam D 93.

47 *C & H Engineering (A firm) v Klucznik & Sons Ltd* (1992) *Times* 26 March.

extremely limited because the court, in assessing costs, has to ignore a Calderbank offer if a payment into court could have been made.[48] However, if the defendant has applied for, but not yet received, a certificate of total benefit from the CRU, a Calderbank offer may be made because a payment into court could not be calculated so as to take into account the amount of benefits.[49] The arrival from the CRU of a certificate of total benefit will often indicate that the defendant intends to make a formal offer or payment in within eight weeks from the date of the certificate. Thereafter, the certificate will lapse.

48 RSC Ord 22 r14(2) and Ord 62 r9(1)(d); CCR Ord 11 r10(2). Thus, a Calderbank offer might be made in proceedings claiming an injunction or in interlocutory steps in personal injury cases. This is, in practice, extremely rare.

49 RSC Ord 62 r9(2).

CHAPTER 12

Summonses and applications

High Court summonses and county court applications are the weapons of the personal injury lawyer. The procedures for taking out either a summons or an application are simple. Examples are given in Part V section D pp437 et seq.

Summons in the High Court

The basic format of the summons is set out in D1 p437. A set of stock forms can be obtained. The basic forms are best put on disk so that the relevant details in each individual summons can be added and the completed form printed out.

Summonses can be heard before a master (in London), registrar in a District Registry, district judge or judge. In fact, the vast majority of summonses are heard by masters. Appeals against a master's decision go to a judge in chambers.

Each day, the masters take it in turn to act as practice master and deal with ex parte and urgent procedural summonses. The procedure in masters' hearings is described in more detail below. A summons may be heard in chambers, either ex parte or inter partes.

Ex parte summons

The High Court has the power to direct that an application made ex parte, ie, without notice to the other side, should proceed by summons, in order to give the other party an opportunity of being heard.[1] Ex parte applications to a judge in chambers are exceptional in personal injury cases. Ordinarily, the following matters are dealt with by ex parte application to a master:

1 White Book 1993 para 32/1–6/2.

- leave to issue and serve a writ out of the jurisdiction[2]
- renewal of the writ[3]
- service out of the jurisdiction of any summons, notice or order[4]
- leave to add as a party the personal representative of a deceased party and to carry on the proceedings[5]
- leave to issue a third (or fourth etc) party notice[6]
- substituted service of a writ and other proceedings.[7]

An ex parte summons needs to be issued and supported by an affidavit. It should then be left in the masters' secretary's department.[8] The summons will be allocated to a master (if one has not already been allocated to the case), who will consider the terms of the summons and the affidavit before making an order.

Summons on notice

This procedure – inter partes – applies to the vast majority of summonses issued in the courts. A single summons can be used to make more than one application. The summons must have the name and address of the defendant or his/her solicitor inserted at its foot and be served (see pp103–7).

Issuing High Court summonses

The procedure for issuing an inter partes High Court summons in London is as follows. The applicant prepares the summons in duplicate and either posts to the court or takes it in person, together with the issuing fee. The court stamps the original summons, certifying that the issuing fee has been paid. The summons is then dealt with by the relevant issuing room (the masters' secretary for masters' summonses) and a summons hearing date will be given.

Applications to judges

The procedure for issuing an inter partes summons and appeal before a

2 RSC Ord 6 rr6 and 7; Ord 11.
3 RSC Ord 6 r8.
4 RSC Ord 11 r9(4).
5 RSC Ord 15 r7.
6 RSC Ord 16 r2.
7 RSC Ord 65 r4.
8 White Book 1993 paras 32/1–6/4.

judge in chambers is contained in RSC Order 32 r2.[9] Five lists are kept. These are: the general list (not more than 30 minutes); the chambers appeals list (appeals from masters or district judges likely to take more than 30 minutes); the list for special appointments (applications and summonses likely to last more than 30 minutes – where a date is fixed); the warned list (special appointments where no date has been fixed); and the expedited list.

All inter partes applications and appeals are entered initially in the general list. Where the hearing is likely to last more than 30 minutes, the parties should apply to have the matter taken out and placed either in the chambers appeals list or the list of special appointments.[10] There is a strict procedure governing these hearings. The latest practice direction merits study before an attendance.[11]

Parties to matters placed in the chambers list are likely to be informed within a matter of weeks that the case can be heard at any time, and put in the daily cause list either as a fixture – ie, before a specified judge – or as a floater.

Applications to masters

The procedure for issuing an inter partes summons to a master is contained in RSC Order 32, r11.[12] A hearing date is written on the summons and it is returned to the applicant, who then has the duty of serving a copy on the other parties to the action. The top copy is retained by the applicant who will place it before the master on the return day. Summonses for extensions of time must be served two clear days before the return date.[13] However, for many kinds of summons this period is longer, for example, for applications to enter judgment under Order 14 the period is 10 clear days.[14]

When a summons is issued in the action, a master is allocated to the case and, from that time onwards, the same master usually hears all further summonses (other than time summonses) on that case. The master's name should be typed on all further summonses at the top, above the names of the parties and just below the court title. The party issuing

9 See also *Listing Statement (Queen's Bench Judge in Chambers)* (1988) *Independent* 25 November; *Practice Note* [1989] 1 All ER 1120.

10 White Book 1993 paras 32/1–6/5 and 32/1–6/6.

11 *Practice Direction (Judge in Chambers in London: Amended Procedure)* [1993] 1 WLR 1303.

12 White Book 1993 para 32/11–13/4.

13 RSC Ord 32 r3.

14 RSC Ord 14 r2(3).

the second summons in a matter is under a duty to notify the issuing officer of the name of the master assigned.

The date and time of the master's summons will depend on the type of summons, the likely length of hearing and its complexity. The applicant must make an accurate assessment of which list (see below) is suitable for the type of hearing applied for.

General list

There is a daily list[15] of summonses heard in chambers, usually between 10.30 am and 12 noon in half-hour blocks. During each thirty-minute session, approximately 12 to 15 summonses are listed. Each summons is supposed to last not longer than 10 minutes, but most last only a minute or two. It is the master's job to get through the list as quickly as possible, so an applicant who cannot quickly produce the documents which the master asks for may be dealt with abruptly. It is best to have a set of pleadings ready, as well as the summons. These summonses are heard in rooms situated round the hall popularly known as 'the bear garden'.

Summonses in this list are put into three categories – short (order 14); short (miscellaneous); and longer (up to 20 minutes) attended by counsel. Generally, these summonses are either those where the parties consent but an order or direction of the court is still required, or are small and simple, contested applications. If counsel attends a 'short summons', the other party is usually offered an adjournment with costs, unless s/he has unreasonably refused a request for transfer to the longer 'counsel's list'. Examples of summonses appropriate to this list are applications for further or amended directions, for the amendment of pleadings, or for further time to comply with the rules.

The short notice list is for applications that are urgent and not expected to last more than 5 minutes. An application to enter the summons in this list must be endorsed for entry on the list on its backsheet and lodged in Room E216 in the Royal Courts of Justice. The master's secretary's listing officer will issue the summons and fax it to all parties concerned and when confirmation of transmission is received from the Court's fax service, the application will be entered in the short notice list. The party who lodged the summons is responsible for collecting the original copy prior to the hearing.[16]

Counsel's list

This list takes place at 12 noon and is used for summonses suitable for

15 White Book 1993 para 32/11–13/4.

16 *Practice Direction (Master's List: Short Notice List)* [1993] 1 All ER 787.

counsel, ie, the more complex, contested applications. Each application has a maximum of 20 minutes, but the court relies on most being dealt with in a rather shorter period and eight or so are usually listed for this one-hour list.

While this list is popularly referred to as 'counsel's list', in fact it is technically still the general list. Solicitors often attend for one party or the other and there is no requirement that both parties be represented by counsel.[17] Examples of summonses appropriate for this list are applications for specific discovery, enforcing interrogatories and contested requests for further and better particulars.

Private room appointments

These applications are made for hearings which will last longer than 20 minutes or which must be heard in private. In the High Court they take place in the master's own room, rather than in the rooms allocated for the hearing of summonses in the morning general or counsel's lists.

To apply for a case to be listed as a private room appointment, a form (obtainable from the masters' secretary's department) must be completed, giving certain details regarding the parties, length of summons, counsel, dates to be avoided and so on – see precedent D2 p438. The summonses in these cases must be given to the masters' secretary's department, together with the specific form requesting a private room appointment. The masters' secretary then arranges a date for the hearing and the applicant collects the summons a few days later from the masters' secretary's room with the return date indorsed on it. Alternatively, the parties may make a request to the master in person for a date. Examples of summonses suitable for this category are applications for an interim payment, for summary judgment, for the staying of proceedings and for an expedited hearing.

Senior master's floating list

The senior master has a list for applications lasting approximately 30 minutes of the following types: for summary judgment; to set aside judgments; those marked by a master 'fit for senior master's list', for reasons of urgency; and those with the consent of all the parties. The senior master's floating list is taken by the senior master on three or four days each week.

17 Counsel's fees are not recoverable for attending unless the master, district registrar or judge has certified the case 'fit for counsel': White Book 1993 para 62/A2/5.

Deputy master's list
A deputy master sits every day during the three court terms. Matters are referred to this list by request of the parties to the masters' secretary or by the assigned master. This usually happens because the master is unable to hear the summons for a long time and s/he agrees to release the summons to the deputy master.

General floating list
This is kept in Room E216 and cases in this list are heard by any Master or Deputy Master who is free. In practice, the Masters' Secretary will use the floating list to transfer cases which cannot be heard by the assigned Master for reasons such as sickness, or overrunning of time on other applications.

Structured settlement's list
Since 30 March 1992 there is a special procedure for approving structured settlements. They are listed on Friday mornings during term time.[18]

The party making the application determines the appropriate type of listing. When the other party receives the summons, s/he can object, perhaps on the ground that the time allocated is too short or the case has been put into the 'short' list, whereas it should be in counsel's list. Where the applicant refuses to relist the hearing for a longer period and, on hearing, the application is adjourned because of lack of time, the other side is likely to be awarded the cost of the adjourned hearing.

If there is any possibility that the defendant may be right in claiming that a summons issued by the plaintiff may require more time than the listing allows, it is usually best to concede, not so much because of the risk of costs but because, if relisting is ordered, the plaintiff's case will have sustained an unnecessary delay. Indeed, one of the increasing difficulties of litigation in the High Court is the length of the time it takes to have a summons heard. Depending on the master, a hearing date will usually take anything from six to 12 weeks and, where a hearing of more than an hour is required, there can be delay of many months. This delay is, of course, advantageous to the defendant and means that the plaintiff's solicitors should be all the more vigilant to ensure that there are no unnecessary adjournments and that defendants are not given too much leeway beyond the various time limits imposed by the automatic directions.

Sometimes it can be as quick to obtain a private room appointment of up to one hour as it is to have a case listed in the general or counsel's list. An experienced solicitor will keep an eye on the time estimates of each type of hearing.

18 *Practice Direction (Structured Settlements: Courts' Approval)* [1992] 1 WLR 328.

Attendance

Rights of audience before the master are not restricted, except for the hearing of a general summons in counsel's list (see above). In many straightforward applications it is sufficient for a clerk to represent the plaintiff. While it is necessary to be cost conscious, it is also necessary not to underestimate the problems which can arise at a hearing and the solicitor should always ensure that the representative has the appropriate skills and experience for the job. On consent applications, it may be necessary only for the applying party to attend. A letter of consent from the other side, dealing with every aspect of the summons, including costs, should be sent to the applicants who will show this to the master.

Orders

At the conclusion of each hearing the master will write the terms of the order on the original summons. The endorsement is often indecipherable but the staff in the order room are usually able to help. Once the terms of the order are clear the party who has obtained the order must draw it up within a reasonable time. If this is not done, the other side can draw the order up and costs may be awarded against the applicant. The order should be typed out in the form set out as shown in D3 p438. An original plus a copy for the court and one for each party should then be delivered or posted to the order room with the original summons. There is no further charge. Provided that the order room staff are satisfied that the order is correct, they will stamp and return it. It is then the solicitor's job to serve a copy immediately on each of the other parties.

Applications in the district registry

Prior to issuing a summons, the solicitor should enquire of the registry whether the state of business will permit the matter to be heard or whether the summons should be issued in the central office, in London. The matter can be transferred to London and vice versa.[19] The procedure for an interlocutory application in the district registry is contained in the White Book.[20]

19 *Practice Direction (Judge in Chambers out of London)* [1972] 1 WLR 4. The considerations applicable for transfer of an action from a District Registry to London were dealt with in *Grey v Durham County Council* [1987] CLY 3109.

20 White Book 1993 para 32/23–24/8.

Applications in the county court

Applications are the county court equivalent, with some notable exceptions, of summonses in the High Court. In contrast to the High Court, most applications to the county court are dealt with by post, rather than by personal attendance. The general practice on interlocutory applications in the county court is contained in CCR Order 13 r1 and County Courts Act 1984 s39.

The application must be heard on notice, except where it is authorised to be made ex parte,[21] and will be heard in chambers, unless otherwise authorised. Two days' notice is required. All applications, unless the circuit judge otherwise directs, must be made to the district judge in the first place, who may refer the matter to the circuit judge. No affidavit evidence is needed, unless required by statute or the court. Counsels' fees will not be recoverable unless the court certifies that the hearing justified the attendance of a barrister (ie, was 'fit for counsel').[22] The trial judge cannot review an order for costs on an interlocutory matter.[23]

An appeal lies from the district judge to the circuit judge within five days of the order or such further time as the latter may allow.[24] An appeal is a rehearing, although the appellant must open the appeal.[25]

A standard county court application is set out in D4 p439. An application is made by sending to the chief clerk of the court the original, a copy for the court and one for each of the other parties to the action. There is no issue fee. The court sends a copy of the application, with the hearing date indorsed thereon, to each party or representative. There is no obligation on the plaintiff's solicitor to notify the defendant's solicitor of the impending hearing.

In the county courts there are only two types of application: the district judges' general list and private room appointments. The district judges' general list operates in a very similar manner to the masters' general list and the same kind of issues are dealt with.

The private room appointment is for any application that will last longer than 10 minutes. These applications may be attended by counsel. There is no special form for such appointments and they should simply be requested by covering letter. It is a usual courtesy to inform the other side if counsel is being instructed to attend a private room appointment.

At the end of the hearing, the district judge makes a note of the order.

21 CCR Ord 13 r1(2).
22 CCR Ord 38 r8.
23 *Flower Bowl v Hodges Menswear Ltd* (1988) 132 SJ 1216.
24 CCR Ord 13 r1(11).
25 *Evans v Bartlam* [1937] AC 473.

The court sends the order to both parties 'in due course' – usually two to three weeks. There are early indications, however, of this practice changing. In at least one county court the district judge makes a clear note in the court file of the terms of the order, and directs that one party draws this order up and takes the draft order to the court office, where the staff check it against the district judge's note and approve and seal the order and allow the party drawing up the order to serve it.

Most district judges' general lists are far less efficient than those of the High Court. It is not uncommon in the county court to wait an hour or two for a two-minute hearing of an application.

Time for compliance

A time summons is used to apply for an extension of the time that the court rules allow for the service of a document.[26] This summons is also useful to compel defendants to do something – for example, provide further particulars of the defence – by a particular time. A precedent is at D5 p440.

A final order indicates that the master will not extend time further, except perhaps in extraordinary circumstances. On a first application, the court rarely makes a peremptory order or attaches a default clause to an order (ie, a provision that the defence will be struck out unless the other side serves the relevant document).[27]

An unless order has the effect of striking out the other party's pleading in the event of non-compliance with the order. Even if the court makes an 'unless' or conditional order which is not complied with, the court has the power to extend the time for compliance, although it will be cautious in this respect.[28] The form of an unless order must be strictly adhered to.[29] A precedent is at D6 p440. The county court can grant an unless order on application or of its own motion at any stage of the proceedings.[30] Unlike the High Court, this can even be done on the first occasion.[31]

26 *Practice Direction (Queen's Bench Division: time summonses)* [1989] 1 WLR 752; and see White Book 1993 paras 3/5/3 and 32/1–6/9.
27 *Siebe Gorman & Co Ltd v Pneupac Ltd* [1982] 1 WLR 185, per Denning MR.
28 *Samuels v Linzi Dresses Ltd* [1981] QB 115.
29 *Practice Direction (Queen's Bench Division: peremptory order)* [1986] 1 WLR 948.
30 CCR Ord 13 r2(1).
31 CCR Ord 13 r2(2).

Tactical applications and summonses

A number of procedural applications are available to both sides and should be kept in mind from the time of service of the proceedings. These can be very useful weapons in the plaintiff's solicitor's hands, but some can be equally useful if used at the right moment by the defendant's lawyers.

The applications to consider here are: for judgment in default; to strike out the whole or part of a pleading; to obtain summary judgment; to consolidate actions; to dispose of a case on a point of law; for a split trial; for interim payment; to stay proceedings; and to dismiss for want of prosecution. Some are more common than others. For convenience, notices of intention to proceed, and withdrawal and discontinuance are also dealt with here.

Judgment in default

Judgment in default of acknowledgment of service of the writ is dealt with in chapter 9 at p108 and judgment in default of defence is dealt with in chapter 11 at p134. Defendants can apply[32] to have such judgment set aside if they give good reason. The penalty is, however, threefold. First, the defendant pays the costs. Second, the plaintiff's lawyers will have exercised decisive control and so will have won a psychological advantage. Third, the defendant's lawyers will be embarrassed at having to explain to their client how judgment came to be entered against them.

Although an application for judgment in default will delay the plaintiff's case if it is not successful, the use of this tactic can ensure that the defendant does not subsequently delay proceedings by unnecessary inaction.

Striking out pleadings

At any stage in the proceedings, the court can order that any pleading, or indorsement on a writ, or part of any pleading or indorsement, can be struck out.[33]

The party applying must give one of four grounds for this. These are that the pleading: discloses no reasonable cause of action or defence; is

32 Under RSC Ord 13 r2 or Ord 19 r3; CCR Ord 9 r6.

33 RSC Ord 18 r19; CCR Ord 13 r5. Failure to comply with an order, for example, to serve further and better particulars ordered, will not justify striking out unless the default was intentional or contumelious: *Grand Metropolitan Nominee (No 2) Co Ltd v Evans* [1992] 1 WLR 1191. A strike-out application will not be appropriate if it involves a difficult point of law which cannot be properly determined upon the facts pleaded: *Lonrho PLC v Tebbitt* [1992] 4 All ER 280.

scandalous, frivolous or vexatious; may prejudice, embarrass or delay the fair trial of the action; or is otherwise an abuse of the process of the court.

Delay may defeat an application to strike out. An application should be made as soon as possible after the offending pleading has been served. In the High Court, a summons to the master is used; in the county court the issue is dealt with by way of application. The summons or application must state precisely the terms of the order being sought and give the relevant grounds. It is not necessary to serve an affidavit, although it may be helpful.

It is rare to find grounds for striking out a defendant's case in a personal injury action, but sometimes such a situation arises and the plaintiff's lawyers should always be alert to seize such an opportunity.

The court will strike out the plaintiff's case only where it is satisfied that the plaintiff has no viable cause of action. Striking out for bringing a claim in the High Court which should have begun in the county court is exceptional.[34] This situation in personal injury cases is even rarer. Where this is a possibility, it is important that the plaintiff's solicitors ensure that the case is as strong as possible prior to the service of the proceedings, which may include procuring an expert's report rather earlier than usual.

Automatic striking out of the plaintiff's claim under CCR Order 17 r11(9) occurs without the need for application by the defendant where the plaintiff has failed to set down for trial within 15 months of close of pleadings (or 9 months of an order to set down). The claim may be reinstated but only where the plaintiff can show the claim has (apart from this) been prosecuted with due diligence, and the failure to set down was 'excusable'. Even so, prejudice to the defendant will usually be fatal.[35]

Summary judgment (Order 14 etc)

On receipt of the defence, the plaintiff's solicitor should consider the prospects for an application for summary judgment under RSC Order 14 or CCR Order 9 r14, with an order for damages to be assessed. The basis for such an application is that the other side has no arguable defence against the plaintiff's claim.

In the High Court, an Order 14 application may be issued at any time after notice of intention to defend has been given. However, the effect of issuing an Order 14 summons before the service of the defence is that the other side does not need to serve the defence until the Order 14 application has been heard.

34 *Rastick v Crickmore* [1994] 1 WLR 420.
35 *Rastin v British Steel* (1994) 17 February, CA (unreported). See also p167.

This weapon is used rather less frequently than it ought to be in personal injury litigation. An application for summary judgment is appropriate wherever facts, either admitted or reasonably incontestable, could lead only to a finding of full liability without any real chance of contributory negligence. The best example would be a plaintiff who was a vehicle passenger in a road accident where a driver was clearly to blame. The possible factual scenarios are infinite, of course, and apply just as much to accidents or diseases at work.

Rather than calling witnesses to give evidence at the hearing, summary judgment is sought by application or summons to the district judge or master, the evidence being given on affidavit. The form of the affidavit must strictly comply with the rules of the court. It must be made by the plaintiff or state that it is made by a duly authorised person.[36] It must verify the facts on which the claim or part of the claim is based and the deponent's belief that there is no defence to the claim, or no defence except as to the amount of damages. No defect in the statement/particulars of claim can be made good by affidavit evidence.[37] The affidavit should clearly set out the source of statements made; the defendant is entitled to object where there has been a failure to do so.[38] Any defects or omissions may be cured by subsequent affidavits.

The court should look at the matter both on jurisdiction and on the merits.[39] It is usual for the summons to be heard in a private room appointment. The affidavit, made by the plaintiff's solicitor, should set out the background to the case, the evidence supporting the plaintiff's account (such as an expert's or police report), and the reasons why it is said that the defendant has no effective defence to the claim. In the county court, if service is effected by the plaintiff's solicitor, an affidavit of service is required, confirming this and that the summons was not returned undelivered.[40]

The defendant's solicitor must be served with the application or summons and affidavit at least seven clear days before the hearing in the county court, or 10 clear days in the High Court. In the High Court, the defendant's solicitors may then serve an affidavit in response – if they intend to rely on it – three clear days before the return date. The defendant need not file an affidavit at all, but can merely argue on the defence or that the statement/particulars of claim or affidavit is defective at the hearing.

36 *Chirgwin v Russell* (1910) 27 TLR 21.
37 *Gold Ores Reduction Co v Parr* (1892) 2 QB 14.
38 *Savings and Investment Bank Ltd v Gasco Investments (Netherlands) BV* [1984] 1 WLR 271.
39 *Les Fils Dreyfus & Cie SA v Clarke* [1958] 1 WLR 300.
40 CCR Ord 7 r10A(4).

In practice, the defendant's solicitors rarely comply with the requirement to serve in advance and usually appear on the day of the application with their affidavit. If an adjournment is necessary the master or district judge has a discretion to award costs.[41] In the county court, there is no similar requirement on the defendant for prior service of an affidavit.

Various orders can be made on the application for summary judgment, namely: judgement for the plaintiff; unconditional leave to defend; conditional leave to defend; and dismissal of the summons. If leave to defend is granted, the master may give ancillary directions for the further conduct of the action.[42]

In the High Court, if the master orders judgment for the plaintiff, the order should be sent to the court's judgment section, together with the pleadings and two copies of the order. In the county court, the court office will send out the judgment to all parties. On obtaining judgment, application should be made for a date for the assessment of damages hearing. This is usually before the master or district registrar in the High Court. In the county court, it will be heard by the circuit judge if the district judge's financial jurisdiction (£5,000) is likely to be exceeded.[43]

The advantage of making an application for summary judgment is to remove the risks of litigation concerning liability, and to do so speedily. Obtaining such an order has a profound effect on negotiations, depriving the defendant of any discount for the risk of losing on liability. It also enables a safe and speedy application for an interim payment.

Interest is recoverable on damages, under the Supreme Court Act 1981 s35A or the County Courts Act 1984 s69, until the date when damages are finally agreed or assessed and judgment entered for that sum. Thereafter, interest is recoverable under the Judgments Act 1838 s17.[44]

There are, however, disadvantages in this course of action. The first is a general disadvantage of interlocutory applications – they divert energy from the principal objective of pressing the whole case on to trial as quickly as possible. The second is that, for most larger cases, it is preferable to have a judge assessing the damages, rather than a master or

41 *Practice Direction (Order 14: return date)* [1970] 1 WLR 258.

42 These include a direction that, within a certain time, the statement of value of the claim must be lodged with the court and a copy served on every other party. Failure to do this may result in the case being transferred to the county court: RSC Ord 14 r6(1).

43 RSC Ord 37; CCR Ord 21 r5(1)(b).

44 In *Thomas v Bunn* [1991] 1 AC 362, the House of Lords decided that interest on damages awarded pursuant to Judgments Act 1838 s17 runs from the date when damages are assessed. Therefore, there is no longer any financial incentive to apply for judgment in default. Interest on judgment debts of over £5,000 can be claimed in the county court: County Court (Interest on Judgment Debts) Order 1991. The procedure is contained in CCR Ord 25 r5A.

district judge. Judges, particularly in the High Court, spend their days making awards, often for very large sums, and are, therefore, accustomed to thinking of damages in substantial terms. Masters and district judges, on the other hand, spend much of their time on procedural minutiae and, generally speaking, their assessments of damages are lower.

Disposal of case on point of law (Order 14A)

Since 1 February 1991, the High Court (there is no corresponding power in the county court) has had the power, on the application of a party or of its own motion, to determine any question of law or the construction of any document where the question can be determined without a full trial; and such determination finally determines (subject to appeal) the entire cause or matter or any claim or issue therein: RSC Order 14A.

The test of whether the question of law or construction is suitable to be determined under Order 14A is whether all the necessary and material facts relating to the subject matter of the question have been fully proved or admitted. There must be no dispute about the relevant facts.

The procedure for the application of Order 14A is ordinarily by way of summons to the appropriate master,[45] but may even be made orally in the course of an interlocutory application to the court.[46] The application may be made at any time after the defendant has given notice of intention to defend and before the full trial of the action has begun. An appeal against the order lies in the ordinary way to the judge in chambers.[47]

Judgment on admissions

The plaintiff can apply for judgment on an admission by the defendants.[48] This may prompt the defendants to amend any pleaded admission, but this will not be permitted if the withdrawal would be unjust to the plaintiff.[49]

Consolidating actions

The purpose of consolidating actions is to ensure that two or more actions

45 RSC Ord 14A r1(4).
46 RSC Ord 14A r2.
47 RSC Ord 58 r1.
48 RSC Ord 27 r3; CCR Ord 9 r6.
49 *Bird v Birdseye Walls Ltd* (1985) *Times* 24 July; and see a useful article in *PMILL* Vol 10 No 2 p15.

are heard simultaneously by the same judge.[50] This procedure is limited to those actions where there is 'some common question of law or fact bearing sufficient importance in proportion to the rest of the subject matter of the actions to render it desirable that the whole should be disposed of at the same time'.[51]

In personal injury cases, the question of consolidation nearly always occurs where separate actions have been commenced by separate plaintiffs against the same defendant arising out of the same occurrence. It is possible to consolidate the actions up to the point when liability is decided, giving conduct to one plaintiff's solicitor. The actions remain separated on the question of quantum.[52] It might be preferable to stay the later actions pending the decision in the 'lead' case.[53] If the lead case fails or is settled, another can be substituted.[54] Actions cannot be consolidated if there are different defendants in each action, even if the claims relate to the same incident.

The application should be made as soon as possible.[55] The nearer one of the cases is to trial, however, the greater the likely objections and the more likely that the court will refuse to consolidate because of the difficulties it would cause the defendants. An application for consolidation should be made by summons to the master in the High Court and by application to the district judge in the county court. The courts usually support consolidation, unless one party will clearly be prejudiced. It is an economic use of the court's time to have one trial for two or more actions, rather than separate trials for each.

Consolidation can be difficult if the statements or particulars of claim differ. It may mean that the defence would then become complicated as it attempts to deal with both cases. Thus, where the pleadings are not likely to overlap to any extent, it may be preferable to obtain, instead, an order that the cases be heard consecutively by the same judge.

Split trials

Trials can be split,[56] so that liability is determined at the first hearing and the issue of quantum, if liability is established, is dealt with at a later hearing. This procedure is not always advantageous to the plaintiff.

50 RSC Ord 4 r9; CCR Ord 13 r9.
51 *Payne v British Time Recorder Co* [1921] 2 KB 1.
52 *Healey v Waddington & Sons Ltd* [1954] 1 WLR 688.
53 *Amos v Chadwick* (1876–7) 4 Ch D 869.
54 *Bennett v Lord Bury* (1879–80) 5 CPD 339.
55 White Book 1993 para 4/9/5.
56 RSC Ord 33 r4(2A); CCR Ord 13 r2(2)(c).

Experience has shown that there may be more judicial sympathy on the issue of liability where the judge hears the evidence of the tragic consequences of the accident. Conversely the authors detect a tendency for larger awards of damages where the court hears the defendant's attempts to resist liability. A case which is weak on liability but strong on damages is likely to be more productive of a settlement if the issues are to be heard simultaneously. Each case depends on its own facts so, for example, if the plaintiff's evidence on damage is shaky, a split trial might be preferable. In general, there are two circumstances where a split trial is often advisable.

The first such situation is where the issue of quantum is complex and will be expensive to try. It may be in both parties' interest to determine liability first to see whether it is necessary to run to the costs of a trial on quantum. The second category of case is where it is foreseen that the evidence on quantum will not be ready for a long time, perhaps because the plaintiff's condition will not be stabilised for some years. A trial on liability alone may be an advantageous means of saving time and costs in the long run and keeping pressure on the defendant. If the trial on liability is successful, an application for an interim payment should be considered immediately. The procedure is explained later in this chapter.

An application for a split trial is made to the master or district judge, unless the case is within a month or so of trial, when the matter is usually referred to the judge in charge of the lists in the High Court, or to the circuit judge in the county court. The courts are now encouraging the use of these applications and have the power to order a split trial of their own motion. A precedent for seeking a split trial is at D10 p443.

Staying proceedings

An application to stay proceedings[57] is the tool of the defendant. It is most commonly used when the plaintiff has failed to co-operate in some aspect of the case. The main examples are failing to: attend a medical examination by the defendant's expert; produce a detailed schedule of damages; give authority to the defendant to obtain the plaintiff's medical records. For the defendant to have any chance of success, the failure must be in relation to something that the plaintiff is obliged to do.

Applications to stay are quite rare. It is usual for the defendant to apply first to the court for an order that the plaintiff carry out the required action within a certain time. Only after the plaintiff has failed to carry out the action is it usual for the defendant to apply for an order either staying proceedings or striking out the plaintiff's claim.

57 Supreme Court Act 1981 s49(3); *White Book 1991* Vol 2 5204; CCR Ord 13 r2(1).

The best policy for the plaintiff's lawyers is, on receipt of the summons, immediately to do that which is required. If not, an affidavit will be required at the hearing explaining the problem and the reasons for the delay, or setting out the principled objection to doing what is sought.

Dismissal for want of prosecution and failure to set down

The court has inherent jurisdiction to dismiss an action for want of prosecution. Because of the draconian effect of CCR Order 17 r11(9) in the county court,[58] which automatically strikes out claims which have not been set down for trial 15 months after close of pleadings (or 9 months after an order to set down), the inherent jurisdiction is unlikely to be much needed in the county court.

If the plaintiff's solicitor has conducted the case properly, an application for dismissal for want of prosecution should never happen. It is the job of the plaintiff's solicitor to ensure that the case is always moving forward and that any pressure by way of interlocutory application is on the defendant. Long delays on the plaintiff's side do occasionally occur, for example where the client has changed solicitor and there has been difficulty in the transfer of papers. If more than 15 months is needed, an application for an extension should be made under CCR Ord 17 r11(9). If the proceedings are still not set down nine months after the date set by the court on such an application, they will be struck out automatically.

Where it is apparent that there has been a lengthy delay and an application for dismissal is made, the first thing to consider is when the matter should have been set down for trial.[59] Any delay after that date will, in particular, have to be justified. If the writ has been issued late, ie, just before expiry of limitation, that is all the more reason why the preparatory stages should have been expedited. Second, the file should be checked to see whether the defendant's solicitors have been made aware of the reasons for the delay. Third, the plaintiff's solicitor should establish whether the case is now ready to be set down for hearing. If not, urgent consideration must be given to what else needs to be done and how long it may take.

Until 1968, dismissal for want of prosecution was virtually unheard

58 As to which see *Rastick v British Steel* (1994) 17 February, CA (unrep).

59 In the High Court where automatic directions apply, the case must be set down within 6 months from close of pleadings: RSC Ord 25 r8(1)(f). Pleadings are deemed to close 14 days after service of the defence or reply (if any): RSC Ord 18 r20. The power to dismiss is contained in RSC Ord 34 r2(2).

of. Since the decision in *Allen v Mc Alpine*,[60] there has been a very hostile climate to delay, particularly when caused by the plaintiff's side.[61] This is fortified by *Rastin v British Steel*[62] which lays down stringent provisions for a plaintiff to reinstate an action struck out under CCR Order 17 r11(9).

There are two sets of circumstances where the courts are likely to order that the action be dismissed for want of prosecution (the CCR Order 17 r11(9) procedure is automatic: the defendant makes no application and there is no hearing). The first situation is when a party has been guilty of 'intentional' or 'contumelious' default. The latter term means deliberate non-compliance with an order of the court. The second circumstance is where there has been an 'inordinate' or 'inexcusable' delay in the prosecution of the action which either gives rise to a substantial risk that it will not be possible to have a fair trial of the issues or is such as to cause serious prejudice[63] to the defendant. The term 'inordinate delay' means materially longer than the time usually regarded by the profession and courts as an acceptable period.[64] In an application by the defendant, 'inexcusable delay' is looked at from the defendant's point of view[65], due allowance being given for illness and accidents. There is no tariff of

60 [1968] 2 QB 229. See also *Sweeney v Sir Robert McAlpine* [1974] 1 All ER 474; *Birkett v James* [1978] AC 297 at 322F.

61 See now *Roebuck v Mungovin* [1994] 2 WLR 290, HL.

62 (1994) 17 February, CA (unreported); see p167 below.

63 Prejudice can be or varying kinds including economic (*Gascoigne v Harringay Health Authority* (1992) *Times* 30 July; (1992) 3 Med LR 291) and is not confined to prejudice affecting the actual conduct of the trial (per Lord Griffiths in *Department of Transport v Chris Smaller Ltd* [1989] AC 1197 at 1209). The plaintiff who is guilty of inordinate and inexusable delay has to take the defendant as s/he finds him (*Antcliffe v Gloucester Health Authority* (1993) 1 PIQR 47, CA.) If the defendant acquiesces in any delay and then applies to strike out the claim for subsequent delay, such acquiescence may not be a bar to striking out the claim, but is a relevant factor together with others such as the length of the acquiescence and extra costs involved: *Roebuck v Mungovin* [1994] 2 WLR 290. Acquiescence will not include negotiating or making a payment-in unless accompanied by an express promise not to seek to dismiss the action (*Draper v Ferrymasters Ltd* (1993) PIQR 356). Delay causing difficulty in recollection is not enough: it must be a significant addition to a substantial risk that there cannot be a fair trial caused by the delay since issue (*Hornagold v Fairclough Building Ltd* (1993) PIQR 400). Without prejudice correspondence can be admitted on application to dismiss for want of prosecution: *Family Housing Association (Manchester) Ltd v Michael Hyde & Partners Ltd* [1993] 1 WLR 354.

64 White Book 1993 para 25/1/6.

65 The defendant's conduct may also be relevant: *Armstrong v Glofield Properties Ltd* (1992) 1 PIQR 358.

periods which do or do not amount to inexcusable delay, since each case depends on its own facts.

Notice of intention to proceed

Where a year or more has elapsed since the last proceeding in a cause or matter, a notice of intention to proceed must be served.[66] The effect of this is that the defendant then has four weeks in which to issue a summons to strike out the action. The notice is simply a letter informing the defendant's solicitors of the intention to proceed.

Reinstatement after strike-out under CCR Order 17 r11(9)

Reinstatement is possible but difficult after automatic strike-out for failure to set down in time. In *Rastin v British Steel*[67] the Court of Appeal made clear that a plaintiff will need to show that apart from the failure to set down, the action was prosecuted with reasonable diligence (though not necessarily free from any criticism whatsoever) and that the failure to set down was excusable. This would be easier if s/he could show that an extension would have been granted if it had been applied for. Absence of prejudice to the defendant is not a sufficient condition but the presence of significant prejudice will usually be conclusive against reinstatement. Only after considering these matters will the Court then consider the availability of suit against an advisor, the expiry of limitation, admissions or payments in.

Withdrawal and discontinuance

Discontinuance applies to the termination of the whole action so that no part of it survives. Withdrawal applies to termination of part only of an action.

It may be that what was a promising claim turns out to be hopeless, or for tactical reasons it is better to withdraw or discontinue and issue afresh. It is preferable to discontinue or withdraw as soon as the decision is made, since any delay may cause the defendants to incur further, unnecessary costs, eg, commissioning experts' reports. To do nothing is to invite an application to strike out (see above), thus incurring more costs. A tactical discontinuance, by agreement (so that, for example, costs lie as they fall),

66 RSC Ord 3 r6.
67 (1994) 17 February, CA (unreported).

should always be explored. Otherwise, costs are usually awarded against the withdrawing or discontinuing party.

In the High Court, the procedures for withdrawal and discontinuance are contained in RSC Order 21. Provided that the plaintiff has not received an interim payment (see below), both discontinuance and withdrawal can be achieved, without leave, at any time up to 14 days after service of the (last) defence.[68] In all other cases, leave is required. The plaintiff may wish to apply for leave to discontinue or withdraw, even though leave is not necessary, as this allows the court to make an order for costs. Otherwise, the defendant is entitled to lodge a bill of costs[69] and sign judgment for costs within four days of taxation. If a matter is withdrawn without leave, in practice, costs will not be executed until the rest of the action is disposed of. Therefore, generally, a stay of execution will be granted. Withdrawal or discontinuance – with or without leave – does not have the effect of barring subsequent proceedings unless the court specifically so orders when granting leave. Notice of withdrawal or discontinuance has to be served in writing.

In the county court,[70] the plaintiff can withdraw or discontinue at any time before judgment or final order and no leave is required. The plaintiff may still apply for leave, so as to obtain a favourable order as to costs. Otherwise, the defendant will be entitled to lodge the bill of costs and sign judgment for costs after 14 days from taxation, if the proceedings involved were worth more than £1,000 or were exceptionally complex.

If a matter is withdrawn or discontinued after being set down for trial, there is a duty on all parties to inform the officer who keeps the list.

Interim payments

An application for interim payment[71] is for a payment on account of damages to be made to the plaintiff prior to the full trial of the action. See the example interim payment summons at D14 on p446 and see also chapter 29.

An application can be made at any stage after the defendant's acknowledgment of service has been lodged, or should have been lodged, although most are made shortly after the close of pleadings, when the nature of the defence is clear. This is because it is usually worthwhile waiting to see if the defendant admits liability. If the defendant's lawyers

68 RSC Ord 21 r2(1).
69 RSC Ord 62 r5(3).
70 CCR Ord 18 r1.
71 RSC Ord 29 r10(1); CCR Ord 13 r12.

are aware that an application for interim payment is in the offing, they may make the tactical decision not to admit liability, so as to make an interim payment application more difficult. The plaintiff's solicitors should, therefore, be wary of mentioning the possibility of such an application in correspondence, over the phone or in negotiations, until the defence is received.

However, where liability is not in issue, whether because of an admission in the defence or because of an open admission in correspondence, the plaintiff's solicitor should write to the defendant's solicitors asking for a voluntary interim payment before issuing a summons. Such a payment can often be agreed, although there may be argument over the amount.

The criteria that the courts apply in considering an application for an interim payment are either that the defendant has admitted liability or summary judgment has been obtained or, if the action proceeded to trial, the applicant would obtain judgment for substantial damages against the defendant (or where there are several, an identifiable one of them).[72] The courts should not be concerned with the use to be made of an interim payment.[73] However, it is usual to state the plaintiff's need in the affidavit; this will be particularly relevant, of course, to the amount sought.

The application is made, at first instance, to the master or district judge, and is usually a private room appointment, attended by counsel.[74] The solicitor must draft an affidavit giving the background to the case, detailing the plaintiff's claim and the progress of the pleadings, before going on to describe why the plaintiff is very likely to succeed in the claim. Any relevant documents, such as police reports, experts' reports and so on, should be exhibited to the affidavit. An outline should be given of the plaintiff's injuries and losses, again appending reports and evidence. The damages claim, including past and future loss of earnings, should be set out in reasonable detail.

The affidavit must be served on the defendant at least 10 days before the application is heard in the High Court or, in the county court, at least 7 days.[75] If the affidavit and supporting arguments are particularly complicated, it is sometimes advisable to ask the master or district judge

72 The standard of proof is the civil standard: *Gibbons v Wall* (1988) *Times* 24 February. A payment into court can be disclosed in an interim payment application: *Fryer v London Transport Executive* (1982) *Times* 4 December.

73 *Stringman v McArdle* (1993) *Times* 19 November.

74 A judge can also hear an interim payment application in chambers: *Smith v Glennon* (1990) *Times* 26 June. This may be preferable in big cases.

75 RSC Ord 29 r10(4); CCR Ord 13 r12(2).

to read them prior to the hearing. However, masters or district judges have a timetable that gives them little time for such reading and many take the view that it is better to leave everything to the hearing itself.

The application may be combined, in suitable cases (see below), with an application for summary judgment. There are two conflicting Court of Appeal decisions as to whether an interim payment can be awarded after granting unconditional leave to defend. According to *Ricci Burns Ltd v Toole*,[76] it can, but *British & Commonwealth Holdings plc v Quadrix Holdings Inc*[77] and *Andrews v Schooling*[78] (both decided after *Ricci*) held to the contrary: an interim payment can be awarded only if the leave to defend is conditional. This issue, therefore, remains open but only just. In practice the court usually makes leave to defend conditional on making an interim payment (as in *Andrews*).

It can be a big morale booster – as well as a financial advantage – for the client to receive an interim payment.[79] However, if liability in a case is so clear that an interim payment is likely to be made, it is also likely that the case can be pushed to an early trial. Unless the plaintiff is in desperate need of an interim payment, it may be a better strategy to devote all effort to an early trial, thus diminishing the need for an interim payment and avoiding even a small risk of losing an application with the likely costs order against the plaintiff.

A peripheral advantage of an interim payment application is that, where there is concern that defendants may have something up their sleeve, such as a secret witness, an interim payment application might draw out the information. This gives the plaintiff's advisers the opportunity to deal with the point early on, rather than having it sprung on them at trial.

It is not clear how much of the estimated damages the plaintiff is entitled to as an interim payment. The payment ordered must not exceed 'a reasonable proportion of the damages' after taking into account contributory negligence.[80] Interest can also be awarded.[81]

Interim payments are available only against a defendant who is

76 [1989] 1 WLR 993.

77 [1989] 3 All ER 492.

78 [1991] 1 WLR 783.

79 It is customary for interim payments to be limited to sums for which the plaintiff can show a need. However, there is no implied restriction in the court rules preventing an interim payment order being made in the absence of need or prejudice: *Schott Kem v Bentley* [1991] 1 QB 61. If a plaintiff is legally aided, the interim payment is exempted from the first charge in favour of the legal aid fund: Legal Aid (General) Regulations 1989 reg 94(a).

80 RSC Ord 29 r11(1).

81 *Independent Broadcasting Authority v EMI Electronics Ltd* (1980) 14 Build LR 1.

insured, or a public authority, or one who has the resources to pay the interim payment sought.[82] An interim payment cannot be given against the Motor Insurers Bureau.[83] In rare circumstances, they can be ordered to be repaid.[84]

Whilst an interim payment is exempt from the first charge to the legal aid fund, it does fall within the definition of a compensation payment and any interim payment over £2,500 will be subject to deduction of benefits paid under the Social Security Administration Act 1992 s81(1). Thus, if a client is in a desperate financial state as a result of his or her injuries, and a first interim payment is needed urgently, it may be better to ask for less than £2,500, as the defendants will not then seek a certificate of repayable benefits from the Compensation Recovery Unit.

The plaintiff can request more than one interim payment and the competent practitioner should always be alive to the possibility of requesting further interim payments.

82 *MV Yorke Motors (a Firm) v Edwards* [1982] 1 WLR 444.
83 *Powney v Coxage* (1988) *Times* 8 March.
84 RSC Ord 29 r17(a).

CHAPTER 13

Close of pleadings

From the time when the pleadings are closed (ie, 14 days after service of the defence, assuming that there is no reply),[1] a number of procedural matters arise. These require consideration by the plaintiff's solicitor, to ensure both that the case moves forward speedily to trial and that the case is run to the maximum benefit of the plaintiff.

High Court directions

After close of pleadings, the court needs to give directions about how the case is to proceed to trial. In most actions, the directions are automatic, but in some cases, it is necessary to apply for a summons for directions.

Automatic directions

In the High Court, under RSC Order 25 r8, most personal injury actions are subject to 'automatic directions'. This procedure avoids the delay which used to be caused in waiting for a summons for directions hearing before the master. The principal exceptions where the automatic directions do not apply are group actions (with many plaintiffs, such as disaster cases, product liability cases and environmental damage cases) and medical negligence cases. Automatic directions provide decisions on eight main issues of pre-trial preparation.

a) Mutual discovery of documents by way of an exchange of lists is required within 14 days of close of pleadings and inspection of the actual documents within seven days thereafter. Exceptions to this are where liability has been admitted or where the action arises out of a road accident; discovery is then limited to disclosure by the plaintiff of any documents relating to special damages.

1 RSC Ord 18 r20; CCR Ord 17, r11(11)(a).

b) Where any party intends to place reliance at the trial on expert evidence, they must, within 14 weeks, disclose the substance of that evidence to the other parties in the form of a written report,[2] which should be agreed if possible.[3]
c) If those reports are not agreed, the parties are able to call as witnesses those experts, the substance of whose evidence has been disclosed, as above. The number of expert witnesses is limited in any case to two medical experts and one expert of any other kind.
d) Any party intending to rely on oral evidence must within 14 weeks serve written statements of all such evidence they intend to adduce. (If the plaintiff is to be a witness, s/he must supply a witness statement.)
e) Photographs, a sketch plan and the contents of any police accident report book can be produced in evidence at the trial and should be agreed if possible.
f) The action will be heard at the trial centre for the place where the action is proceeding, or at any other trial centre that the parties agree in writing. Cases against the Crown are heard only at the Royal Courts of Justice, unless otherwise agreed.
g) The action will be tried by a judge alone, is classified by the courts as a case of substance or difficulty (category B) and must be set down within six months.
h) On setting down, the court must be notified of the estimated length of the trial.

For most personal injury cases, these directions will suffice. Where additions or deletions to the directions are required – eg, if more than two medical experts are needed – an application for further directions has to be made to the master.[4]

If the defendant's solicitors do not comply with one of the directions, the court usually expects a warning to be given, on the expiry of the appropriate time period, before the plaintiff's solicitor issues a summons to strike out the defence. Even then, an application to strike out usually

2 Including letters concerning matters which may arise in evidence: *Kenning v Eve Construction* [1989] 1 WLR 1189.

3 If this direction applies to more than one party, the reports must be disclosed by mutual exchange within the time provided, or as soon thereafter as the reports are available. If the defendant does not seek to adduce, for example, medical evidence, the plaintiff must comply with the direction, notwithstanding that there is no mutual exchange. If defendants request a medical examination, some practitioners insist that, as a condition of allowing the examination, the defendants disclose their report within 28 days of receipt. This is fair on the principle of mutuality, but is not yet supported by authority.

4 RSC Ord 25 r8(3).

results in the defendant being given a further period of seven or 14 days to comply with the direction. This should not discourage the efficient plaintiff's solicitor from issuing a warning on the expiry of the time period and issuing a summons after a further 14 days. If the defendant complies after service of the summons and before the hearing, the plaintiff is nevertheless entitled to the costs of the summons. Care must be taken before issuing a summons that the plaintiff's solicitor's hands are clean. The automatic directions are onerous, particularly in relation to witness statements, and the defendant's reaction to a summons will be to see if there are grounds for a cross-summons in respect of some failure to comply on the part of the plaintiff.

Summons for directions

Where automatic directions do not apply – eg, in respect of claims for injuries resulting from alleged medical negligence[5] or in multiple party cases – an application for directions must be made. This is a straightforward procedural application made by summons to the master in his/her general list. The summons must specify the directions requested. Such a summons will usually make similar provision to the automatic directions.

For proceedings commenced after 1 July 1991 and for all proceedings after 1 January 1992, a statement of the value of the action must be lodged by the plaintiff and a copy served on all other parties not later than the day before the hearing of the summons. Failure to do so will result in the case being transferred to the county court.[6] The substance of a standard directions summons is set out in D11 p444.

It is not necessary to support the application with an affidavit. Where a summons is required, it may be possible to gain the consent of the defendant's solicitors to the application. It is, therefore, advisable to send the solicitors the summons as soon as possible, to give them time to consult with their client and write to the plaintiff's solicitor expressing consent. It is nowadays not advisable to submit a consent order (with a copy of the defendant's letter) to the court. The master has such wide powers to act of his or her own motion (eg, to require further discovery, transfer to the county court, strike out pleadings or even the whole claim) that it is essential for the plaintiff's solicitor or counsel to attend in order to safeguard the plaintiff's interests in relation to any matter the master may raise.

5 RSC Ord 25 r8(5)(b).
6 RSC Ord 25 r6(2A).

A consent order is usually worded as follows: '*upon hearing solicitors for both parties and by consent it is ordered that – (a) lists of documents be exchanged by the parties within 14 days . . . etc, etc.*'

An order by consent without attendance can speed up proceedings, particularly where there is a lengthy delay between the issuing of the summons and the date for the appointment before the master. Costs on a summons for directions are invariably 'in the cause' ie, the costs of the winner will be paid by the loser.

Jury trials

The automatic directions refer all actions, as a matter of course, into the list for trial by judge alone. The plaintiff's lawyers should bear in mind that, at the court's discretion, personal injury cases may be listed before a judge and jury.[7] The Court of Appeal has determined that the judge is given the discretion to decide that a case will be heard by a jury where the circumstances are 'exceptional',[8] for example, where exemplary damages are claimed.[9]

County court directions

Automatic directions

In the county court, the automatic directions have been in force for all new actions (including medical negligence and multi-party cases) commenced after 5 February 1990.[10]

For proceedings commenced on or after 1 October 1990,[11] the following automatic directions apply (though some county courts have adopted minor variations) unless otherwise ordered:

a) There shall be discovery of documents within 28 days and inspection within seven days thereafter.
b) Except with the leave of the court or where the parties agree, (i) no expert evidence may be adduced at the trial unless the substance of that evidence has been disclosed to the other parties in the form of a written report within 10 weeks; and (ii) the number of expert

7 RSC Ord 33 r4; Supreme Court Act 1981 s69(3).
8 *Ward v James* [1966] 1 QB 273. For recent guidance on the procedure, see *Listing Statement: jury list* [1991] 2 QB 103.
9 *H v Ministry of Defence* (1991) *Times* 1 April.
10 County Court (Amendment No 4) Rules 1989.
11 County Court (Amendment No 3) Rules 1990 r17; CCR Ord 17 r11.

witnesses is limited in any case to two medical experts and one expert of any other kind.[12]

c) Any party wishing to rely on oral evidence shall within 10 weeks serve written statements of all such evidence s/he intends to adduce.

d) Photographs, a sketch plan and the contents of any police accident report book can be given in evidence at the trial, and should be agreed if possible.

e) Unless a day has already been fixed, the plaintiff shall, within six months, request the proper officer to fix a day for hearing.

When liability is admitted or where the action arises out of a road accident, disclosure by the plaintiff is limited to any documents relating to special damages. These include documents relating to industrial injury and, for Fatal Accidents Act 1976 claims, documents relating to any claim for dependency on the deceased.

Where a medical report has been disclosed with the particulars of claim[13] and the plaintiff intends to rely on that report, no further report need be produced. If a further report is intended to be relied on, that report should be disclosed and, if appropriate, the statement of special damages amended.[14]

Any orders required which are outside or different from the terms of the automatic directions should be sought by application to the district judge in the usual way.

Where the automatic directions apply, the plaintiff's solicitor is under a duty to set down for trial within 15 months of close of pleadings (or, in default, be automatically struck out): see pp164–7 and 219 et seq.

Pre-trial review

The automatic directions do not apply to cases commenced prior to 5 February 1990, nor to jury trials (extremely rare in PI cases), whenever commenced. In these actions, the court itself sends out a pre-trial review date to both parties. Unfortunately, that is not universal practice and if, once the defence has been received, no pre-trial review date has been given, the plaintiff's solicitor should remind the court by requesting a pre-trial

12 Failure to comply may preclude the calling of the expert: *Croft v Jewell* (1993) PIQR 270.

13 CCR Ord 6 r1(5)(a).

14 CCR Ord 17 r11(7)(b). It is not always necessary to amend pleadings each time fresh reports lead to new developments: *Owen v Grimsby & Cleethorpes Transport* [1992] PIQR Q27.

review appointment. A formal county court application should not be necessary; a letter simply requesting a date should suffice.

Once the court has issued a hearing date, it is sensible to write to the defendant's solicitors inviting them to agree the orders the plaintiff seeks. Notwithstanding the defendant's consent, it is essential for the plaintiff's solicitor or counsel to attend the directions hearing, since the court has such wide powers to act of its own motion. Only by attendance will the plaintiff's interests be protected in relation to any matter the court may raise. Indeed district judges have been known to disregard agreed terms such as those in relation to timetables.

In cases of particular complexity, consideration should be given to the possibility of transfer to the High Court.

Disclosure of witness statements

One of the most far reaching changes to personal injury practice has been the implementation of the requirement to dislose witness statements.[15] The stated objective is to achieve several beneficial results, including:

a) the fair and expeditious disposal of proceedings and the saving of costs;
b) the elimination of any element of surprise before or at the trial as to the witnesses each party intends to call and as to the substance of their evidence;
c) the promotion of a fair settlement between the parties;
d) the avoidance of a trial if possible;
e) the identification of the real issues and elimination of unnecessary issues;
f) the encouragement of admissions of fact;
g) the reduction in the number of pre-trial applications for particulars of pleadings, further discovery and interrogatories;
h) the provision of a framework wherein routine evidence and evidence-in-chief can be given in summary form;
i) the improvement of the process of cross-examination;
j) the concentration of both the parties and the trial judge on the real matters in controversy between the parties.

Defendants will no doubt make use of these objectives, for example, when objecting to the admission of late evidence and when applying for an adjournment with costs.

15 This was proposed by the 'Civil Justice Review' in 1988. It is governed by RSC Order 38 r2A, CCR Order 20 r12A.

The need for disclosure of witness statements makes it essential that all witnesses are properly and fully proofed and that the preparation of the witness statement from the proof is done with care and skill.

Statements can be ordered to be dislosed at any stage of the proceedings, but in most personal injury cases they will be ordered by the automatic directions.[16]

Unless exchange is not ordered (see below), the automatic directions provide for mutual, simultaneous disclosure of witness statements within 14 weeks (in the High Court) and within 10 weeks (in the county court) of the close of pleadings.[17] If the defendants fail to serve statements, the plaintiff should not wait in the expectation that the defendants will be unable to call evidence (they may obtain leave to serve witness statements late). Instead, the plaintiff should apply for an order debarring the defendant from calling any witness whose witness statement has not been served by a specified date, or in the alternative for judgement on the grounds that there is no evidence to sustain a defence.

The statements are intended for use at the trial itself and therefore they should only deal with issues of fact to be adduced at the trial. They are expected to represent what the witness will say 'in chief' at the trial. Accordingly, the statement must contain only statements of material fact of which the witness has direct knowledge. No expressions of opinion are permitted; neither is hearsay evidence. It must contain all the evidence that it is intended the witness will give. Otherwise, it will not be possible to lead such evidence (unless the defendants consent or the court grants leave). It is not necessary to anticipate the evidence of a witness for the defence. A specimen witness statement is at A2 p323.

The statement must set out the witness's name, address, occupation, and his/her relationship to the proceedings. It must be in the first person, be in a clear, straightforward narrative form and as far as possible follow the language of the witness. It should follow a chronological sequence. Each paragraph should be confined if possible to a distinct portion of the witness's evidence and paragraphs should be numbered consecutively.

The statement must be dated and (except for good reason) signed by

16 The requirement to exchange witness statements applies (CCR Ord 20A) to an action in the county court, whenever commenced, where (a) a pre-trial review is held on or after 16 November 1992, or (b) when automatic directions become applicable (ie, when a defence if filed) on or after 16 November 1992. In all other cases where proceedings were in existence on 16 November 1992 there will be no such requirement unless expressly ordered by the court. In the High Court, exchange of witness statements is compulsory for all cases to which automatic directions apply after 16 November 1992: RSC Order 25 r8(1).

17 See RSC Order 38 r2A; CCR Ord 20A.

the intended witness. If the statement is not signed, a letter explaining the reason should accompany the statement. The statement should include a statement that "the contents are true to the best of my knowledge and belief". It should sufficiently identify any documents referred to. Any dates, sums or other numbers should be expressed in figures and not words.

The statement should be on A4 paper and be fully legible. It should normally be typed double-spaced on one side of the paper only. At trial it should be paginated and form part of a paginated bundle of statements.[18] References to any documents mentioned should be given in the margin, where possible.

If it is not possible to obtain a written statement from a witness before the date of disclosure, the court may direct that the party wishing to adduce that witness's evidence provides the name of the witness and the gist of the evidence that s/he is likely to give. At the time of writing it is not clear in what circumstances a plaintiff will be able to rely upon this exception. Each case depends upon its own facts but it is better to err on the side of disclosure than not. Otherwise, it may result in failure to admit the evidence.

Witness statements served pursuant to the rules constitute a 'document' in the proceedings and therefore fall within the amending power of the court under RSC Order 20 r8(1). Amendment will only be allowed in exceptional circumstances, usually to deal with new matters or responses to witness statements from the defendants. The rule will probably exclude amendments to deal with matters which should have been covered in the original statement.

In practice it is envisaged that the witness will be allowed to contradict the evidence of other witnesses in oral evidence without need of a supplementary statement. But a supplementary statement may be ordered[19] if it fills the gap in the witness's own statement or answers the statements of the defendant.

Any objection to the admissibility of the evidence of a witness may be left until the evidence is produced formally at the hearing.

It will be seen from the above that disclosure of witness statements is a major headache for plaintiffs. Although the court does have a discretion to vary or override the requirements of this rule, there can be no doubt that there is a real danger of relevant evidence being excluded because of some slip-up by the solicitor. Conversely, great care must be taken to ensure the

18 See court bundles, p228.
19 See White Book 1993 para 38/2A/10.

exclusion of all unnecessary material which could provide fertile cross-examination topics.

More important, this disclosure gives the defendant the plaintiff's evidence in advance. It remains to be seen whether the effect of this rule change will be to cut down the number of trials. The authors' view is that it could well increase the number of contested hearings.

If the party who has served a statement does not call the witness to whom it relates, then no other party may put that statement in evidence (except by way of Civil Evidence Act notices, see p195 below.)

Where a witness is called, the court (in a non-jury trial) will normally treat the statement as the witness's evidence-in-chief. The witness will be permitted to give evidence about matters that have arisen since the service of the statement. Unless the court grants leave, the witness will not be able to give evidence that contradicts the statement. Once the statement has been referred to in chief, the witness can be cross-examined on all its contents. The statement does not make admissible that which is not otherwise admissible (eg, hearsay).

Once a witness statement has been served, any privilege attached to it disappears.[20] Service of the statement itself does not, unless expressly stated, constitute a Civil Evidence Act notice.[21] Either party can serve a witness statement together with a Civil Evidence Act 1968 notice on the other side if it is or may be necessary to rely upon the evidence contained therein.

If the defendants serve a witness statement that is useful to the plaintiff's case, it is worth considering serving a Civil Evidence Act notice upon them, just in case they do not call the witness. Unless such a notice is served, the witness statement of the witness will not become evidence of the case in the absence of testimony from the witness.

20 *Youell v Bland Welch & Co* [1991] 1 WLR 122, per Phillips J. But there is no waiver of privilege in connected documents: *Balkanbank v Taher* (below).

21 *Balkanbank v Taher & Others* (1994) *Times* 19 February.

CHAPTER 14

Discovery

Plaintiff's list of documents[1]

On receipt of the defence, it is important, tactically, to be immediately in a position to serve the plaintiff's list of documents on the defendant's solicitors. The reason for this is that, as stated above, the automatic directions in both courts require the disclosure of lists of documents by both parties within 14 days of the close of pleadings or transfer to the county court. For most defendants' lawyers, the service of the defence means that the case can be put at the back of the filing cabinet again. Receipt of the plaintiff's list a few days later, however, may encourage them to consider seriously getting rid of the case altogether and reaching a settlement.

In road traffic accidents the defendants do not automatically have to serve a list and the plaintiff's list is restricted to special damage documentation only[2]. If it is felt that discovery is necessary, then an order should be sought.[3]

Where the plaintiff claims permanent loss of earnings and loss of earning capacity, all his/her medical records should be discovered and not just those relating to the injury giving rise to the claim.[4]

Under these orders, it is the duty of both parties to disclose all material documents relevant to the action that are or have been in their possession, custody or power, aside from those they specifically claim as having privilege attached to them.[5]

1 'Document' includes information saved on the hard disc/floppy disc of a computer: *Derby & Co Ltd v Weldon (No 9)* [1991] 1 WLR 652; *Alliance and Leicester Building Society v Ghahremani* (1992) *Times* 19 March; (1992) 32 RVR 198.
2 RSC Order 24 r2(2); CCR Order 17 r11.
3 Under RSC order 24 r3 or CCR Order 14 r1.
4 *Dunn v British Coal Corporation* (1993) PIQR 275.
5 If a party deliberately suppresses a document, this constitutes contumacious conduct which might justify striking out the whole action/defence, even if a fair trial is still possible: *Landauer Ltd v Comins & Co (a Firm)* (1991) *Times* 7 August.

Legal professional privilege, of course, covers (among other things) correspondence between solicitor and client, proofs of evidence, instructions to and advice from counsel and solicitor's correspondence with the experts instructed in the preparation of the case. Public policy privilege covers documents relating to national security and statements given to the police during an enquiry into an officer's conduct. Privilege is too detailed a subject to be dealt with in this book but one aspect of it, of particular importance to personal injury cases, is considered in this chapter (see p186 below).

There is a standard list of documents form produced by Oyez Stationery (Form B9). Alternatively, the format of the standard list set out in precedent E1 (p456) should be put on disk.

In schedule 1 part 1 of the list, all the disclosable documents should be listed, giving sufficient detail of the document so that it can be recognised, including the date. An example would be: '*letter from Johnson & Sons to plaintiff dated 13 October 1993*'. It is also usual to list in this category all the correspondence passing between the parties, and the pleadings. Rather than list them individually, the generic terms 'correspondence passing between the parties' and 'copy pleadings' should be used.

In schedule 1 part 2 there is a standard statement saying:

All correspondence, memoranda relating to communications between the plaintiff and his/her solicitors, and all statements taken from the plaintiff and witnesses, medical and other experts' reports, photographs, communications to and from counsel, draft pleadings, memoranda, notes and any other documents made solely for the purpose of the preparation of the plaintiff's case.

Schedule 2 has to incorporate all material documents that are no longer in the plaintiff's possession, custody or control. Here the standard statement is:

The originals of the copy documents set out in Schedule 1 Part 1 above.

The last part of the form deals with the question of where and when the original documents can be inspected by the other party. The usual phrase is 'at the plaintiff's solicitor's office on notice at any time in office hours'. This facility to inspect is now rarely used and it is usual to ask for photocopies of all relevant documents '*on payment of your reasonable photocopying charges*'. Inspection is unusual unless the list is enormous and the costs of copying all the documents becomes prohibitive.

In many personal injury cases, the plaintiff's only relevant documents are the special damage documentation, ie, wage slips, DSS letter, letters from employers regarding wages, and so on. There will be the rare case where the list is far longer than this, but the plaintiff's solicitor should not be surprised if the list consists of only four or five items.

In the High Court, the lists of documents are exchanged between the parties. In the county court too, since 5 February 1990, the lists are exchanged between the parties (except where the Crown is a party). The plaintiff's list should therefore be sent to the defendant's solicitors and a copy lodged with the county court under cover of letter informing the court that the defendants have been served direct. Though the plaintiff's solicitor can leave it to the defendant's solicitors to request documents from the list, it is accepted practice to send with the list those copies which they are likely to want, with a charge for the copying (needless to say copy documents should not be served on the court at this stage). In sending out the list, the plaintiff's solicitor should specifically request that the defendant's list be sent by return.

Occasionally, privileged documents are inadvertently disclosed to or received by defendants. If the circumstances are such that an obvious mistake has occurred but the defendant is attempting to take advantage of the situation, an injunction can be obtained restraining the use of the information contained in or derived from the documents.[6] A problem that sometimes arises in practice is that an expert's report is accompanied by a letter not for disclosure, giving alternative opinions which might be expressed about the same or similar facts. If the solicitor decides that this letter will not be relied on at trial, the view of the authors is that it need not be disclosed to the defendant's solicitor.[7]

Defendant's list of documents[8]

Defendants' solicitors are under an obligation to ensure that their clients understand the duty of discovery and the importance of preserving documents which might be unfavourable to their case.[9]

If the defendant's list does not arrive within 14 days of the close of pleadings, a letter should be sent, warning the defendant's solicitors that,

6 *Derby & Co Ltd and Others v Weldon and Others (No 8)* [1991] 1 WLR 73; *Pizzey v Ford Motor Co Ltd* (1994) PIQR 15.

7 In *Kenning v Eve Construction Ltd* [1990] 1 WLR 1189, Michael Wright QC, sitting as a deputy High Court judge, ordered that such a letter should be disclosed. However, in *Derby Co Ltd v Weldon (No 9)* [1991] 1 WLR 652, the Court of Appeal refused to order the disclosure of a supplementary report, where the defendants indicated that they did not intend to adduce evidence on the new issues dealt with in the report. It held that the only duty was to disclose expert evidence which it was intended that the witness would give at trial.

8 See footnotes 1 and 5 above.

9 *Rockwell Machine Tool Co Ltd v Barrus (EP) (Concessionaires)* [1968] 2 All ER 98.

if the list does not arrive within 14 days, an application will be made to the court to strike out the defence.[10] The threat should be carried out if nothing is forthcoming, since delay in producing a list of documents is one of the most common ways in which defendants delay the progress of cases.

Discovery can be ordered at any stage of the proceedings. It is, however, generally inexpedient, unnecessary and, therefore, exceptional to do so until the issues have been defined by the pleadings.[11] Nevertheless, there are cases where discovery is needed before particulars can be given: 'It is good practice and good sense that where the defendant knows the facts and the plaintiffs do not, the defendant should give discovery before the plaintiffs deliver particulars.'[12]

As mentioned above, inspection is rare, having been superceded by photocopying unless the list is so long that the cost of copying is prohibitive. In that case, it may be worth going through the originals to decide which are worth copying. If a document is of importance and it is suspicious, then inspection may be necessary to look for erasures, correction fluid, different colour inks, etc, which might not be detectable on a photocopy.

Forcing discovery

If it is thought that there may be documents which the defendant's solicitors have not disclosed, there are a range of weapons available to help extract them. In addition to the obligation to make a formal list of documents under the automatic directions provisions, in both the county court and the High Court, the plaintiff may seek an order for discovery,[13] ie, a direction to any party to make a list of documents which are or have been in his/her possession, custody or power, relating to any matter in question. The county court may, at the same time or subsequently, under CCR Order 14, r 1(5) order this list to be verified by affidavit. The court will do so only where it is necessary in the particular circumstances of the

10 *Chipchase v Rosemond* [1965] 1 WLR 153. If there is a serious risk that a fair trial is no longer possible, the defence can be struck out under RSC Ord 24 r16. Even where a fair trial is possible, if there has been deliberate suppression of a document, the defence can be struck out: *Landauer v Comins & Co (a firm)* (1991) *Times* 7 August.

11 *RHM Foods Ltd v Bovril Ltd* [1982] 1 WLR 661.

12 *Millar v Harper* (1888) 38 Ch D 110 per Bowen LJ at 112. The test of relevancy on the question of discovery of documents is whether those documents might, or could reasonably be expected to, provoke a line of enquiry which would be of assistance to a party: *The Captain Gregos (1990) Times* 21 December, CA.

13 RSC Ord 24 r3; CCR Ord 14 r1.

case.[14] It will not usually make an order until a prior written request by the plaintiff to the defendant has been made.

In the High Court, verification of a list by affidavit requires no order. The defendant must do so if the plaintiff so requests under RSC Order 24 r2(7). This is a useful weapon where there is the slightest doubt about full disclosure by the defendants. It is surprising that plaintiffs' solicitors do not inflict this burden on defendants in High Court cases more often.

If undisclosed documents are suspected, to force the defendants to verify by affidavit is a handy prelude to an application for specific discovery. Such an affidavit can lay the foundation for a telling cross-examination of the defendant's witnesses, causing great embarassment if any attempt is made at court to produce a document previously denied, or to block off any thought on the part of the defendant of manufacturing a document the absence of which is highly embarassing. In work cases (see p187) a defendant's list which reveals the absence of a risk assessment and health and safety policy should encourage the plaintiff's solicitor to require verification on affidavit, thereby allowing plaintiff's counsel the opportunity of damaging cross-examination.

Specific discovery of particular documents can be ordered,[15] though 'fishing expeditions' will not be permitted.[16] If there are reasonable grounds for thinking that there may be further documents of a particular category, then specific discovery will be ordered. An order for a further and better list of documents can also be sought in both the county court and the High Court where it appears from the list itself, from the documents referred to in it, or from admissions made in the pleadings or elsewhere, that the defendants have, or have had, further documents.[17]

Defendants sometimes add at the end of their list: 'Such further or other documents coming into the possession, custody or power of the defendants or their solicitors or insurers herein from the date hereof and not otherwise privileged from production'. This ignores the fact that discovery is a continuing obligation[18] on the defendant and continues to be so from 'the date hereof' until trial. The words add nothing, nor do they excuse the defendant from making further disclosure of relevant documents in the future.

If it is still suspected that there are documents which have not been disclosed, the most effective way to proceed is by way of an application for specific discovery under RSC Order 24 r7 or CCR Order 14 r2. The

14 *Allan v Swan Hunter Shipbuilders Ltd* (1983) 133 NLJ 894.
15 RSC Ord 24 r3; CCR Ord 14 r1.
16 *Re Asbestos Insurance Coverage Cases* [1985] 1 WLR 331, HL.
17 *Jones v Monte Video Gas Co* (1880) 5 QBD 556.
18 *Mitchell v Darley Main Colliery Co* (1882–5) Cab & Ell 215.

test is whether the order is necessary for disposing fairly of the matter.[19] In the High Court, a summons must be issued and an affidavit in support prepared. Standardised examples of both are set out at D15 p447. The affidavit should give a brief background of the case, a history of the pleadings, and then a history of the discovery process. There should be a paragraph for each of the categories of documents sought, showing their relevance to the action and stating the reasons why it is believed that they are in the possession, custody or control of the defendant.

Depending on the number of classes of documents requested, and the complexity of the reasons for non-disclosure, the application should be listed in the master or district judge's general list, or in counsel's list, or for a private room appointment. In many cases, the documents will miraculously appear just before the hearing, in which case the plaintiff's solicitor should insist on obtaining a consent order, withdrawing the summons but with the costs being the defendant's '*in any event*'. If the defendant's solicitors refuse, the summons should go ahead and the costs application be made.

Claims of legal professional privilege

Privilege is a ground for refusing disclosure. It is too big a subject for this book. However, there is one situation not uncommon in personal injury litigation which is worth touching on here. On some occasions, the defendants claim legal professional privilege for an otherwise discoverable document, on the basis that the document has been made in the course of preparing the case for trial. Disputes occasionally arise as to whether privilege attaches to a document coming into existence for more than one purpose.

There is, typically, controversy over reports of investigations into accidents: defendants claim that they were made to help defend them from the litigation, plaintiffs say that they were made to gain information to prevent the accident recurring. In this situation, to qualify for privilege, the sole, or at least, the dominant purpose for which the document was prepared must be submission to a legal adviser for legal advice in view of anticipated litigation. This is, in essence, the rule in *Waugh v British Railways Board*.[20] The time at which the dominant purpose must be judged is when the document was brought into being. A distinction is drawn between anticipated litigation and the mere possibility of litigation. Where a decision has not been taken to defend proceedings,

19 *Dolling-Baker v Merrett* [1990] 1 WLR 1205.
20 [1980] AC 521.

legal privilege does not attach until such a decision has been taken.[21] Accordingly, any documents that came into existence before the defendant instructed a solicitor are not privileged. Ordinary accident reports to employers and insurers, which may be of considerable probative value, are disclosable, however they may be described.

Documents to be disclosed

In most cases, there are a number of fairly standard documents which should be disclosed. Though many of these have been referred to before, it is convenient to list them here. Of course, not all are appropriate to any particular accident. The list should be checked against the defendant's list and, where a document has not been disclosed, an order for specific discovery sought.

Work accidents

- The employer's risk assessment required to be performed in every work situation since 1 January 1993 under Management of Health and Safety at Work Regulations 1992 reg 3, and in specified situations under Health and Safety (Display Screen Equipment) Regulations 1992 reg 2, Personal Protective Equipment Regulations 1992 reg 6, and Manual Handling Operations Regulations 1992 reg 2.
- The employer's safety policy statement required under the Health and Safety at Work Act 1974, s2(3).
- Any accident investigation report, not privileged (see above).
- If the accident involves a machine: all written instructions regarding its use and maintenance; if the machine may have malfunctioned: all maintenance records.
- Receipts, orders, invoices or other correspondence relating to the machine or spare parts for it, or materials used with it (including cleaning where appropriate).
- Receipts for purchase of and records of maintenance of safety equipment.
- The records of this and all other accidents involving the specific or a similar machine or piece of equipment, or occuring in the specific area, or in the same or a similar manner; whether these are recorded in the accident book, daily log, memorandum or wherever else the plaintiff and his/her witnesses think they may have been written down.
- Employers used to be obliged to write to the DSS on a B176 form,

21 *Alfred Crompton Amusement Machines Ltd v Customs and Excise Commrs (No 2)* [1974] AC 405, HL.

giving certain details of the accident, where their employee subsequently had time off to recover. With the introduction of the statutory sick pay scheme, this document is more rarely available now, but should be sought in case it has been used.

- The safety committee's minutes and agendas (if any).
- Any note, report or memorandum from the safety officer and/or safety representative.
- The accident report form (F 2508). Under the Reporting of Injuries Regulations 1985, a report must be made if the injured employee is off work for more than three days or kept in hospital for 24 hours or more.
- Correspondence with the Health and Safety Executive, if any.
- All statements made to the employer by the plaintiff and witnesses after the accident.
- First aid report.
- Plaintiff's medical records held in the defendant's medical centre.
- Records of the plaintiff's earnings, both gross and net.
- If there is a continuing loss and there is doubt as to how much the plaintiff would have continued to earn: wage details in respect of two of the plaintiff's work colleagues in comparable positions, by whom authority has been given to obtain such wage details.

Tripping accidents

- The highway inspector's report for three years prior to the accident.
- All details of accidents that have occurred on that stretch of road over the previous three-year period.
- All contracts for work done by contractors in the vicinity within the previous three year period.

Public transport accidents

- The highway inspector's report.
- The internal investigation report.

Road accidents

For the great majority of road accidents, the only relevant documents are in relation to the plaintiff's special damage claim. That is why the automatic directions specify that the defendant does not have to supply a list. That is not, however, always the case. For example, if the defence is that the vehicle went out of the defendant's control, perhaps because of a mechanical defect after repair, then discovery will be needed of all instructions, invoices, bills, receipts and correspondence with the repairer, MOT certificates, service records etc.

'Non-party' discovery

In many cases, there may be documents that are relevant to the case but are not in the custody, possession or control of the defendant or any other party in the case. A request should be written to what will be referred to in this book as the 'non-party', explaining why a request is being made for the documents, enclosing a written authority from the plaintiff, where that is necessary, and confirming that there is no intention to make them a party to the action (if that is the case). Most non-parties are happy to keep themselves out of the action and willingly disclose the documents requested. There will, however, be those who refuse.

When an innocent non-party becomes involved in the tortious acts of others s/he comes under a duty to assist anyone injured by those acts, by giving full information by way of discovery and disclosing the identity of the wrongdoer.[22] The only way to force the disclosure of documents by a third party is to take out an application for non-party discovery under RSC Order 24 r7A(2) or CCR Order 13 r7(1)(g). Proceedings against the defendant should have been issued first. If the non-party, although innocent, has in some way facilitated the wrong, pre-action discovery can be ordered (see chapter 5 pp46–7). The application should, for example, read:

For an order that Smith & Jones plc serve on the plaintiff's solicitors within 14 days all wages records relating to the employment of the plaintiff from July 1989 to June 1991 and that the costs of the application be costs in the cause.

The application should be served both on the non-party and the defendant's solicitors, together with an affidavit setting out the reasons for the application.

Most applications for non-party discovery are against one of the following bodies.

Health and Safety Executive

The HSE sends an inspector on most serious factory and shop premises accidents. On request, it will usually provide an outline of the information available but will provide full reports only on the plaintiff's obtaining a court order. It is very rare for the HSE to oppose such an order.

A health authority, hospital trust or general practitioner

Once written permission by the client is provided, the plaintiff's medical records are usually produced without argument, but a court application is sometimes necessary to enforce the request. This is less frequently

22 *Norwich Pharmacal Co v Customs and Excise Commrs* [1974] AC 133 at 152.

necessary since the Access to Medical Records Act 1990 allows access by a patient to his/her records after 1 November 1991.

Department of Social Security

The DSS provides all benefit details through the CRU in accordance with its statutory obligation. It is not normally necessary to seek discovery of such details from the DSS. However, discovery of the DSS medical board notes and findings, in appropriate cases, may be sought.[23]

Authenticity of documents

Where discovery by list[24] has taken place in the High Court, the plaintiff is deemed to have accepted the authenticity of every document (including the date and, if a copy, that it is a true copy) contained in the defendant's list and vice-versa, except if: this is denied in the pleadings; the court otherwise orders; or, within 21 days of inspection, a notice of non-admission is served.[25]

In the county court, where discovery has taken place by list and a document is produced from proper custody, it is admitted as authentic without further proof if, in the opinion of the court, it appears genuine and no objection is taken.[26] Such an admission of authenticity does not affect any issue as to whether the document tends to prove the truth of what it purports to state. (See p199 on the use of the Civil Evidence Act to prove the truth of contents of documents.)

Service of a list of documents also requires the person serving the list to produce at the trial originals or copies of the documents contained in the list in his/her possession, custody or power.[27]

23 *O'Sullivan v Herdmans Ltd* [1987] 1 WLR 1047.

24 In both county court and High Court, automatic discovery by exchange of lists does not apply (inter alia) to third party proceedings, nor to defendants where the claim arises out of a road accident or liability is admitted. In such cases, notices to produce are required for relevant documents possessed by the defendants: RSC Ord 27 r5; CCR Ord 20 r3(4).

25 RSC Ord 27 r4(2).

26 CCR Ord 20 r11.

27 RSC Ord 27 r4(3). The county court does not have an equivalent provision. It is possible that this provision could be applied to county court proceedings by County Courts Act 1984 s76 (see Green Book 1994 p70).

Part III

Proceedings after close of pleadings

CHAPTER 15

Review of evidence, merits and quantum

It used to be the practice that a full review of every case was carried out, usually by counsel, at the stage when the pleadings had closed, discovery was complete or nearly so, witness proofs and reports, or the bulk of them, were to hand and the time limit for setting down was approaching. With the introduction of mutual disclosure of witness statements and the 15-month time limit for setting down in the county court, practice has had to change. A review is now necessary:

a) prior to exchange of witness statements;
b) after exchange of witness statements but before exchange of experts' reports; and
c) after exchange of experts' reports.

Legal aid will not fund three reviews by counsel, so the practice is developing of the first two being carried out by the solicitor and the final review by counsel. This chapter is addressed to the final review, but the points made apply equally to all three reviews.

Legal aid

A great many legal aid certificates are limited to 'work done up to, but not including, the setting down of the action, and the completion of the discovery process'. This certificate covers the solicitor carrying out all the usual work up to that stage. That includes obtaining the relevant medical reports, witness proofs, preparing pleadings, going through the discovery process and obtaining photographs and plans. The one restriction is that, if the case goes to taxation, the solicitor will be paid only for work which the taxing master considers to have been 'reasonable' for the prosecution of the action. Where there is any doubt about obtaining a report or its cost, or about some other step in the proceedings, the Legal Aid Board can be asked to give specific approval for the work and cost.[1] If that approval

1 Civil Legal Aid (General) Regs 1989 reg 61.

is given, the taxing master cannot disallow the item as against the legal aid fund, unless the solicitor or assisted person knew, or ought reasonably to have known, that the expenditure was unnecessary before it was incurred.[2] The board's authority must specifically be obtained to instruct leading counsel[3] and also to make any application for pre-action disclosure.[4]

Where the certificate is limited to close of pleadings, completion of discovery or setting down, further authority must be obtained before taking any further steps. This is usually dependent on counsel's opinion on evidence, merits and quantum, which is usually authorised on the original certificate. Commonly certificates bear a financial limit. Expenditure beyond that limit requires specific authority. Failure to obtain such authority will make expenditure beyond the limit irrecoverable, no matter how reasonable the step was.[5] It is vital therefore that the solicitor's financial system alerts the solicitor as any financial limit is neared.

In cases where liability is admitted in the defence or in writing, the Legal Aid Board should be asked to give authority to set down as soon as possible, without awaiting counsel's opinion. Where counsel's opinion is required, it is not necessary to wait for the completion of discovery and all other steps before sending the papers to counsel. To do otherwise might involve a delay of months for little benefit. It is sufficient that the discovery process is largely, if not entirely, complete and that the rest of the case (including exchange of witness statements and experts' reports) is largely up-to-date. Counsel will advise, anyway, on the further work that needs to be carried out before trial.

There will, of course, be the occasional case where counsel's opinion is required at an earlier stage ((a) or (b) on p192) or where it should only be sought after every avenue of investigation has been explored.

Counsel's advice

The decision as to when the thorough analysis of the whole case is to be undertaken is a matter of the solicitor to judge. The review itself is usually done by the barrister who has drafted the pleadings and who will conduct the case at court. In legal aid cases, it is invariably required to be done by counsel.

For the purpose of this book it is assumed that the review is done by counsel in writing in the form of an Advice on Evidence, Merits and

2 Ibid reg 63.
3 Ibid reg 59(1)(b).
4 Under RSC Order 24 r7A(1), Order 29 r7A(1) or CCR Order 13 r7(1).
5 *Drummond v Lamb* (1992) *Times* 24 January.

Quantum. A fairly standard format may be used to ensure that all aspects are covered. These are reflected in the sub-headings below. A solicitor carrying out a review at any of the three stages should use the same subheadings. It is of immense value if a fresh brain is brought to overview the case.

Assuming counsel is instructed to advise on evidence, merits and quantum, the instructions (preceded by an enquiry to counsel's clerk) should state on the outside that the Advice is required by a certain date, since at this stage time will be very short indeed in consequence of the tight timetable imposed by the automatic directions. If necessary the solicitor should, at this stage, make application to the court to extend the timetable so that outstanding steps can be taken. Such an application should not be caused by counsel's delay.

Facts

The initial paragraph of the advice sets out the facts of the case concisely, in no more than half a dozen sentences and usually only two or three.

Pleadings

Next, the state of the pleadings should be reviewed, including commentary on any further and better particulars and interrogatories. Any further pleading steps should be identified and (if possible) drafted. This includes any amendments to the statement or particulars of claim or any reply. It may be necessary to seek particulars of the defence and/or interrogatories. There should then follow a review of remaining major aspects of the case.

Lay witnesses on liability

The next heading of an advice should be 'Evidence on liability and contributory negligence'. This subject has been considered in chapter 6, pp49 et seq. The usual practice at this stage is to consider the plaintiff's evidence, noting in particular any weak areas or areas where further instructions or amendment of witness statements are required. Successive paragraphs deal with each of the potential lay witnesses. Consideration is given to whether they have dealt with all aspects within their knowledge, whether amendment of the statement is needed, and what are the particular dangers or advantages in calling each of them. If witness statements have been exchanged, consideration must be given to how the plaintiff and his/her witnesses will deal with the defendant's statements and whether further evidence is needed in the light of the defendant's statements. The defendant's statements will be analysed and any that can be agreed should be indicated (though the possibility that the witness will not come up to proof because the statement is exaggerated should be kept in mind).

If witness statements have not been exchanged, then advice is required on the draft statements prepared from the proofs, on the statements yet to be prepared and, if necessary, counsel should draft the statements from the proofs provided (legal aid certificate permitting).

Advice should always be given as to any other potential lay witnesses, or categories of witness, who might be contacted and proofed. Thought should also be given to whether any matters disclosed on discovery or any allegations made in the defence or defendant's witness statements have been or need to be put to witnesses. If the plaintiff's character appears likely to be attacked, consideration needs to be given to potential character witnesses.

Sometimes, those giving evidence about the system of work, previous accidents and previous complaints (and complainants) have not been adequately investigated. Safety representatives, shop stewards and workers in the maintenance department responsible for the relevant equipment should not be overlooked.

A witness statement is not evidence until spoken to by the maker in the witness box,[6] so consideration should be given to serving a Civil Evidence Act notice for any helpful witness statement disclosed inadvertently by the defence.[7]

If the plaintiff or witnesses have commented on the defendants' witness statements and documents, the possibility of amending witness statements (see p180) needs consideration.

Where negligence is alleged against a defendant's employee and a helpful witness statement is obtained from that employee, the court has a discretion to admit that statement as evidence if, otherwise, the plaintiff would be obliged to call that employee at trial.[8] Usually, such witnesses should if possible be available at trial.

Civil Evidence Act notices may help to overcome the difficulty of witnesses being unable to attend trial because they are overseas,[9] ill, cannot be traced, have forgotten or are deceased. To be admissible such a notice must be served within 21 days of setting down in the High Court or 14 days before the trial date in the county court.[10] Though Civil Evidence Act notices are not restricted to evidence on matters of liability, it is convenient to deal with them here.

Any one of five grounds will justify service of a Civil Evidence Act

6 See p180.

7 *Youell v Bland Welch & Co Ltd (No 3)* [1991] 1 WLR 122.

8 RSC Ord 38 r21(1); CCR Ord 20 r20(1); *Champion v London Fire and Civil Defence Authority* (1990) *Times* 5 July.

9 A video link should be considered (see p197).

10 RSC Ord 38 r21(1); CCR Ord 20 r15.

notice (an example of such a notice will be found at E5 p460). These are that, at trial, the maker of the statement:

- is dead (if possible a copy of the death certificate should be filed with the notice)
- is 'beyond the seas'
- is unfit by reason of bodily or mental condition to attend as a witness (here a medical report should, if possible, be filed with the notice)
- despite the exercise of reasonable diligence, has not been identified or found
- cannot reasonably be expected to have any recollection of matters relevant to the accuracy or otherwise of the statement to which the notice relates (particularly relevant for keepers of records, such as pay clerks or DSS officials, as well as those suffering from amnesia).

If the other party does not accept the notice, a counter-notice must be served within 21 days. If a statement or document is served under a Civil Evidence Act notice, even if the five grounds set out above do not apply, the statement or document may be put in evidence if the other party fails to issue a counter notice within 28 days.

If a counter notice is served, the solicitor seeking to rely on the notice then has the right to apply, by summons, to the master or district judge for determination of whether the ground is 'made out' and so whether the statement can be admitted as evidence.

Notices to admit facts[11] also require consideration. These have been dealt with more fully in chapter 11 at p143. The question here is whether there are any facts which the defendants should be compelled to agree or disagree. A notice to admit facts is useful, but situations do arise where a notice may force defendants to reveal their true position on some concealed matter, or simply save the plaintiff the expense and trouble of proving some difficult point. Defendant's witness statements should always be read with the possibility of a notice to admit in mind. There may be support for propositions helpful to the plaintiff and a risk of the defendants not calling the maker of a helpful statement.

Any criminal convictions of the defendant which are to be relied on, must be proved by obtaining a certificate of conviction[12] from the appropriate court, if the conviction has not been admitted. Counsel should check that there is a certificate or an admission or remind the solicitor. If necessary, notes of evidence given in the criminal proceedings

11 RSC Ord 27 r2; CCR Ord 20 rr2 and 3.

12 See Prevention of Crimes Act 1871 s18 for the certificate generally and Civil Evidence Act 1968 s11(c) for its admissibility.

may be admitted under Civil Evidence Act 1968 ss2 and 4 and consideration should be given to obtaining them.

An overseas witness can give evidence to an English court via television linkage, under RSC Ord 38, r3. A protocol for the use of video links in court proceedings has been prepared by the Bar Council, and it appears the court will order evidence to be given by video link in appropriate cases.[13] A statement recorded on video can be admitted under the Civil Evidence Act s2, if proved by a person who heard it.

Experts on liability

From the lay witnesses, it is usual for counsel to consider next the expert witnesses and, in particular, the engineer or road traffic accident specialist. The nature of their evidence has been considered in chapter 6 at p50. At this stage counsel should ensure the plaintiff's experts have dealt with all matters raised by the defendants' experts. Counsel should advise whether their reports need to be supplemented by further ones, or whether any other experts need to be called in, such as a meteorologist or a chemist. Sometimes a conference is required to deal with a problem which is apparent from a report. Counsel is not entitled to suggest to an expert how a report should be written,[14] but it is proper to suggest that irrelevant material is excluded or that certain wording is ambiguous and should be clarified.

Plans and photographs

The illustrative value of any available plans and photographs should be considered. If they are helpful, the solicitor should be advised to make sufficient copies – at least four – for the trial and to attempt to agree them with the other side. The defendant should be given at least 10 days before the hearing to inspect and agree them.[15] If the plans or photographs are insufficient or there are none, counsel should consider whether they should be obtained. The precise nature of the plans and photographs desired should be specified and whether these should be done by a professional. Film or video evidence is nowadays becoming more common, though it is rare for the purposes of establishing liability. As the onus is on the plaintiff to prove the case, clarity is important, so good photographers must be used.

13 On video link evidence see White Book 1993 para 38/3/1. The protocol is available from the General Council of the Bar (address, p471) at £2.50 + p&p. The court's jurisdiction to order evidence to be received by video link appears in *R v Horseferry Road Magistrates' Court ex p Bennett (No 3)* (1994) *Times* 14 January.

14 *White v London Transport Executive* [1982] QB 489.

15 RSC Ord 38 r5.

The court has a discretion in rare cases to allow a model, plans, photographs, films and videos to be produced at trial without prior disclosure.[16] Usually such evidence should be disclosed in advance. The utility of such evidence can easily be underestimated.

Documentary evidence

Counsel should then review the process of discovery, ensuring that all the expected documents have been listed and disclosed by both sides and considering whether any further documents which have not been listed might be in existence. Discovery is discussed in more length in chapter 14 p182. Counsel should have particular regard to the possibility of documents relating to alterations made after the accident, and documents relating to the purchase and maintenance of equipment where it was the cause of the accident. In work accidents, as mentioned at p188, consideration should be given particularly to risk assessments and health and safety policy statements.

Where it is suspected certain documents or classes of document have been withheld, counsel will consider an application for specific discovery and/or that the defendant's list be put on affidavit (see pp185–7).

If there has been a refusal to disclose relevant documents, consideration should be given to the merits of an appropriate application (an example can be found at D15 p447) and a challenge to any claim of privilege.

This is the appropriate moment to review how documents are to be admitted. No document can be put into evidence unless it is proved authentic by oral evidence or unless agreed by the parties to be authentic. Where discovery has been by list (or affidavit), the documents described are deemed to be authentic (or true copies, as the case may be),[17], unless the authenticity is denied in a pleading or in a counter notice, served within 21 days of inspection and requiring the document to be proved at trial.

Where discovery is not made by list or affidavit, a notice to admit authenticity of documents (see p191) can be served within 21 days of setting down in the High Court or 14 days before the hearing in the county court.[18] As with discovery, a counter notice must be served within 21 days in the High Court and seven days in the county court, requiring proof at trial, if the documents are not to be deemed authentic. There is likely to be a costs penalty if a counter-notice is served and the document has to be proved unnecessarily. If a notice to produce is served, or deemed to have

16 RSC Ord 38 r5; *McGuiness v Kellogg Co of Great Britain Ltd* [1988] 1 WLR 913, CA; *Morris v British Coal Corporation* (1992) PIQR 366; *Khan v Armaguard* (1994) *Times* 4 March.

17 By RSC Order 27 r4 (see p191).

18 RSC Ord 27 r5; CCR Ord 20 r3.

been served, and the original document is not produced, the plaintiff may call secondary evidence of the contents of the document.

If either the plaintiff or defendant wishes to rely on the contents of a document contained in one of the lists of documents as proving the truth of what it states, unless it is agreed, a Civil Evidence Act notice must be given.[19] This procedure is not used as much as it ought to be by plaintiffs' lawyers. It can be used, for example, to maximise the impact of a helpful description of the accident disclosed in a defendant employer's accident book. Such moves often take the defendants by surprise, counter-notices are overlooked sometimes, embarrassment is caused and more costs run up by the defendants. All useful to keep the pressure on.

Where a document is put in as evidence, the original must be produced at trial. If the original documents are not available, the court will admit secondary evidence (for example, a copy, or sworn testimony about the contents of the original document) only if: either the party wishing to produce the document proves that it has been destroyed or lost and that all reasonable steps to trace it have been unsuccessful; or the original is in the possession of the opposing party who has been served with (or is deemed to have been served with) a notice to produce that original at the trial but has failed to do so. Documents referred to in the pleadings become part of the pleadings and can be looked at by the court without their being put in evidence.[20]

Merits

Unless there are major gaps in the evidence so far collected, it should be possible to express a view about the chances of overall success. First, it is necessary to identify the major issues in the case, and their strengths and weaknesses so far as the plaintiff is concerned. While this may be a relatively straightforward task, the second task of giving an overall percentage chance of success on liability is difficult because it relies on experience and intuition. It is this evaluation that the Legal Aid Board or other funding body will be particularly concerned about as, of course, will be the plaintiff.

Contributory negligence

After an assessment of the overall prospects of success has been made, it is necessary to evaluate the chances of a finding of contributory negligence and the extent of that contribution. Again, this two-stage evaluation is

19 RSC Ord 38 r29(1); *Minnesota Mining & Manufacturing Co v Johnson & Johnson Ltd* [1976] RPC 671.

20 *Day v William Hill (Park Lane) Ltd* [1949] 1 KB 632.

difficult and based on experience and intuition. If contributory negligence is found, experience shows that the most common finding is 25%. Findings of 33% and 50% are less common; 75% or 10% less common still. Other percentages than these are really quite rare in the authors' experience. In driving cases, the usual figure is 25% for failure to wear a seat belt, if using one would have made all the difference. Where it would have made a 'considerable difference', the figure is 15% but, if there is good reason why a seat belt was not being worn, for example if the plaintiff was pregnant or unusually obese, there may be no reduction.[21]

The burden of proof to establish contributory negligence is on the defendants. There are powerful legal authorities available for use against common allegations of contributory negligence in work accident cases.[22] Lord Wright in *Caswell v Powell Duffryn*[23] is authority for a more lenient[24] standard of care by plaintiffs in work cases than others:

'What is all important is to adapt the standard of what is negligence to the facts, and to give due regard to the actual conditions under which men work in a factory or mine, to the long hours and the fatigue, to the slackening of attention which naturally comes from constant repetition of the same operation, to the noise and confusion in which the man works, to his pre-occupation in what he is actually doing at the cost perhaps of some inattention to his own safety.'

Defendants and judges sometimes raise the possibility of 100% contributory negligence, following *Jayes v IMI (Kynoch) Ltd.*[25] This contradicts the purpose of the Law Reform (Contributory Negligence) Act 1945, which presupposes a share of responsibility, and the case may be wrongly decided.[26] No breach of statutory duty can be caused 'solely' through the plaintiff's conduct, without any failure on the part of the defendants.[27]

21 *Froom v Butcher* [1976] QB 286. For passengers not sitting in the front seat, see *Eastman v South West Thames Regional Health Authority* (1992) 1 PIQR 42, CA (a case pre-dating the back seat belt law). For motorcyclists who have failed to fasten their chin strap (10% reduction), see *Capps v Miller* [1989] 1 WLR 839. Rear seat belts were made compulsory in GB and NI from 1 July 1991: Motor Vehicle (Wearing of Seat Belts in Rear Seats by Adults) Regs 1991 (SI No 1255); Road Traffic Act 1988 s14(1) and (2).

22 See, eg, those reviewed in *Munkman on Employers' Liability*, 11th edn, pp608–617.

23 [1940] AC 152, HL.

24 Though where there is contributory negligence, it can sometimes be high where the injured employee was skilled, mature, familiar with the equipment and there were no extenuating distractions: *Gunter v Nicholas & Sons* (1993), 1 PIQR 67, a case where 'contributory negligence' was increased by the Court of Appeal from 25% to 66%.

25 [1985] ICR 155.

26 *Pitts v Hunt and Another* [1991] 1 QB 24 per Beldam J.

27 *Ross v Associated Portland Cement* [1964] 1 WLR 768; *Boyle v Kodak* [1969] 1 WLR 661. But see *Walsh v Crown Decorative Products* (1993) PIQR 194 for a case going the other way.

Lay witnesses on general damages

The next heading should be 'Evidence on damages'. As before, the first task is to review the evidence of the plaintiff, to consider whether all aspects of pre-accident earnings, working, domestic, social, and sporting life and hobbies have been covered. A full picture before the accident and a full picture of the position after the accident is required. The plaintiff's statement should also describe the impact of the accident, the treatment, the pain and suffering, and reaction throughout (see also chapter 3 p29). It is becoming increasingly common in serious cases for defendants to commission a secret video of the plaintiff. They have to apply for leave to admit it, setting out in their affidavit the special reasons for prior non-disclosure, identifying the precise subject matter, and in general terms identifying the issue to which the subject matter relates. This application should be contested on the general principle that all evidence before the court should have been considered by both sides prior to trial. The idea is often to undermine plaintiffs in cross-examination by showing them performing athletic tasks on a secretly taken video after they have testified to their physical incapacity. The effect is intended not merely to diminish quantum, but so to damage a plaintiff's credibility as to cast doubt on the case on liability. The defendants' application has to be made at least 10 days prior to the hearing. If successful the plaintiff will know that a video exists but not what it contains. Often defendants then put forward a lower offer.

The lay witnesses on damages should be assessed. The plaintiff's spouse, parents, relatives, and friends should provide one or, in a very serious case, two good witnesses about the change in the plaintiff since the accident. Any particular achievements of the plaintiff, which are no longer possible, should be amplified by these witnesses and they or the plaintiff should bring to court any cups, medals, certificates or other prestigious proof of pre-accident prowess.

Where care has been, is being or will be given by family or friends, counsel should check that witness statements deal with this in sufficient detail: shopping, cooking, washing clothes and sheets, toilet care, cleaning, gardening, d-i-y, car repair, just spending time talking to an immobile plaintiff etc. This evidence is necesary to sustain a financial claim and a check should be made to see that there is evidence from a care expert, car repairer, gardening firm, decorators etc to put a price on the care given by lay people, together with medical evidence to support the level and kind of care given.

Medical evidence

The medical evidence should be reviewed, to ensure that every aspect of the plaintiff's injuries – both physical and mental – have been covered adequately and every aspect of the defendant's medical evidence has been either accepted or adequately rebutted. It is necessary to review fully the medical evidence, to ensure that the prognosis, including the risk of relapses, epilepsy, diminished life expectancy and so forth, has been fully dealth with. The medical evidence should be compared with the lay witnesses' evidence, to ensure that there is nothing missing from the medical evidence which the lay witnesses have noted, for example, depression, irritability, or a physical incapacity to do some activity important to the plaintiff, but which may have been overlooked by the doctor. The medical reports should be no more than a year old, preferably less than six months unless the plaintiff's condition has resolved.[28]

Reports from the different specialists should be assessed to ensure that there is no inconsistency. If any such inconsistency appears, the medical experts should be invited to speak to each other and if necessary, a joint conference should be held. A particular area where overlap is common is that of future care or treatment. For example, a nursing expert may have been instructed to report on the costs of care and it is absolutely vital that this estimated level of care tallies precisely with the level which the medical experts have prescribed for the plaintiff. By the same token, the medical evidence should support any claim for care since the accident, even if given by family and friends (see above).

The estimated costs of rehabilitation and care should be reviewed carefully. While nursing experts are often familiar with the process of preparing reports and giving evidence to courts, many occupational and physiotherapists, speech therapists and other specialists are not so experienced. They may well under-estimate the level and costs of their services for the future. Where continuous care is being provided to a plaintiff, it is important to ensure that provision is made for relief staff, for recruitment, for holidays for the carers and for the plaintiff and so on.

The medical evidence should also be considered to the extent that it is relevant to liability, for example, in a seat belt case if the lack of a belt might have made no difference to the injuries. In addition, it may be necessary to ask the medical expert to make explicit any implicit finding that the plaintiff will be handicapped on the labour market, ie, suffer a loss of earning capacity.

Since the rules requiring disclosure of the plaintiff's medical report at the outset of proceedings, some of the old battles about mutual disclosure[29] may be over. However, the authorities giving grounds for a

28 See *Kaiser (an infant) v Carlswood Glassworks Ltd* (1965) 109 SJ 537.
29 *Kirkup v British Rail Engineering Ltd* [1983] 1 WLR 1165.

stay of proceedings where a party refuses a medical examination remain relevant.[30] Counsel should consider the extent to which there has been disclosure of the medical evidence and which reports are to be relied on and disclosed. The automatic directions may require amendment if more than two medical experts are needed. Defendants often seek the plaintiff's medical records to see whether there is some underlying condition to which they can attribute part of the responsibility for the plaintiff's continuing injuries. The defendants are entitled to see all the medical records, not just those related to the relevant injury if a claim for future loss of earnings or loss of earnings capacity,[31] or exacerbation of pre-existing condition is claimed. Plaintiff's solicitors occasionally authorise the defendants to peruse a copy of the medical records of the plaintiff without keeping a copy for themselves. Such negligence should be rectified at this stage. Sometimes a letter from the plaintiff's doctor confirming no prior relevant injury or symptoms will avoid the need to disclose the plaintiff's medical records. These records are often used by defendants for other purposes such as cross-examination as to credibility.

In a work accident, it is quite possible that the defendant has medical records of the plaintiff kept at a first aid centre. This possibility should be considered and the solicitor advised to obtain them if they are likely to exist.

The plaintiff's medical records, whether from the receiving hospital, the treating hospital, the general practitioner, or the defendant's medical centre or nurse, should be examined and commented on by counsel. Usually, the documents are almost illegible to a non-medically trained reader. If these records are available, then it is important to ensure that at least one of the plaintiff's medico-legal experts has assessed them in his/her report or a separate letter, especially if they are possibly adverse.

Counsel should be alert to any mental condition emanating from the accident. The limits of compensatable nervous shock[32] were extended in 1983 by *McLoughlin v O'Brian*.[33] Sometimes it may have emerged that the plaintiff has suffered mentally in some way not yet reported on, for example, a fear of travel in a car or some other neurosis. In such cases, a psychiatric report should be recommended. Counsel will be alert to the

30 *Megarity v Ryan* [1980] 1 WLR 1237.

31 *Dunn v British Coal Corporation* (1993) PIQR 275. The authors consider exceptions may be established in the future.

32 Medical evidence is not always needed of nervous shock or psychological disorder: *Whitemore v Euroways Express Coaches* Kemp, Vol II, C4–023. It would, however, be a foolhardy lawyer that failed to see the medical evidence on such an issue.

33 [1983] AC 410. Further refined in *Ravenscroft v Rederiaktiebolaget Transatlantic* [1992] 1 AC 310; *Alcock and Others v Chief Constable of South Yorkshire Police* [1992] 2 All ER 470; *Taylor v Somerset Health Authority* (1993) PIQR 262.

fact that if the plaintiff was not physically injured but suffers a nervous reaction short of an identifiable psychological illness, no damages are recoverable[34] – so no damages for mental suffering, fear, anxiety and the like. Post-traumatic stress disorder has been recognised and compensated in a large number of recent cases.[35] Chronic fatigue syndrome, also known as ME or PVFS, has been accepted as an illness which can be triggered by trauma.[36] A psychiatric report should also be recommended if there is any hint of an allegation of 'compensationitis', or 'malingering' or 'functional overlay'. If defendants make these allegations, they should call their doctor(s) to face cross-examination.[37]

Usually, the plaintiff's medical evidence on the physical injuries give an adequate explanation of the mechanics of the injury, but this is not always possible. In cases where it is not, it is important to have the protection of a psychiatric report to support the plaintiff's claim that s/he is really suffering.

Counsel's next task is to consider the extent to which the defendant's medical evidence[38] can be agreed. If there is any significant discrepancy between the plaintiff and the defendant on their medical evidence, the defendant's medical evidence should be agreed only on the proviso that the plaintiff's evidence is to be accepted on the points of difference. A 'without prejudice' meeting of medical experts[39] is sometimes suggested by the defendants or one of the plaintiff's doctors. In general this should be resisted, since the temptation for an expert to avoid a court appearance by compromising the plaintiff's evidence is an unnecessary risk. There are occasions, however, when the plaintiff's best interest may be served by reaching agreement on what would otherwise be risky medical evidence.

If there is a conflict of medical opinion, the plaintiff's solicitor should consider asking the plaintiff's experts to fortify their opinions by providing copies of relevant parts of current textbooks and articles in journals. These can form useful material in cross-examination of the defendant's expert. Consideration must be given to the extent to which it will be necessary to call the plaintiff's medical experts to give evidence if the defendant agrees the plaintiff's medical reports. There are cases where, even though the medical evidence is agreed, it is still important to have a medical expert to give evidence so as to bring home to the judge a

34 *Nicholls v Rushton* (1992) *Times* 19 June.

35 See the discussion of them in PMILL Vol 5 nos 4 and 5.

36 *Page v Smith* (1993) PIQR Q55.

37 *Stojalowski v Imperial Smelting Corpn* (1976) 121 SJ 118.

38 If a medical report is disclosed accidentally it can be used by the receiving party at trial: *Pizzey v Ford Motor Co. Ltd* (1993) *Times* 8 March.

39 Under RSC Ord 38 r38. And see p225.

particular aspect of the case. In an appropriate case this will not be a significant costs risk.[40]

If the defendants have disclosed no medical evidence but it is feared they might seek leave to do so late, consideration should be given to seeking an order debarring them from adducing medical evidence after expiry of 14 or 28 days.[41]

This stage is an appropriate occasion at which to review whether a split trial should be sought, if it now appears that the medical evidence is so complex and unsettled as to warrant a separate trial on liability first.

Evidence of financial loss

Having considered the medical evidence, financial losses should be reviewed. Loss of the plaintiff's earnings up to date are probably capable of agreement between the two sides on the basis of a letter from the employer. The plaintiff is entitled to rely on his/her medical advisers in deciding if the treatment is necessary and whether s/he is fit to go back to work.[42] Loss of earnings from other sources must not be overlooked (eg part-time work, produce from orchard, allotment, hens, pigs etc). Loss of earnings by carers who have given up time to look after the plaintiff are recoverable[43] and should be claimed.

In some cases, the loss of wages is in dispute and evidence from 'comparators', ie, comparable earners – perhaps workmates of the plaintiff, or employees in the same category as the plaintiff nominated by him/her – is necessary. In some occupations, evidence is required from the Inland Revenue, the plaintiff's accountants or leading members of the 'trade, profession or occupation' as to the earnings, which may include profit as well as income,[44] the plaintiff in business on his/her own account would have had but for the accident.

Counsel should ensure all aspects of remuneration are claimed and supported by evidence, including loss of use of company car, bonuses, tips, free or discounted goods, subsidised meals, pension and holiday pay.

Similar evidence is required about future losses. The evidence for the future should, in addition, deal with the plaintiff's job security and with any prospects for promotion that would have enhanced wages. Both these questions may be dealt with by superior managers (who rarely agree to

40 *Jones v Griffith* [1969] 1 WLR 795.

41 *Lowe v British Steel PLC* (1994) PMILL Vol 10 No 2 p13.

42 *Edward William Southgate v Port of London Authority* (1975) 14 February, unreported, CA.

43 *Donnelly v Joyce* [1973] 3 All ER 475.

44 *Bellingham v Dhillon* [1973] 1 All ER 20.

assist), by trade union officials or leading representatives of professional associations, in appropriate cases.

The disablement employment advisers (formerly resettlement officers) and a growing number of employment consultants are extremely good at giving details of the prospects for obtaining employment in any particular skill and geographical area and as to the wage rates payable.

Employment consultants are particularly useful in providing evidence for a claim for loss of earning capacity. Even though such specific evidence is not essential as a matter of law,[45] damages for loss of earning capacity cannot be maximised without it. Counsel should ensure that a reminder is put in the advice that the plaintiff should continue to make and save as many job applications as possible and retain any documents relating to redundancy or other similar payments. These documents must be diclosed in a supplementary list or a letter.

It is particularly important to review losses which do not flow from inability to earn. These are often overlooked. For example, a valuation is necessary to assess the loss caused to the plaintiff who can no longer tend an allotment. The additional costs of labour to keep the garden as it was, maintain the house inside and out and service the car should be obtained, by letter in the first place, from reputable agencies providing such services commercially, such as gardening firms, building and decorating firms, estate managers, and garages.[46] Generally speaking, the bigger and more prestigious the agency selected, the greater will be its estimate of the labour costs, so maximising the damages claim. It is also more likely that the defendant will accept the valuation of a large and prestigious agency without challenge. Only the labour element is recoverable, of course.

Mention has already been made of the need to have evidence of care by relatives and friends, to have that evidence costed by appropriate agencies and to have that level of care supported by medical evidence (p201).

Valuations should also be sought of the additional costs of taxis, medical prescriptions and other forms of treatment.

The starting point for calculation of future losses is the multiplicand, ie, the annual rate of loss as at the date of trial. Counsel should check to ensure that the necessary evidence to calculate this, reflecting all aspects of continuing loss comprising both loss of income and increase of expenditure, is available.

In the light of the above, the schedule of damages must be reviewed and (probably) reconstructed before being re-served. If the defendants

45 *Patel v Edwards* [1970] RTR 425; *Watson v Mitcham Coardboard Ltd*, CA Kemp and Kemp Vol 2 para 9–745.

46 *Daly v General Steamship Navigation Co Ltd* [1981] 1 WLR 120.

have served a counter-schedule, this too must be considered. If they have not, consideration should be given to seeking an order requiring them to do so (once the plaintiff's schedule has been revised and updated) under CCR Ord 13 r2(2)(a), Ord 17 r11(4)(a). A checklist on evidence of past losses follows. This may also serve as a checklist on the items of special damage for the schedule of damages.

a) Damage to property, eg, clothing, personal possessions, contents of car, watch, rings etc—evidence by receipts, plaintiff, relatives, jeweller etc.
b) Damage to vehicle and associated expenditure, such as:
   - loss of insurance excess;
   - loss of no claims bonus;
   - cost of repairs or replacement (less salvage);
   - replacement car hire and insurance, or alternative means of transport such as bus, train, taxi etc;
   - car recovery costs such as towage and storage;
   - pro rata period of the plaintiff's insurance or AA/RAC subscriptions whilst the car is being repaired/off the road (insurers/AA/RAC should surrender unexpired period if car is a write-off);
   - engineer's fee for valuation purposes;
   - loss of petrol if vehicle a write-off;
   - interest on money borrowed to buy or repair vehicle;
   - loss of use of the vehicle, if no hire of replacement. This must be pleaded. The value of the loss may be calculated from estimating the weekly value of having such a vehicle based on the standing and running costs ascertained by the AA or RAC updated running cost figures, and Glass's or Parker's updated capital value figures.[47] Alternatively the court 'must do the best it can' to come to a reasonable estimate of the damage suffered.[48] Credit must be given for any refund of the standing charges against any award for loss of use.
c) Travelling expenses for medical advice or treatment (but not for legal advice) including taxi, tube and bus fares and use of plaintiff's car on same basis as above. It is not always easy to obtain receipts for such expenditure but the plaintiff's reasonably contemporaneous note is usually sufficient.
d) Medical expenses. The fact that facilities were available under the NHS is no bar to the plaintiff recovering the costs of private

47 *Birmingham Corporation v Sowsbery* [1970] RTR 84.
48 *Dixon's (Scholar Green) Ltd v Cooper* [1970] RTR 222.

treatment.[49] All reasonable medical expenses can be recovered such as:

- operations;
- emergency treatment in hospital;
- prescription charges;
- bandages, aids, prosthetics;
- painkillers;
- physiotherapy;
- osteopathy;
- dentistry;
- psychotherapy;
- nursing care;
- self-conducted therapy such as swimming regularly and thereby incurring admission charges or membership fees for a fitness club.

If the medical expenses have been reasonably incurred, it does not matter if they prove not to have been necessary.[50] Medical expenses may be reasonably incurred even if cheaper treatment is available.[51] Treatment based on medical advice will be reasonable in most cases. Medical evidence that the items claimed were reasonable is necessary. This is sometimes more difficult for 'alternative medicine': acupuncture, chiropractors, homeopaths etc. Evidence in the form of receipts are needed to confirm the actual expenditure, or at least a reasonably contemporaneous note by the plaintiff.

The medical expenses need not have been incurred in relation to professionally qualified medical staff. Payment to unqualified persons for elementary care or mere attendance is also recoverable if reasonable. As noted at p201 medical evidence is required to show that the care and attendance was reasonable; evidence from a professional agency is necessary to cost it. No claim can be made for treatment on the NHS if no expense has been incurred.[52]

e) General expenses/losses. These could include increases in the normal expenses such as: heating and lighting costs incurred through being at home more often; extra cleaning; extra telephone calls/postage; entertaining a plaintiff who formerly entertained him/herself, eg, purchase of computer, video, etc, increased costs of holidays. Correspondingly: loss of use of subscriptions to a sports club or football season ticket, irrecoverable deposit on booked holiday.

49 Law Reform (Personal Injuries) Act 1948 s2(4).

50 *Rubens v Walker* 1946 SC 215 at 216; *SS Baron Vernon v SS Metagama* 1928 SC(HL) 21 at 28.

51 *Rialas v Mitchell* (1984) 128 SJ 704.

52 Administration of Justice Act 1982 s5.

Labour costs of DIY, gardening, allotment, car maintenance previously carried out by plaintiff require estimates from appropriate commercial firms.

f) Court of Protection fees. These are recoverable if the plaintiff's injuries have rendered him or her incapable of managing his or her affairs.

g) If the award is likely to be large: management fees.[53] Evidence will be needed from fund managers as to the likely costs.

h) Loss of earnings (dealt with above).

i) Computation of the annual value of continuing loss as at date of trial for purposes of calculating future loss.

Quantum of damages

The final heading in the advice is 'Quantum of damages'. Often, after a thorough review of the case, so many steps need to be undertaken that it is not possible to evaluate fully the damages likely to be recoverable in the case. Nevertheless, where possible, an estimate of quantum should be given.

Pain, suffering and loss of amenity

The first task is to attempt to evaluate damages for pain, suffering and loss of amenity. A useful starting point is the Judicial Studies Board's *Guidelines for the Assessment of General Damages in Personal Injury Cases*, published at the beginning of each chapter of Kemp and Kemp Volumes 2 and 3. The most up-to-date sources are Current Law, Halsbury's monthly up-daters, Personal Injury Quantum Reports (PIQR) and the *Personal and Medical Injuries Law Letter* (see appendix). These should supplement the more extensive material in Kemp and Kemp Volume 2. Having found a number of cases which are roughly similar to that of the plaintiff on pain, suffering and loss of amenity, each award should be brought up to current value by use of the inflation table in Kemp and Kemp Volume 2. The inflation multiplier must be increased by the current annual rate of inflation for the period between the date of printing of the page and the date of computation.

Where there are multiple injuries, the overall award is usually lower than the sum of awards if each injury were inflicted on a separate plaintiff. Many practitioners have noted that, during the 1980s and early 1990s,

53 *Anderson v Davis* [1993] PIQR Q87; Kemp and Kemp 5-070/3; but contra, *Francis v Bostock* (1985) *Times* 9 November.

awards have failed to keep pace with the real value of money and there is scope to argue for an increase of awards for pain, suffering and loss of amenity. In 1979, the case of *Walker v McClean & Sons Ltd*[54] had criticised the level of awards made after 1973 for being too low.

There are aspects of general damages awards which should not be overlooked, such as the loss of job enjoyment;[55] loss of a good education;[56] loss of status through inability to complete apprenticeship;[57] or loss of the chance to enhance reputation.[58]

Interest in general damages

Next, the interest on the general damages for pain, suffering and loss of amenity should be assessed. Since *Wright v British Railways Board*,[59] the interest rate is at 2% flat per annum from the date of service of the writ or summons. The computation should be made to the nearest week, ie, 1/52nd of 2%. For example, if there has been a two-and-a-half-year delay between issue of the writ and trial, general damages should be increased by 5%.

Past loss

The next computation is that of special damage. The general principle is, of course, that the plaintiff should, as nearly as possible, be put in the same position as s/he would have been had s/he not sustained the injury. Therefore, loss of earnings is recoverable net of tax,[60] as is national insurance.[61] Then, all relevant benefits must be deducted under the clawback of benefits rules (see chapter 6 at pp64 et seq).

Sick pay is usually paid under an agreement that it is to be set off against damages, as are payments received by an employee under a permanent health insurance scheme following incapacity resulting from an accident at work.[62] It should be ensured that sick pay is not deducted twice, ie, from damages and as a result of the clawback provisions. Also, it should be confirmed whether gross or net earnings have been paid. A

54 [1979] 1 WLR 760.

55 *Morris v Johnson Matthey* (1968) 112 SJ 32; *Hearnshaw v English Steel* (1971) 11 KIR 306; *Champion v London Fire and Civil Defence Authority* (1990) *Times* 5 July. See table in Kemp and Kemp Vol. 1 at 5–251.

56 *Jones v Lawrence* [1969] 3 All ER 267.

57 *Dunk v George Waller & Son Ltd* [1970] 2 QB 163.

58 *Marbé v Daly's Theatre* [1928] 1 KB 269.

59 [1983] 2 AC 773.

60 *British Transport Commission v Gourley* [1956] AC 185.

61 *Cooper v Firth Brown Ltd* [1963] 1 WLR 418.

62 *Hussain v New Taplow Paper Mills Ltd* [1988] AC 514.

redundancy payment is deductible from loss of post-receipt earnings, if the redundancy is attributable to some extent to the injury.[63] If it is not attributable, then a redundancy payment is not set off against damages.[64]

There are a number of exceptions to these principles. These exceptions allow the plaintiff to keep the money without giving credit for it against damages received from the defendant. These are: proceeds of private insurance taken out by the plaintiff (though a check should be made to ensure that the insurance company itself will not demand recoupment from any damages received);[65] charitable and benevolent receipts from third parties;[66] pension entitlement, even where the defendant contributed to the pension scheme;[67] assistance from friends and relatives.[68]

Generally, interest on special damages is calculated at half the 'special account rate' on each of those items which is a continuing loss. In respect of those items where the loss has ceased to accrue prior to the date of trial, there is a powerful argument that the full special account rate should be taken.[69]

Future loss

Similar principles apply to the assessment of a future loss as apply to past loss. However, for future loss, a lump sum has to be calculated to represent the present value (at date of trial or settlement) of losses which

63 *Colledge v Bass Mitchells & Butlers Ltd* [1988] 1 All ER 536, CA.

64 *Mills v Hassall* [1983] ICR 330

65 *Bradburn v Great Western Railway Co* [1874] LR Ex 1.

66 *Redpath v Belfast & County Down Railway Co* [1947] NI 167.

67 *Parry v Cleaver* [1970] AC 1; *Smoker v London Fire and Civil Defence Authority* [1991] 2 AC 502.

68 *Liffen v Watson* [1940] 1 KB 556.

69 Interest on special damages is usually calculated at either the whole or half the 'special account rate', a rate which fluctuates (see White Book 1993 p39 para 6/2/12 and Current Law). There are two situations here. The first is where the special damages continue to accrue to the date of trial. In this case, half the interest rate is appropriate (or half the sum at the full rate, or half the period at full rate: *Jefford v Gee* [1970] 2 QB 130). The second situation is where the special damages cease to accrue at a date prior to trial. In this case, it is better to argue that the full rate should be taken from a date halfway through the period of accrual and halfway through the period from accrual to trial: *Prokop v DHSS* [1985] CLY 1037, CA. But note *Dexter v Courtaulds* [1984] 1 All ER 70, CA, a judgment which suggests that the proposition is applicable only in 'special circumstances' (which are ill-defined and somewhat illogical). *Prokop* followed High Court decisions in *Ichard v Frangoulis* [1977] 1 WLR 556 and *Dodd v Rediffusion* [1980] CLY 635, which were cited in *Dexter*. Since then, in *Mendha Singh v Smith Foundries Ltd* (1985) 17 July, unreported, Mars-Jones J preferred and applied *Prokop*, rather than *Dexter*, after full argument on the point.

will accrue in the future. First, the annual net rate of loss as at date of trial or settlement is calculated. This is called the 'multiplicand'. It is calculated on much the same basis as past loss and includes annual rate of earnings loss, annual cost of additional transport expenses, annualised DIY labour costs, annualised loss of allotment produce, and so on. Loss of income is relatively easy to calculate, increased costs are sometimes more difficult to annualise but is simply done by evidence showing the period over which the expenditure is referable from which can be calculated the costs attributable to one year. For example, suppose the labour cost of redecorating a house is £500. It needs painting every five years. The annual cost is £100.

Capital expenditure is more complex. Adaptions which could add nothing to the value of the object adapted (eg, house, car) are recoverable in full less a discount if the purchase is yet to be made. Adaptions which enhance value will only be recoverable to the marginal extent that the plaintiff would not otherwise have made the purchase. There are special rules where purchase of a home is necessitated.[70] These annual costs are taken at their value at the date of trial or settlement. Counsel must ensure, as mentioned above, that no element in the multiplicand is overlooked.

A 'multiplier' is then applied to the multiplicand, a figure less than the plaintiff's remaining years of life expectancy because it takes into account future contingencies (though not the possibility of future inflation). These contingencies include mortality, sickness, the advantage of accelerated payment and, in respect of earnings in particular, the chances of unemployment, promotion and retirement.

Though in most cases there will be a single multiplicand and a single multiplier, in some cases there are several multiplicands, some of which require separate multipliers.[71] Thus, a 30-year-old male plaintiff, whose normal age of retirement would be at 50, and whose injury causes him to lose his job and his allotment, may have a short multiplier for his loss of earnings but a longer one in respect of his allotment if, for instance, it could be said that he had a reasonable expectation of cultivating it until age 70. Such a plaintiff's loss of job, and with it entitlement to enhanced pension, is likely to involve a loss equalling the difference between the pension he will actually receive when he reaches 50 and that which he would have received had he worked to age 50. Again, the computation is of multiplicand and multiplier, but in this case there then needs to be

70 *Roberts v Johnstone* [1988] 3 WLR 1247.

71 In general the approach of averaging the losses over the period and dividing by the number of periods is not in the plaintiff's interest. Note *Brightman v Johnson* (1985) *Times* 17 December; *Housecroft v Burnett* [1986] 1 All ER 332.

applied an additional discount for accelerated payment of the loss[72] since he will receive compensation for it today, aged 30, rather than in the years following his 50th birthday. A further separate calculation may be required to evaluate the cost of this plaintiff's future medical care, on which the level of expenditure may be expected to escalate over the years.

In some cases the rate of loss will differ in different periods during the plaintiff's expected working life. In this situation the overall multiplier should be ascertained and apportioned in proportion to the different loss periods of the plaintiff's total working life.[73]

In a straightforward case where the future loss runs from date of trial to the end of the plaintiff's life expectancy, a rule of thumb for the multiplier is half the plaintiff's life expectancy plus one. Such an estimate should be checked against the examples in Kemp and Kemp.[74] Tables of average life expectancy can be also be found in Kemp and Kemp.[75] The special problem of multipliers and multiplicands in relation to fatal accidents is dealt with in chapter 23, p288.

The rule of thumb for multipliers has come under a great deal of attack in recent years and the plaintiff's counsel and solicitor should always advance their client's case on the higher basis set out below even if ultimately it is compromised on the traditional basis. For one thing claiming on the basis below puts the defendants' at further risk, thus encouraging higher settlement; for another, the new basis is gaining judicial support and may yet be successful in an award of damages.[76]

72 Where an additional discount for accelerated payment has to be made beyond that which is taken into account by fixing the multiplier (ie, where the plaintiff would not, but for the accident and litigation, have received any payment under the particular head of damages until some years, after the actual date of trial), the discount is calculated by deducting between 4 and 5% compound interest per annum: *Mallet v McMonagle* [1970] AC 166 per Lord Diplock at 176D. But see the discussion at pp213 et seq below.

73 *Winwood v Bird* (1986) Butterworths PI Service Vol 3; *Malone v Rowan* [1984] 3 All ER 402; *Brittain v Gardner* Kemp and Kemp paras A–2002, A2–104, *Burke v Tower Hamlets LBC* Kemp and Kemp para A4–103. This is advantageous if the rate of loss increases over the years.

74 Vol 1 para 6–320. The status of actuarial evidence is not clear. In *Mitchell v Mulholland (No 2)* [1972] 1 QB 65 at 76, Edmund Davies LJ stated that it should not be used as the 'primary basis of assessment but as a means of cross-checking the calculations'; see also Lord Pearson in *Taylor v O'Connor* [1971] AC 115 at 140. However, in recent large medical negligence cases, the use of actuaries has been invaluable: eg, *Nicholas Mark Almond v Leeds Western Health Authority* [1990] 1 MLR; and see *O'Brien's Curator Bonis v British Steel PLC* [1991] SLT 447.

75 Vol 1 para 6–340.

76 See the material cited in B. Braithwaite, *Multipliers*, PMILL Vol 10 No 1 p7; 'Scientific Approach to Multipliers', *PMILL* Vol 10 No 3 p18; and C Crook in *PMILL* Vol 10 No 4.

The rule of thumb for multipliers mentioned above is in fact derived from a discount rate for accelerated payment of between 4 and 5 per cent.[77] The plaintiff is receiving now earnings and other moneys that he would not have received (but for the injury) until years in the future. The 'discount rate' is the equivalent of the real rate of return (ie, net of tax and after allowing for inflation) estimated over the desired number of years into the future. The discount rate has been in reality between 2 and 3 per cent for many years. This is consistent with the 2 per cent interest payable on general damages fixed in *Wright v British Railways Board* (see p210) as compensation for loss of the use of this money from writ to trial. However the courts have so far been reluctant to use the lower discount rates.[78]

The effect of a 2 per cent discount rate would be to produce multipliers as high as 25 or even 30. Actuarial tables (which discount for mortality as well as accelerated payment and so are slightly lower than discounted rate tables) based on discount rates of between 1 and 2.5 per cent are to be found in Kemp & Kemp, Vol 2, pp14024–14033. Such rates may be unrealistic but reference to them in negotiations and submissions makes discount rates of 3 or 3.5 per cent attainable. Kemp and Kemp Vol 1 chapter 7 provides a powerful argument in favour of low discount rates and hence higher multipliers.

The 4.5 per cent discount rate is the basis of the traditional multipliers which have been refined into the 'Ogden Tables'[79] which are reprinted in Kemp and Kemp, Vol 1 para 8–029. The Ogden Tables should be used in preference to the rule of thumb referred to above if it becomes necessary to agree to calculating the multiplier on a 4.5 per cent discount rate basis.

These actuarial tables are based on averages; hence if the plaintiff has particular characteristics which might be thought to take her/him out of the average, an actuary may need to be instructed. If the plaintiff is more at risk from the vagaries of life than the average, this option should be forgotten. If the plaintiff appears less at risk, an actuary should be considered, but the courts are reluctant to entertain actuarial evidence.[80]

77 Set in *Cookson v Knowles* [1979] AC 556.

78 Notwithstanding criticism of the 4.5 per cent rate by the Royal Commission on Civil Liability and Compensation for Personal Injury (the Pearson Commission) Cmd 7054 Vol 1, para 648, and by the Law Commission in Paper No 125, *Structured Settlements and Interim and Provisional Damages*, 1992 para 2.21. For an example of rejection of rates other than 4.5 per cent see *Anderson v Davis* [1993] PIQR Q87 per Bell J at Q102.

79 The Joint Working Party of Actuaries and Lawyers, chaired by Michael Ogden, HMSO, 1984.

80 See authorities quoted on p213 above.

Actuarial multipliers need to be discounted for contingencies other than mortality and accelerated payment. 10 per cent is the usual rate.[81]

Pensions pose particular problems in calculating future loss and a variety of methods have been used in the past. A good explanation of the calculations is to be found in Kemp and Kemp at 6–094 et seq.

Handicap on the labour market

Also known as loss of earning capacity or damages for '*Smith v Manchester*', the basic principles for such an award are set out in *Moeliker v Reyrolle*.[82] As a matter of law no specific evidence is required to be directed to this head of damage.[83] However no competent solicitor would fail to prepare evidence focussed on loss of earning capacity where such a claim is appropriate. The evidence required for maximum recovery under this head is the plaintiff's current net wage rate (or that which could reasonably be expected if he was in employment), his prospects for the future and, particularly, evidence of the particular difficulties in seeking and retaining employment by reason of his disabilities. This evidence can be given by the plaintiff and work colleagues, especially managers. It is usual, however, to centre the evidence on that of an employment consultant. Evidence should also be given by the plaintiff of any reasons why he or she might be more likely to be on the labour market than the usual, eg, anticipated move out of big city to area of high unemployment for family reasons; anticipated breaks in employment for child rearing; particular insecurity of job, employer or trade.

In considering the evidence on this head of damage, a check should be made to ensure that disclosure of all the plaintiff's medical records, not just those relating to the accident in question, has been made.[84]

Conclusion

At each stage a review is conducted, it is an extensive task, to be approached methodically and intensively. It is not suited to a busy day at the office between phone calls and meetings.

81 A Judicial Studies Board Paper in June 1991 described 10 per cent as a 'very good guide', though Kemp *Damages for Personal Injury and Death*, 5th ed 1993 p110 suggests it is excessive.

82 [1976] ICR 253, [1977] 1 WLR 132. A recent case is *Robson v Liverpool City Council* (1993) PIQR Q78.

83 See p206.

84 *Dunn v British Coal Corporation* (1993) PIQR 275.

CHAPTER 16

Setting down and applications to fix

High Court

In the High Court, the setting down of an action for trial is governed either by the automatic directions or by an order for directions. Automatic directions provide that an action should be set down within six months of close of pleadings,[1] ie, 14 days after the service of the defence (if there is no reply).[2]

In privately funded cases or where there is an unlimited legal aid certificate (ie, no condition by the Legal Aid Board that counsel's opinion be obtained prior to the setting down of the action), the plaintiff's solicitor should aim to set the case down for trial as soon as possible. There are still likely to be three or four months before the action comes on for hearing, so it is unnecessary for the case to be in a state of total readiness at the time of setting down.[3] In the High Court, the non-jury list is now very quick to reach a hearing date.

Some procedural matters may still be outstanding. Short shrift should be given to the old delaying tactic by defendants, that the action should not be set down because the request for further and better particulars of the statement of claim has not been answered, or some other step has not been taken. When the action is set down, the defendant must be notified within 24 hours.[4]

To set the case down for trial, two copies of a bundle of documents (referred to as the 'pleadings bundle') have to be prepared for the court, sewn in green ribbon. The specified order for the documents is: the notice of legal aid certificate (this may be the first or last document); the writ; statement of claim; further and better particulars of the statement of

1 RSC Ord 25 r8(1)(f).
2 RSC Ord 18 r20(1).
3 The solicitor should take heed of the warning on costs in *Listing Statement (Queen's Bench non-jury list and judge in chambers list)* (1990) *Times* 17 March.
4 RSC Ord 34 r8(1).

claim; defence (and counterclaim); further and better particulars of the defence; reply; interrogatories and answers (if any); all interlocutory orders in chronological sequence (and excluding orders only as to time); third party notices and contribution notices; orders on third party directions; defences to third party notices; replies to third party defences; statement of the value of the action (see the example in at C2 p364); and a note agreed by the parties or, failing agreement, a note by each party giving an estimate of the length of the trial and the list in which the action is to be included.[5] If more than one year has elapsed since the summons for directions, or since the last proceeding in the action, then a notice of intention to proceed must be produced at the time of setting down.

Sewn into each bundle must be a backsheet facing outwards, with the court heading, names, addresses, telephone numbers, document exchange, fax numbers and references of the parties' solicitors, the name of the barrister instructed for the party who is setting the matter down, the estimated length of hearing and an indorsed confirmation that (where appropriate) the case comes under the automatic directions. The backsheet must also be signed in the firm's name and bear (on the right side) the court's stamp showing the £50 setting down fee (cheques payable to 'HM Postmaster General') has been paid.

London[6]

The two pleadings bundles are then either posted or taken to the High Court with the setting down fee. One of the sets is indorsed by the court with the payment and the sets are then lodged with the Crown Office, which issues confirmation that the case has been properly set down, and gives it a 'non-jury number'. On receipt of the court's letter giving the number, the plaintiff's solicitor must write to the defendant's solicitor within two days, confirming the setting down of the action and giving the non-jury number. Unless one of the parties, within 28 days of the matter being set down, applies to the clerk of the lists for an appointment to fix a date for trial, the case is liable to enter the warned list not less than 28 days from being set down.

Short cause list

A question at the setting down stage is whether the case can be put in the short cause list. To qualify for this list, the plaintiff's solicitor has to

5 The note and statement of value are required for all cases after 1 January 1992.

6 *Practice Direction (Trials in London)* [1981] 1 WLR 1296; White Book 1993 para 34/4/1.

certify that the action will last no longer than four hours in court. In those circumstances, the case will go straight into that list without the need for an application to fix and it is likely to be heard within a few weeks of being entered.

Realistically, at the setting down stage few cases are sufficiently clear and complete to predict with certainty that they will last such a short time. Nevertheless, the short cause list is a very useful and speedy tool in appropriate cases.

Outside London[7]

Every action set down in a district registry is immediately listed as being ready for trial. The party setting down the action, having paid the setting-down fee (see p217), must lodge with the two pleadings bundles a statement containing the following particulars: whether an order made upon summons for directions has been complied with, (in particular whether medical or experts' reports have been submitted for agreement, if so, whether they have been agreed and, if not, the number of witnesses to be called, and whether plans and photographs have been agreed); an up-to-date estimate of the length of trial, which should be agreed if possible; and the names, addresses, document exchange numbers, fax numbers and telephone numbers of the plaintiff's and defendant's solicitors and agents, their reference numbers and the names, addresses, document exchange numbers, fax numbers and telephone numbers of counsel, if known. The party setting down must inform all other parties within seven days that this has been done.

As soon as practicable after an action has been set down, the parties are informed of the date on, or period during which, the action is to be heard. Applications for fixed dates etc should be lodged within seven days of setting down. If the case settles, or if it is likely that the case will be delayed, or an application for an adjournment made, the plaintiff's solicitor must inform the court.[8]

Checklist after setting down High Court cases

a) Within seven days of being set down, the court considers whether the case should be transferred to a county court. If so, notice must be issued, either form PF 200 or PF 202 (see pp96–7).

7 *Practice Direction (Trials out of London)* [1987] 1 WLR 1322; White Book 1993 para 34/4/3.
8 RSC Ord 34 r8(2).

b) Civil Evidence Act notices under Order 38 r21 (see p195) should be served within 21 days of setting down.
c) Notices to admit facts (see p144) must be served under Order 27 r2 within 21 days of setting down.
d) As soon as practicable after setting down, a party intending to rely on an expert's report (not just medical) should, after disclosure, lodge a copy of it with the proper officer of the court. Attached to the report should be a note stating: the name of the party for whom the report has been made, the date given and whether or not it has been agreed.[9]
e) At least 14 days before trial (or three weeks of entry in running list): defendants must inform the plaintiff of documents required to be included in the trial bundle. At least 10 days before trial: the plaintiff must serve plans, photographs and videos intended to be relied upon. Two days before trial: plaintiff must lodge two copies of the trial bundle containing witness statements which have been exchanged and experts' reports disclosed and relied on, stating whether each has been agreed or not, and those documents upon which both the plaintiff and defendant wish to rely.

County court

Cases with automatic directions

In the county court, for cases commenced after 1 October 1990 under the automatic directions,[10] the plaintiff's solicitors must set the action down for trial.[11] This must be done within six months from the close of pleadings. As described at pp164–7, failure to do so within 15 months of close of pleadings results in the action being automatically struck out unless an extension is granted.

To set the case down, the plaintiff's solicitor should write to the court requesting the proper officer to fix a date for hearing. The request should include a note, which if possible should be agreed by the defendants, giving an estimate of the length of the trial, the number of witnesses to be called,[12] and, where the claim is valued between £1,000 and £5,000, any

9 *Practice Direction (QBD Personal Injuries Actions)* [1990] 1 WLR 93.
10 CCR Ord 17 r11(3)(d).
11 CCR Ord 17 r11(11)(a): pleadings are deemed to be closed 14 days after delivery of the defence or 28 days after the defence to a counterclaim. If the case is transferred from the High Court, 14 days from the date of transfer: CCR Ord 16 r6(1A).
12 CCR Ord 17 r11(8).

special reason why the case should be heard before a circuit judge.[13] When the proper officer fixes a day for hearing s/he must give at least 21 days' notice to the parties.[14]

At least 14 days before the day fixed for hearing, the defendant must inform the plaintiff of any documents to be included in the court bundle.

At least seven days before the hearing date, the plaintiff should file two copies of a paginated and indexed court bundle comprising the documents on which either party intends to rely or to be before the court. The court bundle should include: particulars of claim and defence, and in respect of each: any request for particulars and the particulars given, and any answer to interrogatories; witness statements and experts' reports which have been disclosed, stating whether each has been agreed;[15] and the legal aid documents required by the court.[16]

Checklist for close of pleadings in county court cases

After close of pleadings

a) Within 28 days – make and serve a list of documents on all other parties.
b) Within 35 days – inspect documents within seven days after a).
c) Within 70 days – disclose experts' reports if it is intended to rely on them.
d) Within six months – request a hearing date and give note of the estimated length of hearing and the number of witnesses. To be agreed, if possible.
e) Within 15 months – action is automatically struck out if no request for hearing has been made.

Before hearing

f) 14 days before – defendants inform plaintiff of documents they require to be in the bundle.
g) Seven days before – plaintiff serves one copy of bundle on the court plus supporting documents (see above).

Cases without automatic directions

In cases where the automatic directions do not apply eg, for cases

13 *Practice Direction (county court listings)* (1991) *Times* 10 July and see the notes to CCR Order 21 r5.
14 CCR Ord 17 r11(10).
15 *Prest v West Cumbria Health Authority* [1990] CLY 3677.
16 CCR Ord 17 r12(3).

commenced before 5 February 1990, when the plaintiff's solicitor has the case ready for trial, a letter should be written to the court certifying that the plaintiff is ready to proceed. At the same time, a letter should be sent to the defendant's solicitors asking them to so certify. They should be warned that, if they do not do so within 14 days or thereabouts, an application will be made to the court asking that it set the case down, notwithstanding the defendants' failure to certify that they are ready for trial.

Unfortunately, county courts are rather unreliable at this stage. The court should send out a standard notice to both parties asking for confirmation that they are ready for the trial to go ahead, and for the estimated length of hearing, the number of witnesses and the dates to be avoided. If one party is in disagreement, the court should notify the other party. In that case, an application should be made straight away to the district judge or circuit judge (depending on the court) for an order that 'the action be set down notwithstanding the defendant's failure to certify the action as being ready for trial and that the costs be the plaintiff's in any event'. If the court fails to take these steps, the plaintiff's solicitor should write requesting that they be taken.

As the hearing date approaches, provided that defendants have had a reasonable time to put their case in order, courts are not generally sympathetic to defence requests for further delays. The most usual reason for defendants saying that they are not ready is that they are waiting for a medical expert to report, often because they have waited until receipt of a plaintiff's report before trying to obtain their own. This should be challenged as an invalid reason for delaying the trial. It will certainly be less arguable now that the medical report is usually to be served with the particulars of claim.

Unfortunately, some county courts are so short staffed that it can take months for them to respond to a request for such a hearing. In others, a hearing date may suddenly arise, sometimes only a couple of weeks ahead, without either party having confirmed the dates to avoid. Whenever a date is given by a court for a hearing, the plaintiff's solicitors should do everything to be ready, since an application to have the date put back does not always succeed and, if it does, it may mean that another date is not given for many months.

Application to fix

In the High Court, if the case is not to 'float' within the court's general list (from about 10–14 weeks later), an application must be made within 28 days of setting down in London, or seven days out of London, to the clerk of the lists for an appointment to fix the date of trial.

There is a standard form for this, obtainable from law stationers, which is self-explanatory. It should be completed and sent to the defendant's solicitor to fill out and sign the defendant's portion and return it to the plaintiff's solicitor. The form is then sent, together with a request for a fixed date, to the clerk of the lists. Following this, a date is set for both parties to attend before the clerk to fix the trial date. The defendant must be notified of this date immediately. At the same time, counsel's clerk must be notified, in order to attend with counsel's diary to ensure that counsel is free for the trial date appointed.

The attendance to fix the date of trial will usually be five to six weeks after the notice. Prior to this attendance, the plaintiff's solicitors should determine whether the case needs a fixed date or can be put into the court's 'Floating List'.

The difference between the two types of dates are that fixtures – referred to as 'AFs' – are given a specific date when the case will be heard. With a 'floating' date (referred to as a 'KP') the case is given a date upon which the case will enter the court list, at the bottom of a list of 'floaters'. Waiting times are published in the daily cause list. The advantage of a fixed date is that solicitors for both sides can organise their experts and witnesses, knowing that the date fixed or the day after will be the date that the case is heard. The disadvantage is that a fixed date takes longer to come on than a KP date. If dissatisfied with a date given by the clerk of the lists, an application can be made to the judge in charge of the lists. This should be done within seven days of learning of the date and two days' notice should be given to the other parties. No formal summons is needed but the clerk of the lists must be informed. The application is usually heard within a few days. If the reasons for obtaining a fixed date no longer apply, eg, if medical evidence is agreed, the solicitors are under a duty to return the case to the general list.

Where the case is given a KP listing, the solicitors for both parties have two choices. They can either wait for the case to move up to the top of the list, when the clerk of the lists will arrange for the case to be heard by the next judge. The main disadvantage of this is that the parties are usually notified only the afternoon before the case comes on. That can be nerve racking and necessitates a flurry of phone calls to make sure that the plaintiff and all witnesses turn up the next morning.

The other, preferable, way of dealing with a KP is that when the case enters the court list, efforts are made to agree with the defendant's solicitors that the counsel's clerks from both parties attend before the clerk of the lists to offer the case up for a fixing on dates convenient to both parties. The date(s) offered must usually be within a few weeks of the request being made but that can be extended if good reasons are given.

The main advantage of taking a KP and then offering it up for a fixed date is that the case comes on much more quickly than a fixed date case, and yet some of the uncertainties of the floater can be avoided. If the case is set down as soon as possible, it means that from issuing and serving the proceedings the trial can be concluded in as little as seven or eight months.

The principal problem with the KP system arises if the defendant's solicitors are not prepared to agree to dates. In those circumstances, an application before the judge in charge of the lists should be made. In recent years the judges in charge of the lists have been determined to have cases heard as speedily as possible and, therefore, objections from defendants, such as that their counsel cannot manage the dates that are convenient to all the experts, may receive a curt response. The same robust line is also taken with the plaintiff who seeks delay.

Finally, if there are good reasons why a case needs a fixture but also needs an early date, eg, the plaintiff has a terminal illness and may not live long, it is possible to apply for an early fixture. The application is made to the clerk of the lists[17] where there is agreement by the defendant's solicitors. Without such an agreement, an application can either go before the master, or the judge in charge of the lists. It is usual to apply to the master first.

17 Fax 071–936 6724.

CHAPTER 17

Preparing for trial

As soon as the trial date is known, the client, all experts, witnesses and counsel's clerk should be notified of the time, date and place of the trial.

Where the case is given a KP listing as a 'floater' in the High Court, there should be notification that the case is likely to be on any day within 28 days after the given date. The witnesses should already have been asked for and have provided a list of the dates when they are unavailable, so that immediate representation can be made if a particular date is to be avoided. The likely delay can be seen in the daily cause list.

The solicitor will be spending more and more time on the case as it comes towards trial. As last minute reports and evidence come in (from both sides), the strengths and weaknesses of the case will become increasingly apparent. All elements should be kept under constant review to ensure that the various loose ends are tied up. The major review of the case described in chapter 15 must be acted on in full. But the solicitor should not regard that review as the last word and assume that no more thinking or checking needs to be done. New loopholes may emerge which need to be closed and new factors can arise which may require further steps to be taken in the final preparation for trial.

Last minute matters

Experts

Expert evidence cannot be relied on unless it has been disclosed according to the automatic directions,[1] or the court has given leave[2] or where the parties agree.

If, for some previously unforeseen reason, further experts need to be brought in at a late stage, efforts must be made to ensure that the relevant

1 RSC Ord 25 r8(1)(b); CCR Ord 17 r11(3)(b).

2 RSC Ord 38 r36; CCR Ord 20 r27.

expert is able to report swiftly, so that there is no adjournment of the hearing date. To minimise the risk of the defendant's solicitors applying for an adjournment on receipt of an up-to-date report, they should be notified that the report is on its way and told its nature. This is a wise course, whether to enable them to make advance arrangements to obtain their own report, or whether the plaintiff's up-to-date report is merely to counter a recent defendant's report. Either way, it gives the defendant less excuse to seek an adjournment, which may be a major preoccupation in the run-up to trial.[3]

The plaintiff's experts should have been sent the reports of the defendant's experts as they came in, with a request for comments. Where there is clear disagreement between the reports of the two sides, the plaintiff's experts should be asked whether they are still confident that they can support their written evidence by oral evidence.

It sometimes happens that the defendant's solicitors arrange for the plaintiff to attend their medical expert but do not then disclose a copy of that expert's report. This may be because it is to the plaintiff's advantage. A useful tactic in such a situation can be to threaten that, unless the report is disclosed, the defendant's expert may be subpoenaed to attend court. That often ensures the production of the report which may then be agreed. The consequences of carrying out the threat if the bluff is called need careful consideration: a hostile doctor in the witness box can be very unpredictable. In any event, where there is disagreement on the two sides, consideration should be given to arranging a 'without prejudice' meeting of the experts. This can be ordered by the court with the object of producing a joint statement indicating the medical evidence which is agreed, and that which is not agreed.[4]

Photographs, plans, videos and films

Sets of the photographs, formal plans, videos and films to be used for illustrative purposes should be sent to the defendants' solicitors earlier rather than later, to be agreed. They are usually uncontentious. If for some reason these things are not agreed, the maker will have to be called to prove them. In the High Court, they will not be admitted unless there has been an opportunity for the other side to inspect and agree them at least 10 days before trial.[5] There is no equivalent rule in the county court, but since

3 For the cost implications of a late adjournment, see *Fowkes v Duthie* [1991] 1 All ER 337.

4 RSC Ord 38 r38. See also p204.

5 RSC Ord 38 r5.

it is possible that the County Courts Act 1984 s76 applies (ie, the High Court rule prevails), it is better practice to disclose at least 10 days before the hearing.

Sufficient sets of the photographs, plans and videos should be made to go round at trial. It is usual to provide two sets for each of the defendants, one for the judge, one for the witness in the witness box and two for the plaintiff's solicitor and counsel. In putting together a set of photographs, if they are loose, it is advisable to mount them on cards, have the cards numbered and then bind them in order to ensure that they are easy to handle.

In the Royal Courts of Justice, a court has been equipped for video. If evidence is to be given live by link, see p197 above. If the equipped court is needed, the clerk of the lists must be informed. In all other courts (or where 8mm or 16mm film is to be used) the equipment must be hired, arrangements made for it to be set up and operated, and the court notified so as to make whatever arrangements are necessary.

Subpoenas and witness summonses

Subpoenas in the High Court or witness summonses in the county court may be necessary, for both reluctant witnesses and willing witnesses who need this formal authority to come to court, eg, doctors and police officers. With lay witnesses, the process should be explained in advance, because the receipt of a subpoena or witness summons may be intimidating.

Where it is necessary to subpoena witnesses, this should be done, preferably a few weeks prior to the hearing. Once the subpoena is issued, it is valid for 12 weeks and must be served not less than four days before the hearing, unless the court directs otherwise.[6] Once served, the subpoena continues in effect until the conclusion of the trial.[7] The county court equivalent of a subpoena – the witness summons – cannot be issued less than seven days before the hearing unless leave is given (application for leave being made ex parte to the District Judge). It must be served not less than four days before the hearing, unless the court directs otherwise.[8]

It is necessary to fill in two forms in either the High Court or county court. There are two types of subpoena: duces tecum and ad testificandum. The first compels a witness to bring documents and the second compels the witness simply to attend. The subpoena or witness

6 RSC Ord 38 r17.
7 RSC Ord 38 r18.
8 CCR Ord 20 r12(4)(a).

summons itself must include the name and address of the witness, the date, time and place of the trial and any documents that the witness is ordered to bring along to the hearing. A standard High Court subpoena is set out at E12 p465.

Along with the subpoena, a praecipe must be completed. A sample High Court praecipe is shown in at E13 p466. This must list all of the witnesses who are being called to give evidence and the date, time and place of the trial. These two documents, with one copy of each, should be either taken or sent to the court to be issued. In the High Court, a subpoena cannot be issued without the court's leave if there is less than four clear days before the hearing date. A standard county court witness summons and a request for the same are at E11 and E10 p464. Leave is also necessary for service in Scotland or Northern Ireland.

In the High Court, it is wholly the plaintiff's responsibility to have the witness summons served. It must be served personally.[9] In the county court, the subpoena can be served by the plaintiff or by the court. In the latter circumstance, the court simply sends the witness summons to the address given, together with a cheque for the witnesses' conduct money, which the plaintiff's solicitor must supply at the time of providing the witness summons. Where the subpoena or witness summons is served by the plaintiff, it has to be served personally, and so it is preferable to arrange for a process server to carry out the job. S/he will keep visiting the witnesses' premises until able to hand the subpoena or witness summons to them personally and will then give the witness the conduct money. The process server should then return the copy subpoena or witness summons with an endorsement on the back confirming that it has been served, describing where the service took place, certifying that the conduct money was offered and giving the server's name and address (see E14 p467).

It is rare that a witness does not comply with a summons, but where that happens and where the witness's evidence remains crucial to the case, an application should be made at the hearing for the case to be adjourned so that the witness can be ordered to attend the court, if necessary by force. It is possible in these circumstances for the court to either imprison or fine the witness for contempt.

Since the automatic directions provide for exchange of witness statements, no witness whose statement has not been exchanged can be called except with leave of the court. This may cause a problem when the witness is hostile but has to be called, perhaps as a witness to the accident. A 'limited' statement may have been taken—ie, the statement given to the police and further questions need to be asked of the witness—but the

9 RSC Ord 38 r17.

witness may have refused to co-operate further. In these circumstances, either the leave of the master or district judge must be sought to call the witness, unproofed[10] or leave of the trial judge sought at trial. Further, RSC Order 38 r5 provides that where one party is unable to obtain a written statement from a witness then it is permissible, unless the court orders otherwise, to give the other party the name and address of the witness and a statement of the nature of the evidence to be adduced.

The court bundle

High Court

The trial bundle of documents (other than the pleadings bundle which was lodged on setting down, see pp216–17) to be used at court is sometimes referred to as the 'agreed bundle' but it can contain documents that are not agreed. It is the plaintiff's solicitor's job to put together the trial bundles (see p219). This should be done about a week or 10 days prior to trial. Bundles must be: firmly secured together; arranged in chronological order, beginning with the earliest; paginated consecutively on the bottom right hand corner; fully and easily legible.

If the bundle of documents has more than 100 pages, it is the responsibility of all the parties' solicitors to prepare and agree an additional 'core' bundle containing copies of the principal documents and to lodge two copies of this bundle with the court at least two but no more than seven working days before the date fixed for hearing. Failure to comply with this direction may result in the documents being rejected and an order for costs.[11]

There are no particular rules governing the form (as opposed to the content) of the trial bundle. Apart from a few basic rules, the way the bundle is put together depends on the solicitor's individual style. The cardinal rule is to try to ensure that, as far as possible, the bundle is put together in a way that is readily understood and is easy to handle. Whether there should be one bundle or more will depend on the size and nature of the documentation and the same applies to the question of whether or not to use a treasury tag or a ringbinder. Ease of handling is important but presentation is more important still. It can affect the attitude of the judge.

At least 14 days before the trial date or within three weeks of an action

10 CCR Ord 17 r4 and Ord 20 r12A(17); RSC Ord 38 r2A(17).

11 See *Practice Direction (evidence: documents)* [1983] 1 WLR 922. This practice direction also deals with affidavits and exhibits for the High Court and Court of Appeal.

being entered on the list, the defendant's solicitors must identify to the plaintiff those documents which they wish to have included in the bundle.

The only plaintiff documents that should be included in the bundle are those that have been agreed as evidence by the defendants or those which are intended to be proved in evidence. Care must be taken that nothing is in the bundle which indicates any compromise of the defendant's position, such as an interim payment order, for example.

Other useful additions to the bundle might be an index, relevant medical records, a schedule of special damages, documents proving special damages, and the statement of value of the action.

At least two clear days before the hearing, the plaintiff must lodge two bundles containing the following documents:

- witness statements which have been exchanged, and experts' reports which have been disclosed, together with an indication of whether the contents of such documents are agreed.[12]
- those documents which the defendant wishes to have included in the bundle and those central to the plaintiff's case.
- where a direction has been given, a note agreed by the parties or, failing agreement, a note by each party giving (in the following order): a summary of the issues involved; a summary of any propositions of law to be advanced, together with a list of authorities to be cited; and a chronology of relevant events.

The court may at any time make further directions about documents required to be lodged.[13]

The bundle should be lodged with the court before the minimum two days beforehand, so that the judge has time to read the papers. Nowadays, judges complain if they are unable to do this (though in reality few have time to do so even if the bundles are available). Make sure that the judge's bundle is in perfect order, as a number of judges are quite finicky and are easily upset by papers that are out of order, badly copied etc.

Each party intending to rely on experts should have sent their reports to the court, whether agreed or not, within a reasonable time of setting down.[14] Nevertheless the expert reports must still be included in the bundle if they are to be relied on. Agreement of expert reports is often reached at the last minute.

12 White Book 1993 Vol 2 para 747; *Practice Direction 28 (personal injury actions: experts' reports)* [1989] 3 WLR 926.

13 RSC Ord 34 r10.

14 See note 12.

County court

At least 14 days before the date fixed for hearing, the defendant's solicitors must inform the plaintiff of the documents they require in the bundle to be provided for the use of the court.

At least seven days prior to the date of the hearing, the plaintiff must file one copy of the paginated and indexed court bundle (see p220), comprising the documents on which either of the parties intend to rely or which either party wishes to have before the court at the hearing, and two copies of the following: any request for particulars and the particulars given; any answers to interrogatories; witness statements exchanged; experts' reports disclosed, indicating if these have been agreed; and any notice of issue of legal aid certificate.[15]

Schedule of financial loss

For actions commenced in the High Court and county court on or after 4 June 1990, the plaintiff must serve a statement of damages claimed with the statement of claim or at a later date specified by the court. The statement or schedule (see pp129 and 205 et seq) must give full particulars of the expenses and losses already incurred and an estimate of any future expenses and losses, including loss of any earnings and of pension rights.[16]

If a further medical report is disclosed, it must be accompanied by a further statement of special damages in the High Court;[17] in practice the schedule will be revised and served several times, the final version being served within a few days before the trial. In the county court, a further statement of special damages need be served only if appropriate.[18]

For actions commenced in the High Court before 4 June 1990, the following procedure applies. A schedule of special damages should be prepared by the plaintiff. It should consist of or include a claim (if appropriate) for: loss of earnings; loss of future earning capacity; medical or other expenses relating to or including the cost of care, attention, accommodation or appliances; or loss of pension rights. This must be served on all the defendants not later than seven days after the case appears in the warned list in London. Within seven days, the defendants have to indicate in writing whether, and to what extent, each item claimed is agreed and, if not agreed, the reason why not and any counter proposals.

15 CCR Ord 17 r12.
16 RSC Ord 18 r12(1A), (1B) and (1C); CCR Ord 6 r1(5), (6) and (7).
17 RSC Ord 25 r8(1A).
18 CCR Ord 17 r11(7)(b).

Where there is a fixed date for hearing, the schedule should be served at least 28 days before that date and the defendant's answer not later than 14 days thereafter. Outside London, the schedule should be served not later than the lodging of the certificate of readiness, and the answer not later than 14 days thereafter. Any failure to comply with these requirements may result in an unfavourable order for costs.[19]

Pre-trial negotiations

The weeks leading up to the trial are the time when the most serious negotiations (see chapter 8 p79) often take place and when the plaintiff's solicitor should be in full command of every aspect of the case. During this period, the defendant will be seriously considering the case and will often combine negotiations with a realistic payment into court usually at least 21 days before the hearing.

The plaintiff's solicitor should be assisted by close liaison with counsel during these negotiations in the run-up to the trial. It is necessary to be aware of the natural instinct to welcome settlement rather than face the hard work and tension of going to trial, and the countervailing desire to be seen as a tough negotiator, bluffing it out to the last moment to get the highest possible award. If settlement is imminent or occurs, the list office must be notified without delay.[20]

Trial brief

It is usual in personal injury cases for the solicitor to instruct a barrister. This is not mandatory in the county court. In the High Court approved solicitors may now conduct litigation.[21]

Briefing counsel has two advantages. The first is that the costs of a solicitor's time preparing for and conducting the trial may be much greater than for a barrister. The second is that there are a significant number of highly experienced personal injury barristers whose experience and up-to-date knowledge are of the greatest value to the client. It is usual to instruct at trial the same counsel who drafted the pleadings in the case, but this is not essential, nor is it always possible because counsel may have other commitments. Leading counsel are usually instructed in fatal accidents and catastrophic injuries cases, those involving a large number

19 *Practice Note (Damages: Personal Injuries)* [1984] 1 WLR 1127.
20 RSC Ord 34 r8(2).
21 Courts and Legal Services Act 1990 ss27–33.

of plaintiffs, where the facts are complex, where the potential value of the claim is very substantial, where some new questions of law may be in issue or where the case is in the public eye. When leading counsel is instructed, it is usual to retain the junior who conducted the pleadings and advised during the litigation leading up to trial.

Because the trial brief is of great importance, sufficient time should be allocated to ensuring that its contents are both comprehensive and correct. The authors have assumed that it is counsel who presents the case at court. Where it is to be another member of the same firm of solicitors, the same process should ensue. If the person handling the case is to present it, the process of preparing the brief obviously need not be carried out but, in note form or, at the very least, mentally, the same considerations should be undertaken, step by step.

The object of the brief is to provide counsel presenting the case for the plaintiff with a complete but concise picture of the case. The following points, dealt with more fully below, should be covered: a summary of the accident and its causes; a précis of the evidence which will be available at court; the solicitor's insights into the case – its strengths and weaknesses; the likely attendance and performance of witnesses; the subtle calculations in the schedule of damages that need emphasis; the arguments on damages which the solicitor feels counsel should be particularly aware of; the 'feel' of negotiations to date; and the solicitor's valuation of each element and the totality of the case.

The brief should list all the documents included with it. These will be all those which the solicitor considers are relevant and which counsel needs to be aware of. This is difficult. On the one hand, counsel should not be burdened with every discoverable document on both sides; on the other, there are likely to be more relevant documents than those in the court bundle. In the end, it is probably better to err on the side of providing too much, rather than too little. The primary documents to send are those which make up the pleadings and trial bundles in the High Court, ie, the court bundle in the county court (see pp216–17, 219–20, 228–30), plus both lists of documents, all party and party correspondence, all counsel's advices, and notices of any payments into court.

The brief should be written on the basis that counsel has no acquaintance with the case, regardless of whether the barrister has dealt with it before. In even the most important cases, barristers can become unavailable through no fault of their own, eg, because a case has unexpectedly gone part heard, and the brief may be switched to someone who has no knowledge of the case.

The instructions start by stating for which party counsel is acting.

Though unnecessary for counsel who has been on the case from the start, it ensures that a barrister who takes over the case at the last minute does not start off on the wrong foot. In all but the smallest cases, counsel's papers are best put into a ringbinder file with numbered dividers to assist in handling the information.

Subheadings in the instructions may be useful:

The accident

A brief outline should be given as to how the accident occurred, what the principal issues will be and where the dispute(s) on liability lie.

The evidence

The evidence on each issue should be described, setting out what witnesses, documents, photographs, plans and videos are relevant and will be available at court. Counsel should be told of the strengths and weaknesses of each aspect of the evidence. The solicitor's views should be set out on liability and contributory negligence, damages, strong or weak points and any particular arguments or aspects that counsel should especially have in mind.

The injuries

A description should be given of the injuries, including a very brief outline of the current position and the prognosis. Mention should be made of which experts each side is using, the position regarding any agreements on evidence, the areas of difference between the parties, their weaknesses and strengths and any special points counsel should bear in mind. If there are any difficulties regarding the timing of the appearance of any witness, counsel should be told.

Financial loss

Unless the figures are obvious, the method of calculation should be explained. Where agreement has been reached on any of the figures, that should be stated. It is important to indicate where the financial loss claim is strong and where it is weak. Any aspects of the claim that are not obvious should be fully explained. Details should be given on how each piece of evidence that is not agreed is to be proved.

Future loss

Where there is a claim for future loss, counsel should be taken through the proposed figures with suggested multipliers and the reasons for each proposed by the solicitor.

Generals

The valuation of each head of the claim and of the case as a whole should be given. This is important and gives counsel an additional perspective on the case. If counsel disagrees, the solicitor will soon be told.

The law

If there are any points of law in the case or case-law beyond the usual, the solicitor should not hesitate to put them in the brief. Two heads are better than one.

Negotiations

Counsel should be told of any negotiations, offers and payments in that have taken place, the line the solicitor has adopted, the 'feel' of the other side, and the client's position regarding settlement.

Other matters

Instructions should be given of the outcome of interlocutory proceedings, if any, and orders to be requested at trial, any issues on costs, whether the plaintiff is legally aided and any points to bear in mind for the conference with the client before the hearing.

Delivery of the brief

The usual time for delivery of the brief is 28 days prior to the hearing. It is generally bad practice to deliver it only a few days before the hearing, not least because full use is then not made of counsel. However, some solicitors hold the brief back as a tool in negotiations since its delivery will increase the costs. This tactic should be adopted only if the case is plainly on the verge of settlement. The benefits of discussion with counsel after delivery of the brief generally far outweigh the advantage of using non-delivery as a bargaining counter.

Pre-trial conference

A pre-trial conference with the client is of the greatest value and should be arranged in every case. Only in the very simplest and most straightforward case can the pre-trial conference be left to the morning of the trial. A conference the night before has little advantage. The pre-trial conference should usually be between one and four weeks before the trial; its timing is dictated by last-minute evidence gathering, negotiations between solicitors, payments into court, availability of counsel, solicitor and client, and a multitude of other factors. In general terms, the earlier the conference is, the better. The more complex the case is, the more time may be required to carry out work identified by the conference. In catastrophic cases, fatal accident cases and other highly complex cases, the pre-trial conference is the last in a series of conferences throughout the litigation. In a more straightforward case, it may be the only opportunity the client has to meet counsel before the trial. Such meetings are essential for clients to have confidence in their legal representatives and to feel more comfortable about the daunting ordeal – as it will appear to them – of the trial.

A note should be made of the conference (of course) and it may be appropriate to let the plaintiff have a copy of it or part of it, eg, in relation to complicated discussions of quantum.

The plaintiff

One of the tasks of the pre-trial conference is to tell clients what they will experience in court. Plaintiffs may have to be reminded that the action is a civil case, which is conducted in what may appear to be a surprisingly informal, if not friendly, manner. Defendants are not treated as if they were arraigned in a criminal court. Clients must be told that, though the questions will be put by counsel, the answers must be addressed to the judge. Answers should be kept short and clients are entitled to take their time and need not fear saying 'I don't know' or 'I cannot remember' where that is the case. Under cross-examination, clients must not argue with counsel but, on the other hand, they should not accept hidden assumptions or words defined in a way not used or understood by them. At all times clients must keep calm.

Experience has shown that certain stereotypes of plaintiff appeal to judges, whereas others do not find favour. Undoubtedly, judges' subconscious reactions to the characteristics of plaintiffs influence their view of liability and quantum. The straightforward, deferential, honest working man and the demure, long-suffering and uncomplaining widow are particular examples to which much sympathy is given. Without necessarily discussing these matters in conference, it is useful to consider how such qualities may be projected. The respectful demeanour, the suit and tie, the use of dark-coloured clothing, the wearing of service uniform (and not just the armed services but police, fire-fighters, ambulance staff and so on) should be considered. Periods in the services, work for the community, the old, the sick, the young and so on and high level sporting achievements, are all particularly useful to emphasise and should have been included in the witness statement.

The converse of this presentational problem should also be considered and explained to the client. The use of enquiry agents and secret filming is now frequent and a plaintiff who claims that the consequences of an indisputable back injury are that s/he cannot climb ladders may well fail on liability, or receive minimal damages if the defendant shows a video of the plaintiff competently painting the house. The defendant may seek to diminish the standing of the plaintiff in other ways as well. A bad sickness or attendance record, previous accidents, disciplinary warnings and the like will not only be relevant to arguments that a plaintiff had pre-existing disabilities, or that his/her earnings would have been diminished in the future for reasons other than disability due to the accident, or that his/her job tenure was insecure, or that there are reasons other than disability which will make him/her unattractive to future employers; such matters will be used, perhaps implicitly, to present the plaintiff as a character to whom sympathy should not be extended.

Consideration has to be given to trade union activities of the plaintiff and any potential witnesses. The object for the plaintiff's representatives is to portray the respectable and responsible face of trade unionism, whereas the defendant will be out to show politically motivated, unreliable trouble makers.

It is tempting, especially for barristers, to assume that the plaintiff is familiar with his/her witness statement(s) and will give testimony in accordance with it. However, the witness statement may have been drafted by the solicitor many months before, under great pressure of work and in the knowledge that over 90% of cases are settled before reaching trial. At the pre-trial conference, therefore, the plaintiff should be taken through the statement and any discrepancies should be explored. By now, the defence, the defendant's witness statements, the expert evidence, the defendant's documents and the medical evidence and records will all be available and the lines of cross-examination by the defendant will be apparent. These should be put to the plaintiff.

Notwithstanding that further witness statements of the plaintiff may have been served, there may still be some updating to do in relation to the client's latest attempts to find work, continuing pain and disability, and so on.

Witnesses

The solicitor handling the case should be reminded by counsel to ensure that the plaintiff's witnesses have refreshed their memory by reading or having read to them their witness statements and that their comments are noted. In most cases it is sufficient to do this on the morning of the trial.

For the pre-trial conference, it is essential to check whether all the witnesses required are ready and available and have been notified and that any requiring subpoenas/witness summonses have been served. Even at this late stage, consideration should again be given to any further witness on liability (though there will be problems in getting the evidence admitted). The availability and order of calling witnesses should be determined.

The reports of engineers or other experts will by now have been supplied to the other side; copies of all the other side's reports should have been received and supplied to the plaintiff's experts and, in turn, their comments should be to hand. Final decisions must be taken on whether each of the plaintiff's experts should be called to give evidence in accordance with their reports (assuming that reports have not been agreed). Sometimes it is worthwhile obtaining an expert's report to ensure that there are no unexplored weaknesses in the case or to provide arguments to rebut points likely to be made by the defendant. At the trial, it may not be necessary to call the plaintiff's expert to give what is, in effect, common-sense evidence, at the risk of irritating the judge and possibly having the attendance disallowed on costs. However, if there is any danger in not calling the expert, that chance should not be taken.

Any conferences with experts for the plaintiff, either separately or with others, so as to elucidate any difficult points, explore any apparent inconsistencies, or to provide the advocate with the fullest understanding of difficult matters should have taken place before the pre-trial conference with the client. Nonetheless the question can be reviewed again.

Documents

Attention should be given at the pre-trial conference to documents. The earliest review of evidence (see chapter 15 p192) will have considered documents but this is a last chance to ensure that matters are in order. Have all the documents requiring agreement been agreed? It is important to check the nature of any agreement: this could be that the document is what it purports to be, that it is a document made by the purported author, that it is evidence of the truth of the content of it, or that the content of it is true. If the bundles have not been prepared, their contents should be discussed. If bundles are ready, they should be checked. Notices (and counter notices) to admit facts, documents and notices under the Civil Evidence Act from both sides should be reviewed.

Quantum

The evidence on quantum must be considered. Medical evidence will have been exchanged and comments obtained from the plaintiff's medical advisers. Often, shortly before trial, there is a flurry of last-minute examinations and further experts' comments. In most cases, an up-to-date medical report, obtained shortly before the trial, will be in the plaintiff's interest. A check should be made that all the plaintiff's doctors have seen all the plaintiff's and the defendant's medical evidence, including any hospital records or GP's records which are available. If there are discrepancies between the plaintiff's doctors, consideration must be given to whether all need be called. Further thought should be applied to the possibility of holding a conference with the doctors, but probably without the plaintiff, to investigate any discrepancies. A 'without prejudice' meeting of experts should also be reconsidered.[22]

As at the review of evidence, a further check should be made to ensure that the medical evidence ties in with evidence from therapists, nurses, architects and those giving evidence of the costs of care, treatment or other services. It is important that the losses being claimed as damages for care, therapy, services and alteration or changes to housing have a solid foundation in the medical evidence about those needs. The necessity of this linkage cannot be overstressed.

Quantum must be re-evaluated. Every element of the calculation of damages must be set out and explained to the plaintiff. The arguments for and against each element, as demonstrated by the latest schedule of damages and the counter schedule, and any arguments which may appear in correspondence should be clearly explained. The best estimate of the band of likely damages in respect of each and every element should be given to the plaintiff. Some bands will clearly be wider than others. The likely award in each band (which is not necessarily the median figure) should be given. The principle of contributory negligence, if it is alleged, should be explained to the plaintiff and the arguments considered. The likely bracket of percentage reduction for contributory negligence, together with an estimate of the likelihood of such reduction, should be given.

22 RSC Ord 38 r38.

Settlement

Having explained all the elements, the way in which judges approach personal injury cases and their differing personalities, a total valuation of the case can be given. It is easiest to express this as upper and lower likely figures. It is then necessary both to consider the chances of winning or losing completely and to discuss the general risks of litigation.

Only at this stage can possible settlement figures be considered. Any offers which have been received or any payments in and the principles of the latter should be explained. It may be that consideration of offers or payments in is the principal purpose of the conference. The plaintiff will expect and is entitled to clear advice and this should be given. The purpose of this exercise is to attempt the most scientific evaluation of what the (unknown) judge is likely to award if the case goes to trial, rather than to consider the amount which the plaintiff, or the lawyers, consider fair. Bearing in mind all the information currently available, the advice should be one of the following:

- that the offer should be rejected
- that although low, it would not be foolish to accept the offer, but a further attempt should be made to seek more
- that the offer is a reasonable one, though it would not be foolish to press for more, or to reject it and go to trial
- that the offer is a very reasonable one and should be accepted.

If the plaintiff wishes to reject the offer, it is essential to emphasise the risks of losing or of achieving less than the offer. In every case, it is vital to give a realistic assessment of the prospects. Bearing in mind that many plaintiffs would prefer their lawyers to make the decision for them, it must be stressed that acceptance is the plaintiff's personal decision. The advice must be neither over-optimistic or the converse; it must be realistic. Many lawyers formulate a 'bottom line', ie, the level below which the plaintiff will definitely not be advised to settle. The authors believe that such an approach should not be applied too dogmatically, since new factors emerge continuously as the trial approaches. The personality of the judge is not known until the night before, and may change on the morning of the trial if the judge allocated is part heard or has emergency business which causes the case to be transferred elsewhere. Witnesses may fail to materialise or may bring powerful new evidence. New documents may appear. Arguments advanced by the other side may suddenly be found to be far more telling than was originally assessed.

Negotiations with insurance companies have been dealt with in chapter 8 pp82–6 and skilled personal injury lawyers will know the characteristics of the leading insurance companies and often of the individuals within them, with whom they frequently deal. Likewise, the approach of defendants' solicitors and counsel is likely to be familiar. Generally speaking, the closer the case gets to trial the more likely the insurance company is to be guided by the advice of its counsel. A settlement before the delivery of the brief to the defendant's counsel may be an attractive saving. As a consequence of the pre-trial conference it may be useful to approach the other side for further negotiations. This may be done through solicitors or through counsel, depending on which tactic is thought to be the more likely to be most productive. (See pp242–4 on negotiations at the door of the court.)

Immediately prior to trial

The solicitor must ensure that all the witnesses are at court. For a fixture, the pressure is less than for a case which floats into the list at 24 hours' notice, when a great deal of urgent telephoning has to be done.

For the advocate, the obvious preparations need to be made. The facts and the documents must be mastered. Consideration must be given to how the documents are to be introduced and, if by witnesses, their witness statements should be annotated at the relevant point as reminders in the course of examination-in-chief. Authorities (ie, reports of the cases to be referred to) on any points of law should be sorted out and a list provided to the court and the other side's counsel. Authorities on quantum derived from Kemp and Kemp Volume 2 (which includes the Judicial Studies Board's *Guidelines for Damages in Personal Injury Claims*) need not be notified until the morning of trial, since in a personal injury case it may be assumed that the other side and the judge will have these volumes with them. Any authorities on quantum which are not in Kemp and Kemp should be notified and photocopies taken to court – such as *Halsbury's Monthly Up-date, Personal Injuries Quantum Reports, Current Law* or *Personal and Medical Injuries Law Letter*. The schedule of damages and counter schedule must be understood and all possible permutations of the calculations considered. The weak and strong points in the damages claim should be noted and the interest calculations performed.[23]

Leading counsel often try to settle a case over the telephone the day before trial. This is less frequent among juniors. An approach to the other side over the telephone needs careful thought, since an indication of weakness may diminish any likely offer. A pretext may be useful.

23 See R M Nelson-Jones 'Personal Injury Interest' *Law Society's Gazette*, annually in September; Nelson-Jones and Nuttal *Tax and Interest Tables* Fourmat, annual.

CHAPTER 18

The trial

Whether the trial takes place in the county court or the High Court, it is the solicitor's job to organise the witnesses outside court, make sure the plaintiff feels as relaxed as possible and deal with any outstanding matters with the solicitor on the other side. Mathematical calculations relating to the various heads of damages (subject to liability) are often agreed with the other side's solicitors at this stage. It is outside court on the first day of the trial that offers of settlement are frequently made in substantial cases, less often in lower value cases. For these reasons it is almost invariably essential that the solicitor running the case attends on the first day. Thereafter it may be possible to leave the case in the hands of a capable assistant whilst remaining available at the end of a phone. Whoever represents the firm will, nowadays, always have a portable phone at court and barristers too are wise to carry one at court (though phones, of course, should be switched off whilst in the courtroom).

Outside the court

The barrister's role at this stage is also, first and foremost, to put the plaintiff at ease. It is then wise to speak to the defendant's barrister. There is always something to discuss, photographs or documents to be agreed, mathematical computations to be resolved, medical witnesses to be interposed in the normal course of evidence in order to release them as soon as is convenient, and so on. Contact of this kind makes it easier for the defendant's barrister to raise the question of an offer. Except in rare cases, no weakness is necessarily implied in asking the defendant's barrister if s/he intends to make an offer. It should, however, be a golden rule that the plaintiff's barrister never makes an offer to the other side. (See pp82–6 on negotiations.)

Any offer from the defendant's counsel must be taken back and discussed fully with the client and solicitor. Advice must be given (see p239). The client must not be put under pressure and as much time as is necessary should be taken. The judge's clerk should be kept informed of the course of negotiations and the judge should be asked for more time before it is needed. Judges often get irritated if they are not kept informed of the needs of the parties for time for negotiation and discussion. The judge must not be told anything about the nature of the negotiations that are taking place, only that time is needed for discussion and the estimate of the amount of time. If more time is required it should be asked for. It is invariably granted.

However presented, the first offer is often an opening bid. Occasionally, it really is the final offer. Invariably the offer will be accompanied by an oral explanation by the defendant's barrister of how s/he sees the case and, in particular, the weaknesses of the plaintiff's arguments on liability and on quantum. These arguments should be attentively listened to, then related back to the client and solicitor and weighed carefully. While it is fruitless for barristers to argue out the case between themselves, it may well be worthwhile to point out some of the weaknesses of the defendant's case and/or the strengths of the plaintiff's case. This may lay the groundwork for inducing a higher subsequent offer from the defendants.

There is little more that can be usefully said about the conduct of negotiations (see pp82–6), since these are very much a matter of personality and experience and depend so much on the circumstances of the particular case. It is, however, the authors' view that no offer should be accepted unless the lawyers are certain that this is the highest and final offer from the defendants.

When an offer has been made and considered by the plaintiff and it is decided to reject it, the advocate should go back to the defendant's barrister and explain the reason for rejection and the basis on which the case is capable of settlement. In some cases, this may involve putting a figure to the defendant's barrister. If negotiations appear to be hopeless, further time should not be wasted, the discussions should be discontinued and the case pressed into court. Some defendants' counsel appear to have a personal rule that they will not make their final offer until everybody is in their seat awaiting the entrance of the judge.

During much of the time spent in negotiations at the door of the court, it is useful (with the consent of the other side) to ask the judge to read the medical reports and other expert reports, indicating which are agreed and which are not.

Barristers can now speak to lay witnesses in exceptional

circumstances.[1] They have always been entitled to speak to expert witnesses outside court and should do so to make clear any points which need clarification and to ensure that nothing new has affected the reports provided.

In court

Opening speeches

If the case is fought the format of the proceedings is relatively standardised.[2] The opening speech by the plaintiff's counsel should describe the circumstances leading up to the accident and the accident itself, shortly, clearly and without ambiguity. Photographs and plans should be used and every effort made to convey the atmosphere in which the accident took place. For example, in a work accident taking place in a deafening iron foundry, the noise and hurly-burly must be discreetly communicated to the judge, who may not immediately be sensitive to it in the quiet calm of the court room. The opening speech will refer to the pleadings, but the judge will have read these and they usually have little importance at trial, except as a basis for the defendant's counsel to cross-examine the plaintiff on inconsistencies between his/her account and the pleadings. The pain, suffering and loss of amenity should be described in concise terms and it is often helpful to give a series of numbered headings to the different ways in which the accident has affected and continues to affect the plaintiff. The judge will usually have read the medical reports but it is worth drawing his/her attention to particular sentences or passages which are relied upon by the plaintiff. The judge should be taken through the schedule and counter schedule of damages, and the areas of agreement and the scope of disagreement under each head should be

1 In civil cases, barristers are now entitled to talk to lay witnesses, provided that: (a) it is in the presence of a solicitor or representative; (b) the barrister considers it is in the interests of his/her lay client; and (c) the barrister has been supplied with a proper proof of evidence of that potential witness (*Code of Conduct of the Bar of England and Wales* 16 March 1991, para 607). The barrister must not (a) put the witness under any pressure to provide other than a truthful account of the evidence, or (b) rehearse, practise or coach a witness in relation to the evidence or the way in which s/he should give it. A barrister need not be accompanied by a solicitor or representative at the county court, provided that the barrister is satisfied, after delivery of the brief, that the interests of the plaintiff and justice will not be prejudiced. The same applies to the High Court if any necessary proofs of evidence have been supplied (*Code of Conduct* para 608).

2 The trial judge may give directions as to which party shall begin, the order of speeches at trial, and, in actions tried without a jury, dispense with opening speeches: RSC Ord 35 r7(1); CCR Ord 21 r5A.

indicated. It is not usual in the opening speech to indicate submissions on quantum unless there are particular reasons for this, eg, to get the judge used to the idea that what appears to be a trivial accident is in fact a very expensive one.

Witnesses

Counsel for the plaintiff then calls the witnesses in the order which is thought to be most effective.[3] Almost invariably, the plaintiff gives evidence first, though there may be good reasons for calling witnesses in a different order. Often medical or indeed other experts may be interposed in the course of other witnesses' evidence in order to release them. The interposition of witnesses should be agreed only if it will not damage the plaintiff's case.

A witness statement is not evidence in the case though it may stand as the evidence-in-chief of the witness in the box.[4] Counsel should nonetheless examine the witness on those parts of his/her evidence which counsel wishes to bring out. This is partly to get the witness acclimatised to giving evidence and partly to give the judge a chance to assess the witness. It may also be to update some matter in the witness statement, or explain some complexity, or to introduce a particular matter on which the witness will be cross-examined in a more helpful way. An expert's report should be put in evidence at the beginning of the maker's examination-in-chief or as the court otherwise directs.[5]

If a witness's statement has been served by a Civil Evidence Act notice and s/he is called to give evidence, the witness still has to give evidence-in-chief before the statement can be admitted, unless the court orders otherwise.[6]

Cross-examination

The cross-examination of the plaintiff should be noted carefully. This will expose the main lines of the defence, if they are not already clear. It is, of course, not possible to seek the plaintiff's instructions while s/he is giving evidence. However, the solicitor may take instructions from other witnesses about matters raised in the course of cross-examination so that counsel can consider dealing with such matters in the examination-in-

3 For evidence by video link see p197.
4 RSC Ord 38 r2A(5)(b).
5 RSC Ord 38 r43.
6 Civil Evidence Act 1968 s2(2)(b).

chief of subsequent witnesses, rather than leaving it to the defendant's cross-examination. With good witnesses, some matters are more effectively left to cross-examination, rather than examination-in-chief.

If the plaintiff or a witness has not given evidence in accordance with his/her witness statement, for example, because s/he is plainly confused, it may (rarely) be possible to admit the witness statement under the Civil Evidence Act 1968. The court has a discretion to dispense with the notice requirements in the interest of fairness.[7] If the circumstances could not reasonably have been foreseen, the application may be allowed.[8]

As the case continues, consideration should continually be given to not calling available witnesses. If evidence given by the plaintiff is unchallenged or his/her answers on some matters clearly convinced the judge in an unshakeable way, then to call further evidence on that particular point may be dangerous. If a party who has served a witness statement does not call the witness, no other party can put the statement in evidence unless a Civil Evidence Act notice has been served.[9]

Re-examination should be as short as possible and in many cases can be avoided altogether. Most judges regard re-examination as an unnecessary irritation.

When all the plaintiff's witnesses have been called, the advocate should check to ensure that all documents relied on have been introduced in evidence by witnesses or else are agreed documents which have been put before the court.

After closing the plaintiff's case, the advocate should be ready for the possibility of the defendant deciding to call no evidence. This is a not infrequent tactic, usually employed because defendants realise that their witnesses are likely to make their case worse, not better. The effect is that the plaintiff's barrister must make his/her closing submissions first, before the defendant. If time is really needed to prepare these, the judge should be asked for a few minutes.

In the usual case, the defence calls witnesses and the plaintiff's barrister's task is to cross-examine. Cross-examination is very much a matter of personal style but the authors' view is that it should be directed only to essential matters, which by then will have become very clear. It should not waste time, neither should it be unnecessarily aggressive, to avoid arousing the judge's sympathies for the defendant's witnesses.

The cross-examination of doctors and experts requires a great deal of preparation. The plaintiff's relevant doctors and experts should be in

7 RSC Ord 38 r29(1); CCR Ord 20 r20(1).
8 *Morris v Stratford-on-Avon RDC* [1973] 1 WLR 1059.
9 White Book 1993 para 38/2A/3.

court, available to give immediate instructions to counsel while cross-examining the defendant's experts. The experienced personal injury practitioner will be aware of those doctors who customarily give evidence only for defendants and make frequent allegations of malingering. Counsel may think it useful to cross-examine to this effect.

Closing speeches

At the close of the defence case, the defendant's barrister will make the first closing submissions. The plaintiff's closing submissions should put the case in the way that s/he thinks most effective and, when dealing with all the submissions made by the defendant, should not simply shadow those submissions. The points should be made shortly and there is no need to review the whole case or all the evidence. The judge will have grasped the critical issues and may indeed indicate specific issues on which s/he would like to hear the plaintiff's submissions.

Judgment and costs

After judgment, if the plaintiff wins, counsel must ask for an order for judgment for the plaintiff in the sum of so many pounds, together with interest[10] totalling so many pounds. Judgements are nowadays payable forthwith so that a period for payment is not needed.

If there is any money paid into court, the order should be '*that the sum in court should be paid out to the plaintiff's solicitors in partial satisfaction and any interest thereon accruing until judgment should be paid out to the defendant's solicitors and any interest thereafter to the plaintiff's solicitors*'.

The plaintiff's barrister should then ask for an order for the plaintiff's costs. There will, of course, be an argument if the damages awarded are less than any amount paid into court. There may be arguments relating to contribution between defendants.[11]

The principles to be applied upon an application for costs were recently restated in the case of *In re Elgindata Ltd*[12] as follows:

- Costs are at the discretion of the court;
- They should follow the event, except when it appears that in the circumstances some other order should be made;

10 If the plaintiff has failed to prosecute the case properly, the court can deduct interest for the number of years delay: *Spittle v Bunney* [1988] 3 All ER 1031.

11 In exceptional cases costs may be awarded against a non-party: *Symphony Group plc v Hodgson* [1993] 3 WLR 830.

12 (1992) *Times* 18 June; (1992) 136 SJ(LB) 190.

- The general rule does not cease to apply because the successful party raised issues or made allegations on which s/he failed, but where that has caused a significant increase in the length of the proceedings s/he could be deprived of the whole or a part of his or her costs.
- Where the successful party raised issues or allegations improperly or unreasonably, the court could not only deprive him or her of his or her costs but might order him or her to pay the whole or part of the unsuccessful party's costs. Conversely, a successful party, who neither improperly or unreasonably raised issues or made allegations on which s/he failed, ought not to be ordered to pay any part of the unsuccessful party's costs.

In a legally aided case, the plaintiff's counsel should ask for a legal aid taxation of the plaintiff's costs.[13] If a legal aid case is lost, the defendant can be granted an order for costs against the plaintiff but in legal aid cases the words '*not to be enforced without leave of the court*' are usually added. The defendant will then be able to enforce costs only where the plaintiff subsequently comes into a large amount of money. This is popularly referred to as a 'football pools order'. Where the plaintiff has paid a contribution into the fund, defendants can ask for a sum equivalent to that amount to be paid to them by way of costs, provided that their costs are equal to or greater than that sum. This happens only rarely.

Where the case is privately funded, the defendant is usually awarded costs against the plaintiff if the claim has failed. In certain circumstances costs can be awarded against legal representatives (see p256).

Counsel should then deal with the scale of costs in the county court. Where the case is commenced in the High Court and transferred to the county court the costs can be awarded on the High Court scale.[14] Counsel will raise any interlocutory orders on costs and any issue on costs in relation to expert evidence. If two counsel are instructed, a certificate for two counsel must be requested.

If the case is unsuccessful[15], an application for leave to appeal should

13 Where one party is legally aided, a court can, at an interlocutory stage of proceedings, order costs in favour of the other party but directing that those costs be set off either against any damages or costs to which the legally aided party had or could in future become entitled in the action: *Lockley v National Blood Transfusion Service* [1992] 1 WLR 492.

14 *Forey v London Buses Ltd* (1992) PIQR 48. The usual order to costs on the High Court scale until date of transfer and on County Court Scale II thereafter.

15 In order to justify an appeal on costs alone the Court of Appeal must be able to say that the judge had not exercised his discretion or had not exercised that discretion judicially: *UK Petroleum Products Ltd v Reg Smith & Sons (Cheadle) Ltd* (1991) *Times* 30 October.

be considered. Where a point of law arises which may give grounds for an appeal, either during a county court hearing or at the end, the trial judge should be specifically asked to make a note of: any question of law raised at the hearing; the facts given in evidence relating to that question; and the decision or determination on that question. A copy of the note requested from the judge on any point of law can be obtained prior to serving the notice of appeal.[16]

If the defendants ask for leave to appeal and ask for a stay of execution, the plaintiff should argue for a suspended order such as '*a stay of execution for 28 days or if Notice of Appeal is lodged within 28 days, until Appeal*'.

16 County Courts Act 1984 s80.

CHAPTER 19

Costs

Successful cases

The purpose of this chapter is to deal with the particular facets of costs common to personal injury rather than other litigation.

After the conclusion of most successful personal injury cases, it is usually preferable to agree costs with the defendant's solicitors. This obviates delay and the need to send the papers off for taxation, which is both time-consuming and expensive.

Because of the standard nature of personal injury cases, there is almost an understood tariff of costs. This assists the solicitor who is economical with time and has the file well ordered and organised. It also means that, where a lot of unnecessary work has been done, that will rarely be paid for by the other side. As with all legal work, the plaintiff's solicitor charges for work done by way of letters out, telephone calls, and time spent in attendances, preparation and perusal of documents. The point has been made already that it is essential (not least for the franchised solicitor) to ensure that all telephone attendances are recorded and that all work done on the file is written up, with a time given for the period spent doing the particular work.

There are two essential elements concerning charging rates. The first is the actual charging rate and the second is the 'uplift' applied to the particular case. These rates differ between the county court and the High Court. The charging rate reflects the cost of doing the basic work in the particular locality of the solicitor's practice. Solicitors in central London have (and are allowed by taxing masters) a higher basic rate than those in small towns, because of the greater overhead costs of premises, staff, and so on. Even within an area like central London, there may be differences between charging rates, and taxing masters allow the big commercial practices to charge more than smaller firms. Equally, county court work is thought of as rather 'second rate' and, therefore, the charging rates have always been lower. The new county court scales provide that for scale II cases (exceeding £3,000) the High Court system of taxation applies. The amounts allowed are at the taxing officer's discretion. These rules apply when the event giving rise to taxation occurred on or after 1 July 1991. For the lower scale and scale I cases, there are set fees that are published periodically.

Once the hourly charging rate is determined, the telephone charges and letters are charged at one tenth of that rate, ie, ten telephone calls or letters equal one hour's attendance.

The next step is to apply the 'uplift' to the costs. This depends solely on how hard it is to do the work. The lowest figure is 50%. This is supposed to represent the profit margin for the partners in the practice. Unfortunately, personal injury cases are considered to be relatively simple and so they often attract only the minimum uplift. In more complex or larger cases, sometimes an uplift of 60% or even 75% may be accepted, but the percentage is rarely higher than this in a personal injury case.

A specimen letter setting out a plaintiff's solicitor's costs following settlement of a claim is given at B55 p361.

The principle is that the losing party should pay for all work reasonably done and disbursements reasonably incurred in the pursuit of the action. In deciding what is reasonable, the taxing officer considers whether the 'sensible' solicitor, given the knowledge at the time when the work was done or disbursement incurred, would have been reasonable in doing so in the interest of the client.

Where the case is privately financed, the client can be charged those costs that are not met by the defendants. In most cases the costs recovered from the other side will cover or almost cover the plaintiff's solicitors costs (including profit). Some firms never therefore charge their clients. When it is borne in mind that on taxation only 60–70 per cent of the chargeable costs are allowed against the losing defendant, it will be appreciated that such firms' actual costs are significantly lower than their chargeable costs, usually because of efficiency and high and fast turnover of cases.

Legal aid cases

Where the case is legally aided, no claim can be made against the legal aid fund where proceedings have been commenced unless the costs have been taxed by the court. That means, if there are major costs that cannot be claimed against the defendant or if it is impossible to reach a satisfactory agreement with the defendant, a bill must be drawn up and the costs put through the taxation system.

Where it is possible to reach agreement with the defendant, the plaintiff's solicitor must complete and send to the Legal Aid Board Form CLA26. This provides all necessary detail to the Legal Aid Board. It is convenient to write a covering letter such as at B27 p345. The Certificate can then be discharged on what is known as a 'book entry'.

Where there is no statutory charge, the solicitor can withhold sufficient of the damages and settlement to cover costs and send the balance to the client. Where there is a statutory charge the whole recovered sum should be sent to the Legal Aid Board for them to make the retention and send the balance to the client.

Once the board has processed the details of the settlement its accounts department automatically checks to see whether any payments have been made, on account of costs or disbursements, during the case. In those cases where such payments have been made, the interim payments made on the settled case will be deducted when the next routine payment is made to the solicitor's firm on its various legal aid cases.

For certificates issued on or after 25 February 1994 legal aid rates are capped (see pp75–6).

Taxation of costs

Bills

In cases where agreement cannot be reached on the costs, a bill must be drawn up. This is a specialist job which is beyond the scope of this chapter. Many solicitors send their papers to an independent costs draftsperson although larger firms may have a full-time employed specialist. This service usually costs between 6 and 7.5% of the profit costs. The costs draftsperson also usually gives different rates, depending on whether the solicitor wants to be charged on a percentage of the bill as drawn or as taxed. The solicitor's experience with the amounts that are usually taxed off by the court will determine which is preferable. Finding a good costs draftsperson who is able to provide the bill within a few weeks and who ensures that the costs claim is maximised is difficult. Solicitors should beware of any costs draftsperson where the taxing officer does not take anything off the bill. That usually implies that too little has been asked for.

Once the bill has been drafted, it should be lodged with the court's taxing office within three months of the judgment or court order.[1] In legal aid cases, failure to do so may result in all of the costs being disallowed or

1 RSC Ord 62 r29(1); CCR Ord 38 r20(1).

reduced.[2] With the bill, all the relevant papers (put together by the costs draftsperson) should be lodged, including the original court order allowing the bill to be taxed. In large cases, ie, those where the costs are over £20,000, the court will not accept the supporting papers until it is ready to deal with them – to prevent the court being swamped by documents. In those cases, the court initially requires only the bill, the original court order (together with a copy) and a statement of parties.

Bills in successful legally aided cases have three columns for the costs to be paid by the defendants and three for the costs to be met by the legal aid fund, and ultimately by the client from the damages money. In a successful privately funded claim on behalf of a minor, the bill has to have six columns if the solicitor intends to claim costs against the infant plaintiff. In unsuccessful cases, the bill has only three columns for payment by the legal aid fund.

Taxation hearings

On lodging the papers in successful cases, the solicitor should forward a copy of the bill to the defendant and a copy to the plaintiff, who will almost certainly have a financial interest in the taxation outcome.

The court allocates a taxing officer to consider the bill and, in successful cases where the Legal Aid Board is the paying party, a date is given for the taxation hearing. In unsuccessful cases, the taxing officer provisionally taxes the bill and it is only if the solicitor disputes the bill that a hearing will be fixed if requested. The length of time between lodging the papers and receiving a hearing date varies from court to court and from case to case, but it can be anything from a couple of months to a year.

At the hearing in successful cases, both parties are usually represented and the proceedings are adversarial, with the taxing officer being the arbitrator. In legal aid cases, the defendant's representative attempts to persuade the officer to transfer as much of the costs as possible into the legal aid fund column. It is the plaintiff's representative's job to oppose such representations. The client must be given notice of the date of the taxation hearing and told of the right to attend. Experience shows the client's presence discourages taxing officers from reducing (in effect) the plaintiff's damages. It is also open to counsel to attend the hearing, although usually the plaintiff's representative will defend counsel's fees.

2 Civil Legal Aid (General) Regs 1989 reg 109.

The procedure is broadly the same in the county court as in the High Court, except in the county court the district judge will hear the taxation.[3]

Basis of taxation

There are now only two bases for the taxation of costs to be paid by the defendant. They are the standard basis and the indemnity basis. Unless otherwise ordered, the costs are taxed on an indemnity basis. In fact, the order made is almost invariably for standard costs, except in infant cases. On the standard basis, the taxing officer allows a reasonable amount for all costs reasonably incurred which reflect steps in the action. If there is any doubt about reasonableness, the paying party is entitled to the benefit.[4] On the indemnity basis, the costs are allowed unless they are of an unreasonable amount or have been unreasonably incurred. If there is any doubt, the paying party is not entitled to the benefit. Unless otherwise ordered by the court, costs in legal aid cases are taxed on the standard basis.[5]

Where the bill being taxed is claiming money from both the defendant and the legal aid fund, the only costs to go into the fund columns are those standard costs, reasonably incurred, unrelated to a step in the court action. A good example is the cost of obtaining an early opinion from counsel, solely for the purpose of enabling the Legal Aid Board to consider whether the legal aid certificate should be extended.

Obtaining payment

Following the hearing, the plaintiff's representative takes the bill and all the papers from the court and then completes the bill. This means finalising all the figures following the taxation, and putting in the legal aid summary, where necessary.

The bill is then returned to the taxing office of the court, with the taxing fee of 5% of the costs, for the 'allocator' to be drawn up. This is the formal court document which confirms the amount of costs payable by the defendant and the legal aid fund.

During the taxation, the officer checks to see whether each disbursement has been paid for by the plaintiff's solicitors. Where no voucher confirming payment is among the papers, s/he will note the initials 'qv' against the amount. On relodging the bill following the

3 See CCR Order 38 r2(2) and Green Book Part 3, County Court Costs.
4 RSC Ord 62 r12(1).
5 Civil Legal Aid (General) Regs 1989 reg 107(4)(c).

taxation hearing, the court expects to be given a voucher receipted by the recipient for each of these items. The only exception is that the courts allow solicitors to certify that vouchers up to £200 have been paid, without the need for lodging a receipted voucher.

The allocator should then be sent to the defendant's solicitors requesting the defendant's proportion of the bill. Recently the courts have held that interest is chargeable on the plaintiff's costs from the date of judgment to the date of payment. Some defendants, as a result, pay the solicitors a reasonable proportion of the likely costs figure, on account, to save the interest.[6]

Where the case is legally aided and the taxation process completed, damages (if not already passed on), costs and interest received are sent by the plaintiff's solicitors to the Legal Aid Board. The board then sends a cheque to be paid to the plaintiff's solicitors, covering both the inter partes costs and the costs met from the legal aid fund, together with a cheque payable to the plaintiff. The money payable to the plaintiff is the damages awarded less any costs that are payable out of the fund. The Legal Aid Board keeps the interest payable on the costs and disbursements.

Unsuccessful cases

Legal aid

Where the case is unsuccessful and it is legally aided, a bill must be drawn up and taxed, unless the costs to be claimed from the legal aid fund are less than £500 in total and proceedings have not been issued. That applies only where the case is abandoned at a relatively early stage.

Taxation of costs in an unsuccessful case is much the same as that described above in relation to successful cases. The main difference is that the defendant has nothing to do with the taxation process and the only party attending the hearing is the plaintiff's representative.

Following the hearing, the bill is completed in the same way as above, the allocator obtained, and the allocator sent to the Legal Aid Board for payment. The board deducts any money paid on account during the case, prior to payment.[7]

6 *Hunt v R M Douglas (Roofing) Ltd* [1988] 3 WLR 975. If a payment in is accepted without a court order or judgment, interest on costs is not recoverable for cases settled after 1 October 1991: RSC Ord 62 r5, CCR Ord 38 r1(3). Where judgment is obtained in default with damages to be assessed, interest under Judgments Act 1838 s17 runs from date of assessment: *Thomas v Bunn* [1991] 2 WLR 27, HL.

7 For certificates made after 25 February 1994, the fees payable by the Legal Aid Board in an unsuccessful case are capped (see pp75–6).

Under Legal Aid Act 1988 s17, where a legally aided party loses the case, the court can make an award of costs against the assisted person only to the extent that it is reasonable in all the circumstances, depending on the loser's means and conduct through the case. In this situation, the judge often takes as guidance the amount of contribution that the legally aided party paid towards his/her certificate, and limits the costs to this amount. Under s18 of the Act there is a provision, in certain circumstances, for a non-legally aided winner to claim costs from the Legal Aid Board where the loser was suing under a legal aid certificate. A 'football pools order' is where the balance of costs awarded to the winner is marked 'not to be enforced without leave of the court'.

Privately funded cases

Where the case is not legally aided, the plaintiff has to pay the bill and, indeed, is usually ordered to pay the defendant's costs.

The defendant usually sends a draft bill and the plaintiff must decide whether to negotiate an agreement on those costs or whether to force the defendant to put the bill through the taxation process. The main disincentive of taking the latter course is that the plaintiff has to pay the costs of taxation, which can be a few hundred pounds.

Review of taxation

In the county court[8] if a party wishes to challenge any decision made on taxation, then the proper procedure is to seek a reconsideration by the district judge who heard the taxation, and if that is not satisfactory, to apply for a review by a circuit judge. Appeal may be made from the judge to the Court of Appeal. A request for reconsideration must be made within 14 days of the taxation. There is no prescribed form, but objections ought to be set out and sent to other persons heard on the taxation. An application for review by the judge must again be made within 14 days on notice.

In the High Court[9] a party dissatisfied with a decision of the taxing officer (other than a decision on provisional taxation or on wasted costs) may apply in writing with a notice of objections within 21 days of the decision for a review of the decision. A party dissatisfied with the decision of the taxing officer may apply for a review to a judge within 14 days after

8 CCR Order 38 r24.
9 RSC Order 62 r33.

the taxing officer's decision. Appeal lies from a judge to the Court of Appeal.

Costs against lawyers

Costs may be awarded against a party's solicitors or counsel. The Court of Appeal has recently given guidelines for making such 'wasted costs orders'[10] in *Ridehalgh v Horsefield and Another.*[11] The court expressed concern that such orders were threatening to become a new and costly form of satellite litigation. Costs orders against legal representatives may only be made in respect of conduct which is 'improper, unreasonable or negligent'.

'Improper' covers (but is not confined to) conduct which would ordinarily be held to justify disbarment, striking off, suspension from practice or other serious professional penalty. It includes conduct which would be regarded as improper according to the consensus of professional (including judicial) opinion, whether or not it violates the letter of a professional code.

'Unreasonable' describes conduct which is vexatious, for example, designed to harrass the other side rather than advance the resolution of the case, and it makes no difference that the conduct was the product of excessive zeal and not of an improper motive. The acid test is whether the conduct permits of a reasonable explanation.

'Negligent' should be understood in an untechnical way to denote

10 The Supreme Court Act 1981 s51(6) as amended provides that in any proceedings in the Court of Appeal, High Court and county court: 'the court may disallow, or as the case may be order the legal or other representative concerned to meet, the whole of any wasted costs or such part of them as may be determined.' Since 1 October 1991 personal liability is extended to all representatives, not just solicitors. The test is simple negligence, not gross misconduct or neglect: see *Gupta v Comer* [1991] 2 WLR 494. 'Wasted costs' are those incurred because of any improper, unreasonable or negligent act or omission by a legal or other representative which the court considers unreasonable to expect the other side to pay: s51(7). Before the order is made the legal representative concerned must be given a reasonable opportunity to contest the order in court: RSC Ord 62 r11(4). The courts have been keen to exercise their new powers both at the hearing (RSC Ord 62 r11) or on taxation (RSC Ord 62 r28) – for cases against counsel see *Antonelli v Wade Gerry Fair (a firm)* (1992) *Times* 29 December; *Fozal v Gofur* (1993) *Times* 9 July; for a case against solicitors see *Philex PLC v Golban* (1993) *Times* 9 July.

These rules apply to county court proceedings by virtue of CCR Ord 38 rr1(3) and 19A.

11 (1994) *Times* 28 January.

failure to act with the competence reasonably expected of ordinary members of the profession. Negligence must be proved.

A legal representative is not to be held to have acted improperly, unreasonably or negligently simply because s/he put foward on instructions a claim or defence that was bound to fail. It is incumbent on the court to bear prominently in mind the peculiar vulnerability of legal representatives acting for assisted persons. It is only when all allowances have been made and an advocate's conduct of court proceedings was quite plainly unjustifiable that it would be appropriate to make a wasted costs order.

The question of a wasted costs order should ordinarily be left until after the end of the trial. The applicant or the court can initiate the enquiry. The procedure to be adopted depends on the circumstances of the case, but it should be fair and as simple and summary as fairness permits. The court has a two-stage discretion.

At the initial stage, the court should not automatically invite the legal representative to show cause. The costs of the inquiry as compared with the costs of the claim are a relevant consideration. A causal link between the conduct complained of and the costs incurred is essential. After inquiry and hearing the representative, an order to show cause should not be made unless an apparently strong prima facie case has been made out. The burden of proof is not on the legal representative to exculpate him or herself.

Even if the court is then satisfied that the legal representative has acted improperly, unreasonably or negligently so as to waste costs, it is not bound to make an order, but it will have to give sustainable reasons for not doing so.

CHAPTER 20

Handling the award

The receipt of a substantial sum of money by award or settlement requires forethought. The plaintiff's advisers should consider the advantages and disadvantages of a structured settlement, the effect of an award or settlement on the plaintiff's tax position, the way in which a lump sum may be invested, and the possibility of setting up a trust to minimise any loss of income support.

Structured settlements

A structured settlement is an agreement whereby a defendant pays damages to a plaintiff in the form of future annual payments in place of part of the traditional lump sum. The defendant finances this by the purchase of a life annuity, or life annuities, from an insurance company. There are in effect two back-to-back agreements which result in the payment of the agreed sums from the insurance company to the defendant, and then from the defendant to the plaintiff. Recently a defendant health authority has self-funded such a structure. The annual payments under a structured settlement agreement are guaranteed for the lifetime of the plaintiff. The payments may also be linked to the increase in the retail prices index and guaranteed for a minimum period. Whereas the income produced by the investment of the conventional lump sum is taxable (which is, in theory, taken into account when assessing the sum), the payments under a structured settlement are not liable to tax in the hands of the recipient. This follows an agreement between the Inland Revenue and the Association of British Insurers in 1987 whereby, provided that an agreement is so worded to make it clear that the periodic payments under the structured settlement are the instalments of an antecedent debt created by settlement of judgment, the payments are to be regarded as capital receipts and therefore not subject to income tax.

On 14 July 1989, the High Court approved the first structured settlement in *Kelly v Dawes*.[1] In this case, the plaintiff was a patient under the jurisdiction of the Court of Protection and so the court's approval was required. Potter J stated that, although it is not necessary for all such settlements to have the court's approval, at the very least the following should be available to the plaintiff's advisers before a settlement is reached:

1) A detailed opinion of counsel, assessing the value of the claim and its constituent elements on a conventional basis, and the appropriate lump sum figure or bracket for settlement on that basis. Careful consideration of the plaintiff's life expectancy based on the medical opinions should be included.

2) A report by accountants or other financial experts as to the fiscal and investment advantages to the plaintiff of the structured settlement proposed, with particular regard to the life expectancy of the plaintiff and the likely future costs of care.

3) A draft of the form of agreement proposed, together with confirmation that the Inland Revenue regards such an agreement as within the scope of any revenue provisions or practice on which the value of the structured settlement depends.

4) Where appropriate, confirmation of the approved terms of the agreement by the Court of Protection conditional on the approval of the settlement by the court.

5) Material to satisfy the court that there are sufficient funds available outside the structured provisions to meet any foreseeable capital needs of the plaintiff, whether by means of a lump sum element in the settlement or by reason of other resources available to the plaintiff.

6) Material to satisfy the court that the agreement involves secure arrangements by responsible insurers, whether one of the well-known tariff companies or one of the syndicates operating under the rules and protection of the Lloyds' market.

Potter J emphasised that this was not a checklist and that the information required was a matter of individual consideration in every case. Where the appropriate Inland Revenue approval (referred to in (3) above) cannot be obtained, the settlement should expressly provide for the contingency that the Inland Revenue does not recognise the agreement as tax advantageous.

The model agreement

The Inland Revenue has accepted a model agreement, with four alternative forms of attached schedule which allow four different types of periodical payments, as follows:

1 (1990) *Times* 27 September.

a) Basic terms

The settlement consists of a lump sum plus a series of pre-set amounts to run for a fixed period. This might be attractive to someone receiving a retirement pension.

b) Indexed terms

As in (a), but the payments are linked to the retail price index.

c) Terms for life

A lump sum plus a series of pre-set amounts to run until the plaintiff's death. There is an option to make the number of payments subject to a pre-set minimum so that they will continue in the event of the plaintiff's early death.

d) Indexed terms for life

As in (c), except that the periodical payments are linked to the retail price index. This is the most frequently chosen option.

Advantages to the defendants

The initiative on structured settlements has come from defendants' insurance companies because they have seen the vast savings made in the USA and Canada. In *Kelly v Dawes*, the plaintiff settled for less than the conventional lump sum payment because of the tax advantages of the settlement. It has become accepted that the defendant is entitled to a discount on the damages as conventionally assessed in return for co-operation in implementing a structure, and the cost of administering it. This is usually calculated as a percentage of the amount of the award going into the structure, and can be as high as 10%–15%. Any discount over 8% to the defendant, however, more than offsets the financial advantage of the structure's tax-free status to a basic rate taxpayer at current tax rates. Agreements provide either for a fixed number of payments and/or for them to cease on the death of the plaintiff. Therefore, if the plaintiff dies earlier than envisaged, the defendant's insurance company or self-funding defendant gets an unexpected windfall. The plaintiff's estate gets nothing unless s/he dies within the guarantee period.

Advantages and disadvantages to the plaintiff

The plaintiff benefits from a structured settlement because s/he can plan for lifetime needs in full knowledge of what his/her income will be. The annual payments can be tailor-made to some extent, for example to anticipate higher care costs when the plaintiff is older. The principal advantage is therefore one of certainty. The plaintiff is not exposed to the disadvantages of possible falling investment yields, higher taxes or increasing RPI inflation. The payments, being guaranteed for life, do not cease at the end of the period estimated as the plaintiff's life expectancy. The plaintiff is also saved the costs of managing the fund, which may not have been fully recoverable as a head of damage.

However there are also considerable disadvantages to the plaintiff in a structured settlement, some of which have only become apparent at a time when annuity rates have fallen. There is a discrepancy between the discount rate used by the courts to calculate multipliers and the rate of return on structured settlements. The courts assume that lump-sum compensation will be invested to produce a real (ie, after inflation) net-of-tax income of 4–5% pa (see pp212–14). This is approximately the rate that can be obtained by investing 70%–80% in equities and the rest in gilts or cash. The rate of return available in 1994 on structures compares with the return on index-linked gilts (the security backing the annuity), currently 2–3% gross. In short, if annual payments of income are translated into a lump sum with an implied rate of return of 4.5%, yet the sum is in turn invested in a structure with an underlying yield of, say, 3%, before the addition of the 'capital' element, then there will be a shortfall in the annual income produced. The only way for a lump sum to meet the financial demands expected of it is in fact to invest it in the way envisaged by the courts, but this would involve the plaintiff in what might be considered an unacceptable degree of risk.

This problem would be remedied if the courts used a discount rate derived from the return on index-linked gilts, as suggested in the Law Commission's Consultation Paper No 125 on structured settlements, or if damages were calculated on the basis of providing the annual sums required directly by way of a structured settlement, without calculating the lump sum first by conventional methods.

Another disadvantage is that the plaintiff loses flexibility. The structured settlement is irrevocable and unchangeable and yet in a lifetime a plaintiff's needs can vary in a completely unpredictable way: health may improve or deteriorate, new treatments or equipment may become available. There is arguably limited usefulness of having certainty on one side of the equation if there is unpredictability on the other. With the lump sum there is the scope to review and change investment policies to adapt to changing circumstances. Conversely, if the plaintiff's needs are completely predictable, and the structured settlement can produce sufficient income, it is an ideal solution.

The high amount of the defendant's discount can negate the benefits of the tax-free status of the structured settlement, making it even more difficult for the plaintiff to meet income needs. Similarly, intermediaries who charge on a commission basis, generally 3%, for setting up the structured settlement reduce commensurately the amount of money available to provide the annuity. In large cases in particular, it would be advantageous to use an intermediary charging on an hourly rate fee basis.

Index-linking to the RPI gives the plaintiff exposure to the possibility that the costs of care will rise by more than the RPI. This can be considered likely because care is essentially a wages cost, and historically wages have increased by on average 2% pa more than the RPI.

There is at present no satisfactory answer to the problem of the security of future payments under a structured settlement.[2] Life companies can collapse and structured settlements are not covered by the statutory compensation scheme under the Policyholders' Protection Act 1975. Where the defendant is a health authority, there is no guarantee of its continued existence for the lifetime of a given plaintiff. As yet there is no legislation in place to guarantee that payments will continue to be made for or on behalf of the defendant.

If the plaintiff dies before the estimated life expectancy expires, the insurance company gains, and the plaintiff's estate suffers a loss.

Independent advice

The practice of using intermediaries to set up structured settlements acting on joint instructions for both plaintiff and defendant has become familiar. However, until the size of the discount and the amount of the annual payments has been ascertained, there is clearly a conflict of interests. The Law Society has recommended that the plaintiff should take independent advice. The Ethics and Guidance Department also recommends that arrangements by which the remuneration is on a contingency basis and the package advisor receives a commission on the purchase of the annuity, but nothing if the matter does not proceed, should be approached 'with great caution'. Advice under such conditions would not be demonstrably impartial.

2 Though guidelines were given for the protection of policyholders under the Insurance Companies Act 1982 and the Policyholders' Protection Act 1975 in *Scher v Policyholders' Protection Board* (1992) *Times* 18 August.

Tax

No tax is payable on an award for damages for personal injuries or death.[3] Where a plaintiff loses only part of his/her income, that part is always 'the top slice' when assessing liability for tax and so calculating the net loss.[4]

The income produced by investing the capital is liable to tax and, if the plaintiff's award is substantial, it increases the plaintiff's post-trial tax liability. The court should take this into account in assessing the plaintiff's future loss but only in exceptional cases, where justice requires, is a special allowance made.[5]

Investments

Where the damages are substantial, the client may need assistance in deciding how to invest the money. The regulations regarding investment advice have become increasingly rigorous in recent years and, for a solicitor even to contemplate giving that advice, the firm must be regulated by the Law Society in the conduct of investment business.

Because of the complexities and risks of investment, unless the firm specialises in this subject, it is wisest to avoid giving the client specific investment advice. The best course of action is to state that financial advice ought to be obtained and to refer the client, in the first place, to his/her bank or building society manager. Even recommending named accountants or financial advisers involves the solicitor in the slight risk of a negligence action if the client receives bad advice, because it may be said that the solicitor should have investigated the adviser's competence more thoroughly.

Management of the plaintiff's investment may be recoverable as a head of damage in itself (see p208).

Income support

An award of damages may affect clients who are in receipt of income support, which is the major non-contributory means-tested social security benefit payable in the UK. Entitlement depends, among other things, on

3 Income and Corporation Taxes Act 1988 ss148 and 188; *British Transport Commission v Gourley* [1956] AC 185.

4 *Lyndale Fashion Manufacturers v Rich* [1973] 1 WLR 73.

5 *Taylor v O'Connor* [1971] AC 115 per Lord Reid at 129; *Hodgson v Trapp* [1989] AC 807.

the income and capital resources of the claimant. The claimant is not entitled to income support if his/her capital[6] exceeds a prescribed amount (£8,000, in the year 1994 – 95).[7] There is a tariff income to be taken into account for capital between £3,000 and £8,000 – viz, £1 for every £250 or part of capital in excess of £3,000.[8] An award of damages or a settlement is treated as capital, and so the client and his/her family may find the entitlement to income support reduced,[9] if the value of damages or settlement is between £3,000 and £8,000, or extinguished if the value exceeds £8,000. If the claimant loses income support, s/he also loses entitlement to full housing benefit and maximum council tax benefit and (while that operated) community charge benefit.

This problem can be overcome by holding the money on trust. If a personal injury award or settlement is placed on trust for the claimant, the capital value of such a trust is not taken into account in assessing the claimant's capital.[10] The claimant is not treated as having deprived him/herself of such capital.[11]

The trust can be simple. Independent trustees must be appointed. The trust should give the trustees power to advance capital in their absolute discretion from time to time (unspecified). Payments out of the trust by the trustees, if voluntary and not made at regular intervals, should be treated as capital payments and not income.[12] Therefore, payments made, for example, for a holiday or a wheelchair should not disentitle the claimant. As each payment depends on its own circumstances, it is difficult to advise whether a particular payment will be treated as income or capital. As a rule of thumb, payments will not be allowed (ie, will be treated as income) if their effect is to top up the income of the claimant from income support or other benefits. There is, however, a disregard of the first £10 per week of income paid from such a trust.

Drafting a trust should only be entrusted to a solicitor or counsel familiar with trusts in this setting. Such drafting would be outside the range of specialisation of most personal injury counsel.

6 This includes capital of the claimant's partner, child or dependent young person: Income Support (General) Regs 1987 reg 23(1).
7 Social Security Act 1986 s22(6) and Income Support (General) Regs 1987 reg 45 as amended.
8 Ibid reg 53.
9 Since the establishment of the Compensation Recovery Unit, the DSS will know about all the plaintiffs who are claiming benefit prior to the settlement of their claims.
10 Income Support (General) Regs 1987 reg 46(2) and Sch 10 para 12.
11 Ibid reg 51(2)(b).
12 Ibid reg 48(9).

CHAPTER 21

Appeals

This chapter explains the procedures for making appeals. The first question is whether the appeal can be funded. In private or trade union funded cases, discussions should be held with the client and, where appropriate, the union, to determine whether the benefits of an appeal are likely to outweigh the costs.

In a legally aided case, an application must be made to the Legal Aid Board. The certificate does not cover counsel's opinion or indeed any work on an appeal. The board should, therefore, be asked to authorise an opinion from counsel and the solicitor should set out the reasons why an appeal is thought appropriate. If counsel's advice is positive, the board should then be asked to extend the certificate to fund the appeal as soon as possible. A certificate to appeal, or an amendment to an existing certificate, can be obtained from the area director very quickly.[1]

There are time limits, set out below, for lodging an appeal. Often, if a solicitor waits for the granting of legal aid before setting down the notice, the case will be out of time. The registrar of appeals may or may not consider the time needed for obtaining legal aid a good enough reason to waive the time limit. It is, therefore, better to draft, serve and set down the notice within the appropriate period. It can always be withdrawn.

If the error is a mere slip in drawing the order, application should be made to the master or judge who made the order under the 'slip rule' for it to be corrected.[2] This is much more convenient than an appeal.

Appeals follow the path set out below.[3]

1 *Legal Aid Handbook 1993* notes for guidance para 4–11.

2 *Mecuminger IRO GmbH v Trip-Lite Ltd* (1992) *Times* 9 July.

3 Interlocutory appeals shortly before trial are discouraged by the Court of Appeal. *Ashmore v Corporation of Lloyds* [1992] 1 WLR 446 at 453; *Croft v Jewell* (1993) PIQR 270.

Appeals from district judge

There is no appeal from an award of a district judge to whom proceedings have been referred for arbitration under County Courts Act 1984 s64, although the award may be set aside on grounds of misconduct or legal error by the judge.[4] In applications to set aside by the district judge notice, with grounds, must be served within 14 days after the day on which the arbitration award was entered as a judgement of the court.

There is a right of appeal from the district judge to the circuit judge from a judgment or final order.[5] The party appealing must show grounds and notice of appeal must be served within 14 days of the judgement or order appealed against being made.[6] The circuit judge exercises an appellate discretion.[7]

A notice of appeal against an interlocutory order must be served within five days, unless the judge directs otherwise.[8] The circuit judge hears the matter de novo and makes such decision as is considered just. The hearing is in chambers unless otherwise directed.

Appeals from circuit judge to Court of Appeal

Time and leave

Notice of appeal must be served not later than four weeks after the date of judgment or order,[9] and not, as in appeals from the High Court, when it was sealed or otherwise perfected.[10] If leave is granted by the Court of Appeal, time for service is extended by seven days.[11]

It may be necessary to obtain leave to appeal. Under the County Court Appeals Order 1991[12] and the Supreme Court Act 1981 s18, leave is required, inter alia, to appeal most interlocutory judgments or orders[13] for claims of less than £5,000 or where the claim cannot be quantified and where the circuit judge was acting in an appellate capacity. If leave is required, it must be obtained before serving the notice of appeal.[14] Leave

4 CCR Ord 19 r8.
5 CCR Ord 37 r6.
6 CCR Ord 37 r6(2).
7 For procedure, see *Practice Direction (district judges: appeals)* [1991] 1 WLR 206.
8 CCR Ord 13 r1(10) and (11).
9 RSC Ord 59 r4(1).
10 RSC Ord 59 r19(3).
11 RSC Ord 59 r4(3).
12 SI 1991 No 1877.
13 RSC Ord 59 r1A.
14 *Cumbes v Robinson* [1951] 2 KB 83.

should be obtained as quickly as possible, preferably at the hearing. Otherwise, an extension of time should be sought. Unless the time limit for serving notice of appeal has expired, the application for leave must be made to the county court before the Court of Appeal.[15] Leave need not be given by the trial judge.[16] The detailed practice and procedure for applications to the Court of Appeal are contained in the White Book 1993 paras 59/19/1–13.

Applications to the Court of Appeal for leave to appeal must be within seven days from refusal of leave. These are made ex parte, in writing, setting out the reasons why leave should be granted. If necessary, an application to extend time for appealing should be included and, if the time for appealing has expired, the reasons why the application was not made in time. This should be supported by affidavit. The court (a single Lord Justice) may grant the application on paper or direct that it be renewed in open court either ex parte or inter partes.

The application should be a notice of ex parte application[17] with a draft notice of appeal annexed to it. Guidance on the procedure is provided in the decision in *R G Carter Ltd v Clarke*.[18] The civil appeals office replies by letter, acknowledging the setting down of the application and stating the time limit for supplying and describing the bundle of documents required by the court. If the single Lord Justice directs that the application be heard in open court, the relevant parties are notified by the civil appeals listing office. If the application is refused, the solicitor should write to the registrar of civil appeals within seven days to renew the application, which will be heard ex parte (unless otherwise directed) in open court.

If leave is granted, otherwise than after a hearing inter partes in open court, any party affected may apply to have the grant of leave reconsidered inter partes in open court. Application must be made by summons within seven days of being notified.

Stay of execution

If an application for stay of execution pending appeal is necessary, it should be made with the application for leave to appeal. The latter does not operate as a stay of proceedings and, therefore, an application must be

15 RSC Ord 59 r14(4).
16 *Warren v T Kilroe & Son Ltd* [1988] 1 WLR 516.
17 White Book 1993 para 59/14/19.
18 [1990] 1 WLR 578.

made specifically to the court which made the order appealed from or to the Court of Appeal.

The solicitor should obtain copies of the trial judge's signed notes of evidence and note of the judgment. The judge is under a duty to give reasons for the decision as part of the judgment.[19] County courts are obliged to begin transcribing the trial judge's notes of evidence immediately they are served with the appellant's notice of appeal.[20] If the judge has no notes of the judgment, counsel's notes[21] or the solicitor's notes must, unless otherwise directed, be submitted to the judge for approval or other comment. These notes should form part of the bundle of documents (see below). References to payments into court should be excluded.[22]

Notice of appeal

The district judge, as well as the party or parties affected by the appeal, must be served with the notice of appeal.[23] The notice need not be stamped, sealed or otherwise authenticated by the court. Service may be by fax.[24] No leave is required where a statement of value exceeding £5,000 is served with the notice.

The notice must contain:[25] the ground(s) of the appeal; the order which the appellant wishes the Court of Appeal to make; the list in which it is proposed to set down the appeal;[26] and after the signature of the solicitor for the appellant, the following statement:

No notice as to the date on which this appeal will be in the list for hearing will be given: it is the duty of solicitors to keep themselves informed as to the state of the lists. A respondent intending to appear in person should inform the Registrar of Civil Appeals, Room 136, Royal Courts of Justice, WC2 of that fact and give his address; if he does so he will be notified to the address he has given of the date when the appeal is expected to be heard.[27]

See also the sample notices of appeal at E17 p470 (county court) and E18 p471 (Court of Appeal).

19 *Banaskiewicz v Mulholland* (1985) *Times* 19 April.
20 *Greenwood and Others v Wearden and Another* (1990) *Times* 24 March.
21 Counsel is under a duty to take a note: *Letts v Letts* (1987) *Times* 8 April.
22 RSC Ord 59 rr12A and 19(4A).
23 RSC Ord 59 r19(2).
24 *Hastie & Jenkerson v McMahon* (1990) *Times* 3 April, CA; RSC Ord 65 rr5(1)(c) and 2B.
25 For form of notice, see White Book 1993 para 59/3/4.
26 White Book 1993 para 59/3/7.
27 *Practice Note* [1953] 1 WLR 1503.

Respondent's notice

Respondents who wish to cross-appeal or contend that the decision appealed from should be varied or affirmed on different grounds, must serve a respondent's notice within 21 days after service of notice of appeal. The notice should specify the grounds and form of order desired. Two copies of the respondent's notice must be lodged with the registrar by the respondent within four days of either the date of service of the respondent's notice or the date of notification that the appeal has been set down. One notice must be indorsed with the fee, the other with the certificate of service.[28]

Setting down an appeal

This is the process by which the appeal is entered in the records of the Court of Appeal. This must be done within seven days of serving the notice of appeal, unless time is extended. The solicitor must lodge with the registrar of appeals at the civil appeals office: the judgment or order appealed from or copy and two copies of the notice of appeal appropriately stamped or indorsed with receipt of the fee and service respectively.

Within four days of setting down, notice must be given to all parties specifying the list (see below) in which the appeal is set down and any extension of time allowed.[29] The papers are then referred by the civil appeals office to an office lawyer, who scrutinises them. If the appeal was not validly instituted or the court has no jurisdiction to entertain the appeal, the appellant's solicitor is informed by letter and the appeal is not set down. The civil appeals office cannot guarantee that it will notify solicitors or litigants of defects in time for them to be rectified before the relevant time limits expire. Therefore, the solicitor should not delay in setting the appeal down.[30]

Amendment

The notice of appeal and respondent's notice may be amended without leave at any time before the appeal appears in the list of forthcoming appeals. Thereafter, leave is required.[31]

28 RSC Ord 59 r6.
29 RSC Ord 59 r5(4).
30 *Practice Statement: (Civil Appeals: Setting Down)* [1990] 1 WLR 1436.
31 RSC Ord 59 r7.

Extending time

A circuit judge has power to extend or abridge time for appealing if the application is made within four weeks.[32] The Court of Appeal or a single Lord Justice has a discretion to extend or abridge time, whether the time for appealing has expired or not.[33]

Fresh evidence

The Court of Appeal has power to receive further evidence on questions of fact.[34] Three conditions must be satisfied.[35] (a) It must be shown that the evidence could not have been obtained with reasonable diligence[36] prior to the trial. (b) The evidence must have, or would have had, an important influence on the result of the case. (c) The evidence must be apparently credible, though it need not be incontrovertible. If the fresh evidence has arisen within 14 days of judgment, it is possible to apply to the county court for a rehearing.[37]

Enquiries and information

Enquiries concerning the setting down of appeals or applications or about other Court of Appeal procedural matters should be made to the civil appeals general office (Royal Courts of Justice, room E330; telephone 071–936 6409 and 071–936 6916).

Enquiries about listing should be made to the civil appeals listing office (Royal Courts of Justice, room E329, telephone 071–936 6195 and 071–936 6917). For enquiries about applications to a single Lord Justice, telephone 071–936 6891; and to the registrar, 071–936 6917.

Processing the appeal

The civil appeals office, when acknowledging the setting down of an appeal, writes to the appellant's solicitor (or the appellant, if not represented). S/he will be informed of the reference number allocated to the appeal on the list in which it has been entered and the date when it is

32 RSC Ord 59 r15.
33 RSC Ord 3 r5.
34 RSC Ord 59 r10(2).
35 *Ladd v Marshall* [1954] 1 WLR 1489.
36 For a generous interpretation of 'reasonable diligence' see *Wood v Gamlings* (1993) PIQR 76.
37 CCR Ord 37 r1.

intended to include the case in the list of forthcoming appeals. The letter will have the following four enclosures. Annex A: a form to be completed by the appellant's solicitor giving details of the solicitors and counsel appearing for each party. Annex B: a list of documents which must be included in each set of appeal bundles. Annex C: a copy of *Practice Statement* 22 October 1986, setting out the court's requirements concerning the form and content of the bundles to be used by the Court of Appeal. Annex D: a time estimate form to be completed by the appellant's counsel.

The list of forthcoming appeals is the sole list of pending appeals and is printed in the daily cause list. Once a case enters the list of forthcoming appeals, it has a strict and important timetable (see below).

Bundles

Two or three copies of the appeal bundles (depending on the number of judges), must be lodged within 14 days, unless the registrar of civil appeals grants an extension. This can be applied for by writing to the registrar before the 14 days' time limit expires. The bundle should contain the following documents:[38] the notice of appeal; the respondent's notice; any supplementary notice;[39] the judgment or order of the court below; the pleadings; the notes of the judge's reasons for judgment; the relevant notes of evidence; any list of exhibits or schedule of evidence; and any relevant affidavits and exhibits as were in evidence in the court below.[40]

The appellant's solicitor is obliged to provide the respondent with a copy of the bundle index and details of any transcripts that have been bespoken, but is under no obligation to provide the respondents with appeal bundles and transcripts.[41] In practice, they are provided to respondents who agree to pay the additional costs incurred.

Length of hearing

A written certified estimate by the appellant's counsel should arrive at the civil appeals office and a photocopy be sent to the respondent's counsel within 14 days, unless extended by the registrar of civil appeals. Counsel have a uniform tendency to underestimate hearing times. A realistic estimate should be given. The respondent's counsel is deemed to have

38 For detailed guidance of the form and content of bundles, see *Practice Direction (Appeals: Documentation)* [1986] 1 WLR 1318 and White Book 1993 para 59/9/14.

39 Given under RSC Ord 59 r7.

40 RSC Ord 59 r9.

41 *Di Salvo v Hughes* (1988) *Times* 16 June.

adopted the appellant's counsel's time estimate unless s/he provides one. The certified estimate must be placed and kept with counsel's papers. Counsel is under a duty to review the time estimate each time s/he advises on or does anything in connection with the appeal.

The appeal can be listed for hearing any time after the period of 14 days, unless extended by the registrar. In practice, the appeal is added to the list of forthcoming appeals well in advance of the anticipated hearing date. Counsel's clerk should keep in touch with the civil appeals office.

Any default in these procedures result in the appeal being listed for the appellant to show cause why it should not be dismissed for failure to comply with RSC Order 59 r9.

Listing in the Court of Appeal

Appeals are divided into three categories: first and second fixtures and those on the short warned list ('SWL cases'). First fixtures usually commence on the day fixed or on the next sitting day. If this cannot be achieved, a fresh date will be fixed. Second fixtures comprise a list of cases which act as floaters to the first list. They are given 'hear by' dates.[42] SWL cases are shorter, relatively straightforward appeals.

The parties' solicitors are notified by letter from the civil appeals office that the case has been assigned to the SWL. If objection is taken, for example, because the case requires more than 48 hours' preparation or because expert witnesses require a fixed date, an application for a fixture should be made to the registrar of civil appeals immediately. Counsel's skeleton arguments must be lodged with the civil appeals office within 14 days of the receipt by the solicitors of that letter. If not, the case is automatically listed for the counsel in default to explain why. If longer than 14 days is required, application should be made to the registrar prior to the expiry of the 14-day period. The solicitor is under a duty to inform counsel immediately that the case has been assigned to the SWL and the date on which the skeleton arguments are due.

When the skeleton arguments have been lodged, the listing office notifies counsel's clerks by telephone of the date from which the SWL case will be 'on call'. It will remain in the SWL, liable to be heard at worst with half a day's notice or at best 48 hours' notice. If substitute counsel requires more than half a day but less than 48 hours to prepare the appeal, the registrar of civil appeals designates that the case requires 48 hours'

42 White Book 1993 para 59/1/13.

notice. If this has not been done, the solicitor should apply to the registrar for the case to be so designated.[43]

Once the case is called on for hearing, counsel instructed is under an immediate personal professional duty to take all practicable measures with a view to ensuring that the lay client is represented by counsel fully instructed and able to argue the appeal. If there is any doubt about availability, s/he should contact his/her instructing solicitor and the brief should be returned and given to a counsel whose availability is certain. The court has the power to make a wasted costs order (see p256) against counsel who has failed in this duty under Supreme Court Act 1981 s51 (as substituted).[44]

Skeleton arguments and other aids to the court

Either a skeleton argument should be prepared or counsel should write to the registrar of civil appeals explaining why one is not necessary. The registrar will then grant a special order.

The purpose of the skeleton argument is to identify points, not expound on them. The facts should be set out very briefly. Points of law should be stated and the authorities cited in support, with references to the particular page(s) where the principle concerned is enunciated. The official law reports should be used unless specialist reports are required. Their need must be explained and photocopies may be attached to the skeleton argument. Only the leading cases should be cited. For questions of fact, the basis on which it is contended that the Court of Appeal may interfere with the findings of the trial judge should be concisely stated, with cross-references to the relevant passages in the transcripts or notes of evidence. These, together with the cited authorities, should be clearly tied in with the grounds of appeal. There must also be a separate chronology.

Unless the registrar of civil appeals orders otherwise, the final deadline is 4pm on the 14th day prior to the fixed date. If the civil appeals office is closed on that day, it is the working day preceding the 14th day. For SWL cases, the operative day is the 14th day following receipt of the letter of notification by the appellant's solicitors (see section on listing, above). Four copies of the skeleton arguments must be lodged with the office, together with a separate document giving the chronology of the case, and one copy sent to each of the opposing counsel by counsel's clerk. If counsel

43 *Practice Note: presentation of appeals* [1990] 2 All ER 318.

44 *Practice Direction (Court of Appeal: Short Warned List)*[1992] 1 WLR 371, as amended by *Practice Direction (Appeals: Short Warned List) (No 2)* [1992] 1 WLR 485.

experiences difficulty in obtaining a copy from the other side, s/he should contact the registrar. It is common to withhold skeletons until the other side is ready to exchange. Supplementary skeleton arguments may be lodged in exceptional circumstances.

Lists of authorities must be lodged with the head usher's office for the Court of Appeal not later than 5.30pm on the working day before the hearing is due to commence. The list should give an accurate description of the law report, statute or other book, together with the page(s) to be referred to.[45] Photocopies of the rarer reports should be made in adequate numbers and given to the usher on the morning of the appeal. It is becoming frequent nowadays for counsel to photocopy all authorities, and provide them to the court in tabulated lever arch files. If so, the usher should be informed that the authorities will be provided in this way.

Dismissal of appeals by consent

Dismissal by consent can be effected without a hearing by sending a signed request for dismissal by consent to the registrar of civil appeals. It must set out the appeal number and names and addresses of the parties and the following words:

We, the solicitors for the above-named appellant [*and respondent*], *who* [*is*] [*are*] *sui juris, hereby request the dismissal of the appeal in the above matter with* [*costs*] [*no order as to costs*] *or* [*specify order as to costs required*].

If the agreement is that either there be no order as to costs or that costs should be less than full taxed costs, the solicitors to all parties must sign or the parties in person, if not represented. The registrar then initials the dismissal by consent, with the effect that the appeal is dismissed.[46]

The hearing

In most cases the court will have read the notice of appeal, any respondent's notice, the judgment, and any skeleton arguments. At the beginning of the hearing, the presiding Lord Justice will usually state what other documents or authorities have also been read. Counsel is notified if any opening is required. Counsel for the appellant is otherwise expected to

45 Ibid and *Practice Direction* [1989] 1 WLR 281; White Book 1993 para 59/9/16. Official Law Reports are expected to be cited rather than specialist: *In Re D (A Minor)* [1992] 1 WLR 315.

46 For settlement on terms, see White Book 1993 para 59/1/15. Once dismissed, there is no jurisdiction to entertain a fresh appeal: *Ogwr BC v Knight and Others* (1994) *Times* 13 January.

proceed immediately to the ground of appeal which is in the forefront of the appellant's case. In citing authorities which have been pre-read, counsel should go to the passage in the judgment where the principle relied on is found. Similarly, counsel should refer to the notes of evidence outlined in the skeleton argument and, so far as possible, avoid reading the evidence at length. In considering quantum, the court will not generally examine the party's physical condition.[47]

Solicitor and counsel are under a duty to warn the client that the procedure may appear shorter than expected but that their case has been just as fully considered. This is an important point. Whereas the full hearing before a county court judge may have been difficult for the client to follow, the Court of Appeal proceedings are totally baffling for most people.

If the appeal is successful, the order for costs of the court below will usually be reversed and costs will include interest, usually from the date of the original judgment.[48]

The Court of Appeal can reverse, or vary in favour of the respondent, any appealable determination of the trial court whether on law or fact. In considering an appeal on a question of fact, the Court of Appeal will not readily differ from the findings of the trial judge.[49] Neither will it readily alter an assessment of quantum, unless the judge proceeded on a wholly erroneous estimate.[50] If the damages awarded by a jury are excessive or inadequate, the Court of Appeal may substitute 'such sum as appears to the court to be proper'.[51]

The court is slow to interfere with a trial judge's findings as between experts[52] and will interfere with an award of contributory negligence in a road traffic case only if the trial judge's assessment is plainly wrong.[53]

Appeals from masters or district registries

To a High Court judge in chambers

This is a complete rehearing, with the appellant opening the appeal. Notice of the appeal must be issued within five days – or seven days in the

47 *Stevens v William Nash Ltd* [1966] 1 WLR 1550.

48 *Kuwait Airways Corporation v Iraqi Airways Company and Another (No 3)* (1994) *Times* 19 February, CA.

49 *Benmax v Austin Motors Co Ltd* [1955] AC 370.

50 *Wilson v Pilley* [1957] 1 WLR 1138.

51 RSC Ord 59 r11(4).

52 *Joyce v Yeomans* [1981] 1 WLR 549.

53 *Hannam v Mann* [1984] RTR 252.

district registries – of the decision or order.[54] The notice must be indorsed with an estimate of the length of hearing. Any alteration to the time estimate must be notified to the listing officer, Judge in Chambers Listing Office (Royal Courts of Justice, room W15), before 12 noon on the day preceding the hearing. It is not necessary to draw up the order appealed from. Time may be extended.[55]

In London

All appeals are initially placed in the general list. Where the appeal is likely to last more than 30 minutes, the parties should apply to have the matter taken out of the general list and put in the chambers appeals list or, if necessary, the expedited list (see below). All applications are published in the daily cause list and the chambers list. Applications remaining in the general list are heard on Tuesdays and Thursdays, returnable at 10.30 am if attended by counsel and not before 12 noon, if not.

Cases in the chambers appeals list are listed in the daily cause list by the clerk of the lists, who prepares the following day's lists at 2 pm. They may be listed on any day of the week, particularly on Fridays when short cases are needed. Fixtures are given in exceptional circumstances. Effort is made to give seven days' notice.

The parties may apply to a judge for an expedited special appointment of an appeal. The application may be made at the hearing of the matter in the general list. The grounds for seeking expedition must be shown. If granted, the parties should immediately apply for a special appointment on an early fixed date to the clerk of the lists.

In advance of the hearing, a bundle must be lodged in room 119. For floaters, this must be not later than 48 hours after notification that the case is in the warned list; for fixtures, not later than five days before the hearing. It must be paginated, in chronological order and indexed. It should contain: the notice of appeal, copies of all affidavits, any pleadings, any relevant order, and in complex cases, a skeleton argument and/or chronology. The originals of affidavits should be 'bespoken' (ordered to be produced from the court office) or produced at the hearing.[56]

Outside London

Judges of the Queen's Bench Division sit in chambers at any court where

54 RSC Ord 58 r3.
55 RSC Ord 3 r5.
56 *Listing Statement (Queen's Bench Judge in Chambers)* (1988) *Independent* 25 November; *Practice Direction of the Lord Chief Justice* [1989] 1 WLR 359; White Book 1993 paras 58/1/2–58/1/6.

sittings of the High Court are held. The matter may be dealt with in the district registry, for example, in order to save costs. The solicitor should enquire of the registry whether the state of business is such that it will permit the matter to be heard there. The matter can be transferred to and from a district registry to London. The notice of appeal should bear the title of the district registry and should be issued in the registry at which the appeal will be heard. Thereafter, the London practice and procedure should be followed.[57]

To the Court of Appeal

In cases where there has been a trial by a master with the consent of the parties[58] or an assessment of damages, an appeal lies direct to the Court of Appeal.[59]

Appeals from a High Court judge in chambers

There is a right of appeal to the Court of Appeal against any order made by a judge in chambers.[60] The majority of orders made in chambers are interlocutory[61] and, therefore, leave to appeal is required either from the judge or from the Court of Appeal (see below). For the practice and procedure see sections on appeals from the county court (above) and appeals from the High Court to the Court of Appeal (below).

Appeals from the High Court

The procedure is, in most respects, the same as for appeals to the Court of Appeal from the county court, (see above) with two important differences.

Leave is generally not required (save, in particular, for interlocutory appeals). The notice of appeal must be served not later than four weeks after the date on which the judgment or order was sealed or otherwise perfected. This differs from the county court, where time runs from the date of judgment or order or when damages are assessed. The appellant from the High Court may serve the notice of appeal before the judgment

57 *Practice Direction (Judge in Chambers: outside London) (no 3)* [1976] 1 WLR 246; White Book 1993 58/1/7.

58 RSC Ord 36 r11.

59 RSC Ord 58 r2(b).

60 Ibid r6.

61 White Book 1991 para 59/1/25.

has been drawn up unsealed. In such a case the seven-day limit for setting down runs from the date on which the judgment or order is sealed.[62]

Second, the transcript of the judgment should be lodged. This is sometimes the official shorthand note or, on other occasions, the judge can hand down a signed copy of a written judgment.[63]

The Court of Appeal has complete discretion as to costs but as a general rule costs follow the event.

A leapfrog appeal from a High Court judge direct to the House of Lords can be made if all the parties consent; or if the House of Lords grants leave; or if the judge grants a certificate. This will only be proper if the case involves a point of law of general public importance.

Appeals from the Court of Appeal

Appeal to the House of Lords lies only with leave of the Court of Appeal or the House of Lords.[64] The application to the Court of Appeal for leave should be made at the hearing of the appeal. If not, the application should be lodged with the registrar of civil appeals. It should include the title of the action, the name of the applicant, the date of the order of the Court of Appeal and a brief statement of the grounds. The written application is referred to the Lord Justices who heard the appeal and an order is drawn up. If further comment is required, the matter is dealt with inter partes in open court. If leave is refused, application may be made to the House of Lords, by petition, within one month from the date on which the order appealed from was made.[65]

Appeals to the House of Lords are permitted only on a point of law of public importance. Thus, personal injury cases go to the House of Lords only where some principle of the law concerned with liability or on the assessment of damages is at issue.[66] Personal injury cases in the House of Lords are, therefore, very rare.

62 Ibid para 59/4/2.

63 *Practice Statement (Court of Appeal: note of judgment under appeal)* (1990) *Times* 12 July.

64 Administration of Justice (Appeals) Act 1934 s1.

65 See further White Book 1993 Vol 2 paras 16–001 to 16–116.

66 When the Court of Appeal has drawn the same inferences from the facts as the tribunal of first instance (whether or not the facts are in dispute), the House of Lords cannot substitute its own inferences unless it can be shown that both courts were plainly wrong: *Hicks v Chief Constable of South Yorkshire* (1992) 1 PIQR 433.

Part IV

Special problems

Introduction

Part IV of the book considers in broad outline a number of specific issues that arise in the course of personal injury litigation. These may be infrequently met by the practitioner who is not a personal injury specialist, but knowledge of these areas is required by the practitioner who does personal injury work to any extent.

CHAPTER 22

Limitation of actions

This chapter outlines the basic information in relation to the time limits for suing in a personal injury action and summarises the relevant provisions of the Limitation Act 1980. For a full treatment of the problems of limitation see Redmond-Cooper, *Limitation of Actions* Sweet & Maxwell 1992.

The time limit

An action is brought on the day when the writ is issued or the action is commenced in the county court.[1] The Limitation Act 1980 provides that, in any action claiming damages for negligence, nuisance or breach of statutory duty which consists of, or includes, a claim for damages in respect of personal injuries to the plaintiff or any other person, the time limit for the issue of proceedings is three years from: the date on which the cause of action accrued,[2] or if later, from the 'date of knowledge' (see below) of the person injured.[3] If the injury was caused by a trespass to the person, the limitation period is six years with no provision for extension.[4] It is crucial to establish the limitation date at the first interview.[5]

If the person injured dies during the three-year period, the cause of action survives for the benefit of his/her estate under the Law Reform (Miscellaneous Provisions) Act 1934 and for his/her dependants under the Fatal Accidents Act 1976 – provided the cause of action has not been otherwise barred (for example, struck out) – for three years from: the date

1 *Deerness v John R Keeble & Son (Brantham) Ltd* [1983] 2 Lloyd's Rep 260.
2 The day of the accident does not count: *Marren v Dawson Bentley & Co Ltd* [1961] 2 QB 135.
3 Limitation Act 1980 s11(4).
4 *Stubbings v Webb* [1993] 2 WLR 120.
5 *Thompson v Brown* [1981] 1 WLR 744; *Donovan v Gwentoys Ltd* [1990] 1 WLR 472.

of death, or the date of the personal representative's or dependant's 'knowledge', whichever is the later. Where the person dies outside the three-year period (and the claim under the Fatal Accidents Act is not otherwise barred), the court may exercise its discretion under Limitation Act 1980 s33 to disapply the limitation period.

The 'date of knowledge' of a person means the date on which s/he first had knowledge of the following: that the injury in question was significant;[6] that the injury was attributable in whole or in part to the act or omission which is alleged to constitute negligence, nuisance or breach of duty; the identity of the defendant;[7] and, if it is alleged that the act or omission was that of a person other than the defendant, the identity of that person and the additional facts supporting the bringing of the action against the defendant. However, knowledge that any acts or omissions did or did not, as a matter of law, involve negligence, nuisance or breach of duty is treated as irrelevant.[8]

An injury is to be regarded as significant if the potential plaintiff would reasonably have considered it sufficiently serious to justify instituting proceedings for damages against a defendant who did not dispute liability and was able to satisfy a judgment.[9] A person is deemed to have knowledge which s/he might reasonably have been expected to acquire, ie, constructive knowledge, from facts observable or ascertainable by him/her; or from facts ascertainable by him/her with the help of medical or other appropriate expert advice which could have been obtained by taking all reasonable steps.[10]

If the writ has to be amended to include new defendants, it has to be served on those defendants within the limitation period, otherwise it will be time-barred.[11]

6 *Stubbings v Webb* [1993] 2 WLR 120; and see also *Broadly v Guy Clapham & Co* (1993) *Times*, 6 July; (1994) 4 MLR 328 as to the extent of knowledge required and the role of medical advice. See also C Lewis, *PMILL* Vol 10 No 3 p23.

7 A little more time may be allowed if the identity of the defendant is not readily available: *Simpson v Norwest Holst Southern Ltd* [1980] 1 WLR 968.

8 Limitation Act 1980 s14(1) and see *Dobbie v Medway HA* (1994) *Times*, 18 May.

9 Ibid s14(2). The test is partly subjective and partly objective: *McCafferty v Metropolitan Police Receiver* [1977] 1 WLR 1073 at 1081. It is not necessary to have sufficient knowledge for a statement of claim to be drafted: *Wilkinson v Ankliffe (BLT) Ltd* [1986] 1 WLR 1352 at 1365.

10 Ibid s14(3). This is an objective test of what the plaintiff ought reasonably to have known, taking into account such matters as the plaintiff's age, background, intelligence and disabilities.

11 *The Kyriaki* [1993] 1 LLR 137.

Beyond the time limit

An action may be brought, without leave of the court, after the expiry of the limitation period. It is up to defendants to raise the limitation defence.[12] Almost invariably they do so. Nevertheless, it is usual not to mention any limitation problem in the particulars or statement of claim but to wait to see if it is raised in the defence and, if so, respond by way of a reply (see chapter 10 p138 and sample pleading at C18 p417).

Persons under a legal disability

Persons regarded as being under a legal disability are exempt from the time limit.[13] A person is treated as under a disability if s/he is an infant or of unsound mind.[14] A person is of unsound mind if s/he is a person who, by reason of mental disorder within the meaning of the Mental Health Act 1983, is incapable of managing or administering his/her property and affairs.[15] It is not necessary for the plaintiff to have been a formal or an informal patient but, if this is the case, s/he is conclusively presumed to be of unsound mind. This is dealt with in more detail in chapter 28 p308.

The three-year period begins to run for such potential plaintiffs only from the age of majority of an infant or, for persons of unsound mind, from the time when s/he becomes capable of managing or administering his/her property and affairs.

If a disability occurs after the cause of action has accrued, it does not interfere with the three-year period.[16] However, the court is directed to have regard to the duration of any such disability in considering disapplication of the time limit.[17]

12 *Dismore v Milton* [1983] 3 All ER 762, CA. See White Book 1993 Vol 1 para 18/8/16, where it is argued that the plaintiff has a duty to plead all facts relating to the date of knowledge in the statement of claim, because of RSC Ord 18 r12(4)(a).

13 *Turner v W H Malcolm Ltd* (1992) *Times* 24 August; (1992) 136 SJ (LB) 236. In exceptional circumstances where under the inherent jurisdiction of the court there is found to be an abuse of the process, a plaintiff who is under a disability can have his or her claim struck out even though the limitation period has not expired: *Hogg v John Hamilton and Northumberland HA* (1992) PIQR 387, CA.

14 Limitation Act 1980 s38(2).

15 Ibid s38(3).

16 *Purnell v Roche* [1927] 2 Ch 142.

17 Limitation Act 1980 s33(3)(d).

Extending the time limit

In personal injury cases, the court has an equitable discretion under Limitation Act 1980 s33 to 'disapply' the limitation period. In considering whether to extend the time limit in this way, the court must have regard to all the circumstances of the case and in particular to: the length of and reasons for delay on the part of the plaintiff; the effect of the delay on the cogency of the evidence; the conduct of the defendant; the duration of any disability arising after the accrual of the cause of action; the extent to which the plaintiff acted promptly and reasonably once s/he knew that negligence had probably been committed; the steps taken by the plaintiff to obtain medical, legal or other expert advice and the nature of any such advice. The onus is on the plaintiff to satisfy the court that the discretion should be exercised to disapply the time limit.

The application to disapply the limitation period can be dealt with at an interlocutory stage by a master or a district judge,[18] or at a preliminary hearing either before or at the trial.[19] In practice, defendants usually apply at an interlocutory stage to stay the action on the ground that it is out of time.[20] The plaintiff should then respond by making an application at the same time to have the limitation period disapplied under s33. This requires a supporting affidavit setting out the facts relied on. Such an application may be made in addition to the prior argument that, on the facts, the limitation period had not actually expired (because, for example, the date of knowledge brings the issue of proceedings within three years). The court is directed to have regard to 'all the circumstances of the case'.[21] It is usually to the plaintiff's advantage to delay such a hearing, at least until discovery has been completed. It is not generally advisable to delay such a hearing until trial, when no costs will be saved and the plaintiff's negotiating position will be weakened by the possibility of losing on limitation, as well as by the usual risks of litigation.

18 RSC Ord 32 r9A.
19 *Buck v English Electric Co Ltd* [1977] 1 WLR 806.
20 White Book 1991 para 18/8/16.
21 *Donovan v Gwentoys Ltd* note 4.

CHAPTER 23

Fatal accidents

Since 1983, running a fatal accident case has been little more complicated than an ordinary personal injury case. Establishing quantum of damages, however, is more complex and its intricacies are thoroughly dealt with in Volume 1, Part II of Kemp and Kemp. The first part of this chapter sets out a brief working summary on both liability and quantum.

Liability

The evidence on liability in fatal cases is gathered in much the same way as in an ordinary case. The difference is that there is usually no evidence from the victim. In some cases, such as those where the victim had a disease, s/he may have consulted the solicitor prior to death. If so, notice will need to be served to admit the deceased's statement or proof into evidence under the Civil Evidence Act 1968 (see p195). This emphasises the vital importance of preparing a full and adequate proof of evidence at the outset of every case and getting the client to correct, date and sign it (see p23).

There is often one additional important source of evidence in fatal cases and that is an inquest (see pp47–8). Where an inquest is held, the solicitor or counsel should attend having given notice to the coroner's officer, both to take the fullest possible note of evidence and to ensure that, as far as possible, the questions helpful to the claim are asked. After the inquest, the coroner's notes should be obtained, as should copies of all statements and photographs. The ground should be laid for obtaining these by personal introduction to the coroner's officer at the inquest.

Other causes of action should be considered. For instance, the survivors may have personal causes of action because they were passengers in the car, or perhaps because they sustained psychological shock and injury by seeing or learning of the deceased's injuries and death, under the principle in *McLoughlin v O'Brian*.[1] Such personal injury claims can be combined with the writ and pleadings for the fatal accident claim. The form of pleading a fatal case is exemplified at C15 p404.

Contributory negligence, of course, applies to fatal cases just as to others.[2] So does the possibility of obtaining interim payments[3]. In cases where children are likely to be the beneficiaries, any settlement must be approved by a master or the judge[4].

In a fatal accident case, the victim's family may require a great deal of care and attention because of the trauma of their loss. In these cases, even more than the ordinary personal injury case, the solicitor must keep in touch throughout the conduct of the litigation.

Damages

For deaths occurring after 1 January 1983 there are two kinds of claim: under the Law Reform (Miscellaneous Provisions) Act 1934, and under the Fatal Accidents Act 1976 (both as amended). (Claims in respect of deaths prior to that date are not considered in this book.)

Law Reform Act

Under the Law Reform (Miscellaneous Provisions) Act 1934, the deceased's estate inherits the deceased's right to sue in respect of the cause of death. Any recovery under the Law Reform Act which duplicates a head of recovery in respect of the same beneficiary under the Fatal Accidents Act 1976 is deducted from it.

Usually the litigation is commenced, after death, in the name of the estate. If the litigation was commenced by a client who dies, it is an easy matter to amend the writ or summons to substitute those acting on behalf of the estate as plaintiffs in place of the deceased[5]. In order to conduct the litigation on behalf of the estate, the executors must obtain probate in the usual way and administrators must obtain letters of administration. The essential facts relating to these matters must be pleaded.

1 [1983] 1 AC 410.
2 Law Reform (Contributory Negligence) Act 1945 s1(1) and Fatal Accidents Act (FAA) 1976 s5.
3 See RSC Order 29 r10 or CCR Order 13 r12. The affidavit in support must give the statutory particulars required by FAA 1976 s2(4).
4 RSC Order 80 r11; CCR Order 10 r10.
5 RSC Order 15 r7; CCR Order 5 r11. The personal representatives should usually make an ex parte application to the master or district judge for an order to continue the litigation.

There are four heads of claim under the Law Reform Act.

First, special damages, ie, loss of earnings of the deceased and damage and loss to property occurring from the date of the cause of action until the date of death.

Second, pain, suffering and loss of amenity sustained by the deceased between the date of the cause of action and death. In the case of immediate death or immediate loss of consciousness followed by death, there will be no or negligible[6] recovery under this head. In some accident cases, the period of suffering prior to death may be relatively short. In disease cases, there may be months or years of increasing incapacity or ill health prior to death.

Third, damages for the deceased's awareness, if any, that his/her life has been shortened.

The final head of damages is for funeral expenses.

Fatal Accidents Act 1976

Under the Fatal Accidents Act, the claim is brought by the dependants of the deceased for loss of support. Dependants include spouses and former spouses, children and parents, persons treated as children and/or as parents, grandparents and grandchildren, and co-habitees of opposite sex who have lived together for more than two years.

The claim under the Fatal Accidents Act is for the following three heads.

a) First there is the value of the dependency (see below);
b) Secondly there are the funeral expenses; and
c) Thirdly damages are recoverable in respect of bereavement sustained by a surviving spouse, the parents of a legitimate child or the mother of an illegitimate child. Bereavement is assessed at £3,500 for causes of action accruing before 1 April 1991. For causes on or after that date, it is £7,500.[7] Bereavement damages are recoverable for the death of each child under 18 years at the time of death.[8] If there is more than one bereaved, the sum is shared. It is arguable that interest at the higher special damages rate is payable on bereavement damages.[9]

6 In *Davies v Hawes*, Kemp & Kemp Vol 3 M2–032, Ogden J awarded £750 for pain and suffering when the deceased did not regain consciousness between accident and death.

7 Damages for Bereavement (Variation of Sum) (England and Wales) Order 1990.

8 *Doleman v Deakin* (1990) *Times* 30 January; (1990) LS Gaz 4 April 43.

9 *Khan v Duncan* (1989) 9 March, unreported, Popplewell J.

Dependency

The dependency in a Fatal Accidents Act case consists of past loss from the date of death to trial and future loss from the date of trial onwards. It is assessed mathematically by establishing a multiplicand and a multiplier, as in an ordinary personal injury case (see chapter 15 pp211–14). The principles specifically in relation to fatal accidents are set out below.

Multiplicands

The multiplicand is the annual value of the dependency. Nowadays this is generally assessed in the ordinary case as two-thirds of annual income for a deceased breadwinner leaving a spouse and no children and as three-quarters for a deceased leaving a spouse and two children.[10] However, these proportions can be and are varied in particular cases displaying particular features, and the plaintiff's lawyers should be alert to exploit variations from these usual situations which may allow a higher proportion of dependency. Another method of checking the value of the dependency is to take the deceased's annual income and deduct from it the 'living expenses' spent exclusively on his/her own maintenance.

The value of the dependency may be greater than the loss of the relevant proportion of the deceased's annual income, since the deceased may have provided services. These services may include do-it-yourself maintenance of the home, maintenance of the car, maintenance of the garden, produce from an allotment, child care, domestic cleaning and so on. The loss of these services needs to be valued commercially for the future, even though some or all may have been provided voluntarily by neighbours or relatives up to trial. The consideration of these costs is similar to that in a non-fatal case, as described in more detail at pp201 and 206.

These various heads of loss, expressed as multiplicands, each require application of an appropriate multiplier.

Multipliers

The multiplier is assessed from the date of death, rather than from the date of trial (thus being different from the ordinary personal injury case). The number of pre-trial years for which special damages are awarded should then be deducted to produce the multiplier for future loss. Damages recoverable for loss attributable to the period between death and trial will bear interest, whereas damages attributable to future loss will not. The approach to multipliers (apart from the fact that they are taken from the date of death rather than the date of accident) is much the same

10 *Harris v Empress Motors Ltd* [1984] 1 WLR 212 at 216.

as in a non-fatal case and this subject is considered more fully at pp213–14.

The multiplier for loss of earnings is usually taken to reflect the deceased's likely years of earning up until the anticipated date of retirement. However, the possibility of further earnings after the date of retirement should be considered, particularly for a deceased who had a job with an early retirement age or a deceased who was fit and had skills easily exercisable after retirement.

A loss or diminution of pension by reason of the accident or ill health, which would have been sustained after retirement by a deceased who died prior to retirement, is recoverable, though the calculation is usually not easy.[11]

The multipliers for the various services provided by the deceased may each have different figures to reflect the fact that the deceased would have been likely to have ceased providing them at different points in his/her life. Precise instructions should be taken about each of these matters to establish the deceased's plans and abilities prior to death.

All these losses necessarily relate to the deceased's age at death. The deceased's life expectancy is the base factor from which each multiplier is established. The basis of computation of the multiplier is described at pp213–14.

The great difficulty in making predictions for the very young or those who had not established themselves in a trade, profession or education is exacerbated because the victim is dead. In such cases, evidence should be sought from school teachers, relatives, employers, authoritative friends (such as religious leaders, scout masters etc) and others who may give worthwhile predictive evidence based on their knowledge of the deceased.

Calculations of future loss of earnings cannot take into account increases in earnings because of inflation[12], but the claim can and should take into account likely increases in real income attributable to promotion or advancement[13]. Again this is made more difficult by the absence of evidence from the deceased. Therefore, investigations should be made of evidence likely to demonstrate that the deceased would have been promoted at various stages. Having established the overall multiplier for lost income, the multiplier can then be divided into separate periods with a separate multiplicand for each, to reflect increased earnings by reason of promotion for each period within the overall multiplier.

Just as different multipliers are taken for different losses sustained by

11 *Auty v National Coal Board* [1985] 1 WLR 784.

12 *Lim Poh Choo v Camden and Islington Health Authority* [1980] AC 174.

13 *Malone v Rowan* [1984] 3 All ER 402.

the dependants, so too different multipliers may be applied where the dependency may change over the years. If the deceased was single at the time of death but was likely to have married and had children, then a reasonable estimate should be made of the dates of those events. Likewise any prospect of divorce should be considered.[14] The overall multiplier should be divided accordingly and applied to the differing rates of dependency throughout those differing periods within the overall multiplier. Likewise, for example, if the dependant is likely to leave home and get a job, the multiplier for that dependant may be reduced to that time scale.

Deductions and apportionment

From the losses sustainable under both the Law Reform Act and the Fatal Accidents Act, no deductions are to be made for money which has accrued, or will or may accrue, to any person from his/her estate as a result of death.[15] Therefore, any beneficial pensions or insurance money received as a consequence of the death are not deductible.[16]

Where an award is made to a surviving adult and to children, it must be apportioned. There are no rules of apportionment except that most of the damages is generally paid to the surviving parent. This is done on the basis that the parent will use it to look after the children, and little is given to each of the children, though the younger will be given more than the elder because their expectation of life is greater. Examples of apportionment from decided authorities may be found in Kemp and Kemp Vol 1, chapter 23. A worked example of a fatal accident schedule of damages is given at C24 p432 to demonstrate some of these principles.

14 *Martin v Owen* (1992) *Times* 21 May.
15 Administration of Justice Act 1982 s2.
16 Fatal Accidents Act 1976 s4; *Wood v Bentall Simplex Ltd* (1992) *Times* 3 March; (1992) PIQR 332; and *Stanley v Saddique* [1992] 1 QB 1 at 10.

CHAPTER 24

Disease cases

There is no fundamental difference between a personal injury case which results in a traumatic injury and one which results in a disease. However, many diseases are the result of prolonged exposure to some hazard. Such prolonged exposure is usually found in the work environment, but more and more cases are being taken on behalf of clients made ill by their living environment which has been polluted by some nearby enterprise.

Where the disease is the result of momentary exposure, the case is really no different to run than an ordinary accident case, except that specialised expertise may need to be brought in to prove causation, if there is room for doubt as to the nature of the disease and its attribution to the incident. See p126 on pleading disease cases.

Prolonged exposure

The real problems in disease work arise in prolonged exposure cases. Such cases are complicated and should not be undertaken lightly by an inexperienced practitioner. Evidence to support the plaintiff about the conditions which it is alleged gave rise to the illness many years before may be difficult to obtain. The system of work which involved the causative exposure may have been commonplace at the time. There may be problems over limitation with arguments over the 'date of knowledge' (see p282), and the court's discretion under Limitation Act 1980 s33 (see pp283–4) may have to be relied on. Causation may be difficult where the client is an employee who worked for a number of employers in the same trade and was exposed by each to the factors giving rise to the disease, or if a number of factors apart from the work (or other) environment may arguably be causative of the disease or of its symptoms (eg, lung disease to which smoking may have contributed).

Experts are needed to demonstrate safe systems of work and to establish the level of knowledge of a hazard arising from the system which was available to the employer (or polluter) at various periods of time. Expert medical evidence is required to show that the disease was caused by the exposure. Some diseases are notoriously difficult to demonstrate in a living patient, particularly where the condition may be overlaid by other conditions (eg, asbestosis or pneumoconiosis, particularly if overlaid by emphysema). One client complaining of a progressive disease caused by exposure to some hazard often indicates that there may be other victims and the solicitor should investigate this.

A detailed examination of this subject is beyond the scope of this chapter, but examples of such diseases are: leukaemia from living near nuclear installations; heavy metal poisoning from eating fish or drinking water polluted by escapes from toxic waste treatment plants or dumps; noise-induced deafness from working near machines; asthma and welder's lung from welding operations; pneumoconiosis from mining in silica-bearing rocks or working in iron and steel foundries which use silica sand for mouldings; work-related upper limb disorders in journalists, secretaries and other operators of word processors and in chicken trussers; dermatitis in woodworkers and others; and headaches and constipation in workers with solvents.

Collecting evidence

It is essential to draw on the huge body of knowledge and expertise which has been built up on many industrial diseases themselves, the processes which give rise to them, and the means by which their incidence can be avoided or minimised. Contact should be made initially with the Association of Personal Injury Lawyers (see p473 for address).

The first step is to establish a full history of the client's exposure to the causative hazard. There must be a complete chronology of his/her working history, showing the nature of the work, the place of work, the name and address of the employer(s), the names and addresses of any potential witnesses, and a full description of the work undertaken by the plaintiff and others. The chemicals, dust, fumes and processes giving rise to the hazard must be described in detail. The duration and intensity of exposure must be examined. The manufacturer of machines and substances should be identified as far as possible.

All warnings given by all possible defendants and all instructions, advice and information must be fully particularised, the giver of each identified and the absence of such warnings and information noted. The presence or absence of pre-exposure tests for susceptibility must be investigated. Demonstrations, training, or other guidance on how to perform the work safely must be explored. Advice (or lack of it) about what to do if symptoms occurred must be considered. All possible forms of protection, by containing the hazard and/or the plaintiff, need to be investigated. After advice from experts, this is one area which is likely to require further investigation when the solicitor is fully appraised of the safety measures available to a reasonable defendant. The attitude of the defendant to health and safety matters should be dealt with in detail. All relevant complaints must be logged and complainants identified. All previous occurrences of contraction of the disease must likewise be explored. General practitioner and hospital records for the client must be obtained and his/her consent for this given immediately. All available literature must be gathered by the solicitor, particularly from the Health and Safety Executive.

Discovery in such cases must be pursued rigorously. This concerns not only substances, machines and systems but also the defendant's potential sources of prior knowledge. Records should be obtained from the Department of Health and discovery sought from the Health and Safety Executive. The relevant experts, both on the conditions giving rise to the contraction of the disease and on the disease in the plaintiff, must be instructed early and their advice sought on other steps and investigations which the solicitor should carry out.

In recent years, schemes of no-fault compensation have been established which pay out on a fixed tariff. The schemes apply to the workers (and former workers) in particular industries who have contracted particular diseases. It is necessary to prove only the existence of the disease or disability. Some schemes include a loss of earnings element, others are restricted to a one-off lump sum. There is, for example, a pneumoconiosis scheme for former mine workers agreed between British Coal and the mining unions, which also covers some other lung diseases, such as asbestosis in such workers. There is a deafness scheme for those who worked in the engineering and shipbuilding industries which was negotiated by the Iron Trades Insurance Companies and Messrs Robin Thompson & Partners. (There are other schemes for other diseases and trades.) Solicitors concerned with industrial diseases need to be familiar with these schemes (which are outside the scope of this book). They must weigh up with the client whether, bearing in mind the level of disability, the strength of the case on causation, and the prospects of proving negligence or breach of statutory duty, it is more beneficial to claim under the relevant scheme or pursue a claim for damages.

CHAPTER 25

Liability for products and premises

Product liability

The principles of litigation for injuries caused by defective products are the same as for other personal injury cases. However, the defendants and the causes of action are difficult and require a brief consideration. This chapter contains a summary of the legal provisions affecting liability for defective products. Since this book does not deal with medical negligence, there is no discussion of special statutory provisions dealing with liability for medical products.

Breach of contract and negligence

An action may be brought by the buyer of defective goods against the seller. Express terms of the contract are unlikely to be helpful and so statute has implied terms: the Sale of Goods Act 1979 governs products supplied for money and the Supply of Goods and Services Act 1982 applies to services. In both statutes, the implied terms are the same.[1] The goods have to be of merchantable quality, unless the seller or supplier has indicated a specific defect or the purchaser has examined the goods and the defect should have been discovered. Liability is strict.[2] The Sale of Goods Act 1979 s14(3) provides that goods must also be reasonably fit for the purpose for which they are bought. The Unfair Contract Terms Act 1977 ss6(1) and 7(3A) prevent a retailer who sells to a consumer from excluding liability under the 1979 and 1982 Acts.

In spite of the contractual provisions, negligence remains the principal means of recovering compensation for injury sustained from defective

1 Sale of Goods Act 1979 s14 and Supply of Goods and Services Act 1982 s4.
2 Sale of Goods Act 1979 s14(2), Supply of Goods and Services Act 1982 s4(2) and Supply of Goods (Implied Terms) Act 1973 s10 (hire purchase agreements).

products. The principles are stated in *Donoghue v Stevenson*[3] – the snail in the ginger beer bottle case, known to all law students. The law here is so extensive, well known and thoroughly dealt with in other textbooks that the application of the law of negligence to product liability cases will not be dealt with here.

Consumer Protection Act 1987

The much newer principles to be found in the Consumer Protection Act 1987 do, however, require consideration. (See p120 for pleading the Act.)

Products or produce made after 1 March 1988 are now subject to the provisions of the Consumer Protection Act 1987, introduced following the European Product Liability Directive[4]. The Act does not apply to agricultural produce or game that has not undergone an industrial process. Part I of the statute provides a cause of action in personal injury claims. The Act must be construed to comply with the directive, but the directive has no effect on common law liability or other statutory provisions.

The Act creates liability for producers of goods causing 'damage', ie, death, personal injury or any loss of or damage to any property, including land. The minimum damages that can be claimed are £275. The damage is regarded as having occurred at the earliest time at which a person with an interest in the property had knowledge of the material facts about the loss or damage. The three-year limitation period for personal injury and damage to property can be extended under the Limitation Act 1980, with a 15-year maximum – irrespective of the date of knowledge.[5] The remaining part of this section explains the main provisions of the Act.

Where damage is caused, wholly or partly by a defective product, the following persons may be liable without proof of negligence and if two or more are involved they will share liability jointly and severally: the producers of the product; any persons who, by putting their name on the product or using a trade mark or other distinguishing mark in relation to the product, have held themselves out to be the producers of that product; and any persons who have imported the product into an EC member state in order to supply it to another in the course of business.[6]

The supplier of the product is liable for the fatality or injury if the following action has been taken. First, the person who suffered the injury has requested the supplier to identify one or more of the above persons

3 [1932] AC 562, HL.
4 85/374/EEC.
5 Limitation Act 1980 s11A.
6 Consumer Protection Act 1987 s2(2).

(whether they are still in existence or not). Second, that request has been made within a reasonable period after the incident occurred and at a time when it was not reasonably practicable for the injured person to identify all those persons. Third, the supplier has failed, within a reasonable period after receiving the request, either to comply with the request or to identify the person who supplied the product.[7]

A product is defective if the safety of the product is not such as 'persons generally are entitled to expect'.[8] This includes the safety of products comprised in that product. It extends to protect against risks of damage to property, as well as risks of death or personal injury.

What 'persons generally are entitled to expect' depends on the circumstances of each case and involves consideration of: the manner in which, and the purposes for which, the product has been marketed, its get-up, the use of any mark in relation to the product and any instructions for, or warnings with respect to, doing or refraining from doing anything with or in relation to the product; what might reasonably be expected to be done with, or in relation to, the product (this includes misuse to which the product may be put); and the time when the product was supplied by its producer to a customer.

Section 4 provides certain statutory defences. The onus of proof is on the defendant to show:

(a) that the defect is attributable to compliance with any requirement imposed by or under any enactment or with any Community obligation; or

(b) that the defendant did not at any time supply the product to another; or

(c) that the following conditions are satisfied, that is to say:

(i) the only supply of the product to another by the defendant was otherwise than in the course of a business of that person; and

(ii) that section 2(2) above does not apply to that person, or applies to him by virtue only of things done otherwise than with a view to profit; or

(d) that the defect did not exist in the product at the relevant time; or

(e) that the state of scientific and technical knowledge at the relevant time was not such that a producer of products of the same description as the product in question might be expected to have discovered the defect if it had existed in his products while they were under his control; or

(f) that the defect:

(i) constituted a defect in a product ('the subsequent product') in which the product in question had been comprised; and

7 Ibid s2(3).
8 Ibid s3(1).

(ii) was wholly attributable to the design of the subsequent product or to compliance by the producer of the product in question with instructions given by the producer of the subsequent product.

Damages will not be awarded for injury or fatalities caused by property not ordinarily intended for private use, occupation or consumption, or property not intended by the injured or deceased person to be for his/her own private use, occupation or consumption.[9] Private use is not defined, but this Act is of little benefit for accidents at work, in respect of which the Employer's Liability (Defective Equipment) Act 1969 is relevant.

Employer's Liability (Defective Equipment) Act 1969

Employers are liable for personal injuries sustained by their employees in the course of their employment, caused by defective equipment. The latter must be provided by the employer (including public authorities), for the purposes of the employer's business. The defect must be attributable, wholly or partly, to the fault of a third party, whether identified or not. If all these elements are proved or admitted, the employer is liable, regardless of fault. Equipment has been defined to include any plant and machinery, vehicle, aircraft and clothing. It has also been held to include a ship[10] and a flagstone.[11] The equipment must be defective, not just unsuitable or inadequate. For example, soap provided at work that was materially more of an irritant than other soaps and caused dermatitis was held to be defective.[12] See pp120 and 137 on pleading the Act.

Liability for defective premises

People injured by the defective state of premises may have an action in negligence. They may also sue under the Factories Act 1961 or one of the other statutes or regulations which apply to accidents at work.

The Occupiers' Liability Act 1957 may also assist (see p120 on pleading it). Liability arises to lawful visitors, who may be invitees or licensees under s1(2) of the Act, persons entering premises under contractual rights under s5(1) (eg, workmen), or persons entering under general legal rights, rather than by personal or implied permission of the occupier, under s2(6) (eg, firefighters). The question, 'who is the occupier?', so as to determine the proper defendant, is not always easy to

9 Consumer Protection Act 1987 s5(3).
10 *Coltman v Bibby Tankers Ltd, The Derbyshire* [1988] AC 276.
11 *Knowles v Liverpool City Council* (1994) PIQR 8, HL.
12 *Ralston v Greater Glasgow Health Board* [1987] SLT 386.

answer. The 'control test' is helpful but not always conclusive. In each case, an occupier must be entitled to control at least part of the premises, and must have done something by way of control or established a right of control. There may be more than one occupier of premises at any one time.

The occupier of premises owes the common duty of care to all visitors.[13] That is such 'as in all the circumstances of the case is reasonable to see that the visitor will be reasonably safe in using the premises for the purposes for which he is invited or permitted . . . to be there'.[14] The character of the visitor in question is relevant to the standard of care owed to him/her.[15] Thus, a child or blind person requires a greater standard of care. Under the Occupiers' Liability Act 1984, an occupier has a duty of care, reasonable in all the circumstances, to protect anyone whom the occupier has reasonable grounds to believe may come into the vicinity of a danger on the premises.

In addition to the 1957 Act, there is the Defective Premises Act 1972 (see p120 on pleading it). This Act imposes a duty on, among others, architects and engineers who undertake work for, or in connection with, the provision of a dwelling, to carry out their work in a professional manner so that the house is fit for habitation.[16] The Act does not apply to houses constructed under the National House Building Council scheme. The limitation period is six years from the time when the building is completed, unless further work is carried out later.[17]

Liability in nuisance and under the principle of *Rylands v Fletcher*[18] should also be considered in relevant cases. The reader is referred to the standard textbooks on these subjects.

13 Occupiers' Liability Act 1957 s2(1).
14 Ibid s2(2).
15 Ibid s2(3).
16 Defective Premises Act 1972 s1(1).
17 Ibid s1(5).
18 (1868) LR 3–4 HL 330.

CHAPTER 26

Motor drivers and owners

Road traffic accidents are familiar and frequent sources of personal injury litigation. This chapter briefly describes compensation payable by drivers and owners of vehicles involved in such accidents. See p114 on pleading such cases.

The Road Traffic Act 1988 s143 requires the drivers of motor vehicles to be insured against their liability to third parties and the owner of a vehicle is liable if s/he causes or permits a driver to drive the vehicle without insurance against third party risks.[1] Problems arise sometimes in spite of these laws. These may be where: the insured's insurance company denies liability under the policy or security (for example, a cover note); the driver was not insured; the driver cannot be traced; or the insured's insurance company is in liquidation (see pp92–4). These situations are dealt with below.[2]

Investigating the insurance

The solicitor must first try to find out if the defendant driver was covered by an insurance policy or security. Where the police have been involved, they may have served a form HORT 1 which requires, among other things, the production of the driver's insurance details. This information should be obtained from the police. The Road Traffic Act 1988 s154 requires drivers to give particulars of their insurance certificate or security if required. If there is no certificate, the driver must include the name of the insurer, the policy number, the vehicle covered and the period of cover. It is an offence to fail to comply with such a request or to give a false reply without reasonable excuse. If the driver was not insured, or liability is not covered by the terms of the policy, or the person will not give this

1 *Monk v Warbey* [1935] 1 KB 75.
2 More detailed consideration can be found in *Bingham's Motor Claims Cases* 10th edn.

information, the solicitor should contact the Motor Insurers Bureau (MIB).

Suing an insured driver

Once it is established that the driver had an insurance policy in existence, the solicitor must give notice to the insurance company within seven days following the commencement of proceedings against the driver. The solicitor should then proceed with the action against the driver in the usual way.

Refusal to pay by insurers

If the insurers refuse to pay any damages awarded against a driver who appears to be insured by them, proceedings may then be brought directly against the insurance company under the Road Traffic Act 1988 s151 for recovery of the judgment debt. This requires:[3] the appropriate notice to have been given; that the judgment is in relation to damage covered by compulsory insurance under the Road Traffic Act 1988 s145, ie, death or bodily injury to the third party; that liability is covered by the terms of the policy or security; that the policy has not been validly cancelled; that the claim is for less than £250,000; and that the insurance company has not obtained a declaration of entitlement to avoid. It is of course only in small cases that it would be advantageous to enforce judgment against the driver personally, rather than pursue the insurers.

Motor Insurers Bureau

All authorised insurers are required to be members of the MIB. The bureau is not itself an insurance company and exists to compensate persons who have been injured by uninsured drivers (the first agreement), untraced drivers (the second agreement), or foreign motorists visiting Britain, or where the insured's insurance company has become insolvent.

Uninsured drivers

Where the negligent driver was uninsured or the identity of the insurer cannot be ascertained, notice of bringing proceedings must be given to the

3 The insurance company has to plead the absence of notice as a defence: *Baker v Provident Accident and White Cross Insurance Co Ltd* [1939] 2 All ER 690.

MIB by a 'section 151 notice' (under the Road Traffic Act 1988 s151), within seven days following the commencement of proceedings. For this reason, and because of delays in postal service and the county court, it is better to issue and serve in person in an uninsured driver case, as the MIB is strict and will refuse to accept proceedings if the 'section 151 notice' is not served within the time-limits. Proof of service is therefore crucial.[4] If the driver had some form of contract of insurance with an identified insurance company, the notice is served on the insurer.[5]

The notice must be accompanied by a copy of the writ or summons. The plaintiff should issue and serve the summons by post and send a copy to the MIB.[6] Otherwise, the court will not be able to return a copy within seven days. The MIB accepts service by fax.

An injured party, or the estate of a deceased party, (but not a knowingly uninsured passenger)[7] will be compensated by the MIB where a judgment has been obtained in the United Kingdom for damages, costs and interest, resulting from a road traffic accident. Thus, damages for pain, suffering and loss of amenity are recoverable, as are damages for lost employment. Property claims for over £175 may be recoverable.

Where an insurance contract exists, the insurer concerned will usually act as agent for the MIB. If no policy exists, the bureau may appoint an insurance company to act as agent. The MIB may waive the requirement of obtaining judgment. Interim payments cannot be obtained against the MIB.[8] If the MIB disputes its liability under this agreement, it can be joined as a party to proceedings.[9]

Untraced motorists

Where the problem is that the negligent driver cannot be traced, so his/her insurers cannot be discovered, an application[10] to the MIB must be made in writing within three years from the date of the event giving rise to the death or injury. The MIB will nominate an insurance company to handle the case. Payment is made for fatality or bodily injury to any person caused by, or arising out of the use of, a motor vehicle on a road in Great

4 *Stinton v Stinton and MIB* (1993) PIQR 135.
5 First agreement para 5(1)(a).
6 CCR Ord 3 r3(1A) and Ord 7 r10A. See p473 for address.
7 *Stinton v Stinton* (1992) *Times* 5 August.
8 *Powney v Coxage* (1988) *Times* 8 March.
9 The MIB has not taken the point of privity of contract and this has received judicial acknowledgement: *Albert v Motor Insurers Bureau* [1972] AC 301, per Lord Donovan.
10 Under schedule 2 to the agreement.

Britain.[11] It has to be shown that, on the balance of probabilities, the untraced driver was responsible. The applicant must assist the MIB as reasonably required in carrying out its investigation. An appeal may be made against the decision of the MIB, provided that the applicant gives notice within six months from the date of receipt of the notice of decision. Under the MIB agreement, the MIB cannot be sued in disputes over such claims.[12] Nonetheless the injured person is well advised to appoint an experienced personal injury solicitor to look after his or her interest. As always the insurance company will be looking to escape as cheaply as possible. The claim needs to be maximised and tough negotiations may be involved.

Foreign motorists

Where someone has been killed or injured by a foreign motorist in the United Kingdom, the driver's name, registration number of the vehicle, and details of the green card should be given to the MIB as soon as practicable. The bureau will deal with the claim and proceed against the foreign insurance company.

Claims against a motorist who is a member of a visiting foreign military force should be made to the Ministry of Defence.[13]

11 Second agreement para 1(1)(c).
12 *Persson v London Country Buses* [1974] 1 WLR 569.
13 Visiting Forces Act 1952 s9(2); and see *Littrell v USA* (1993) *Times*, 24 November.

CHAPTER 27

Multi-party or group actions

Increasingly there are circumstances where a number of potential plaintiffs are affected by the same tragedy. Often many have different solicitors. Common situations involve drugs with damaging side-effects, rail, air or maritime disasters, and environmental pollution cases. In such instances, a plaintiff's solicitor should seek the help of the disaster co-ordination service of the Law Society.[1] It is not within the scope of this book to review in detail the existing procedures for group actions. A very useful guide to the procedures is the *Guide for Use in Group Actions* (see bibliography p474). The authors consider that the relatively minor changes to the system made to accomodate group actions have proved largely inadequate to protect the interests of the increasing number of members of the public injured by these tragedies.

The Legal Aid Board designates one area office to handle all legal aid applications concerning a particular product or disaster, if the potential number of legal aid applications makes it appropriate. For less obvious cases, this is often the first indication that the solicitor may have that the case is a potential group action, though notices of group actions are regularly placed in the *Law Society's Gazette*.

Steering committee

The Law Society's co-ordination service registers enquiries by solicitors and potential plaintiffs and sets up an initial meeting of solicitors. This meeting is advertised in the *Gazette* and appoints a steering committee for the litigation, including a chair, secretary, press officer, and a liaison officer (to deal with foreign countries, if plaintiffs or defendants or courts concerned are abroad). An attempt is made, in setting the size of the committee and the firms appointed to it, to reflect matters such as

1 Information Co-ordinator, The Law Society, 50–52 Chancery Lane, London WC2A 1SX. See p473 for telephone and fax nos.

numbers of clients represented, expertise in handling this sort of case, regional presence, and so on. Firms rather than individuals are appointed to the committee, to allow substitution and continuity. Payment is on the usual time basis.

The steering committee undertakes much work and is responsible usually for generic research, discovery, liaison with experts, conducting party and party correspondence, conducting negotiations to establish the principles of settlement and, most important, co-ordination of the group.

Regular meetings are held. Where there are more solicitors than are practicable to form a steering committee, a smaller group is elected from all the solicitors involved. Those with the greatest number of clients are the most likely to be elected. All this is invariably done by agreement. If problems arise, the matter can be referred to the judge allocated to the case (see below).

The committee appoints lead solicitor(s) (or a group administrator) to handle the essential preparatory and interlocutory work, referring decision-making back to the committee or group, and reporting to all solicitors by way of bulletins at every step. By the same token, each solicitor for a registered plaintiff must inform the steering committee of each step that is taken and send copies of all pleadings and documents. Counsel, or a team of counsel, is usually instructed by the steering committee.

The inexperienced practitioner will be greatly assisted in the conduct of the case by participation in the group. Indeed, such a grouping is not merely useful, it may be vital. It allows the solicitors to pool information and witnesses (especially expensive experts), to share the costs and to prevent defendants picking off plaintiffs one by one. Second, the grouping gives the solicitors a combined influence much greater than the sum of the parts. This is particularly important when it comes to dealing with powerful multinational corporations or seeking changes in the law. A co-ordinated grouping can also better handle the press, use of which may well be a powerful weapon in achieving satisfactory settlement. The defendants in such cases are very sensitive to adverse publicity, since they need to advertise to customers the safety of their operations. A well-organised solicitors' committee can exert formidable pressure, particularly media pressure, and often obtain a speedy settlement of the claims at levels much higher than the damages which might have been obtained otherwise.

Court procedure

The High Court has now recognised the use of solicitors' committees and they have been used in cases since the Opren litigation in the mid-1980s, although the procedure has not yet found a place in the White Book. Group actions are usually retained in the High Court. This is because the value of an action is defined to include the value of all the claims in an action, whether multiple claims of one plaintiff or the aggregate of the claims of several plaintiffs. Therefore, many group actions begun on behalf of many plaintiffs for quite small individual claims are properly begun in the High Court, without the need for an application for transfer from the county court.[2] Where it is not possible to join all the plaintiffs on the same writ, because for example, their identity and number are unkown, and the value of the individual claims is less than £50,000, proceedings must be commenced in the county court. Separate arrangements will then be required for transfer to the High Court.

On application to the senior master, a High Court judge is usually allocated to the case, to deal with all interlocutory matters as well as the trial. Directions are given by the judge on a summons to which is attached a schedule setting out the multiplicity of orders sought (some of which may be agreed).

The judge usually orders the solicitors' steering committee to prepare a register of plaintiffs so that the defendants know who is claiming against them. S/he may set a date after which no claim can be brought, unless the latecomer is within the primary limitation period. Failure to complete the registration form may result in exclusion. Provision will be made for the sharing among the solicitors of costs common to all plaintiffs who are or who become registered ('generic costs'), so that the first plaintiffs to come to trial do not run the risk of bearing all these costs if they lose.[3] A successful plaintiff, on an interlocutory application is entitled to all the costs for the application and not a proportion.[4] 'Master' statements of claim are provided for, so that the shorter individual statements of claim can be drafted by incorporating such allegations from the master statement of claim as may be relevant in the shorter individual case. Likewise, a master defence may be permitted, with individual defences to each claim.

Orders giving the time for service of pleadings, documents, lists and the like will be given, but the periods are usually significantly longer than in the ordinary personal injury case. If a 'cut-off' date is imposed, it

2 High Court and County Courts Jurisdiction Order 1991 art 9(1)(c) and (3).
3 *Davies v Eli Lilly & Co* [1987] 1 WLR 1136.
4 *Nash v Eli Lilly* [1992] 3 Med LR 353.

simply bars claimants from taking part in the group litigation. It does not destroy the claim in itself.[5] The statement of claim may require certain documents to be served with it, eg, medical reports, authority for the defendants to obtain the plaintiffs' medical records and so on. All plaintiffs may be ordered to submit to a reasonable medical examination by the defendants.

Where a registered plaintiff takes a settlement or payment in to court, s/he must pay to the steering committee the element of costs which represents the generic costs, to be held pending the outcome of the litigation and the payment of further generic costs.

To avoid increasing individual costs and thus strengthening the defendants' bargaining position, experience suggests it is very important to obtain a direction at an early stage, perhaps when the group action order is made, for the generic issues to be defined and tried before any individual cases.

Legal aid

The Legal Aid Board has set up a multi-party action committee, to oversee the running of multi-party actions. The committee was set up in 1992 and by the end of 1993 had only taken two actions under its wing. The key feature of this arrangement is that where 10 or more certificates in one action are issued, the Legal Aid Board notifies the committee and a decision is made as to whether the claim will come under the committee's remit. Where this is the case the committee invites tenders. Applicant solicitors have to set out the background to the claims, the firm's systems, their own expertise in the field, and their charging arrangements.

The committee will determine (on the basis of the tenders and interviews) which firm(s) should get a contract to undertake the general work on the case.

Legal aid in group actions is a subject too complex for this book and is beset with difficulties.[6] Reference should also be made to the current edition of the *Legal Aid Handbook*.

5 *A, B and Others v John Wyeth & Brother Ltd* (1992) *Times* 20 October.

6 See, eg, *A, B and Others v John Wyeth and Brother Ltd (No 2)* (1993) *Times*, 1 December, where the Court of Appeal upheld the striking out of benzodiazepam cases on the basis that they were vexatious and an abuse of process, because the irrecoverable costs incurred (and likely to be incurred) by the prescribing doctors, who were also being sued, were out of all proportion to the possible benefits to the plaintiffs from the litigation.

CHAPTER 28

Persons under a legal disability

People who do not have full legal capacity include all young people under the age of 18 (infants) or persons of unsound mind.[1] A person is of unsound mind if s/he, by reason of his or her mental disorder,[2] is incapable of managing and administering his or her property and affairs.[3] This is essentially a medical question of fact on which the plaintiff has the burden of proof.

However, a person is conclusively presumed to be of unsound mind in two specific situations.

Firstly, the presumption of unsound mind operates while s/he is liable to be detained (ie, detained compulsorily) or subject to a guardianship order under the Mental Health Act 1983 (otherwise than by virtue of ss35 or 89).

Secondly, the presumption operates while s/he is receiving treatment as an in-patient voluntarily, (ie, not 'sectioned') in any hospital within the meaning of the Mental Health Act 1983 or in a mental nursing home within the meaning of the Nursing Homes Act 1975. This means undergoing treatment without being liable to be detained under the 1983 Act (otherwise than by virtue of ss35 and 89), being treatment which follows without any interval during which s/he was liable to be detained or subject to guardianship under legislation prior to or under the Mental Health Acts 1959 and 1983.[4]

RSC Order 80 r1 is equally convoluted because it defines a person under a disability as a 'patient'. It defines a patient as someone who is 'incapable of managing and administering his property and affairs'. It is important to note that a patient need not be a patient in a hospital.

1 Limitation Act 1980 s38(2).
2 As defined by Mental Health Act 1983 s1.
3 Limitation Act 1980 s38(3) as amended.
4 Limitation Act 1980 s38(4). For a useful article see Gordon R Ashton, 'Mental Incapacity and Civil Justice': *Law Society's Gazette* 28 April 1993 p18.

Neither need the patient be under the care of the Court of Protection (although the test is the same as for receivership).

If a person was under a disability on the day that the right of action accrued, then time does not begin to run and the person can bring proceedings up to 6 years from the date when s/he ceases to be under a disability.[5]

If civil proceedings are contemplated on behalf of a patient against persons such as nurses and doctors for acts done in pursuance of the Mental Health Act 1983, leave is required under s139 of the Act. The application should be made to a judge in chambers supported by an affidavit.[6]

Proceedings may not be brought by persons under a legal disability except under the aegis of their 'next friend'. This is usually the person's parent, but may be any adult willing to act. There must be no conflict of interest. The next friend may be substituted by an order of the court. If proceedings have been commenced and the plaintiff becomes a patient, an application must be made by a solicitor to the court for the appointment of a person to be next friend.[7] The object of having a next friend is to give security for the costs to the defendant and to make up for the lack of capacity and judgment in the conduct of the litigation.

Legal aid is now available for infants, whose own resources and income are assessed, rather than that of their parents.[8] Legal aid is available for patients in the same way as for all other adults but is granted to the next friend.

Principles

Issuing proceedings

The next friend must signify consent and undertake to pay costs, in a standard form, and the plaintiff's solicitor must certify that the next friend has no conflict of interest with the patient, again in standard form, before the court allows an infant's or patient's case to commence. An example of a statement of claim is at C11 p394.

5 Limitation Act 1980 s28(1) and *Turner v W H Malcolm and Another* (1992) *Times* 24 August; (1992) 136 SJ (LB) 236, CA, where it was decided that a brain-injured plaintiff could not have his writ struck out for delay.

6 RSC Ord 32 r9(1)(b). This rule does not apply to health authorities, NHS trusts or informal patients: *R v Runighan* [1977] Crim LR 361.

7 RSC Ord 80 r3(5).

8 Civil Legal Aid (Assessment of Resources) (Amendment) Regs 1990 reg 4(2).

Statutory limitations

One important difference in an infant's case is that the statutory limitation period begins only when the child reaches the age of 18. For example, a child who has an accident on its eleventh birthday has 10 years from that date within which to commence proceedings. The limitation period is also extended during the period when the patient is of 'unsound mind'[9] (see also chapter 22 p281).

Payments into court

Leave is required to accept a payment into court if the plaintiff is under a disability.[10]

Settlements

No infant's or patient's case, no matter how small, may be settled without the authority of a court order.[11] Any settlement negotiated on a child's behalf must, to obtain legal protection, be sanctioned by the court. Therefore, in a case where no settlement is agreed but proceedings have begun, an originating infant settlement summons should be issued and an application to the master should be made to determine whether the negotiated figure is reasonable. If proceedings have already been issued, a summons for an infant settlement should be issued either before the circuit or district judge in the county court or the High Court master. If the settlement or compromise is agreed at or during the trial, it is made to the trial judge.

Practice and procedure

In the High Court, applications for approval are made to masters and appointments are made in their own private rooms. If the application is to the judge, the matter is heard in chambers. The procedure is paralleled in the county court. As the master may prefer to hear the facts of the case and the evidence before being informed of the terms of the compromise, the amount must not be stated on the summons. At the hearing, the plaintiff's solicitor should have: the summons; a copy of CFO form 320, completed on the first side; a copy of the infant's birth certificate; any pleadings; if

9 Limitation Act 1980 s28.
10 CCR 1981 Ord 10 r10(1); RSC Ord 80 r10(1).
11 Ibid.

liability is disputed, evidence relating to liability; medical reports; schedule of damages and supporting documentation; consent of the next friend; and the approval of the settlement by the next friend.

If liability is in dispute,[12] the master must be told the extent to which this can be established by evidence. Where counsel has advised, the opinion may be shown to the master, as may police reports, memoranda of convictions, accident reports, witness statements and so on, ie, all the available material to establish liability (see below).

When considering quantum, the master should be shown the medical evidence dealing with pain, suffering and loss of amenity. Infant plaintiffs or patients usually need not attend but, if cosmetic injuries are sustained or if the case is complex, the master may require their attendance. Plaintiffs who are not infants or patients should attend if they possibly can, as should the next friend in all cases. The reports should be up to date, as if at trial.

The test applied is whether the settlement is a reasonable one and for the benefit of the infant or patient, having regard to all the circumstances of the case. The district judge or master will place weight on counsel's opinion and will wish to be assured that counsel has seen the plaintiff and next friend in conference and considered any visible injuries or disability. If the master is not satisfied, the summons may be adjourned to give the parties further opportunity to negotiate.

If the settlement is approved, the order[13] directs by and to whom and in what amounts the money is to be paid and how the money is to be applied or otherwise dealt with. The procedure should have been explained to the next friend in advance. Payment out should be sought for expenditure incurred properly by the next friend. The plaintiff's money will be invested until s/he is old enough or becomes capable of managing her/his own affairs (as the case may be) save for necessary expenditure to sustain the plaintiff whilst under a disability. It is an appropriate moment to ask for payment out for any immediate expenses for the plaintiff such as for an educational course, or a bicycle for a child.

Following the hearing, the order as minuted by the master on the summons, and court forms CFO 320 and CFO 212 must be taken to the action department – within seven days or the time allowed by the order – for the order to be sealed and for the CFO 212 to be checked from the CFO 320. After this, the CFO 212 will be sent by the court to the court funds

12 Usually, the master does not require an affidavit from the plaintiff's solicitor except in cases of exceptional difficulty.

13 White Book 1993 Vol 2, Queen's Bench Masters' Practice Forms PF174 and PF175, paras 374 and 375.

office and the CFO 320 will be retained in the action office. The solicitor should draw up the order promptly.

For control of the money recovered by a person under a disability see RSC Order 80 r12 and CCR Order 10 r11. The money will be available for the infant to take out at the age of 18 or for the patient when s/he is no longer subject to disability.

Costs

In cases where the settlement is approved by a master, the usual order is to direct costs to be taxed on the standard basis, with the plaintiff's solicitor waiving any further costs. In more complicated cases, the defendant may agree or be ordered to pay on an indemnity basis.[14]

The next friend is liable to pay costs of an unsuccessful application or an unnecessary, frivolous or vexatious one. Where an order for costs is made against a next friend of a legally aided infant or patient, s/he has the benefit of Legal Aid Act 1988 s17(1). The costs ordered will not exceed the amount which is reasonable, having regard to the resources of the parties and their conduct. The means of the next friend are deemed to be the means of the infant or patient.[15]

14 White Book 1993 para 62/16/2.
15 Civil Legal Aid (General) Regs 1989 reg 133.

CHAPTER 29

Small claim arbitration

Any claim worth less than £1,000 will be automatically referred for arbitration in the county court by the district judge on receipt by the court of a defence to the claim. Furthermore, the plaintiff or defendant can make a voluntary request for arbitration even if the value is over £1,000 (CCR Order 19 r9). Such a request must be contained in the plaintiff's particulars of claim, or in the defence or counter-claim and on notice to all parties.

The Lay Representation (Rights of Audience) Order 1992 allows the litigant a free choice of representative at arbitration hearings, although the circuit judge or district judge may refuse to hear a lay representative if s/he behaves 'in an unruly manner'.[1] The lay representative can be disqualified where s/he has misled the court or demonstrated an unsuitability to exercise the right of audience.

The district judge may, after considering the defence – or upon application by either party – order that the matter be referred to trial in the county court if:

a) a difficult question of law or facts of exceptional complexity exist;
b) fraud is alleged against any party;
c) the parties are agreed the dispute should be tried in court; or
d) it would be unreasonable for the claim to proceed to arbitration having regard to its subject-matter, size of the counter-claim, circumstances of the parties or interests of any other person likely to be affected by the award.[2]

There are restrictions on costs allowed in arbitration proceedings. No costs are allowed between parties except:

- the costs on the summons;
- the costs of enforcing the award; and

1 CCR Order 19 r1(8).
2 CCR Order 19 r3.

- such costs as the district judge may direct where there has been unreasonable conduct on the part of the opposing party in relation to the proceedings or claim.

However, certain expenses may be allowed. They are:

a) expenses reasonably incurred by parties or witnesses travelling to or from the hearing or in staying away from home;
b) a sum not exceeding £29 in respect of expert fees; and
c) a sum not exceeding £29 in respect of witnesses' or parties' loss of earnings to attend hearings.

The district judge will be the arbitrator unless the court orders otherwise, although, with the consent of the parties, an outside arbiter can be ordered.

When a matter is referred for arbitration, the district judge provides the timetable for directions and estimates the length of the hearing. The normal timetable is for discovery 14 days before the hearing, and exchange of experts' reports and a list of witnesses to be called seven days before the hearing. The parties are given 21 days' notice of the hearing date.

The arbitration hearing is informal, evidence is not taken on oath and strict rules of evidence do not apply unless ordered otherwise. The hearing is held in private.

The arbitrator's award is final and may be set aside only on grounds of an error in law or misconduct by the arbitrator. An application to set aside must be made within 14 days of the date the award was entered as a judgment of the court.

In October 1993 the Lord Chancellor's Department made proposals to extend the arbitration scheme by including *all* claims not stated to be over the small claims limit. That limit is likely to be increased, thus taking in more and more PI litigation. The proposals specify fixed legal costs at a level not quantified at the time of writing. Medical evidence would be in the form of a GP's letter unless the district judge (to whom all cases would be allocated) orders further medical evidence at a preliminary hearing, which would be held in every case. Discovery would be limited to documents on which the parties intend to rely. No costs would be recoverable after the preliminary hearing except for a standard £29.50 for attendance of party or witness and £112.50 for attendance of an expert.

The authors are deeply concerned that these proposals, if implemented, would deprive an increasing number of injured plaintiffs of access to justice. The failure to provide for solicitors' costs and the very low level of payment to experts and witnesses would effectively mean that the plaintiff with minor injuries is denied legal representation.

CHAPTER 30

Criminal injuries

Very rarely is a civil action against an uninsured attacker worth pursuing. However, personal injuries or death caused by criminal violence may justify an application for compensation to the Criminal Injuries Compensation Board (CICB). The CICB's criteria for assessment and its practice and procedure is set out in its scheme dated February 1990.[1]

Major revisions to the scheme were to have come into effect on 1 April 1994. There is resistance to the changes and judicial review proceedings were brought to quash the new scheme. These failed on 23 May 1994 but an appeal was lodged. The new scheme has been suspended pending the outcome of the litigation. Both schemes are therefore summarised. Claims submitted before 1 April 1994 will be dealt with under the old scheme in any event.

The 1990 scheme

Anyone who has sustained personal injury directly attributable to a crime of violence, or suffered injury attributable to the apprehension (or attempted apprehension) of an offender (or suspected offender) or the prevention (or attempted prevention) of an offence, or to giving help to the police, is entitled to make a claim to the CICB. Claims can also be made by dependants and relatives of a criminally injured person who has since died. Friends of the deceased may claim for funeral expenses resulting from criminal injury.

The time limit for a claim is three years from the date of the incident giving rise to the injury, but the application should be made as soon as possible. Delay is dangerous. Costs are not usually recoverable. For

1 Changes in the scheme from time to time do not give rise to retrospective relief. If the scheme in force at the time of the applicant's injury does not cover the injury sustained, then compensation will be refused: *R v CICB ex p P* (1993) PIQR 314.

relatively modest claims, it is not worthwhile instructing lawyers, whereas in larger claims it is.

Conditions

In order to be eligible, applicants must report the crime to the police within 3 months of the event, or have a reasonable explanation for not doing so. They must assist in any prosecution that arises, otherwise compensation may be withheld or reduced. The conduct and character of the applicant is also assessed. If the CICB decides that the applicant was in some way responsible, an award may be reduced[2] or refused. Applications may be rejected where the applicant has: a conviction for a serious crime of violence or some other very serious crime; more than one recent conviction for less serious crimes of violence; or numerous convictions for dishonesty of a serious nature. Each case is judged on its own merits.

Compensation

The evidence required to establish liability and quantum under the criminal injuries compensation scheme is much the same as at common law. Therefore, as a rule of thumb, as much evidence as possible should be gathered in order to gain the maximum award of damages, as if running ordinary personal injury litigation. However, certain differences should be noted. The 1990 scheme does not allow the CICB to compensate for loss of or damage to clothing or other property, unless relied on by the victim as a physical aid. Compensation for net loss of earnings is limited to one-and-a-half times the gross average UK industrial wage at the date of assessment (as published by the *Department of Employment Gazette* and adjusted as considered appropriate by the CICB). Social security benefits are deducted in full. Pension payments may be deducted. Damages paid as a result of a compensation order are also deductible.[3] In fatal cases, loss of dependency and bereavement expenses are recoverable under the principles of the Fatal Accidents Act 1976. Only funeral expenses are recoverable by the victim's estate. The lower limit of compensation does not apply to funeral expenses. The minimum award is £750 for applications received after 1 February 1990. Guideline figures for awards are published by the CICB but should be treated as guidance, not as immutable figures. No interest is payable on CICB awards. Sometimes the board's decisions are reported in *Current Law*, *Personal*

2 *R v CICB ex p Gambles* (1994) *Times* 5 January.
3 1990 Scheme paras 19–21.

and Medical Injuries Law Letter, *Personal Injury Quantum Reports*, Halsbury and Kemp & Kemp. The board also produces an annual report which gives details of selected decisions.

Making a claim

The usual procedure, as set out below, after the application has been made, is for the CICB staff to prepare the case. However, the solicitor may decide to prepare the case on behalf of the client, which should shorten the whole process. The decision whether to instruct a solicitor may rest on funding – legal aid is not available for CICB representation – or it may be that there are difficulties in the case which make it desirable that a solicitor should run it. If a civil claim is also being pursued, the evidence and reports for that claim may be made available to the CICB.

Applications[4] must be made on a standard form, which, together with details of the current scheme and guidelines, is available direct from the CICB (see appendix for address). Once the application is received, an acknowledgment is sent, giving the applicant a personal reference number which must be quoted in subsequent communications with the CICB. A case file is opened. The board's staff scrutinises the form and then reports to see if the CICB is liable and if enough information has been given to assess compensation. If more information is required, the case is investigated and the applicant must agree to the CICB contacting police, hospital, doctor, employers, or anyone else who can give relevant information. Sometimes, photographs are required or, if these would not be helpful, a personal examination may be necessary.

When the investigation is completed, a brief summary, together with the application form, reports and correspondence, are sent to a single member of the board, who decides whether to make an award, reject the application or make a 'reduced' award. These awards may be made by designated staff. Board members or designated staff may refer the case for an oral hearing if they consider that they cannot make a just and proper decision.

The member then returns the file to the case-working officer, who notifies the applicant of the decision and sends the requisite forms and explanatory notes. The notes inform applicants that they may apply for an oral hearing within three months of the date of notification of the single member's decision. An extension may be granted before the end of the three-month period if it is in the interest of justice to do so. The application is then considered afresh and not by that single member.

4 Ibid paras 22–27.

Otherwise, awards must be accepted in writing. Part I of the form is for acceptance and Part II is for applying for an oral hearing. If the applicant requests a hearing, the CICB notice must be signed personally and not by someone on the applicant's behalf.

Hearings

Application

An application for a hearing should be supported by reasons, with any additional evidence. If the reasons suggest that the initial decision was based on incomplete or erroneous information, the application may be remitted to the CICB member who made the initial decision, or, if made by a designated member of staff, it will be remitted to a member of the board. Thereafter, if dissatisfied, the applicant may still apply for a hearing within three months of the matter being reconsidered.

An oral hearing is granted in only three circumstances. First, where no award was made, on the sole ground that it would be less than the current minimum award, and it appears that the board *could* make an award.

Second, where an award was made, but applying these principles the board might make a larger award.

Third, where no award or a reduced award was made and there is a dispute as to the material facts or conclusions, or it appears that the decision may have been wrong in law or principle.

The principles are the same as those applied by the Court of Appeal in deciding whether to alter the assessment of damages by a trial judge. So, an assessment of quantum will not be altered unless the initial judgment proceeded on a wholly erroneous estimate, ie, if a significantly different award is appropriate.[5]

The application for a hearing is scrutinised by a member of the board's staff and, if it appears likely to fail the above criteria, it is reviewed by not less than two other members of the board. The application for a hearing is refused where it is decided that, were any disputed facts or conclusions resolved in the applicant's favour, it would not make any difference to the decision, or that an oral hearing would serve no useful purpose. Such decision is final. These principles mean that few applications for an oral hearing are successful. Given the lack of generosity often shown by single board members in the past, this is regrettable.

Procedure

When an application for an oral hearing is granted, the board's staff

5 *Wilson v Pilley* [1957] 1 WLR 1138.

prepares a bundle of documents to be used at the hearing and sends it to the applicant or solicitor. This bundle includes: the application form; the letter containing the initial decision; the form requesting a full hearing; the medical reports; documents concerning special damages; a copy of the scheme and notes on procedure at the hearing.

The evidence must be checked to see if further evidence on eligibility or medical evidence is required. If so, the board must be told within 28 days of receiving the explanatory notes. The CICB must have copies of all medical evidence and documents intended to be relied on, at least 14 days prior to the hearing. Failure to do so may result in the postponement of the hearing or, even worse, refusal to accept the late evidence. In practice, late evidence is usually accepted, provided that it is not too complicated. Four photocopies should be produced.

A summary of the issues is prepared by the CICB and sent to the applicant or solicitor with a list of witnesses to be invited by the board. When the case is ready for hearing, a notice of listing, giving the time, date and place, is sent. On the day of the hearing, police statements and previous convictions (if any) are disclosed to the applicant. Applicants may present their own case or be represented by a lawyer, trade union representative or friend. Legal costs are never awarded, but the CICB may award the applicant and witnesses expenses for attending the hearing.

The hearing itself takes place in private. The burden of proof is on the applicant. The CICB is represented by an advocate who is a member of the board's staff. The procedure is flexible and, in less complicated cases, is usually semi-inquisitorial. After the applicant has given evidence in chief, s/he is cross-examined by the board's advocate; then the members ask questions. The applicant's advocate (or, if in person, the applicant) has the right to ask questions after this. If the case is complicated and if it would help, the board should be asked to adopt the strict adversarial procedure. There will be at least two members sitting and they will have considerable experience in personal injury work. Given the need to show that the original assessment was wholly erroneous, it is wise to cite relevant cases on quantum as in a civil personal injury trial.

The members will have read the papers and do not wish to be told the obvious. Hearings are remarkably quick, and this sometimes causes clients to feel that they have not been given a fair hearing. It is, therefore, important that the advocate and the client are prepared for this.

The principles of res judicata and abuse of process do not apply to the CICB.[6] The Board must, however, give reasons showing the basis of fact

6 *In re G (A Minor)* (1992) *Times* 18 June.

on which it relied in making its award.[7] It can make a nil award if the damages assessed are less than the benefits received.[8]

The only way to challenge the decision of a full hearing of the board is to apply for judicial review, with all its attendant difficulties. The board can reopen a case if a serious change has occurred in the applicant's medical condition attributable to the original injury and if injustice would occur if the original assessment were allowed to stand.[9]

The 1994 'tariff' scheme

This scheme[10] is intended to deal with applications received on or after 1 April 1994 (see p314). It will be administered by the Criminal Injuries Compensation Authority (CICA) and appeals will go to a Criminal Injuries Appeals Panel (CIAP). The main changes from the 1990 scheme are noted below.

Time limits

Applications must generally be received by the CICA within one year of the incident giving rise to the injury, instead of three as previously. Any application for review of a decision by the CICA must be made within 90 days. An appeal must usually be submitted within 28 days of notification of the review decision by the CICA.

Withholding or reducing an award

As with the 1990 scheme, the CICA can withhold or reduce an award because the applicant failed to inform, co-operate with or give reasonable assistance to the police, or because of conduct before, during or after the event, or because of the applicant's character. The tariff scheme sets out a more systematic appraisal of the applicant's character by operating a penalty points scheme with proportionate reductions depending upon the gravity and number of previous convictions.

Compensation – the tariff

The essential feature of the new scheme is the substitution of a tariff of fixed awards in place of the use of common law principles of loss and

7 *R v CICB ex p Cummins* (1992) *Times* 21 January; (1992) PIQR 281; and *R v CICB ex p Powell* (1994) PIQR 77.
8 *R v CICB ex p Lazzani* (1993) PIQR 421.
9 1990 Scheme para 13.
10 A copy of the tariff scheme and a guidance leaflet can be obtained from the CICA (see p473 for address).

damage in each individual case. The scheme has 25 bands, ranging from £1,000 for, say, a chipped front tooth requiring a crown, to £250,000 for quadriplegia. The full list setting out the tariff payment for 160 different injuries may be obtained from the CICA. Thus the most marked distinction between the 1990 and 1994 schemes is that under the latter nothing is recoverable for financial loss, past or future. This will mean substantially smaller awards in many (if not most) cases, with consequent injustice to victims.

Reopening the case

The assessment (or Panel finding on an appeal) is normally regarded as final. There is no provision for a provisional assessment, but if the applicant's medical condition has changed materially, the authority can reopen a case within three years of the final decision and thereafter if this can be done without involving extensive enquiries. It remains to be seen what this means in practice.

Review

If the applicant is dissatisfied with the CICA award, s/he can apply for a review within 90 days. This must be in writing and supported by reasons, together with any other relevant additional information. A 'review' simply means that the award is reconsidered by a more senior member of the CICA.

Appeal

An appeal against a review goes to a single member of the CIAP. It must be made in writing within 28 days and supported by reasons together with any other relevant additional information. An (oral) hearing will only be granted by the single member where the evidence appears to justify an award where none was made, or a higher award if a lower one was made, or appears to suggest that the decision might be wrong where material facts or conclusions were in dispute.

Procedure at the hearing is similar to that under the 1990 scheme but the CIAP may withhold expenses and/or reduce any award previously offered if the request for a hearing is considered to be frivolous.

Members of the appeal panel will no longer be restricted to practising QCs experienced in dealing with personal injury cases but drawn from a 'broad constituency' including the legal and medical professions, the business and commercial world and other professional or responsible groups. They will be appointed by the Secretary of State.

Part V

Precedents

A Proof and witness statements

A.1 Proof of John Smith of 15 High Street, Haxby, York.

1 I am a teacher, born on 3 February 1959. National Insurance number YZ 321999. I am married and have two children aged three and fifteen months.

2 I work in the English department of Monkthorpe School, Manor Lane, York and I am on scale 2. I have worked for this comprehensive school since 1985 and teach children from 11 up to 'A' level standard.

3 While the school is only 25 years old there have been major structural problems due, apparently, to subsidence. The Johnson Building where most of the English teaching is carried out was out of bounds for perhaps three months over the last two years while they tried to rectify the problem. The last time it was closed was in summer 1991, when the headteacher, Ms Graham, told us the problems had been resolved.

4 In January 1992 I noticed that cracks were beginning to appear in the walls in the classroom where I do most of my teaching, room 3A. I complained twice to Mr George, the head of the English department, once toward the end of January in the staff room and again about a fortnight later while we were both on playground duty. On both occasions he just shrugged and ignored me. I then came across Ms Graham, only a couple of days later just outside her office. I think this was on Friday 17 February. I told her about the problem and she said she would see what she could so. I was told by Ms Shepherd, deputy head of English, that the school had been inspected by the education authority maintenance department during the Christmas holidays. She is not prepared to be involved in my case, however.

5 On Tuesday 10 March 1992 at about 10am I was teaching the 3rd years and I went to lean against the wall, next to the window overlooking the playing fields. In doing so a part of the wall suddenly gave way, and I fell out through the hole onto the playing field. If it were not for the fact that I fell into the sand of the adjacent infants sand pit, my injuries would have been far worse as I had fallen some 15 feet from the first floor level.

6 I was immediately taken to the casualty department of York Hospital in Main Road, York (my no is RD 132567) where I was diagnosed as suffering from a fractured femur of the left leg. I also had sustained grazing and bruising to my left thigh and arm.

7 My left leg was put into plaster, I was discharged late that afternoon and have been seen another four times since then in out-patients. The consultant, Mr Jones, has told me that I should come out of the plaster at the end of April 1992.

8 I lost no wages and have received no benefits during my time off work so far. I will inform my solicitor if the position changes.

9 The expenses I have incurred to date are as follows:

Damaged trousers bought from M & S in June 1991	£ 46.00
Travelling expenses to and from hospital, four-and-a-half return trips at £8 return	£ 36.00
Excess on insurance for cancelled holiday	£ 50.00
Total	£132.00

10 The holiday was booked for my wife and me to go to Paris over Easter, while my parents looked after the children.

11 The injury has not only stopped me doing work around the house, putting an additional burden on my wife, but has stopped me playing in my Sunday league football team and attending my evening class in pottery. It has proved very difficult and embarrassing to have sexual intercourse with my wife and this has caused some tension between us.

........................(signed) ....(dated)

I have initialled all changes I have made to the above.
(Proof taken on 29th March 1992 by Mary Doyle)
Ref MD/SMITH/V906027

A.2 Statement of John Smith of 15 High Street, Haxby, York YK7 3Z

1 I am a teacher, born on 3 February 1959. National Insurance number YZ 321999. I am married and have two children aged three and fifteen months. I am the Plaintiff in these proceedings.

2 I work in the English department of Monkthorpe School, Manor Lane, York and I am on scale 2. I have worked for this comprehensive school since 1985 and teach children from 11 up to 'A' level standard.

3 While the school is only 25 years old there have been major structural problems due, apparently, to subsidence. The Johnson Building where most of the English teaching is carried out was out of bounds for perhaps three months over the last two years while they tried to rectify the problem.

The last time it was closed was in summer 1991, when the headteacher, Ms Graham, told us the problems had been resolved.

4 In January 1992 I noticed that cracks were beginning to appear in the walls in the classroom where I do most of my teaching, room 3A. I complained twice to Mr George, the head of the English department, once toward the end of January in the staff room and again about a fortnight later while we were both on playground duty. On both occasions he just shrugged and ignored me. I then came across Ms Graham, only a couple of days later just outside her office. I think this was on Friday 17 February. I told her about the problem and she said she would see what she could so.

5 On Tuesday 10 March 1992 at about 10am I was teaching the 3rd years and I went to lean against the wall, next to the window overlooking the playing fields. In doing so a part of the wall suddenly gave way, and I fell out through the hole onto the playing field. If it were not for the fact that I fell into the sand of the adjacent infants sand pit, my injuries would have been far worse as I had fallen some 15 feet from the first floor level.

6 I was immediately taken to the casualty department of York Hospital in Main Road, York (my no is RD 132567) where I was diagnosed as suffering from a fractured femur of the left leg. I also had sustained grazing and bruising to my left thigh and arm.

7 My left leg was put into plaster, I was discharged late that afternoon and have been seen another four times since then in out-patients. The consultant, Mr Jones, has told me that I should come out of the plaster at the end of April 1992.

8 I lost no wages and have received no benefits during my time off work so far. I will inform my solicitor if the position changes.

9 The expenses I have incurred to date are as follows:

Damaged trousers bought from M & S in June 1991	£ 46.00
Travelling expenses to and from hospital, four-and-a-half return trips at £8 return	£ 36.00
Excess on insurance for cancelled holiday	£ 50.00
Total	£132.00

10 The holiday was booked for my wife and me to go to Paris over Easter, while my parents looked after the children. This holiday had to be cancelled because of my injuries. It was very disappointing to both of us.

11 The injury has not only stopped me doing work around the house, putting an additional burden on my wife, but has stopped me playing in my Sunday league football team and attending my evening class in pottery. It has proved very difficult and embarrassing to have sexual intercourse with my wife and this has caused some tension between us.

12 The contents of this statement are true to the best of my knowledge and belief.

......................(signed) ....(dated)

B Specimen correspondence

Clients

B.1 Letter before initial interview

Ref WR/MF/SMITH/S123.94

Dear Mr Smith,

Further to your telephone conversation with this office, I write to confirm your appointment to see me on Monday 3 May 1994 at 3.30pm. The appointment is likely to last about an hour.

I would be grateful if you would bring with you every document you have which relates in any way to the accident, your employment (including wage slips and contract of employment) and any details you have from the DSS (if you have been claiming benefits); also anything which relates to your injuries such as out-patient's card and the name, address and phone number of your doctor etc.

If it appears that there is a reasonable chance of winning your case and you come within the legal aid limits, I would certainly be happy to take on your case within the legal aid scheme. If you do not come within those limits, we can discuss the possibilities of financing the case at the meeting. If, having heard my advice, you decide not to go ahead with the case, I will not charge for the initial meeting.

A plan is enclosed showing the location of the office and I look forward to meeting you. I would be very grateful if you could telephone me if you run into any difficulty in keeping the appointment at 3.30pm.

Yours sincerely,

William Roberts
For Leigh, Gall and Ayed

B.2 Letter after initial interview

Dear Mr Smith,

Ref WR/MF/SMITH/S123.94

Thank you for instructing Leigh Gall & Ayed to deal with your case. We shall do our best to ensure that everything proceeds as smoothly as possible. The solicitors' professional organisation, the Law Society, require that we give you certain information at the start of your case in writing and this rather formal letter is written with this in mind.

I shall personally be responsible for looking after your case. I am a qualified legal executive. I may be assisted from time to time by other members of staff in the Personal Injury Department. If for any reason you are not satisfied with the service which you receive and remain unhappy after discussing it with me, you can raise the matter with Marianne France, who is one of the firm's joint managing partners.

I am writing to you separately about the question of costs in your case.

Our office is open from 9.30am to 5.30 pm each weekday. If it is difficult for you to visit during these hours, it may be possible to arrange to meet outside normal office hours. If you are disabled, home visits can be arranged. Generally, the switchboard only deals with incoming telephone calls during office hours. Please write to me with any query at any time. If something urgent arises please feel free to telephone me. If we need to meet to discuss something face to face it is best to make an appointment through my secretary.

If there is anything that you would like to discuss at this stage regarding the arrangements for the conduct of your case or you would like any other information, please do not hesitate to contact me.

Yours sincerely

William Roberts

For Leigh, Gall & Ayed

B.3A Costs letter to privately funded client after interview

Dear Mr Smith,

Ref WR/MF/SMITH/S123.94

Second letter

As I indicated in the letter accompanying this one, I am writing this letter to make clear the position regarding costs. As we discussed, it does not appear that you are eligible for legal aid and so you have decided to pay for the conduct of the case yourself. I attach a note of the implications of this decision. I would ask you to read it carefully and to sign it, date it and return it to me if you agree to the terms set out in it. This will mean that you have entered into a binding agreement with Leigh, Gall and Ayed on the terms set out in the note, including the hourly charging rates. Once you have entered the agreement by signing, it will restrict your right to challenge the rates.

We discussed all these matters at our meeting on 3 May 1994 but if you have any queries you would like to discuss with me before signing, please do not hesitate to contact me. Needless to say, I will not charge for any such discussion.

I enclose a second copy of the note on costs for you to keep.

Yours sincerely

William Roberts
For Leigh, Gall and Ayed.

B.3B Costs note for privately funded client

A note about your legal costs and charges

Introduction

The purpose of this note is to explain how we charge for the work we do on your behalf. Unfortunately, it is difficult to explain some aspects without being formal or technical. We apologise for the complexity of what follows but our terms of costing and charging clients are usual for solicitors undertaking personal injury work. The solicitors' professional body, the Law Society, expect us to explain these things at the outset. We feel that it avoids misunderstanding if you have full information about our charges at the beginning of a case. If there is anything in this note that you do not understand please do not hesitate to speak to the lawyer who is dealing with your case.

The hourly charging basis

At present we are not allowed to charge you on a 'no win – no fee' basis. We charge according to the time we spend on your case. All time spent by solicitors, legal executives, litigation clerks and other staff such as our in-house scientists and damages chartered accountant is charged at a rate per hour. We do not charge for time spent on your case by general office staff carrying out tasks such as photocopying.

The hourly charge rate is made up of two separate parts. The first is a basic rate which lawyers call the 'expense' rate. This covers our overheads only, that is, it contains no element of profit. The expense rate for each member of staff is calculated in accordance with a formula suggested by the Law Society. [William Roberts'] current expense rate is £85.00 per hour excluding VAT. We hope not to have to review our current rates before May 1995. [William Roberts] will work with other staff on your case whose time may be charged at a lower rate. Although he will still have to charge for some time spent supervising other staff, it will be cheaper for you than if he does absolutely everthing on your case.

The second part of the hourly rate is the profit element which lawyers call 'uplift'. It is a percentage of the expense rate. In assessing the total hourly rate we charge we take into account current rates allowed by the court officials appointed to assess the amounts that may reasonably be charged by solicitors. There are a number of discretionary matters which may be taken into account and which cannot be fully assessed until the work has been completed. These include the complexity of the matter, its importance to you and the value of the claim as well as the skill, specialised knowledge and responsibility required of the lawyer. Because of this we will not fix the percentage uplift to apply in your case until the work has been completed but it will be no less than 50% and may be substantially more. Please see the section on **interim billing** in this leaflet for further information on the costs you will be asked to pay before the case is finally concluded.

Disbursements

It is inevitable that we will incur some 'disbursements'. These are specific payments made on your behalf. The most substantial ones are likely to be medical and other experts' fees and barristers' fees. VAT has to be added to most disbursements. If you ask us to, we will consult you to discuss the likely charges before instructing a barrister or expert.

My estimate

If is very difficult to estimate the costs of your case at this stage. We are required to do so however and my best estimate is that our costs (including disbursements but exluding VAT) will be in the region of [£7500]. I will let you know if this estimate changes significantly. It is harder to estimate the defendants' costs but they are likely to be fairly similar.

Payment

(i) Initial payment

Like other solicitors, we do need to ask all clients for money on account of costs and disbursements at the beginning of the case. This is held in our client account in your name until a bill is delivered to you or a disbursement paid. Any interest accruing on your money held by us is credited to you.

(ii) interim billing

As your case progresses we will send you interim bills on account from time to time. This will normally be at three or six month intervals. You may tell us how frequently you would like to be billed and you may also ask at any time for an estimate of the costs incurred since the last bill was delivered. **Bills on account are not an exact costing of the full amount due.** They give a broad indication of the work done taken from our computer time records.

At the end of the case the full costs over the whole period will be calculated. There is a rule that if you win your case and costs are to be paid by the other side, we are unable to charge them any more than you have been charged for the same work. Sending out interim indications as bills on account during your case helps us maximise the amount of costs recovered for you from the other side when the final bill is delivered.

When an expense is incurred or a bill is delivered, the amount will be transferred from our client account holding your money to our office account which holds our own money, not clients' money. If the amount by which your account is in credit exceeds a disbursement or interim bill on account, the balance will, of course, remain to the credit of your account. If it does not, we will ask you to pay the balance due on the bill promptly and may ask you for a further sum on account.

If you have difficulty in paying for work as it goes along and in particular if you fear that you might have to deprive yourself of treatment or therapy that you need because of this, please speak to us and we will do our best to assist. We cannot work for free but in limited circumstances we may defer delivering bills on account.

(iii) Final payment

We normally expect bills to be met within 30 days and reserve the right to charge interest at 2% per annum above the XYZ Bank rate for borrowing if bills are not paid within 30 days. If you would like to know the interest rate that applies at any time, please ask.

The other side's legal costs

Just as we will consider your best interest in trying to obtain the maximum compensation for you, we will try to ensure that as much as possible of your own legal costs is paid by the other side. The general rule is that the successful person's costs will be paid by the other side. However, it is unfortunately only in the rarest case that **all** legal costs will be recovered from the other side, even though you have won your case.

If you succeed, at the end of the case your legal costs are usually assessed on 'the standard basis'. This means that a reasonable amount of all costs reasonably incurred will be allowed (if we cannot agree the costs with the other side, the court decides) with any doubts to be resolved in favour of the person who has to pay. The standard basis usually works out at between 70% and 90% of your full costs, although sometimes we do recover a better percentage from the other side. As our client, you are liable to pay our full costs and will therefore be liable for any shortfall. The same principles apply if you lose; in addition to your own legal costs you will usually have to pay the other side's costs on the standard basis.

There are some specific circumstances in which the usual rules may not apply such as if an offer of settlement or payment into court is made by the other side. We will explain any particular circumstances to you if they arise during the course of your claim.

Interest

As mentioned above any interest accruing on the money you pay to us on account of costs and disbursements until it is used will be added to your fund. Interest will accrue unless your fund is under £50 or is used within less than a month of receipt.

If your case succeeds, it is likely that the other side will have to pay interest on your costs from the date on which the case ends until the date they pay your costs. This interest will belong to you only to the extent that you have funded the case as it has progressed. The current rate at which this interest is payable is 8% per annum. Unfortunately, the same rule applies if you lose your case; that is, you will most probably have to pay interest on the other side's costs from the date on which the case ends until the costs are paid.

If an acceptable settlement of your costs can be negotiated, it may be to your advantage to forego part of the entitlement to interest to avoid delay and a formal 'taxation' hearing.

Taxation

The procedure by which the court assesses solicitors' costs is confusingly known as 'taxation'. This is nothing to do with the Inland Revenue. Full details of the taxation procedure will be given to you at the end of the case. A formal taxation hearing, which you will have the right to attend, will only be necessary if the costs cannot be agreed between the parties to the litigation.

When your case ends it may be necessary to prepare a document known as a 'bill of costs' for the taxation procedure. The bill of costs has to be prepared in an old-fashioned and formal style. It sets out in detail the work done on your case and the amounts claimed from the other side. We generally ask outside specialists known as 'law costs draftsmen' to prepare the bill of costs. This is mainly because an experienced costs draftsman will be able to cost the case in a way designed to maximise the amount that will be paid by the other side.

Costs draftsmen charge a percentage of the costs on the bill. We will ask you to pay the draftsman's fees. As we would otherwise have to charge you for the time we would spend preparing a formal bill of costs, and taking into account the likelihood that the other side will end up paying more towards your costs, we believe that the use of a costs draftsman ultimately results in a saving for you.

More information
Please do consult us if you would like any more information about legal costs. If asked, we will provide you with advance estimates for your legal costs but because each case is different it is difficult to predict with accuracy the amount of time we will need to spend on your case. What we can do, if you wish, is tell you each time an agreed limit has been reached.

If you believe the costs you are asked to pay are excessive, please talk to the lawyer dealing with your case. We also have an 'in-house' complaints procedure. If you remain dissatisfied, in certain circumstances you may ask the Law Society of the court to assess whether or not the costs are reasonable. If you would like further details of these procedures, please let us know.

Agreement
A second copy of this leaflet is enclosed for you to keep. Please sign and return this one to show that you accept the terms upon which we charge. This will mean that you have entered into an agreement with Leigh, Gall and Ayed on the terms set out in this leaflet, including the hourly charge rates. Once you have entered into this agreement your right to challenge the hourly rates will be restricted.
Signed .... Dated ....

B.4 Letter on grant of legal aid

Ref MD/Maloney/P915084

Dear Mr Maloney,

You have now been granted a legal aid certificate. I am required by the Legal Aid Board to advise you about the implications of legal aid. I apologise for the fact that this letter is so formal and complex but you will remember that we discussed these matters when we last met. Please read this letter carefully and keep it for your future reference

1) The effect of the certificate is that from the date of issue the Legal Aid Board (not you) pay me for the work that I do on your case within the scope of the certificate. Any contribution you have to make you pay direct to the Board when they ask you.
2) The certificate states what aspects of your case it covers. It has a limitation on it as you see. This is nothing unusual and we shall have to apply to have the certificate extended as the case progresses. Please note that the certificate is not retrospective and does not cover any work done before the date on which it was issued. In fact in your case there was no chargeable work done before the certificate was issued.
3) If your succeed in 'recovering' or 'preserving' property, ie if you win your case and end up with money as damages, the Legal Aid Board has first call on that money so as to cover the costs of running the case. This is called the 'statutory charge'. It will amount to my firm's costs (including expenses such as barristers and experts' fees and VAT) less (i) any contribution you have paid, and (ii) any costs recovered from your opponent.

4) If your claim is successful, your opponent will probably be ordered to pay towards your costs in addition to paying damages. Unfortunately, the amount recovered for costs will generally not cover all your costs – only a proportion which generally works out at around 65% to 80%. However, in some cases if the costs are agreed there will be no shortfall and your contribution will also be refunded. If there is a shortfall you are expected to make this up out of your damages, which effectively puts you in the same position (if you win your case) as a private client.

5) There are some situations which increase the likely shortfall between your costs and the costs of the other side may be ordered to pay if your claim succeeds and therefore increases the 'statutory charge'. For example it may be that your case is sufficiently complex for two barristers to be involved rather than one or an unusually expensive expert's report needs to be obtained. There may also be occasions when the court will order that some costs need not be paid by the other side even if your claim succeeds. If one of these situations arises, I will write and tell you, where possible in advance. Obviously, the longer your case takes the more work is done and so the higher the 'statutory charge' may be. I will **not** write routine letters to you simply saying that the 'statutory charge' is likely to be higher because another six months have elapsed – rather this is something that you should bear in mind throughout. I will write and ask for your authority to take a step in the proceedings which will significantly increase costs, such as instructing counsel or an expert.

6) I must give you an estimate of the costs of your case. This is very difficult at this stage but I estimate my firm's costs will be in the region of £7,500 if the case does not settle before trial. I will let you know if this estimate changes significantly. As this letter makes clear either the defendants or the Legal Aid Board will meet the bulk of these costs.

7) If you are in the end unsuccessful in your case against the defendant(s) you will not be expected to contribute to the costs beyond any contribution you have made during the case. In certain (unusual) circumstances you may be ordered to pay towards the other side's costs. If so, the court will generally put an upper limit on the sum that has to be paid to the other side. This upper limit is usually fixed at the amount of the contribution you have already paid to the Legal Aid Board so that you will have to pay no more.

8) There is always the possibility that the other side may not be able to pay the money it is ordered to do so as damages or costs. (This is most improbable since, in your case, we know the defendant was insured.)

9) If the Legal Aid Board decide at any time that your claim does not have sufficient prospects of success or that you have not co-operated with them, or us, they can discharge your certificate. This means that from the date of discharge your costs are no longer covered. In extreme circumstances the Board may revoke your certificate which means that it is treated as never having existed and you become personally liable for all the costs since the certificate started. These are merely possibilities and I have to warn you of

them. If the circumstances occurred which made it a likelihood that legal aid would be withdrawn, I would discuss them with you well in advance.

10) You must tell the Legal Aid Board (and me of course) if you change your address. You must also let the Legal Aid Board know if your income or capital (or that of the partner/spouse) increases or decreases so that they can, if appropriate, reassess your contribution or entitlement to Legal Aid.

If there is anything in this letter which is not clear or that you would like to discuss please do phone me at the office, or make an appointment with my secretary to come and see me.

Yours sincerely,

B.5 Letter sending proof of evidence

Ref MD/SMITH/V 906027

Dear Mr Smith,

Please find enclosed a copy of the 'proof of evidence' that I have written for you, following our discussions at the meeting on Monday. I would be grateful if you would read it through carefully and make and initial any amendments or alterations that you feel are necessary and then sign it at the foot of the proof. Please return it to me in the enclosed stamped addressed envelope. I also enclose a duplicate copy which you can keep.

It is important that you check through the proof carefully as this will form the basis for various legal documents and may also be sent to various experts and counsel. If therefore there are any inaccuracies they must be corrected now.

I look forward to receiving the proof returned, duly signed.

Yours sincerely,

B.6 Franchisee's letter outlining case plan

Ref MD/SMITH/V906027

Dear Mr Smith,

I write to set out how I intend to proceed with your case. The steps to be taken are as follows:

1) Gather in the medical reports on your injuries
2) Gather in information on actual and projected financial losses to draft the schedule of special damage and financial losses
3) Consider whether it is necessary to obtain other expert reports from perhaps an accident reconstruction expert and, if necessary, obtain these reports
4) Send the papers to a barrister expert in accident litigation for the Court documentation to be drafted
5) Issue a writ in the High Court and serve the Court documentation on the defendant to your action. The Court rules require that this documentation is served with supporting medical evidence and the schedule of financial loss

6) Receive the defence and proceed to discovery (when the relevant documents are disclosed by both parties)
7) Update medical and financial reports and schedule of financial loss if necessary
8) If necessary, ask counsel to advise in the case, either in writing or in a meeting, on the claim's value and merits, and whether or not the evidence is sufficient to move towards a trial date. At this point counsel will let us know what else he or she thinks needs to be done before a trial date is obtained.
9) Obtain a trial date.

I will of course send you copies of all relevant documents as they are received and I will ask you to comment on them.

Please note that we cannot proceed to trial until and unless we can get a firm medical prognosis and we cannot accurately value a claim until we know the extent of the damage. The above plan may need to be modified as we proceed in the light of circumstances which may arise. In some cases where evidence is complicated for whatever reason, I may have to ask counsel to advise on more than one occasion. In other cases, I do not have to ask counsel to advise at all.

At present, I estimate we should reach trial in about 18 months provided no major problems arise.

In due course, please confirm that you have received this plan and approve its contents. If there are any aspects of it that you do not understand, or any questions you wish to raise on it, just ask me. It is generally best if we communicate by letter, and delays will be avoided if you respond as quickly as possible to my letters. I will try to do the same. If you need to see me to discuss something, my secretary will be happy to arrange an appointment for you to come to the office or, if this is impracticable, I could come to see you. If an emergency arises, please do not hesitate to phone me.

Yours sincerely,

B.7 Letter advising 'no case'

Ref MD/BROWN/V 906026

Dear Mr Brown,

I have now had an opportunity to consider fully your case and have taken on board everything that you told me at the meeting on Monday 3 May 1994 together with all the documents that you sent on to me.

Having considered all the evidence I am sorry to have to inform you that I take the view that there is no realistic prospect of pursuing a successful claim in your case.

The reason for my opinion is that the part of the pavement where you fell is unlikely to be considered sufficiently dangerous for the council to be held liable. As I mentioned to you at the meeting, the courts consider a difference in height of less than one inch as being acceptable. In your case the defect was at best a quarter of an inch as you told me and as the photographs you sent me seem to confirm.

I will therefore be filing your papers and can confirm that there is no charge for this advice or for our initial discussion.

Finally, I must warn you that if you do intend to pursue the claim, despite my advice, proceedings must be issued by 2 November 1996. This is three years from the date of the accident. A claim commenced after that date is very likely to be struck out for not coming within the statutory three-year limitation period.

I am sorry once again that my advice is not more optimistic. If you want to discuss any of the above please do not hesitate to write or phone my secretary to make an appointment with me. I return to you the documents and photograph you provided to me.

Yours sincerely,

B.8 Letter sending medical report

Ref MD/MALONEY/P915084

Dear Mr Maloney,

I have now received the expert's report from Mr Verygood and enclose a copy. I would be grateful if you could read through the report carefully. Please provide me with any comments you would care to make, including a note of any inaccuracies and any part of the report you do not agree with.

You will see that Mr Verygood says that your fracture is serious and that it will be some time before a full prognosis (ie, a forecast of how the fracture will turn out and what effect it will have on your life) can be made.

He recommends that he sees you again in nine months' time and I have put this in my diary and will write to him for an appointment nearer that time. I would like your confirmation that this is in order.

While we wait for that further medical report I shall be continuing to progress the other aspects of your case.

I enclose a sheet of paper bearing my reference and a stamped addressed envelope.

Yours sincerely,

B.9 Letter seeking client's authority to issue proceedings

Ref MD/MALONEY/P915084

Dear Mr Maloney,

I have now received the necessary documentatior. to commence legal proceedings against the defendants. I will be sending the papers to counsel for him/her to draft a court document known as 'the particulars of claim', which sets out your case in legal language.

The issuing and commencement of proceedings is the start of the formal court process and although we have discussed the position I would be grateful if you would write, confirming that you are in agreement that we should start the legal proceedings. If you have any queries please do not hesitate to contact me at the office.

Yours sincerely,

B.10 Letter re payment into court or offer

Ref MD/MALONEY/P915084

Dear Mr Maloney,

I have just received notification from the defendants that they have paid the sum of £7,000 into court.

The significance of the payment in is, as I explained at out meeting last week, that you have until 13 September to decide whether to accept the offer (that is, 21 days from the receipt of the notice of payment). If you accept the offer the defendants will pay their own and nearly all my costs.

If you do not accept the payment in by 13 September and the case then goes to trial, and if you are awarded a sum equal to or less than that paid into court, it is highly likely that the court will order you to pay the defendants' costs from the date of the payment in up until the end of the case. My best estimate is that this could quite easily come to five or six thousand pounds, though it could conceivably be more.

However, my advice is still that your claim is worth between £12,000 and £15,000 and I remain of the view that you are much more likely to win than to lose. Even if the court were to make a deduction for contributory negligence, which I think is unlikely, I consider that it would be extremely unlikely, as I told you, that such a deduction would be more than 25%. So my view is that the payment into court does not come within the proper bracket and thus my firm advice is to reject it.

If you want to discuss the matter please do not hesitate to phone me at the office or to arrange an appointment with my secretary to come in and see me.

Yours sincerely,

B.11 Letter confirming accepted offer

Ref MD/MALONEY/P915084

Dear Mr Maloney,

I am pleased to say that, following our discussions, the defendants' insurers have now agreed to pay to you the sum of £12,500 which you authorised me to accept on the phone yesterday in settlement of your claim. We are now in the process of having an order issued by the court to that effect and I should be in receipt of the cheque within the next two or three weeks.

As I have informed you, I will be able to send you £10,000 at this stage until the costs position has been determined. It is certainly possible that I may be able to reach agreement with the defendants on costs which would mean that you would be entitled to the full balance of the monies due to you. If, however, it is impossible to reach agreement with the defendants, it may be a good few months before the courts have gone through the costs in a process known as 'taxation' which will determine how much has to be paid by the defendants and how much by yourself. You will be entitled to attend that taxation and I will let you know the hearing date as soon as we have it, if that is the case.

If any monies are deducted from you, they will come out of the £2,500 I will retain from the £12,500 paid by the defendants. You will recall that this is in consequence of the operation, by the Legal Aid Board, of the statutory charge.

Yours sincerely,

Defendants

B.12 Initial letter to other side in road case

Ref MD/JONES/A914193

Dear Sir/Madam,

Re: Rose Jones of 16 Albany Road, Cardiff. DOB 31.1.60. NI number YZ 223991B.

We are instructed by the above-named in respect of a road accident which occured on 6 October 1993. Our client was driving her Volvo motor car, registration number H232 MLN, along Albany Road, Cardiff in a southerly direction when a Vauxhall Nova motor car, registration number G192 KNV, which we believe to have been owned and driven by yourself, came straight out of Dartmouth Road and hit our client's vehicle in the middle nearside.

As a result of the accident our client sustained whiplash injuries to her neck and shoulders.

The accident was caused by your negligent driving and we therefore claim, on behalf of our client, damages for personal injuries and all losses and expenses incurred as a result of the accident. We recommend that you pass this letter to your insurers as soon as possible.

The plaintiff is employed by Huge Gaskets Ltd of 13 New Industrial Estate, Greenbelt, Kent.

We would suggest that you or your insurers contact the Compensation Recovery Unit, Department of Social Security, Reyrolle Building, Hebburn, Tyne and Wear NE31 1XB (telephone 091-489 2266) and complete form CRU1 as soon as practicable.

Yours faithfully,

B.13 Initial letter to the other side in work accident case

Ref MD/MALONEY/P915084

Dear Sir/Madam,

Re: James Maloney of 31 Dean Street, London, SE5. DOB 30.1.65. NI number: YZ 220991B.

We are instructed by the above-named in respect of an accident at work which occurred on 13 May 1993. Our client is employed by your company as a fitter and his works number is B16143.

The accident occurred at your factory in Rason Road, Sutton at about 10am. The accident occurred when the pipe he was preparing gave way, falling on top of him.

As a result of the accident our client sustained a broken collar bone and bruising.

The accident was caused by the negligence and/or breach of statutory duty by yourselves, your servants or agents in, inter alia, not providing a safe system for our client to work within. We therefore claim on behalf of our client damages for personal injuries and losses and expenses incurred as a result of the accident.

We would suggest that you contact the Compensation Recovery Unit, DSS, Reyrolle Building, Hebburn, Tyne and Wear NE31 1XB (telephone 091–489 2266) and complete form CRU1 as soon as practicable and pass this letter on to your insurers as soon as possible. Please acknowledge receipt.

Yours faithfully,

B.14 Initial letter to other side in tripping case

Ref MD/LS/HARTIGAN/Q91 1242

Dear Sir/Madam,

Re: Helen Hartigan of 15 Flowers Close, Hitchin. DOB 29.1.60. NI number YZ 220991B.

We are instructed by the above named in respect of an accident which occurred on 7 June 1993. Our client was walking along the London Road, Hitchin in a northerly direction when, outside number 17, she tripped and fell over a paving stone which we understand to be your responsibility.

We have been to the scene of the accident and have measured the defect in the pavement which is clearly well over one inch.

As a result of the accident our client sustained a broken hip.

The accident was caused by the negligence and/or breach of statutory duty of yourselves, your servants or agents and we therefore claim on behalf of our client damages for personal injuries and all losses and expenses incurred as a result of the accident.

The plaintiff is employed by The Florists, Little Harbottle, Suffolk.

We would suggest that you contact the Compensation Recovery Unit, DSS, Reyrolle Building, Hebburn, Tyne and Wear NE31 1XB (telephone 091–489 2266) and complete form CRU1 as soon as practicable and pass this letter to your insurers. We would be grateful if you would acknowledge receipt.

Yours faithfully,

B.15 Letter to other side re failure to respond

Ref MD/FRY/B912986

Dear Sir/Madam,

Re: Katherine Fry of 40 Tatersall Corner, Manchester M23.

We refer to our letter dated 14 March 1994 and note we have not heard from you. We enclose a copy of that letter in case it has gone astray.

Unless we hear from you within the next fourteen days we will advise our client to commence proceedings immediately.

We would once again urge you to pass the correspondence to your insurers.

Yours faithfully,

Insurers

B.16 Initial letter to insurers

Ref MD/PRICE/9011298

Dear Sir/Madam,

Re: Our client - June Price. Your insured - Holly Hunter. Policy number - ATL/ 34518924.

We are instructed by the above named in respect of a road accident which occurred on 5 June 1993. The other driver involved in the accident was Ms Hunter who we understand was insured by yourselves at the time, under the policy number given above.

We enclose a copy of the letter we have sent to your insured and we would be grateful if you would confirm that your insurance covered Ms Hunter for the accident concerned.

Yours faithfully,

B.17 Response to insurers' standard letter

Ref MD/SMITH/C910298

Dear Sir/Madam,

Re: Our client - Smith. Your insured - Hunter.

Further to your letter dated 13 March 1994, we would be happy to supply you with the various documents and information you have requested, on confirmation that liability is admitted. If you are not prepared to admit liability, we will have no alternative but to advise our client to commence proceedings.

Yours faithfully,

B.18 Letter to other side enclosing High Court pleadings

Ref MD/VINCENT/C914986

Dear Sir/Madam,

Re: Harry Vincent of 18 Norbert Close, Halifax.

Further to our previous correspondence, we are now able to send to you the writ, statement of claim, medical report, schedule of special damages, notice of issue of legal aid and acknowledgment of service, all served in accordance with the rules of the Supreme Court.

We would suggest that you pass this letter and documentation on to your insurers immediately.

We look forward to receiving the defence within the time set down by the rules.

Yours faithfully,

Police

B.19 Request to police for accident report

The Superintendent,
Process section.

Ref MD/GILL/9829

Dear Sir/Madam,

Re: Road traffic accident on 13 October 1993 at Chestnut Close, Canterbury.

We are instructed on behalf of Peter Gill of 13 Mall Lane, Canterbury in connection with the above street accident. The two vehicles involved in the accident were a Honda Accord, registration number B219 AFC, owned and driven by Mr Gill, and a Rover 2000.

We enclose a remittance of £44 and should be obliged if you would forward a copy of the police report and statements. If proceedings are pending or have been concluded we would be grateful if you would inform us of the name and address of the defendant, any charges laid against him/her, the hearing date, the court, the outcome if any, and details of the defendant's insurers.

In the event of any delay in furnishing the report, we ask that the original is not destroyed until after the conclusion of our client's litigation. We would be grateful if you would confirm this.

Yours faithfully,

B.20 Request to interview police officer

Ref MD/JOHNSON/319XL

Dear Sir/Madam,

Johnson v Patel

Thank you for sending on the police report dated September 1993. We have now had a chance to read through the report and in the light of the contents thereof we would like to interview PC 132 Rose on behalf of our client Patricia Q. Johnson of 17A Balham Drive, London SE17.

We enclose the interview fee and would be grateful if you would let us know through whom the arrangements should be made for the interview.

Yours faithfully,

B.21 Obtaining defendant's details from police

Ref MD/DEANS/QT9 4BL

Dear Sir/Madam,

Re: Joan Deans of 3 St John's Crescent, Portsmouth.

Further to your letter dated 18 January 1994 informing us that the police report is not yet available, we would be grateful if you would provide us with the name, address, vehicle registration and insurance details of the driver of the vehicle that hit our client.

Yours faithfully,

Legal Aid Board

B.22 Initial letter accompanying application for legal aid

Ref MD/HODGKISS/P9140159

Dear Sir/Madam,

Re: Our client: Peter Hodgkiss of 19 Paling Close, Upshot.

We are instructed on behalf of the above-named in respect of his personal injury claim for damages following an accident on 23 August 1993. We enclose an application for legal aid, together with supporting documentation.

The accident occurred while our client was at work at 10 Dray Road, Upshot. His employers are Joseph Man & Sons, a company. At about one o'clock in the afternoon on the day of the accident our client was in the process of loading a lorry with a fork lift truck when another truck reversed into the one being driven by our client, knocking Mr Hodgkiss onto the floor. As a result of the accident our client sustained fractured bones in his right hand.

There can be little doubt that the employers were to blame for the accident in that they are vicariously liable for the negligent driving of the driver of the other truck and were in breach of their statutory duties under the Factories Act 1961, the Management of Health and Safety at Work Regulations 1992 and the Workplace (Health, Safety and Welfare) Regulations 1992.

We would estimate the value of the claim to be £7000 for the injury and £3,500 for the loss of earnings and other financial losses.

We would therefore ask that legal aid be granted to enable us to commence proceedings.

Yours faithfully,

B.23 Disputing limitation on the legal aid certificate

Ref MD/HARP/H9199

Dear Sir/Madam,

Re: Our client Helen Harp. Certificate no L18/234165.

We have just received the legal aid certificate dated 5 March 1994 from which we see that you have limited the scope of the certificate to our obtaining counsel's opinion.

As we pointed out to you in our initial letter applying for legal aid, this case is very straight forward, involving a pedestrian hit by a vehicle while walking across a pelican crossing.

We take the view that there can be little doubt that this claim will succeed and, taking into account our experience of personal injury work, we consider it to be a waste of resources and time for counsel's opinion to be obtained at this stage. We would therefore ask that you delete the limitation from the certificate to allow us to commence proceedings and pursue the case through to trial as speedily as possible.

We attach to this letter our form CLA30 duly completed. We would ask you kindly to read this letter in conjunction with that completed form.

Yours faithfully,

B.24 Sending counsel's opinion to Legal Aid Board

Ref MD/MURDOCH/912814

Dear Sir/Madam,

Re: Hope Murdoch of 5 Brechin Gardens, Lampeter. Certificate no L16/342516.

In accordance with the limitation on the legal aid certificate we now enclose counsel's opinion on the merits, evidence and quantum.

You will see that counsel takes the view that this claim has a good chance of succeeding and that the value of the claim is between £10,000 and £15,000. In these circumstances we write to ask that the limitation be removed from the certificate to enable us to pursue the case to trial.

We attach to this letter our form CLA30 duly completed which we would ask you kindly to read in conjunction with this letter.

Yours faithfully,

B.25 Request for approval for use of expert

Ref MD/GREEN/J91298

Dear Sir/Madam,

Re: Peter Green. Certificate no L15/365718.

We write to ask your approval to obtain a report under this certificate from Ms Helen Fry, a leading care expert whom we have instructed on several occasions in the past and in whom we have confidence.

As you will be aware from your file, this action relates to Mr Green's personal injury claim following the very serious injuries he received in a road accident last June. He is now severely disabled.

We would like to obtain an expert's report from Ms Fry who will be reporting on the issue of the care, aids and adaptations that Mr Green will require to be able to live at home. We have discussed the matter with the expert and the estimate of her fees is £500. We would therefore ask that you authorise the obtaining of such a report.

We attach to this letter our form CLA31 duly completed, which we would ask you kindly to read in conjunction with this letter.

Yours faithfully,

B.26 Request for approval for leading counsel

Ref MD/SULLIVAN/J999814

Dear Sir/Madam,

Re: David Sullivan of 35 Carrick Street, Liverpool. Certificate no L61/345167.

We write to ask for approval to appoint leading counsel to represent the plaintiff at the hearing of the action. The leader we have in mind is Ms Marianne Merion, QC who is a member of the Association of Personal Injury Lawyers and is a specialist in personal injury work.

As you will be aware from your file, the basis of this action is that Mr Sullivan lost his right arm as a result of an accident at work.

The reason that approval for a leading counsel is being requested is that the claim is valued at £500,000. Mr Sullivan was a successful artist and the defendants are challenging various aspects of the case including his earnings history and his continuing ability to paint. We enclose a short written opinion from junior counsel confirming the necessity for a leader in this case.

We would therefore be grateful if you would authorise our instructing leading counsel to represent the plaintiff at the hearing. We attach to this letter our form CLA31 duly completed. We would ask you kindly to read this letter in conjunction with that completed form.

Yours faithfully,

B.27 Covering letter for Form CLA26 on conclusion of case

Ref MD/SARGEANT/J91406

Dear Sir/Madam,

Re: John Sargeant. Certificate no L45/561435

This case has now settled for the sum of £10,000 plus costs. The defendants have paid to us those monies, which we continue to hold.

We have been able to reach agreement with the defendants regarding our costs which we set out below:

Profit costs	£2,000 + VAT
Counsel's fees	£ 400 + VAT
Disbursements	£ 550 + VAT
Interest on Costs	£nil

We have received a cheque from the defendants for our costs and we confirm that no claim will be made against the legal aid fund and that no green form was signed by Mr Sargeant.

We enclose form CLA26 duly completed and ask for confirmation that we can pay the damages to our client and that the certificate will be discharged.

Yours faithfully,

Note: This letter should be sent when the costs have been agreed between the parties and where there is no claim on the legal aid fund.

Medical reports

B.28 Initial letter requesting medical report

Ref MD/BONE/90409

Dear Mr Jones,

Re: Gay Bone of 4 Joseph's Avenue, Deal, Kent. Hospital no 34512/HY.

We are instructed by the above-named in respect of an accident which occurred on 13 January 1994. We write to ask that you provide us with a medical report in relation to the injuries sustained by our client.

The accident occurred when Ms Bone was knocked down while crossing Talbot Road at its junction with Bule Street, Deal. As a result of the accident, our client sustained a fractured pelvis and fractured right tibia. Ms Bone worked as a barmaid.

We would be grateful if you would provide us with a medical report detailing the injuries, the present position, the prognosis, and the cost of any treatment likely to be needed now or in the future. Please send our client an early appointment for examination and we would be grateful if you would send to us a copy of the appointment letter.

We will of course be responsible for your reasonable fees in relation to the report and look forward to receiving it in due course.

We have written to the treating hospitals asking that they forward to you a copy of the medical records with any X-rays involved. If the documents do not arrive in due course please let us know and we will chase them up.

Yours faithfully,

B.29 Letter to medical records officer

Ref MD/BONE/90409

Dear Sir/Madam,

Re: Gay Bone of 4 Joseph's Avenue, Deal, Kent. Hospital no 34512/HY.

We are instructed by the above-named in respect of an accident which occurred on 13 January 1994. Immediately following the accident our client, who had sustained a fractured pelvis and right tibia, was admitted to your hospital for treatment.

Our client was kept in your hospital for four days and was then seen regularly in your out-patient department.

We have asked Mr Jones, a consultant orthopaedic surgeon of 35 Harley Street, London, W1 to provide us with an independent medical report in relation to these injuries.

To assist the expert in providing us with a medical report we would be very grateful if you could send to him a copy of all the medical records in relation to the treatment received by our client. We would also be grateful if you would send a copy of the X-rays or scans that were taken.

We shall of course be responsible for any reasonable copying and postage fees. We confirm we have no instructions to take any proceedings against your authority. Finally, we enclose an authority from our client for you to release the records.

Yours faithfully,

B.30 Authority to release medical records

Dear Sir/Madam,

Re: Hospital no 23456/78.

I write to authorise you to make available a set of my medical records and X-rays to my solicitors, Messrs Grey & White of 13 Time Square, High Wycombe, under reference MD/HUMPHRIES/98914 relating to the treatment I received following my accident on 5 December 1993.

I am grateful to you for your assistance.

Yours sincerely,

Beverly Humphries

Solicitors' reference MD/HUMPHRIES/98914

Note: This letter should be typed on plain paper with the client's address in the top right-hand corner.

B.31 Request for final medical report

Ref MD/WILLIAMS/97417

Dear Ms Johnston,

Re: Michael Williams of 6 Belfast Road, Barry.

Thank you for kindly providing us with your interim report of 2 September last year on this case. The case is due to go to trial in the next few months and I would like you to provide us with a final report for our use in the case.

I would be grateful if you could send our client an early appointment for examination and would ask you to provide us with a report dealing particularly with the present position and the prognosis. If you still think an operation may be necessary at some time in the future, could you kindly estimate the cost at today's value, and give us your best estimate of when the deterioration might occur and when thereafter an operation might be advisable. I appreciate how difficult these estimations are but the court is required to make them.

I would be grateful too if you would set out the levels of care, attention and therapy my client will need, since I propose to instruct a care expert to cost these matters when your report is to hand.

In preparing your report I would be grateful if you would pay especial attention to the client's employment prospects and any future disabilities that are likely to affect his work position, social life or health.

I will of course be responsible for your reasonable fees and I look forward to receiving your report in due course.

Yours sincerely,

B.32 Notification to expert witness of hearing date

Ref MD/PAUL/91977

Dear Mr Peters,

Re: John Paul of Grate Street, Grantham.

We have now received notification that the trial date has been listed for 3 May 1995 at the Grantham County Court at 4 High Street, Grantham. The case has been listed for two days and we are likely to need you to give evidence on the first day.

It is certainly possible that the defendants will agree your evidence prior to the hearing, or indeed that the case will settle. I would however be grateful if you would note this date in your diary to ensure that you are free to attend the court if necessary. If you have any problems with the particular date I have mentioned, it may be possible to have your evidence taken on the other day of the trial. I would however be grateful if you could notify me of this straight away.

I confirm that we will be responsible for your reasonable fees in appearing at the hearing, together with any preparation fee. If you impose a late cancellation charge in the event of the case settling before trial, please let me have the details forthwith so that I can put the defendants on notice.

I would be grateful if you would acknowledge receipt of this letter and confirm your availability for the hearing.

Yours sincerely,

Other experts

B.33 Request for engineer's report

Ref MD/GREEN L 91/9894

Dear Sir/Madam,

Re: Laura Green of 3 Fry Rd, Leeds.

We are instructed by the above-named in respect of an accident on 5 March 1994. We write to ask that you prepare a report for us for our use in the court case that has evolved following the accident.

Our client is a machine operator and works for Scrooge plc at their premises, Station Road, Leeds. The company is involved in the making of widgets. On the day of the accident our client was operating her widget-making machine and in pulling the lever to close the hood of the machine the hood fell off and hit her head.

I enclose a copy of the pleadings, my client's proof and letters from three witnesses.

I would be grateful if you would arrange to inspect the locus in quo with my client and would ask that you provide us with a report explaining how the accident happened, the likely causes of the accident and your support for the claims of negligence and/or breach of statutory duty as set out in the pleadings. If you consider that any of the allegations are not supportable it would perhaps be helpful if you could state that in a separate letter. If there are further allegations that should be made please state those in the main report.

Please would you provide me with an estimate of your costs so that I can obtain confirmation from the Legal Aid Board that they are prepared to pay that fee? On confirmation that you are happy to go ahead with this report, I will obtain details from the defendant's solicitors regarding the person through whom the inspection facilities should be arranged.

Yours sincerely,

B.34 Request for care expert's report

Ref MD/VINCENT/9104/98

Dear Ms Smith,

Re: Peter Vincent of 2 Green Street, Lytham.

I am instructed by the above-named in respect of an accident on 4 July 1992. As a result of the accident our client sustained very severe injuries and he is now seriously incapacitated. I write to ask that you produce a care report for our use in the court action which has ensued from the accident.

My client, having lost his legs in the accident, is wheelchair bound. I would be grateful if you would arrange an appointment to go and see my client at his home. His telephone number is 0123-456789 and I have written to him confirming that you will be contacting him.

I enclose the medical reports of Mr Sym of 10 September 1992 and 4 August 1993 together with that of Mr Path of 14 January 1994. You will see the level of care, attention and therapy the doctors are advising at present.

Please would you provide me with a full report, detailing the limitations on my client's activities, the aids and adaptations needed in the house to ameliorate his time at home, any building works necessary, the care and assistance he needs at home in terms of his personal care, the housework, the maintenance of the property and the garden, together with details of the additional costs necessarily incurred in enabling him to travel both locally and on a wider basis.

You will appreciate that it is important that your report and the medical reports are consistent and it may be that a consultation with counsel, yourself and the doctors is the best way forward especially if you consider that there are elements of care, attention and therapy which you think necessary which are not presently reflected in the medical reports.

I look forward to receiving your report and would be grateful if you could, at this initial stage, let me know your likely fee so that I can obtain authority for this expenditure from the Legal Aid Board.

Yours sincerely,

B.35 Request for road accident expert's report

Ref MD/BENNET/91039

Dear Ms Piper,

Re: Timothy Bennet of 4 Peters Gate, Broadway.

I am instructed by the above-named in respect of a road accident that occurred on 8 July 1993. I write to ask that you provide us with a road accident report.

The accident occurred at the junction of Main Road and High Street, Broadway at approximately 10am on the day of the accident. Mr Bennet was walking across the junction, travelling on the north side going from east to west, with the pedestrian lights showing the green man. A Mercedes motor car jumped the lights and knocked him down.

I enclose a copy of the pleadings, my client's proof, the witness proof, the police report and a rough sketch plan prepared by my client showing the various positions of the people and vehicles involved in the accident.

I would be grateful if you would prepare an accident report describing your views as to how the accident occurred, where the various people involved in the accident were placed at the time the accident happened and your estimate as to the speed of the various vehicles involved. Please give your expert opinion about the cause of the accident and any support you can give to the allegations of negligence in the particulars of claim.

If you have any doubts regarding the allegations made by counsel in the particulars of claim I would be grateful if you could let me know in a separate letter. If you consider there are any further allegations of negligence please mention them in your report.

You may well want to meet with my client at the scene of the accident and I have warned him that you may be contacting him. His telephone number is 0546–75645.

I look forward to receiving your report and photographs of the locus in quo. I would be grateful if you could let me know what your fee is likely to be, so that I can have this approved by the Legal Aid Board.

Yours sincerely,

B.36 Request for employment expert's report

Ref MD/DOORS/9103914

Dear Mr Stevens,

Re: John Doors of 13 Southvale, Peterborough.

I am instructed by the above-named in respect of an accident on 25 May 1993. I write to ask that you provide me with an employment report for our use in the ensuing court action that has arisen following the accident.

My client was very severely injured on the day of the accident when the car in which he was a passenger went into the crash barrier on the M1. His injuries are right-sided hemiplegia.

At the time of the accident my client was working as a car mechanic. His working history up to that time was that he left school at the age of sixteen and had worked for three different garages as a mechanic before commencing the current job with Len's Autos, High Road, Peterborough in 1989 when he was aged 23.

I enclose copies of the pleadings, my client's proof and the medical reports. You will see from those documents that he has been unable to return to work until now, but that the doctors are saying that he may be able to do a job involving light duties in the near future. You will see from his proof that he is suggesting that he would be interested in doing the following jobs: telephonist, receptionist or filing clerk.

I would be grateful if you would provide a report giving an assessment as to his chances of finding work in these fields and his likely earnings. Would you set out his likely career pattern if the accident had not occurred? I would finally be grateful if you would compare the wages that he would have earned, as against the wages that he is likely to earn.

I have told my client that you may well need to contact him to clarify certain points and his telephone number is 0234–675456.

I look forward to receiving your employment report and would be grateful if you could let me know now your likely fee so that I can obtain authority for this expenditure from the Legal Aid Board.

Yours sincerely,

Department of Social Security

B.37 Request to Compensation Recovery Unit

Ref JONES L/MD/91469

Dear Sir/Madam,

Re: Laura Jones of 2 Knowles Crescent, Oxbridge.

NI No YE PBLM 96 B. DOB 2.7.55.

We are instructed by the above-named in respect of an accident which occurred on 15 October 1993. She is employed by the Oxbridge City Council.

We would be most grateful if you would forward, in duplicate, details of all benefits paid to our client since the date of the accident, together with the total amount paid to date. If a certificate of total benefit has been issued may we please have a copy?

We confirm that this information is requested pursuant to The Law Reform (Personal Injury) Act 1947/Social Security Act 1989 s22.

Yours faithfully,

Witnesses

B.38 Letter to lay witness with questionnaire

Ref MD/JONES/917

Dear Ms Philips,

Re: My client – Roy Jones of 17 New Road, Ilford, Essex.

I am instructed by the above-named in respect of an accident in which he was hit by a Volvo motor car on 16 September 1993 at 10am. The accident occurred when Mr Jones was walking across the High Road where it joins at the Roundhouse Roundabout, Ilford, Essex.

I have been asked to advise Mr Jones in relation to a possible claim against the driver of the Volvo.

I understand that you were a witness to this accident. I would be most grateful if you would answer the questions raised in the enclosed questionnaire, and draw a sketch plan, if appropriate, on the paper attached.

I enclose a stamped addressed envelope for your reply. I look forward to hearing from you and thank you for your assistance.

Yours sincerely,

Questionnaire for Ms Philips

1 Your full name
2 Your address
3 Your telephone number
4 Your date of birth
5 Your job
6 The date of accident
7 The time of accident
8 The place where accident occurred
9 Please give a description of exactly what you saw.
10 State where you were positioned. (It may assist you to draw a plan of the accident spot and where the various people were stationed. A sheet of paper is enclosed for this purpose.)
11 Please state who you think was to blame for the accident, giving your reasons for your view.
12 Please confirm whether you would be prepared to give evidence if this case went to court.

Signature . . . Date . . .

Ref MD/JONES 917

Note: The questionnaire should be spaced out appropriately to give adequate space for descriptions, reasons etc.

B.39 Request to take detailed statement

Ref MD/JONES/917

Dear Ms Pound,

Re: My client – Roy Jones of 17 New Road, Ilford, Essex.

Further to your kindly providing me with a written statement, it is now clear that this case is likely to go to trial and we will be wanting you to give evidence at the hearing.

I would like to take more details from you and would therefore ask that you telephone my secretary so that we can arrange either for you to come to my office at a time convenient to you or so that I could meet you at home or at work, again at a time convenient to you.

If you have any travelling expenses or loss of earnings as a result of the time spent with me I will be more than happy to pay those costs. If you do have loss of earnings I would be grateful if you could provide me with either a wage slip or a letter from your employer confirming the amount.

Yours sincerely,

B.40 Notification to witness to attend court

Ref MD/JONES 917

Dear Ms Pound,

Re: My client – Roy Jones of 17 New Road, Ilford, Essex.

I write to inform you that the court hearing in this case has now been fixed for 5 October 1994 and this will be heard at the Swindon County Court at 10.30am.

The case has been listed for hearing for two days and I would like you to attend the hearing on the afternoon of the first day. If you have any problems with this specific time, I may be able to re-arrange the scheduling of the different witnesses to put you on the other day of the hearing. Please let me know if this is a problem.

A witness summons will be served on you in the next few days by our process server. She will be telephoning you to work out a time for service. The witness summons is a formal document from the court requiring you to attend. It may be useful to you to show it to your employers so as to get time off more easily.

On the day that you are required at court I would be grateful if you could arrive at 1.30 pm which will give us the opportunity to have a short discussion prior to your giving evidence.

Yours sincerely,

Employers

B.41 Request for wage details

Ref MD/MOYNE/910765

Dear Sir/Madam,

Re: Melinda Moyne (Pay roll no A79632).

We are instructed by the above-named, an employee of your company, in connection with her road accident on 17 October 1993, as a result of which she sustained serious injuries.

To assist in the preparation of our client's claim for loss of earnings as a result of the accident, we would be obliged for the following information:

1 dates of our client's absence(s) from work attributable to the accident;

2 details of her net and gross earnings week by week for the period of 13 weeks prior to the accident; if any of those weeks were untypical please extend the period accordingly;

3 details of changes of wage rates or deductions during the period of absence with an estimate of the weekly net and gross earnings that would have been produced thereby;

4 details of gross and net earnings week by week for six weeks from her return to work;

5 any sick pay awarded to her, including any which may be refundable to yourselves, should she be successful in her claim. If this is the case please send a copy of the contract of employment or other agreement or document setting out this provision;

6 any other losses in respect of earnings which have resulted or may result from the accident or period off work such as overtime, bonuses, commission, pension contributions and entitlement etc.

We look forward to receiving the information requested above, and thank you in advance for your co-operation. We confirm that you have no involvement in the claim. A stamped addressed envelope is enclosed for your reply.

Yours faithfully,

Meteorological Office

B.42 Request for weather report

Ref MD/PERVIS/919456

Dear Sir/Madam,

Re: George Pervis of 15 Shepherd's Bush, London, W6.

We are instructed by the above-named in relation to a road accident that occurred on 15 January 1993, at approximately 5 am. The accident took place at Shepherd's Bush Roundabout, London, W6.

We are making a claim, on behalf of our client against the driver of the other vehicle involved in the crash and we are keen to know the exact weather conditions, not only at the time of the accident but also for the preceding twelve hours.

We would be very grateful if you could supply us with as detailed information as possible for both 14 and 15 January 1993, including a description of the rainfall, cloud cover, and temperature. We shall, of course, be responsible for your reasonable fees.

Yours faithfully,

Health and Safety Executive

B.43 Request for HSE report

Ref MD/JONES/91LQ491

Dear Sir/Madam,

Re: Melissa Jones of 2 Connecticut Close, York.

We are instructed by the above-named in relation to a potential claim against her employers, Bigsby, Brown & Co of 2 High Road, York, following an accident at work on 13 December 1993.

The accident occurred at 2 High Road, York at about 10.15am. Our client was in the process of operating the lathe on which she worked, when a component in the lathe exploded and a piece flew off into her eye.

We understand that an officer from the Executive attended the scene of the accident to carry out an investigation. We would be very grateful if you could provide a statement of your findings together with any other documents relating to the case that relate to the incident. We will of course pay any reasonable fee incurred in producing the information.

If you are unable to send certain documents without the necessary court order, please list the documents in your possession.

Yours faithfully,

Motor Insurers Bureau

B.44 Uninsured driver

Ref MD/SMITH/91099177

Dear Sir/Madam

Re: John Smith of 5 Browning Road, London, E5.

We are instructed by the above-named in relation to a road accident that occurred on 16 January 1993. The owner of the vehicle, Mr Alan Brook of 13 Clapham Street, London SW5, who caused the accident appears to have been uninsured and we write to notify you under the terms of the MIB agreement of our having issued proceedings against him two days ago. We enclose a copy of the writ/summons.

The accident took place at the junction of Broadbent Road and Fry Street, Manchester 23. Our client was walking in an easterly direction along Broadbent Road. When he arrived at the junction, the lights were green for pedestrians travelling in his direction and he started to walk across the junction. While doing so he was knocked down by a motor car. The accident was clearly caused by the negligence of the driver of the Vauxhall motor car because the driver must have driven through a red light to have hit our client.

After the accident, Mr Brook gave his name and address to the police but they have written to us saying that he has failed to disclose his insurance details. We enclose a letter from them confirming this. We have also had no response from him to our two letters before action.

Proceedings were commenced on 13 June 1994 and we enclose a copy of the particulars of claim. Please confirm that you will accept this letter as notification under the terms of the agreement.

Yours faithfully,

B.45 Untraced driver

Ref MD/JONES/91444

Dear Sir/Madam

Re: Peter Jones of 10 Manor Road, Hanley, Middlesex.

We are instructed by the above-named who was injured by a hit and run driver in an accident on 18 May 1993. We write to ask that you accept this case under the terms of the 'Untraced Drivers Scheme'.

The accident happened in London Road, Hanley. Our client was walking across a pedestrian crossing when the driver of a Golf GTI motor car drove straight across the pedestrian crossing knocking him to the ground. The driver did not stop and neither the client nor any witness took his registration number. We enclose a copy of the letter from the police confirming they have been unable to locate him. We therefore ask that you accept the case under the MIB agreement.

The injuries and losses sustained by our client were as follows: fractured left tibia; cut left ear; bruised left thigh and arm.

We look forward to hearing from you.

Yours faithfully,

Defendant's solicitors

B.46 Letter enclosing pleadings

Ref MD/SMITH/914096H

Dear Madam,

Re: Smith v Bailey.

On behalf of the plaintiff, please find enclosed a copy of the letter and documents we have today served on the defendant in this case. We look forward to receiving the defence within the time set down by the rules.

Yours faithfully,

Note: This letter should be sent to the defendant's solicitors if they have not yet given notice that they will accept service of the proceedings.

B.47 Extending time

Ref MD/DEANS/9142987

Dear Sir,

Re: Deans v Berry.

Further to your letter dated 3 May 1994 we write to make it plain that we are not prepared to grant you a general extension of time for service of the defence. We are prepared to grant you an extension of 14 days. If you need further time thereafter you will have to take out a time summons.

Yours faithfully,

B.48 Letter enclosing plaintiff's list of documents

Ref MD/HERBERT/91404

Dear Madam,

Re: Herbert v Curry and Co.

We write to acknowledge receipt of the defence enclosed with your letter dated 5 June 1994.

Please find enclosed the plaintiff's list of documents. We will be happy to supply you with copies of any of the documents listed in schedule 1 part 1 on confirmation that you will pay our reasonable copying charges.

Yours faithfully,

B.49 Letter notifying setting down in High Court

Ref MD/TIDY/9109412

Dear Sir/Madam,

Re: Tidy v Bone.

Please note that this action has now been set down and has been allocated the non-jury number 91 2356. We shall be taking out the application to fix in due course and we will send to you details of the hearing as soon as we have them.

Yours faithfully,

B.50 Letter enclosing application to fix

Ref MD/STONE/H402

Dear Sir/Madam,

Re: Stone v Garner.

Please find the application to fix in duplicate which you will see is returnable on 3 October 1994. Please complete the details on the top copy and return it to us. The other copy is for your own file.

Yours faithfully,

B.51 Letter re failure to comply with automatic directions

Ref MD/HORSE/989

Dear Sir/Madam,

Re: Horse v Jones.

You have failed to supply us with the defendant's list of documents within the time set down by the automatic directions. Unless you serve that document within the next seven days we will take out an application to strike out the defence.

Yours faithfully,

B.52 Letter re defendant's request for medical examination

Ref MD/DOWNS/90491

Dear Sir/Madam,

Re: Downs v Elliot.

Further to your letter requesting facilities to have our client examined by Dr Brown, we write to confirm that you may have the facilities provided that you undertake (i) to pay the plaintiff's reasonable travelling expenses and loss of earnings; (ii) to disclose a copy of the report within 28 days of receipt; and (iii) not to make any payment into court until after the report is disclosed.

Yours faithfully,

B.53 Request for facilities for expert

Ref MD/GERRY/LK9177

Dear Sir/Madam,

Re: Gerry v Tunes Ltd.

We write to ask that facilities be granted for our expert, Mr John Dixon, to examine the locus in quo.

Please confirm that you are prepared to grant those facilities and we would ask that you notify us of the telephone number of the person through whom the arrangements should be made.

Yours faithfully,

B.54 Letter enclosing bundle

Ref MD/BALL/040601

Dear Madam,

Re: Ball v Cox.

Please find a draft bundle of documents for use at the court hearing. If you want us to include any other documents please let us know by 30 September 1994, otherwise we will assume that you are content with the bundle as it stands.

Yours faithfully,

B.55 Statement of costs following settlement

Ref MD/EVANS/58114

Dear Sir/Madam,

Re: Evans v Chapman.

Further to the settlement of this action we set out below our costs for possible agreement.

Telephone calls – 60 @ £7 per call			£ 420
Letters out – 80 @ £7 per letter			£ 560
Attendances, preparations etc – 12 hours @ £70 per hour			£ 840
			£1820
Care and attention @ 50%			£ 910
			£2730
VAT at 17.5%			£ 477.75
		Total	£3207.75
Disbursements liable for VAT:			
Counsel's fees –	£1200		
Engineer's fees –	£ 750		
VAT at 17.5% –	£321.25		
		Total	£2271.25
Disbursements not liable for VAT:			
Court fees	£120		
Police report	£ 33		
Medical reports	£600		
		Total	£ 753

Our total costs are therefore £6232

Please let us know if you are prepared to agree these costs or whether we will need to have a formal bill drawn to lodge with the court for taxation.

Yours faithfully,

C Pleadings and ancillary documents

C.1 Capacity and description of parties on pleadings

Administrator/ administratrix	'AB, administrator of the estate of CD, deceased' (RSC Order 15 r14)
Attorney-General:	'Her Majesty's Attorney-General'
Charity Commissioners:	'The Charity Commissioners of England and Wales'
Club, incorporated:	*Corporate name*
unincorporated:	'AB and CD on their own behalf and on the behalf of all other members of the club . . .'[1]
Company:	*Registered name*
Corporation:	*Corporate name*
Executor:	'AB, executor of the will of CD, deceased'[2]
Firm:	[*Individual's name*] trading as Business Names *alternatively:* Business Names (a trading name) *alternatively:* Business Names (a firm)
Government department:	*The name of the appropriate authorised department or, if there is reasonable doubt, the Attorney-General.*[3]
Hospital:	*The name of the appropriate authority eg* 'XY District Health Authority' or 'Oxbridge Hospital Trust'
Individual, in his/her own capacity:	'J Starkey (a male)' *or* 'John Starkey' P Rivers (a female) *or* 'Pamela Rivers'
Minor, if suing:	'AB a minor, by CD his father and next friend'

1 *Campbell v Thompson* [1953] 1 QB 445.
2 RSC Order 15, r15.
3 See White Book 1993 Vol II, para 607 for list of authorised departments.

if sued:	'AB a minor by CD his guardian ad litem'
City:	'The City Council of [*name*]'
City of London:	'The Mayor and Corporation of the City of London'
County council:	'The County Council of [*name*]'
London borough:	'The London Borough of [*name*]'
District:	'The District Council of [*name*]'
Community:	'The Community of [*name*]'
Partnership:	'AB (a firm)'
Patient, if suing:	'AB, by CD his next friend'
if sued:	'AB, by CD, his guardian ad litem'
Police force:	*Chief Officer of Police*
School, state:	*Name of education authority*
private or grant-maintained:	*Name of school*
Trade union:	*Name of Trade Union*
Trustees:	'AB and CD (suing as trustees of the estate of EF, deceased)'.

C.2 Statement of value (form PF 204)

IN THE HIGH COURT OF JUSTICE 19 No.
QUEEN'S BENCH DIVISION
[DISTRICT REGISTRY]
Between

Plaintiff

– and –

Defendant

To the master [district judge] of [insert Central Office or District Registry as appropriate.]

STATEMENT OF THE VALUE OF THE ACTION

Tick appropriate box

☐ The value of this action for the purpose of article 7(3) of the High Court and County Courts Jurisdiction Order 1991 is not less than £25,000; or

☐ The value of this action is less than £25,000 but by reason of one or more of the criteria mentioned in article 7(5) of that Order it is suitable for determination in the High Court; or

☐ The action is for relief other than a sum of money but the plaintiff can reasonably state that it is of financial worth to him of not less than £25,000; or

☐ The action is for relief other than a sum of money but the plaintiff cannot reasonably state that it is of financial worth to him of not less than £25,000 but by reason of one or more of the criteria mentioned in article 7(5) of that Order it is suitable for determination in the High Court; or

☐ The action has no quantifiable value but by reason of one or more of the criteria mentioned in article 7(5) of that Order it is suitable for determination in the High Court; or

☐ The action is suitable for trial in a county court.

Dated

Signed

[Solicitor for the plaintiff/defendant/party acting in person]

C.3 Specimen writ endorsements

Road accident

The Plaintiff's claim is for injuries suffered and losses and expenses incurred as a result of an accident on the 5th September 1993 at the Redhill roundabout, Redhill, Surrey caused by the negligent driving of the Defendant.

Work accident

The Plaintiff's claim is for injuries suffered and losses and expenses incurred as a result of an accident on the 5th September 1993 at 59 High Street, Cambridge whilst employed by the Defendants and caused by the negligence and/or breach of statutory duty of the Defendants, their servants or agents.

Tripping

The Plaintiff's claim is for injuries suffered and losses and expenses incurred as a result of an accident on the 5th September 1993 in High Road, Oxford caused by the negligence and/or breach of statutory duty of the Defendants, their servants or agents.

Fatal accident

The Plaintiff is the widow and administratrix of the estate of the late John Williams who died in an accident on the 5th September 1993 in Russett Road, Derby caused by the negligent driving of the Defendant and the Plaintiff claims on behalf of herself and the Plaintiff's estate and on behalf of her children, James Williams, date of birth 12th August 1987 and Alice Williams, date of birth 4th February 1990 under the provisions of: (a) The Fatal Accidents Act 1970; and (b) The Law Reform (Miscellaneous Provisions) Act 1934.

Claim against police

The Plaintiff's claim is for damages under the Fatal Accidents Act 1976 and the Law Reform (Miscellaneous Provisions) Act 1934 for loss arising out of an accident caused by the negligence of the Defendant or his constable, servant or agent in the driving of a police patrol car on the 19th February 1994.

C.4 Certificate of Value

All writ endorsements should conclude as follows (pursuant to *Practice Direction (Personal Injuries Action: Indorsement on Writ)* [1991] 1 WLR 642):

This writ includes a claim for personal injury but may be commenced in the High Court because the value of the action for the purposes of article 5 of the High Court and County Courts Jurisdiction Order 1991 exceeds £50,000.

(Note: this certificate of value must be signed by the plaintiff's solicitor. Claims of less than £50,000 which are intended to be High Court actions should be issued in the county court and an application made to transfer accompanied by the Statement of Value of the Action (C.2 p364).)

Statements of claim/particulars of claim

C.5 Factory accident (statutory duty and negligence pleaded separately – Provision and Use of Work Equipment Regulations and Management of Health and Safety at Work Regulations both pleaded)

IN THE OXBRIDGE COUNTY COURT Case No. 1234

BETWEEN:

JEANNIE LONGO Plaintiff

– and –

EXPRESS PRESS LIMITED Defendants

PARTICULARS OF CLAIM

1 At all material times the Plaintiff was employed by the Defendants as a machine operator at their premises at the Towpath, Burchill, Surrey.

2 The Defendants' said premises were at the material time and still are a factory within the meaning of the Factories Act 1961 and/or the provisions of the Provision and Use of Work Equipment Regulations 1992 (hereinafter 'Equipment Regs'), the Management of Health and Safety at Work Regulations 1992 (hereinafter 'Management Regs') applied.

3 On the 15th November 1993 the Plaintiff, in the course of her said employment at the said premises, was operating a rise and fall 'loose' knife punching press when, whilst she was applying bolt resin powder to the two 'Vee' belt drives of the electric motor which operated the main driving pulley of the said machine, her thumb and middle fingers on her right hand were caught in a nip of the machinery causing her to sustain injuries and to suffer loss and damage.

4 The Plaintiff's said injuries were caused by the breach of statutory duty and/or the negligence of the Defendants, their servants or agents.

PARTICULARS OF BREACH OF STATUTORY DUTY

The Defendants were in breach of their statutory duty in that they, their servants or agents:

(1) Failed to provide suitable work equipment contrary to Regulation 5(1) of the Work Equipment Regulations 1992;

(2) Failed to ensure that the said punching press was only used for operations and under conditions for which it was suitable, contrary to Regulation 5(3) of the Work Equipment Regulations 1992;

(3) Failed to maintain the said punching press in an efficient state, efficient working order and in good repair contrary to Regulation 6 of the Work Equipment Regulations 1992;

(4) Failed to ensure that the use of the said punch press was restricted to those persons given the task of using it, contrary to Regulation 7(1)(a) of the Work Equipment Regulations 1992;

(5) Failed to ensure that the Plaintiff had adequate health and safety information and written instructions pertaining to the use of the said punch press, contrary to Regulation 8(1) of the Work Equipment Regulations 1992;

(6) Failed to ensure that the Plaintiff had adequate training in the use of the said punch press, contrary to Regulation 9(1) of the Work Equipment Regulations 1992;

Further, if the said machine was provided for use in the said premises before 1st January 1993 (which the Plaintiff is unable to ascertain until after discovery herein):

(7) failed to fence every moving part of any prime mover securely as required by Section 12(1) of the Factories Act 1961;

(8) failed to fence every part of the transmission machinery of the said press as required by Section 13(1) of the Factories Act 1961;

(9) failed to fence securely every dangerous part of the said press as required by Section 14(1) of the Factories Act 1961;

(10) failed to provide fencing or other adequate safeguards of substantial construction, constantly maintained and kept in position, as required by section 16 of the Factories Act 1961;

(11) failed to make and keep safe every place at which the Plaintiff had at any time to work as required by Section 29(1) of the Factories Act 1961;

(12) failed to ensure that effective measures were taken
   (a) to prevent access to any dangerous part of the punching press; and/or
   (b) to stop the movement of the punching press before any part of the Plaintiff entered the danger zone, contrary to Regulation 11(1) of the Work Equipment Regulations 1992;

(13) Failed to ensure that all control systems of work equipment were safe, contrary to Regulation 18(1) of the Work Equipment Regulations 1992;

(14) Failed to take appropriate measures to ensure that the said punching press was so constructed or adapted that maintenance operations which involve the risk of health or safety can be carried out without exposing the Plaintiff to a hazard, contrary to Regulation 22 of the Work Equipment Regulations 1992;

(15) Failed to ensure that the punching press incorporated appropriate warnings or warning devices, contrary to Regulation 22 of the Work Equipment Regulations 1992.

PARTICULARS OF NEGLIGENCE

The Plaintiff repeats the allegations of Breach of Statutory Duty herein as allegations of negligence and further the Defendants were negligent in that they, their servants or agents:

(a) failed to guard, fence or cover adequately or at all the two 'Vee' belts on the said press;

(b) failed to provide a safe and effective means for applying the said belt resin powder to the said belts without requiring the Plaintiff to handle the said belts;

(c) failed to replace the belts on the said machine when the said belts were defective;

(d) failed to heed and act upon properly or at all the complaints made by the Plaintiff prior to her said accident regarding the noise emanating from the said belts;

(e) failed to heed and act upon properly or at all the complaints made by the Plaintiff prior to her said accident regarding the defects in the on/off switch fitted to the said machine;

(f) failed to inspect, maintain and repair properly or at all the on/off switch of the said machine;

(g) failed to ensure that the said belts and motor did not recommence operation after the said off switch had been applied;

(h) failed to prevent the Plaintiff having to apply the said belt resin powder to the said belts whilst they were in motion;

(i) failed to provide safe plant and equipment for the Plaintiff's use;

(j) failed to provide a safe place to work;

(k) failed to keep a safe system of work;

(l) failed to have any or any adequate regard for the Plaintiff's safety and exposed her to an unnecessary risk of injury;

(m) negligently failed to heed or act upon duties in criminal law under the Management Regulations, in particular,

  (i) failed to make a suitable and sufficient assessment of the health and safety risks to which the plaintiff was exposed; further or alternatively, failed to review any such assessment as was made (as was the Defendants' duty under Regulation 3);

  (ii) failed to give effect to appropriate arrangements for the effective planning, organisation, control, monitoring and review of preventative and protective measures (as was the Defendants' duty under Regulation 4);

  (iii) failed to appoint a competent person to assist the Defendant to undertake the necessary measures to comply with his obligations under the Regulations (as was the Defendants' duty under Regulation 6);

(iv) failed adequately or at all to provide the Plaintiff with information on:

(1) the risks to her health and safety that were or should have been identified by the risk assessment hereinbefore referred to at paragraph (i) above;

(2) the preventative and protective measures hereinbefore referred to at paragraph (ii) above; (as was the Defendants' duty under Regulation 8).

(v) failed to provide the Plaintiff with any or any adequate health and safety training (as was the Defendants' duty under Regulation 11).

5 By reasons of the matters aforesaid, the Plaintiff who was born on the 10th November 1939 and who was aged about 50 at the date of the said accident, has sustained injury and suffered loss and damage.

PARTICULARS OF INJURY

Please see attached medical report.

PARTICULARS OF SPECIAL DAMAGE

The plaintiff is handicapped upon the labour market.

Please see attached schedule of damages.

6 Further the Plaintiff claims interest pursuant to Section 69 of the County Courts Act 1984 on the amount found to be due to her at such rate and for such period as the Court thinks fit.

AND the Plaintiff claims:

(1) DAMAGES in excess of £5000

(2) INTEREST pursuant to Section 69 of the County Courts Act 1984.

PARTICULARS

(a) Interest on general damages found to be due from the date of issue of the Summons to the date of judgment or earlier payment at such rate and for such period as the Court shall deem just.

(b) Interest on special damages at the full rate in the special circumstances that the Plaintiff has lost earnings and has incurred expenses which will be irrecoverable from the Defendants until the trial herein.

A BARRISTER

Dated 7th day of December 1993 by Grey, White and Partners, 1 The Place, Burchill, Surrey TNQ 7R, Solicitors for the Plaintiff.

To the District Judge and the Defendants.

C.6 Factory accident (statutory duty and negligence pleaded together – Provision and Use of Workplace Equipment Regulations, Personal Protective Equipment Regulations, and Management of Health and Safety at Work Regulations pleaded, as well as Abrasive Wheels Regulations)

IN THE HIGH COURT OF JUSTICE 1994 G. No. 10511
QUEEN'S BENCH DIVISION
BIRMINGHAM DISTRICT REGISTRY
(Writ issued 26th June 1994)

BETWEEN:

ERNEST GUEVARA Plaintiff

– and –

MAN AUTOMATIC LATHES LIMITED Defendants

STATEMENT OF CLAIM

1 At all material times the Plaintiff was employed as a setter turner by the Defendants at their premises at Barnes Lane, Coventry, a factory within the meaning of the Factories Act 1961. The Personal Protective Equipment Regulations 1992 were binding on the Defendants.

2 On or about the 24th May 1994 the Plaintiff, whilst in the course of his employment, was sharpening a parting off tool on a Kyoto Grinding Wheel, an operation to which The Abrasive Wheel Regulations 1970 and/or the Provision and Use of Work Equipment Regulations 1992 apply, when the said wheel shattered and the Plaintiff lost the sight of both eyes when fragments of the said wheel entered them. The Plaintiff is unable to say until after discovery herein whether the said machine was first provided for use before or after 1st January 1993.

3 The said accident was caused by the negligence and/or breach of statutory duty of the Defendants, their servants or agents.

PARTICULARS OF NEGLIGENCE AND/OR BREACH OF STATUTORY DUTY

A. Whenever the said machine first came into use

(a) In breach of Regulation 8 of the Abrasive Wheels Regulations 1970 and/or negligently failing to correctly mount the grinding wheel.

(b) In breach of Regulation 4(1) of the Personal Protective Equipment at Work Regulations 1992 and for negligently failing to provide goggles or other effective and suitable eye protection for the plaintiff

(c) In breach of Regulation 7(1) of the Personal Protective Equipment at Work Regulations 1992 and/or negligently failing to maintain in an efficient state, efficient working order and in good repair or to replace, the goggles with which he was provided on or about June 1993.

(d) In breach of Regulation 9 of the Personal Protective Equipment at Work Regulations and/or negligently failing to inform, instruct and train the Plaintiff adequately and appropriately for him to know the risk of working without goggles and/or action he could have taken to ensure the goggles with which he was provided in or about June 1993 were maintained or replaced.

(e) In breach of Regulation 5 of the Provision and Use of Work Equipment Regulations 1992 and/or negligently failing to ensure that the said machine is so constructed or adapted as to be suitable and safe for sharpening a parting off tool and/or failing to have regard to the risk to the Plaintiff in using it and/or failing to ensure the said machine was only used for operations and under conditions for which it was suitable and safe.

(f) In breach of Regulation 6 of the Provision and Use of Work Regulations 1992 and/or negligently failing to maintain the said machine in an efficient state, in efficient working order and in good repair.

(g) In breach of Regulations 8 and 9 of the Provision and Use of Work Equipment Regulations 1992 and/or negligently failing to ensure the Plaintiff had adequate health and safety information and/or training and/or written instructions in the use of the said machine and/or risks thereof.

(h) Causing or permitting the Plaintiff to operate the said wheel when there was an excessive gap between the wheel and the rest.

(i) Causing or permitting the Plaintiff to operate a wheel which was worn.

(j) Failing to inspect the said wheel and/or its alignment regularly, sufficiently often or at all.

(k) Failing to maintain the said wheel and/or rest in time or at all.

(l) Failing to replace the said wheel.

(m) Failing to warn the Plaintiff in time or at all that the said wheel was unsafe and/or failing to immobilise the said wheel.

(n) Failing to heed in time or at all the previous accidents which have occurred whilst sharpening parting off tools, in particular the accident suffered by Mr Moon on or about the 11th May 1994.

(o) Failing to provide and/or maintain safe and adequate plant and machinery.

(p) Failing to provide and/or maintain a safe system of work for the Plaintiff.

(q) The Plaintiff will further rely on the happening of the said accident as evidence in itself of the negligence and/or breach of statutory duty of the Defendants, their servants or agents.

(r) Failing to heed and/or act on the oral warning shortly before the accident by Mr D Deal to Mr R Vickers that he should get the wheels trimmed up as they were in a bad state.

(s) Failing to heed adequately or at all the many oral requests by Mr D Bumpton to shop-floor supervisors to correct the wheels when they needed it.

(t) Failing to motivate and operate a system of maintenance that did not rely on requests to correct the wheels but was preventive.

(u) Failing to inspect or have any or any adequate system of inspection, maintenance or repair of the goggles provided to the Plaintiff.

(v) Failing to have any or any adequate system of so supervising the Plaintiff as to ascertain and prevent him working without goggles on the grinding wheel.

(w) Negligently failing to heed or act upon duties in criminal law under the Management of Health and Safety Regulations 1992, in particular,

  (i) failing to make a suitable and sufficient assessment of the health and safety risks to which the Plaintiff was exposed; further or alternatively, failing to review any such assessment as was made (as was the Defendant's duty under Regulation 3);

  (ii) failing to give effect to appropriate arrangements for the effective planning, organisation, control, monitoring and review of any identified necessary preventative and protective measures (as was the Defendant's duty under Regulation 4);

  (iii) failing to appoint a competent person to assist the Defendant to undertake the necessary measures to comply with his obligations under the Regulations (as was the Defendant's duty under Regulation 6);

  (iv) failing adequately or at all to provide the Plaintiff with information on:

    (1) the risks to his health and safety that were or should have been identified by the risk assessment hereinbefore referred to at paragraph (i) above;

    (2) the identified necessary preventative and

protective measures hereinbefore referred to at paragraph (ii) above (as was the Defendant's duty under Regulation 8);

(v) failing to provide the Plaintiff with any or with any adequate health and safety training (as was the Defendant's duty under Regulation 11).

B. If the said machine first came into use prior to 1st January 1993

(a) In breach of Regulation 9(1) of the Abrasive Wheels Regulations 1970 and/or negligently failing to train the Plaintiff in accordance with the Schedule of the said Regulations.

(b) In breach of Regulation 10 of the Abrasive Wheels Regulations 1970 and/or negligently failing to provide and/or keep in position a guard at the said wheel when in motion.

(c) in breach of Regulation 11 of the Abrasive Wheels Regulations 1970 and/or negligently failing to provide and/or maintain a guard which enclosed the whole of the said wheel except such part thereof as is necessarily exposed for the purpose of work being done at the said wheel.

(d) In breach of Regulation 13(i)(a) of the Abrasive Wheels Regulations 1970 and/or negligently failing to properly secure the rest on the said wheel.

(e) In breach of Regulation 15(i)(b) of the Abrasive Wheels Regulations 1970 and/or negligently failing to adjust the rest so as to be as close as practicable to the exposed part of the said wheel.

C. *If the said machine first came into use after 1st January 1993*

(a) In breach of Regulation 11 of the Provision and Use of Work Equipment Regulations 1992 and/or negligently failing to ensure that measures were taken to prevent access to any dangerous part of machinery.
(b) In breach of Regulation 12 of the Provision and Use of Work Equipment Regulations 1992 and/or negligently failing to take measures to ensure that the exposure of the plaintiff to fragments of the grinding wheel being ejected and/or the grinding wheel disintegrating was prevented and/or controlled.
(c) In breach of Regulation 20 of the Provision and Use of Work Equipment Regulations 1992 and/or negligently failing to ensure that the grinding wheel was stable.
(d) In breach of Regulation 24 of the Provision and Use of Work Equipment Regulations 1992 and/or negligently failing to ensure the said machine incorporated appropriate warnings or warning devices.

4 By reason of the facts and matters aforesaid the Plaintiff has suffered personal injury loss and damage.

PARTICULARS OF PERSONAL INJURY

The Plaintiff who was born on the 7th January 1959 attaches a medical report.

PARTICULARS OF SPECIAL DAMAGE

1	Loss of earnings from 24th May 1994 to 21st June 1994 (4 weeks) and continuing at £200 per week	£800.00
2	Travelling and incidental expenses	£ 25.00
	TOTAL	£825.00

AND the Plaintiff claims:

(1) DAMAGES

(2) INTEREST pursuant to Section 35A of the Supreme Court Act 1981.

PARTICULARS

(a) Interest on general damages found to be due from the date of issue of the Summons to the date of judgment or earlier payment at such rate and for such period as the Court shall deem just.

(b) Interest on special damages at the full rate in the special circumstances that the Plaintiff has lost earnings and has incurred expenses which will be irrecoverable from the Defendants until the trial herein.

A COUNSEL

SERVED this 28th day of June 1994 by Black & Blue of McLagan House, 2, The Street, Birmingham B9 7OR.

Solicitors for the Plaintiff.

C.7 Lifting case (pleads Manual Handling Operations Regulations 1992, also relies on the Manual Handling Directive as against a state employer)

IN THE SEVENOAKS COUNTY COURT Case No 492

BETWEEN:

GILLIAN STUBBS Plaintiff

– and –

BILLSHIRE REGIONAL HEALTH AUTHORITY Defendants

PARTICULARS OF CLAIM

1 At all material times the Plaintiff was employed as a nursing auxiliary by the Defendants at their Geriatric Hospital premises, Sevenoaks, in Billshire.

2 The Defendants are an emanation of state on whom the Manual Handling Directive 90/269 and Framework Directive 89/391 are binding.

3 On or about the 13th May 1994 the Plaintiff was engaged with Sister Gregory in endeavouring to move the Defendants' patient Mrs Bloggis who weighed approximately 22 stone and suffered from senile dementia. During the course of this endeavour the Plaintiff's back was injured.

4 On or about the nights of the 11th, 12th and 13th of September 1994 the Plaintiff was engaged inter alia in moving the Defendants' patient Mr Baldman who was extremely heavy together with other heavy patients as a result of which the injury to her back was exacerbated.

5 The said operations were an operation to which the Manual Handling Operations Regulations 1992 applied.

6 The said injury to the Plaintiff's back was caused by the negligence and/or breach of statutory duty of the Defendants, their servants or agents.

PARTICULARS OF NEGLIGENCE

(a) Failing to provide and/or maintain a safe system of work.

(b) Failing to provide any mechanical hoist equipment to move patients.

(c) Failing to provide sufficient numbers of strong staff to move patients.

(d) Failing to heed that the Plaintiff's back was likely to be susceptible after her accident on the 13th May 1984.

(e) Failing to provide and/or maintain a safe place of work for the Plaintiff.

(f) Failing to provide and/or maintain any or any adequate and safe plant and equipment.

(g) The Plaintiff will further rely on the happening of the said injuries as evidence in themselves of the negligence of the Defendants, their servants or agents.

(h) Failing to heed the complaints of the Plaintiff and others about the weight of Mr Baldman and Mrs Bloggis and about the lack of lifting equipment.

(i) The Plaintiff relies on the following failures by the Defendants as negligence.

PARTICULARS OF BREACH OF STATUTORY DUTY

(a) In breach of Regulation 4 of the Manual Handling Operations Regulations 1992 failing to avoid the need for the plaintiff to handle manually the said patients, alternatively if the Defendants prove the said need to have been unavoidable, failing to make a suitable and sufficient assessment of such manual handling in conformity with Schedule 1 of the said Regulations and/or failing to take any or any appropriate steps to reduce the risk of injury to the plaintiff to the lowest practicable level.

(b) To the extent that the duties imposed by Regulation 4 of the Manual Handling Operations Regulations 1992 referred to in (a) are qualified by the words 'reasonably practicable' and to the extent the Defendants prove they fulfilled the duties so qualified, the Plaintiff will rely on the corresponding duties in the Manual Handling Directive 90/269 which are not so qualified, namely Articles 3(1) and (2), and 4.

(c) In breach of Article 3 of the Manual Handling Directive 90/269, failing to use appropriate means, in particular mechanical equipment in order to avoid the need for the plaintiff to handle manually the said patients and/or to reduce the risks of doing so.

(d) In breach of Article 6(2) of the Manual Handling Directive 90/269 and/or Articles 10 and/or 12 of the Framework Directive 89/391, failing to properly train and inform the Plaintiff how to handle patients correctly and the risks to which she was exposed.

(e) In breach of Articles 5(1), and 6 and 9 of the Framework Directive 89/391 failing to ensure the Plaintiff's health and safety at work, and/or failing to take the necessary measures to prevent, avoid, evaluate and combat the risk to the Plaintiff.

(f) In breach of Article 6(3)b of the Framework Directive 89/391 failing to take into account the Plaintiff's unsuitability (pursuant to Article 5 and Annex II of the Manual Handling Directive 90/269) to manually handling patients by reason of her small stature and build.

(g) In breach of Article 11 of the Framework Directive 89/391 and Article 7 of the Manual Handling Directive 90/269 failing to consult the Plaintiff and/or her union representative and/or failing to allow them to participate in discussions in relation to patient handling by nursing staff, in particular geriatric patient handling at residential homes.

5 By reason of the facts and matters aforesaid the Plaintiff has suffered personal injury, loss and damage.

PARTICULARS OF PERSONAL INJURY

The Plaintiff who was born on the 14th June 1950 sustained injuries to her back, pain and shock and she continues to suffer. She is handicapped on the labour market. A medical report is attached.

PARTICULARS OF SPECIAL DAMAGE

A Schedule is attached.

AND the Plaintiff claims:

(1) DAMAGES in excess of £5,000

(2) INTEREST pursuant to Section 69 of the County Courts Act 1984.

PARTICULARS

(a) Interest on general damages found to be due from the date of issue of the Summons to the date of judgment or earlier payment at such rate and for such period as the Court shall deem just.

(b) Interest on special damages at the full rate in the special circumstances that the Plaintiff has lost earnings and has incurred expenses which will be irrecoverable from the Defendants until the trial herein.

A COUNSEL

Dated 2nd October 1994 by Grey, Green & Co of 142 London Road, Sevenoaks, Billshire.

Solicitors for the Plaintiff who will accept service of all proceedings on her behalf at the above address.

To: the District Judge and to the Defendants.

C.8 Workplace Regulations case to which Factories Act 1961 ss28 and 29 no longer apply

IN THE BROMLEY COUNTY COURT Case No. 579

BETWEEN:

ERNESTO GARRY MANSFIELD Plaintiff

– and –

HARPERS LAMINATORS LIMITED Defendants

PARTICULARS OF CLAIM

1 At all material times the Plaintiff was employed as a production worker by the Defendants at their premises at Iveston Industrial Estate, Leadgate, Consett, in the County of Durham and the Plaintiff was a lawful visitor thereto.

2 The said premises were and still are a factory within the meaning of the Factories Act 1961 and to which the provisions of the Workplace, Health, Safety and Welfare Regulations 1992 applied. In about February 1993 the said premises were modified by creation of the opening referred to in paragraph 3 below.

3 On 10 February 1993 at approximately 11.50 hours the Plaintiff, in the course of his employment at the said premises, was assisting with the transfer of a quantity of laminate sheets on a frame from unit 3 to unit 2 when whilst pushing the frame through a crude opening made in the wall between the two units, the left front wheel of the frame buckled causing the laminate sheets and the support bar of the frame to drop onto the Plaintiff's right leg, causing him to sustain injury and suffering, loss and damage. The said operation was one to which the Manual Handling Operations Regulations 1992 applied.

4 The Plaintiff's said injuries, loss and damage were caused by the Defendants' breach of their statutory duty and/or negligence.

PARTICULARS OF BREACH OF STATUTORY DUTY

The Defendants:

(a) Failed to provide a suitable system of maintenance of the frame as required by Regulation 5(2) of the Workplace, Health, Safety and Welfare Regulations 1992;

(b) Failed to heed and/or act upon the Workplace (Health, Safety and Welfare) Regulations 1992, Regulation 12 in that the surface of the floor between units 2 and 3 was unsuitable because it was uneven and not smooth;

(c) Failed to provide suitable work equipment for carrying the said laminate sheets, as required by the Provision and Use of Work Equipment Regulations 1992, Regulation 5;

(d) Failed to maintain the said frame adequately as required by the Provision and Use of Work Equipment Regulations 1992, Regulation 6;

(e) Since working with the defective frame involved a specific risk, failed to ensure that the Plaintiff was designated and trained for the purpose as required by the Provision and Use of Work Equipment Regulations 1992, Regulation 7;

(f) Failed to provide any or any adequate information and instructions as required by the Provision and Use of Work Equipment Regulations 1992, Regulation 8;

(g) Failed to provide any or any adequate training in the use of the said frame contrary to the Provision and Use of Work Equipment Regulations 1992, Regulation 9;

(h) Caused and/or permitted and/or required the Plaintiff to undertake a manual handling operation which involved a risk of injury, contrary to the Manual Handling Operations Regulations 1992, Regulation 4(1)(a);

(i) Alternatively, failed to carry out an assessment of risk of the manual handling operation, contrary to the Manual Handling Operations Regulations 1992, Regulation 4(1)(b)(i);

(j) Failed to reduce the risk of injury or attempt to do so as required by the Manual Handling Operations Regulations 1992, Regulation 4(1)(b)(ii);

(k) Failed to provide information as required by the Manual Handling Operations Regulations 1992, Regulation 4(1)(b)(iii).

PARTICULARS OF NEGLIGENCE

The Plaintiff repeats the allegations of breach of statutory duty and further that the Defendants were negligent in that they, their servants and/or agents:

(a) Failed to heed and/or act upon a prior oral complaint made by Mr Neil Robinson to Mr William Curry about a faulty weld on a similar frame;

(b) Failed to examine, inspect, repair and/or maintain the said frame adequately and/or at all prior to the Plaintiff's accident;

(c) Failed to make good the floor at the base of the said wall, or in any way ensure that the said section of floor was reinstated adequately and/or at all and was smooth and level with the surrounding floor surface;

(d) Failed to examine, inspect, repair and/or maintain the said floor adequately and/or at all;

(e) Failed to mark/rope off or otherwise ensure that the said floor was not accessible;

(f) Failed to provide a safe route for the said frame between units 2 and 3;

(g) Failed to give any or any adequate warning of the said hazards;

(h) Exposed the Plaintiff to a danger or a trap;

(i) Failed to provide a safe place of work;

(j) Failed to provide a safe system of work;

(k) Failed to provide adequate and safe plant and equipment;

(l) Failed to have any adequate care for the Plaintiff's safety and exposed him to an unnecessary risk of injury.

The Plaintiff will rely upon the maxim 'Res ipsa loquitur'.

5 By reason of the matters aforesaid the Plaintiff, who was born on 16th February 1971, has suffered injury, loss and damage.

PARTICULARS OF PERSONAL INJURY

Particulars of the Plaintiff's injuries are set out in the medical report annexed hereto.

PARTICULARS OF SPECIAL DAMAGE

Details of the Plaintiff's claim for special damage are set out in the schedule attached hereto.

6 Further, the Plaintiff claims interest pursuant to section 69 of the County Courts Act 1984 on the amount found to be due to him at such rate and for such period as the Court thinks fit.

AND the Plaintiff claims:

(1) DAMAGES up to and exceeding £5,000

(2) INTEREST pursuant to Section 69 of the County Courts Act 1984.

PARTICULARS

(a) Interest on general damages found to be due from the date of issue of the Writ to the date of judgement or earlier payment at such rate and for such period as the Court shall deem just.

(b) Interest on special damages at the full rate in the special circumstances that the Plaintiff has lost earnings and has incurred expenses which will be irrecoverable from the Defendants until the trial herein.

ANTHONY BROWN

Served this day of 1993 by

Solicitors for the Plaintiff who will accept service or all proceedings on his behalf at the above address.

To: the District Judge and to the Defendants.

C.9 Occupational disease case (pre-1st January 1993)

IN THE IPSWICH COUNTY COURT Case No. 1141

BETWEEN:

MARILYN DAWN Plaintiff

– and –

CHICKEN LIMITED Defendants

PARTICULARS OF CLAIM

1 The Plaintiff was employed as a production worker by the Defendants from about November 1979 at their premises at Dark Road, Ipswich, in Suffolk, a factory within the meaning of the Factories Act 1961.

2 In about February 1990 the Plaintiff contracted tenosynovitis from bagging chickens on a conveyor belt in the packing room. In about September 1990 the Plaintiff recontracted tenosynovitis from cropping, drawing and removing the lungs of chickens in the E.V. Room. In about August 1991, and in September 1992 and in December 1992 the Plaintiff recontracted tenosynovitis from packing chickens in the packing department.

3 The said tenosynovitis was caused by the negligence of the Defendants, their servants or agents.

PARTICULARS OF NEGLIGENCE

(a) In breach of Section 29 of the Factories Act 1961 and/or negligently failing to make and/or keep safe the Plaintiff's place of work.

(b) Causing or permitting the Plaintiff to undertake work involving constant fast and repetitive hand movements for an excessive number of hours continuously, daily and/or weekly.

(c) Failing to enlarge the Plaintiff's jobs so that she was not restricted solely to tasks involving constant fast and repetitive hand movements.

(d) In relation to the tasks required by the Defendants to be done, failing to rotate those tasks sufficiently and/or amongst sufficient jobs and/or sufficiently frequently.

(e) Requiring the Plaintiff to work at too fast a speed and/or failing to provide her with any or any adequate rest periods.

(f) Failing to use power tools to remove chicken 'innards'.

(g) Failing to take any or any reasonable steps to ascertain the Plaintiff's susceptibility to tenosynovitis at the outset of her employment and/or regularly and/or sufficiently often thereafter.

(h) Failing to heed the Plaintiff's visits to the Defendants' nurse at the outset of each said outbreak of tenosynovitis and frequently thereafter complaining of and exhibiting symptoms.

(i) Failing to heed the Plaintiff's absences from work after each said outbreak of tenosynovitis.

(j) On the Plaintiff's return to work after each outbreak of tenosynovitis putting her back on work which involved constant fast and repetitive hand movements.

(k) Failing to take the Plaintiff off work which required constant fast and repetitive hand movements.

(l) Failing to provide and/or maintain proper suitable and adequate training and supervision.

(m) Failing by suitable and adequate training to ensure that the Plaintiff carried out the said job in such a way that the risk of her contracting tenosynovitis was minimised.

(n) Failing to warn the Plaintiff adequately or at all of the danger of contracting tenosynovitis.

(o) Failing to properly treat the Plaintiff's condition.

(p) Failing to heed the fact that many of the Defendants' employees including the Plaintiff had developed tenosynovitis.

(q) Failing on many occasions to heed the fact that many of the Defendants' employees had complained of tenosynovitis and/or symptoms in their hands, wrists and arms and/or that these symptoms were caused by their work.

(r) Failing to heed and/or enquire into the prevalance of tenosynovitis in the poultry processing industry.

(s) Failing to provide and/or maintain a safe system of work.

(t) The Plaintiff will further rely on the said outbreaks of tenosynovitis as evidence in itself of the negligence of the Defendants, their servants or agents.

(u) Failing to heed the requests for job rotation proposed by the shop stewards.

(v) Failing to warn the Plaintiff in time, adequately or at all of the dangers of the work and the seriousness of the potential injuries she might suffer by undertaking or continuing the work.

(w) (i) Failing to maintain an adequate system of keeping, inspecting and considering hand, wrist and arm injury records.

(ii) Failing to maintain such records over as long a period as possible.

(iii) Destroying such records after four years.

4 By reason of the facts and matters aforesaid the Plaintiff has suffered personal injury, loss and damage.

PARTICULARS OF PERSONAL INJURY

The Plaintiff who was born on 4th February 1961 suffered pain and swelling in her wrist. The condition recurred as pleaded. She has been treated by a variety of means. She may require surgical intervention. If she continues her work her condition may become chronic and untreatable. She continues to suffer from pain and discomfort in the wrist. She has difficulty with fine movements and in carrying heavy objects such as shopping. She has difficulty in carrying out her domestic work. She cannot wash, wring out or hang up clothing. Sexual relations are interfered with. She cannot knit and dressmake as before. She has difficulty in doing her hair. She is handicapped on the labour market and she continues to suffer. Please see attached medical report.

PARTICULARS OF SPECIAL DAMAGE

A Schedule is attached.

AND the Plaintiff claims:

(1) DAMAGES in excess of £5,000

(2) INTEREST pursuant to Section 69 of the County Courts Act 1984.

PARTICULARS

(a) Interest on general damages found to be due from the date of issue of the Summons to the date of judgment or earlier payment at such rate and for such period as the Court shall deem just.

(b) Interest on special damages at the full rate in the special circumstances that the Plaintiff has lost earnings and has incurred expenses which will be irrecoverable from the Defendants until the trial herein.

A COUNSEL

Dated 4th July 1994 by Grey, White and Partners of 1, The Place, Burchill, Surrey.

To: the District Judge and the Defendants.

C.10 Road accident

IN THE GOSCOTE COUNTY COURT Case No 419

BETWEEN:

RICHARD HARRIS Plaintiff

– and –

MR S M PATCH Defendant

PARTICULARS OF CLAIM

1 On or about 11th November 1993 the Plaintiff was riding his bicycle along the A607 Melton Road towards East Goscote in Leicestershire when as he rode past the mount of Chestnut Way, he was struck by a car, registration number NPO 270R, driven out of Chestnut Way by the Defendant.

2 The said accident was caused by the negligence of the Defendant.

PARTICULARS OF NEGLIGENCE

(a) Failing to keep any or any proper lookout.

(b) Failing to observe or heed in time adequately or at all the Plaintiff, his bicycle, the bicycle's lamps, the signs, markings and layout of the mouth of Chestnut Way.

(c) Driving from a minor into a major road when it was unsafe to do so.

(d) Driving too fast.

(e) Failing to warn the Plaintiff in time adequately or at all of the movements of the Defendant's car.

(f) Failing to stop at the mouth of Chestnut Way.

(g) Failing to accord precedence to the Plaintiff.

(h) Failing to stop, slow down, swerve, or so to manage or control the Defendant's car so as to avoid the accident.

(i) The Plaintiff will further rely on the happening of the said accident as evidence in itself of the negligence of the Defendant.

(j) The Plaintiff will further rely on the Defendant's conviction of Driving Without Due Care and Attention on the 2nd April 1994 at the Leicester County Magistrates' Court as evidence of the negligence of the Defendant. The said conviction arises out of and is relevant to the issues in this action.

3 By reason of the facts and matters aforesaid the Plaintiff has suffered personal injury, loss and damage.

PARTICULARS OF PERSONAL INJURY

The Plaintiff was born on the 28th April 1947. He will be handicapped on the labour market. Two medical reports are attached.

PARTICULARS OF SPECIAL DAMAGE

A Schedule is attached.

AND the Plaintiff claims:

(1) DAMAGES in excess of £5,000

(2) INTEREST pursuant to Section 69 of the County Courts Act 1984.

PARTICULARS

(a) Interest on general damages found to be due from the date of issue of the Summons to the date of judgment or earlier payment at such rate and for such period as the Court shall deem just.

(b) Interest on special damages at the full rate in the special circumstances that the Plaintiff has lost earnings and has incurred expenses which will be irrecoverable from the Defendants until the trial herein.

A COUNSEL

Dated etc.

C.11 Road accident, infant, provisional damages

IN THE HIGH COURT OF JUSTICE 1994 D No:
QUEEN'S BENCH DIVISION

(Writ issued on the 14th day of February 1994)

BETWEEN:

CHARLOTTE DAWSON (An infant, suing by her mother and next friend, Christine Dawson) Plaintiff

– and –

TREVOR DAWSON Defendant

STATEMENT OF CLAIM

1 At all material times the plaintiff was a rear seat passenger in a Ford Fiesta motor car registration number E104 KLJ driven by the defendant.

2 On the 4th November 1993 at about 18.00pm the said Fiesta was being driven along the Welling Road, Tamworth when at about 300 yards south of the junction with East Road the Defendant lost control and the car left the road and collided with trees whereby the Plaintiff sustained injury and suffered loss and damage.

3 The Plaintiff's said injuries, loss and damage were caused by the negligence of the defendant:

PARTICULARS OF NEGLIGENCE

The defendant was negligent in that he:

(a) Failed to maintain any or any adequate control of the said motor car;

(b) Drove too fast in the circumstances;

(c) Failed to keep any or any proper look-out;

(d) Failed to brake, swerve, slow down or so manage the said motor car so as to avoid the said collision;

(e) Failed to continue along the said road;

(f) Drove onto the verge and into the trees at the side of the said road;

(g) Failed to have any or any adequate regard for the Plaintiff's safety and exposed her to an unnecesary risk of injury.

The Plaintiff will rely upon the maxim 'res ipsa loquitur' at the trial of this action.

4 By reason of the matters aforesaid the Plaintiff who was born on the 4 August 1990 and who was aged 3 at the date of the said accident, has sustained injury and suffered loss and damage.

PARTICULARS OF INJURY

The Plaintiff sustained multiple severe injuries which included nervous shock, severe pain, loss of her left eye, extensive frontal skull fractures, fractures to her right arm, lacerations to her right hand, and prominent residual scarring. She required numerous and skilled surgical procedures. Her intellect has been altered and she has a growth lag. Prognosis is guarded. She will almost certainly require corrective surgery in the future for bony defects in the skull and facial skeleton. She continues to suffer. She is handicapped upon the open labour market.

The particulars of injury and claim for special damages and future loss do not take into account the chance that at some indefinite time in the future the Plaintiff may as a result of the Defendant's negligence develop a serious deterioration in her physical condition. If she has a further accidental head injury, even if relatively trivial, the effect upon the Plaintiff could be devastating. Further she has an increased chance of suffering from epilepsy.

In the event of an award of provisional damages being refused, the Plaintiff will contend that such chance of further disability includes a risk of a further head injury occuring and a 10% chance of her suffering from epilepsy. If the former occurred, the effects upon the Plaintiff would be devastating; if the latter, she would be epiliptic. A preliminary medical report is attached.

PARTICULARS OF SPECIAL DAMAGE

Please see attached schedule.

5 Further the Plaintiff claims interest pursuant to section 35A of the Supreme Court Act 1981 on the amount found to be due to her at such rate and for such period as the Court thinks fit.

AND the Plaintiff claims:

(1) DAMAGES on the assumption that the Plaintiff will not at a future date as a result of the act or omission giving rise to the cause of action develop the condition of severe brain damage and/or epilepsy which would severely increase the Plaintiff's present disability;

(2) AN ORDER for the award of provisional damages (under section 32A of the Supreme Court Act 1981) so that if at a future date the Plaintiff develops such conditions, she shall be entitled to apply for further damages;

(3) INTEREST pursuant to Section 35A of the Supreme Court Act 1981.

PARTICULARS

(a) Interest on general damages found to be due from the date of the Summons to the date of judgement or earlier payment at such rate and for such period as the Court shall deem just;

(b) Interest on special damages found to be due at the full rate in the special circumstances that the Plaintiff has incurred expenses which will be irrecoverable from the Defendants until the trial herein.

A. HACK

Served the day of 1992 by Child, Brain & Partners, Balfour Street, London WC1.

Solicitors for the Plaintiff.

C.12 Tripping case (against utility)

IN THE BOW COUNTY COURT Case No 712

BETWEEN:

SEAN KELLY Plaintiff

– and –

TOWER GAS BOARD Defendants

PARTICULARS OF CLAIM

1 On or about 6th April 1994 the Plaintiff was walking to his home at 394 Hackney Road, Bethnal Green, London E2, when his foot slipped on a piece of loose rubble at the edge of a hole which had been dug by the Defendants, their servants or agents, and was situated in the pavement outside the said house causing the Plaintiff to fall to the ground.

2 The said accident was caused by the breach of statutory duty and/or negligence of the Defendants their servants or agents.

PARTICULARS OF BREACH OF STATUTORY DUTY AND/OR NEGLIGENCE

(a) In breach of section 8(1)(a) of the Public Utilities Street Works Act 1950 failing to ensure that the hole and/or rubble was adequately fenced and guarded;

(b) In breach of section 8(1)(e) of the Public Utilities Street Works Act 1950 and/or negligently failing to ensure that the rubble was not carried away;

(c) Failing adequately or at all to fence over, in-fill, or otherwise render the hole and/or rubble safe;

(d) Failing to provide a safe, level, even and continuous surface to the pavement;

(e) Failing to leave the site safe before leaving the same;

(f) Failing to warn the Plaintiff in time adequately or at all of the presence of loose rubble;

(g) Failing to provide and/or maintain safe means of access to the Plaintiff's home;

(h) The Plaintiff will further rely on the happening of the said accident as evidence in itself of the negligence of the Defendants, their servants or agents.

3 By reason of the facts and matters aforesaid the Plaintiff has sustained personal injury, loss and damage.

PARTICULARS OF PERSONAL INJURY

The Plaintiff who was born on 5th August 1914 sustained a broken right femur which was plated under general anaesthetic. He was wheelchair bound for a month and continues to use crutches. He is unable to look after himself and continues to live in a council home which distresses him greatly as does his loss of independence. He experienced pain, shock and continues to suffer. A medical report is attached.

PARTICULARS OF SPECIAL DAMAGE

A schedule is attached

AND the Plaintiff claims:

(1) DAMAGES in excess of £5,000

(2) INTEREST pursuant to Section 69 of the County Courts Act 1984.

PARTICULARS

(a) Interest on general damages found to be due from the date of issue of the Summons to the date of judgment or earlier payment at such rate and for such period as the Court shall deem just.

(b) Interest on special damages at the full rate in the special circumstances that the Plaintiff has lost earnings and has incurred expenses which will be irrecoverable from the Defendants until the trial herein.

A COUNSEL

Dated etc

C.13 Tripping case (against council)

IN THE BLOOMSBURY COUNTY COURT Case No 1243

BETWEEN:

STEPHEN ROCHE Plaintiff

– and –

THE LONDON BOROUGH OF CAMENDOWN Defendants

PARTICULARS OF CLAIM

1 The defendants are and were at all material times the Highway Authority in respect of the highway known as Hazel Street, London NE1.

2 At all material times and in breach of their duty under section 41 of the Highways Act 1980 the defendants failed to repair and/or maintain the said highway properly and/or at all in that the pavement outside the Royalty Hotel had deteriorated leaving therein (inter alia) a hole at least 1 inch in depth measuring 17 inches by 14 inches. The surround of the said hole had broken and was wobbly and unstable.

3 On the 18th February 1994 at about 9.30am the Plaintiff was walking along the said pavement towards Exeter Square when he tripped in the said hole and fell heavily onto the said pavement causing injury, suffering, loss and damage.

4 The Plaintiff's said injuries, loss and damage were caused by the breach of statutory duty and the negligence of the Defendants.

PARTICULARS OF BREACH OF STATUTORY DUTY AND/OR NEGLIGENCE

The Plaintiff repeats the allegations of breach of statutory duty set out in paragraph 2 and further the Defendants were negligent in that they, their servants or agents:

(a) Failed to pack, fill in or cover the said hole or to make the surface of the same smooth and level with the surrounding pavement;

(b) Caused and/or permitted the said hole to grow to such a depth and size that it was dangerous;

(c) Failed to examine, inspect, repair and/or maintain the said pavement which was a hazard, as aforesaid;

(d) Failed to fence off, rope, or otherwise warn against the presence of the said hole, adequately or at all;

(e) Failed to ensure that the said pavement was safe for pedestrians;

(f) In the premises, failed to have any or any adequate regard for the Plaintiff's safety and exposed him to an unnecessary risk of injury.

5 Further and in the further alternative by reason of the matters aforesaid, the Defendants, their servants or agents were guilty of nuisance in that they rendered the use of the said highway dangerous.

6 By reason of the matters aforesaid, the Plaintiff, who was born on the 31st October 1951 and who was aged 42 at the date of the said accident, has sustained injury and suffered loss and damage.

PARTICULARS OF INJURY

See attached medical report.

PARTICULARS OF SPECIAL DAMAGE

See attached schedule.

AND the Plaintiff claims:

(1) DAMAGES up to £5,000.

(2) INTEREST pursuant to Section 69 of the County Courts Act 1984.

PARTICULARS

(a) Interest on general damages found to be due from the date of issue of the Summons to the date of judgment or earlier payment at such rate and for such period as the Court shall deem just.

(b) Interest on special damages at the full rate in the special circumstances that the Plaintiff has lost earnings and has incurred expenses which will be irrecoverable from the Defendants until the trial herein.

A COUNSEL

Dated etc

C.14 Animal injuries case

IN THE RUGBY COUNTY COURT CASE No 1234

BETWEEN:

ANDREW JACKSON Plaintiff

– and –

H ISLOP (Male) Defendant

PARTICULARS OF CLAIM

1 At all material times the Plaintiff was a pedestrian and the Defendant was the owner and the keeper of a tan-coloured mongrel dog.

2 The said dog was permitted to roam loose on the public highway and at about 4.45pm on the 27th day of February 1994 the said dog was roaming in Howl Road, Rugby in the County of Warwickshire.

3 The said dog constituted a danger to road-users and as the Plaintiff passed the said dog it attacked and bit the Plaintiff.

4 The said dog was of a fierce and mischievous nature, and accustomed to attack and bite mankind, and the Defendant wrongfully kept the said dog, well knowing that it was of such fierce and mischievous nature and so accustomed.

PARTICULARS

5 (a) The dog attacked John Eddison on 3rd August 1993 in Howl Road;

(b) the dog attacked PC Robert Owen on 14th November 1993 in Howl Road.

6 At the trial of this action, the Plaintiff will rely upon the following convictions of the Defendant, pursuant to the Civil Evidence Act 1968. On the 25th day of May 1994 at Rugby Magistrates' Court, the Defendant was convicted of four offences of causing the said dog to be upon a road without being held on a lead.

7 In consequence of the matters aforesaid, the Plaintiff, who was born on 6th July 1970, sustained injury and suffered loss and damage as hereinafter set out.

PARTICULARS OF INJURY

Please see attached medical report.

PARTICULARS OF SPECIAL DAMAGE

Please see attached schedule of special damages.

8 Further the Plaintiff claims interest pursuant to Section 69 of the County Courts Act 1984 on the amount found to be due to him at such rate and for such period as the court thinks fit.

AND the Plaintiff claims:

(1) DAMAGES in excess of £5,000

(2) INTEREST pursuant to Section 69 of the County Courts Act 1984.

PARTICULARS

(a) Interest on general damages found to be due from the date of issue of the Summons to the date of judgment or earlier payment at such rate and for such period as the Court shall deem just.

(b) Interest on special damages at the full rate in the special circumstances that the Plaintiff has lost earnings and has incurred expenses which will be irrecoverable from the Defendants until the trial herein.

PHILIP BRIEF

DATED the 28th day of May, 1994 by Grey, Green & Co, of Mansfield House, Rugby Road, Rugby.

Solicitors for the Plaintiff who will accept service of all proceedings on his behalf at the above address.

To: The District Judge and to the Defendants.

C.15 Fatal accident (industrial disease)

IN THE HIGH COURT OF JUSTICE 1993 F. No. 716
QUEEN'S BENCH DIVISION
Writ issued the 14th November 1993

BETWEEN:

JAYNE ANN FLEMING
(Widow and Executrix of
the estate of Ray Fleming,
deceased) Plaintiff

– and –

SOOT, ASH, SMOKE AND COMPANY LIMITED
Defendants

STATEMENT OF CLAIM

1 The Plaintiff is the widow and executrix of the Estate of Ray Fleming, deceased, who died on the 22nd day of March 1993, probate of whose will was granted to her out of the Bournemouth Probate Registry on the 16th day of June 1993, and she brings this action for the benefit of the estate of the deceased pursuant to the Law Reform (Miscellaneous Provisions) Act 1934 and for the benefit of the dependents of the deceased, pursuant to the Fatal Accidents Act 1976.

2 The deceased was born on the 10th July 1938.

3 The deceased's employment history was as follows:

(i) 1953–54	Apprentice moulder, employed by Ivor and Chalk Ltd of Rochester.
(ii) 1954–57	Shear operator, employed by the Defendants or their predecessors in title, in Erith.
(iii) 1957–59	National Service in the army. Rifleman.
(iv) 1959–60	Shear operator, employed by the Defendants at Erith.
(v) 1960–72	Press operator, employed by the Defendants.
(vi) 1972–78	Foreman, employed by the

	Defendants.
(vii) 1978–91	Yard buyer/quality control foreman, employed by the Defendants.
(ix) 1991 on	Employed by Benjamin Franklin Limited in the same capacity.

In none of the aforesaid employments save those with the Defendants was the deceased exposed to the inhalation of asbestos dust and fibre.

4 The provisions of the Factories Act 1937, and thereafter the Factories Act 1961, and Regulations made thereunder applied to the premises occupied by the Defendants in Erith.

5 In the course of his employments with the Defendants the deceased was exposed to the inhalation of airborne dust and fibre, particularly (i) when, as a shear operator, he operated a guillotine to cut old steel pipe-work which was covered in asbestos lagging, usually an inch or two thick, and often greyish white in colour and crumbling, and which he used both to chop off and manually to remove, causing clouds of asbestos dust to be liberated; and when he worked in the vicinity of other shear operators who were engaged in a like task; (ii) when, as a press operator he crushed the doors of old gas or electric cookers, which had incorporated asbestos rope; (iii) when as foreman, he worked overseeing shear machine operators who were engaged in shearing; when, again as foreman, he oversaw the processing of steel pipes and steel materials from the Andrews and Robertson asbestos factory; (iv) when, as yard-buyer he was present when articles containing or lagged with asbestos were accepted by the Defendants for processing (which continued until in or about 1984/85); and (v) when the Andrews and Robertson asbestos factory, which contained pre-formed asbestos sections, was bought by the Defendants and demolished; and (vi) when pockets of asbestos debris which had been sealed or hidden under concrete road slabs at the Defendants' premises were exposed as the slabs were broken up by the passage of lorry traffic across them, and new foundations dug for the roadways.

6 The exposure aforesaid was caused by the negligence and/or breach of statutory duty by the Defendants, their servants or agents

PARTICULARS OF NEGLIGENCE

The Defendants were negligent and/or in breach of their common duty of care under the Occupier's Liability Act 1957 in that they:

(a) caused or permitted the deceased to be exposed to conditions in which the Defendants knew or ought to have known that;

 (i) asbestos was present in visible quantities at or around the machinery and on the materials with which the deceased had to work at their premises; and

 (ii) asbestos dust was injurious to health;

(b) failed to provide the deceased with any or adequate good breathing apparatus or to instruct him adequately or at all to use breathing apparatus whenever he ran the risk of inhaling asbestos dust;

(c) failed to advise and/or insist that the deceased wore a mask or respirator when he ran the risk of inhaling asbestos dust;

(d) failed to provide any sufficient and suitable protective clothing;

(e) failed to lay down any sufficient system or to provide any or adequate equipment to render asbestos dust and fibre harmless to the deceased;

(f) failed to warn the deceased of the known or suspected dangers or asbestos dust (until in or about the mid 1980s);

(g) failed to provide information to the deceased as to the methods that might be used to protect him from inhalation of asbestos dust, and the need to employ them;

(h) failed to provide adequate dust extraction units at their premises and in particular at or beside the shearer guillotines and in those areas where asbestos was forcibly removed from scrap metals;

(i) failed to devise, institute and implement any adequate safe system of work for stripping asbestos dust from old pipework, for removing asbestos debris, and for preventing, minimising or damping down the liberation of asbestos dust into the atmosphere at the deceased's place of work;

(j) failed to make any or proper enquiry or to obtain proper and sufficient expert advice as to:

(i) the known or suspected dangers of asbestos dust and/or

(ii) methods or systems capable of protecting the deceased against contracting asbestos related disease;

(k) continued to employ the deceased in successive tasks which exposed him to the inhalation of asbestos dust and fibre;

(l) caused or permitted the deceased to be exposed thereby to an unnecessary and avoidable risk of physical harm;

PARTICULARS OF BREACH OF STATUTORY DUTY

The Defendants, their servants or agents:

(i) in breach of Section 1 of the Factories Act 1937 failed to remove accumulations of asbestos dust and refuse daily by a suitable method from the deceased's place of work;

(ii) in breach of Section 4 of the Factories Act 1937 and thereafter Section 4 of the Factories Act 1961, failed to make effective and suitable provision for rendering harmless dust injurious to health that was generated in the course of work;

(iii) in breach of Section 47 of the Factories Act 1937 and thereafter Section 63 of the Factories Act 1961, failed to take all practicable measures to protect the deceased against the inhalation of injurious dust and to prevent its accumulation;

(iv) in breach of Section 26 of the Factories Act 1937, and thereafter Section 29 of the Factories Act 1961, failed to provide the deceased with a safe place of work by reason of the facts and matters particularised above;

(v) in breach of Regulation 7 of the Asbestos Regulations 1969, failed to provide, maintain and use equipment producing such an exhaust draught that asbestos did not enter the air of the deceased's place of work;

(vi) in breach of Regulation 8 of the Asbestos Regulations 1969, failed to provide the deceased with respiratory protective equipment and/or protective clothing;

(vii) in breach of Regulation 8 of the Asbestos Regulations 1969, failed to keep walls, floors, ceilings and surfaces clean and free of asbestos dust and waste.

7 By reason of the matters aforesaid, the deceased suffered pain and injury, and contracted a fatal mesothelioma, and he, his estate and dependants have thereby suffered loss and damage and have been put to expense.

PARTICULARS OF INJURY

In about January 1992, the deceased developed pains in his left side, and a persistent dry cough. Bronchoscopy and a thoracotomy were performed in February 1992, revealing a mesothelioma.

The deceased suffered much mental distress on learning of the diagnosis.

Pain increased, with increasing breathlessness and lethargy. Steroid treatment was commenced; but weight loss continued. Sleep was difficult. Special food was needed; and the deceased rapidly became unable to work or to attend to his hobbies of garden and home maintenance or badminton. He became totally dependent upon the Plaintiff for his support and care, whilst at home. In the last month of his life he required in-patient palliative treatment, and had only the prospect of an imminent and painful death to contemplate.

It was a matter of particular distress to the deceased that he would miss the birth of his first grandchild in April 1993.

The deceased declined until his death on 22nd March 1993.

PARTICULARS OF SPECIAL DAMAGE

Please see the Schedule served herewith.

PARTICULARS PURSUANT TO THE FATAL ACCIDENTS ACT 1976

A *Persons for whom this claim is brought*

(i) The Plaintiff, Jayne Ann Fleming, widow of the deceased who was born on the 15th October 1938, and who married the deceased on the 12th July 1961.

B *Nature of the claim*

The deceased was at this death employed by Benjamin Franklin Limited at a gross salary of £21,000 per annum (£15,000 net). He would have remained in employment until retirement age, and would have been entitled to pension thereafter. The Plaintiff was dependent upon his income for her maintenance and support, and her dependency is claimed at two-thirds of the deceased's net income and prospective pension.

C The deceased provided services by way of home, garden and car maintenance, repair and improvement upon which the Plaintiff was dependent. He was a keen DIY worker, attending to all the domestic wallpapering and painting, and to many plumbing and electrical repairs. He had constructed a greenhouse; and regularly mowed the lawn, dug, weeded and planted the garden for an average of some 5 hours per week. The value of his services in these respects will be assessed upon expert evidence at trial, but is unlikely to be less than £1,500 per annum.

D Bereavement: £7,500

E Funeral expenses and headstone: £3,941

8 The Plaintiff claims interest to be assessed pursuant to Section 35A of the Supreme Court Act 1981 for such periods and at such a rate as shall seem just to the Court, and in particular claims to be entitled to interest at full rate upon the sums claimed in respect of bereavement from the date of death of the deceased, and upon funeral expenses from the date of the incurring of those expenses.

AND the Plaintiff claims:

(1) DAMAGES for the benefit of the estate of the deceased, pursuant to the Law Reform (Miscellaneous Provisions) Act 1934;

(2) DAMAGES, pursuant to the Fatal Accidents Act 1976 for the benefit of the dependant of the deceased;

(3) INTEREST to be assessed thereon pursuant to Section 35A of the Supreme Court Act 1981.

BARRY STIRRE

Served this 30th day of November 1992 by Alternative Advocacy & Co, of 17 Riding Street, Bournemouth, Solicitors for the Plaintiff.

C.16 Amended particulars of claim

(Note: underlinings and crossings out should be shown in red)

IN THE SUNDERSET COUNTY COURT Case No 463

BETWEEN:

ROGER FULLER Plaintiff

– and –

SUNDERSET BOROUGH COUNCIL First Defendants

– and –

GREEN EQUIPMENT LIMITED Second Defendants and Third Party

AMENDED PARTICULARS OF CLAIM

1 At all material times the Plaintiff was employed by the First Defendants as a light tractor driver.

2 On or about the 5th August 1993 in the course of his said employment the Plaintiff was driving a John Deere tractor with which he was cutting the grass in Grey Road, Sunderset when the seat of the tractor became detached, throwing the Plaintiff against the back of the tractor and on to the ground.

3 The said John Deere tractor was purchased by the First Defendants from the Second Defendants prior to the said accident.

3 This accident was caused by the negligence of the First and/or Second Defendants, their servants or agents.

PARTICULARS OF NEGLIGENCE

(a) Failing to maintain and/or repair the tractor and/or the tractor seat and/or the bolts/mountings securing the seat in time, sufficiently often, regularly, thoroughly, adequately or at all;

(b) Failing to inspect the tractor and/or the tractor seat and/or the bolts/mountings securing the seat in time, sufficiently often, regularly, thoroughly, adequately or at all and/or to heed the condition thereof in time, adequately or at all;

(c) The tractor seat and/or the bolts/mounting securing the seat was/were defective/loose/worn;

(d) Failing to warn the Plaintiff in time, adequately or at all of the risk of the seat becoming detached from the body of the tractor;

(e) Failing to provide and/or maintain safe and adequate plant and equipment of safe and sound construction and/or design;

(f) Causing, permitting or requiring the Plaintiff to drive the tractor when it was unsafe so to do;

(g) The First Defendants failed ~~Failing~~ to provide and/or maintain a safe system of work;

(h) The First Defendants failed ~~Failing~~ to provide and/or maintain a safe place of work;

(i) The Plaintiff will further rely on the happening of the said accident as evidence of the negligence of the First and/or Second Defendants, their servants or agents.

(j) Failing to provide and/or maintain a safe, secure seat.

(k) The Second Defendants supplied the First Defendant with the tractor defective in the respects referred to above and/or not fit for use and/or not safe and of sufficient strength, construction and design.

(l) As against the First Defendant the Plaintiff will rely on the provisions of the Employer's Liability (Defective Equipment) Act 1969.

4 By reason of the matters aforesaid the Plaintiff suffered pain, injury, loss and damage.

PARTICULARS OF PERSONAL INJURY

The Plaintiff whose date of birth is 11th April 1958 suffered a severe strain to his back and a direct bruise to the right renal region. He has developed increasing low back pain which still continues. He probably has a bulging intervertebral or prolapsed disk. The pain radiates down the front of his right thigh. He has pain in both shoulders. He experiences back pain when driving, turning over in bed, sitting down, coughing, sneezing and first thing in the morning. There is significant restriction of spinal movements and limitation of straight leg raise. In the long term, lumbar spondylosis must be expected with continuing periods away from work for physiotherapy and corsetry. It is possible that his symptoms will deteriorate and he may be subjected to a laminectomy for removal of the offending disc. The Plaintiff had his left leg amputated as a child and in the accident he grazed the stump of his left leg which causes him continuing pain. He has to use a stick. Since the accident he has been unable to play as goalkeeper in football. He experienced pain, suffering and shock. He is handicapped on the labour market. A medical report is appended hereto.

PARTICULARS OF SPECIAL DAMAGE

Loss of earnings from 5.8.93 to 22.3.94;
32 1/2 weeks at £74 per week £2372.50
Due allowance will be made for sickness payments made by the First Defendants to the Plaintiff. Travelling expenses were incurred attending for medical treatment. A fuller schedule will be provided as soon as it is to hand.

AND the Plaintiff claims:

(1) DAMAGES in excess of £5,000

(2) INTEREST pursuant to Section 69 of the County Courts Act 1984.

PARTICULARS

(a) Interest on general damages found to be due from the date of issue of the Summons to the date of judgment or earlier payment at such rate and for such period as the Court shall deem just.

(b) Interest on special damages at the full rate in the special circumstances that the Plaintiff has lost earnings and has incurred expenses which will be irrecoverable from the Defendants until the trial herein.

A COUNSEL

Dated this 24th day of March 1994, by Pink & Co of Hayrick House, Prince's Square, Newcastle under Lyme.

Solicitors for the Plaintiff who will accept service of all proceedings on his behalf.

A COUNSEL

Re-dated this 5th day of June 1994 by Pink & Co, as above.

To: the District Judge and to the Defendants.

C.17 Further and better particulars

IN THE PILSBURY COUNTY COURT Case No. 342

BETWEEN:

CHARLES HILL Plaintiff

– and –

(1) MAURICE STOKES LTD
(2) STOKES & CO plc. Defendants

FURTHER AND BETTER PARTICULARS OF THE PARTICULARS OF CLAIM PURSUANT TO A REQUEST BY THE FIRST DEFENDANT

1 UNDER PARAGRAPH 2

Of: 'At all times material to this action he was contracted to the First Defendants . . .'

REQUEST

Please state whether it is alleged that the contract was written or oral. If the contract was written, please identify the document or documents. If the contract was oral please state its terms.

ANSWER

Oral. All its terms were implied save for pay which was express.

2 UNDER PARAGRAPH 3 PARTICULARS

Of: '(h) Failed to provide a safe system of work.'

REQUEST

(a) State what positive allegations are made against the First Defendants not particularised elsewhere in the Particulars.

(b) State what a safe system would have been.

ANSWER

(a) The First Defendants provided a system which was unsafe and exposed the Plaintiff to the risk of injury.

(b) This is not for the Plaintiff to prove. A safe system would not have exposed him to the risk of injury.

3 UNDER PARAGRAPH 8 (PARTICULARS OF INJURY)

Of: 'For a considerable period of time the Plaintiff required the assistance of his girlfriend to look after him after his discharge by reason whereof her earnings were reduced.'

REQUEST

Please identify the Plaintiff's girlfriend and state the period she is alleged to have looked after the Plaintiff; the nature of the services she provided; the nature of the Plaintiff's girlfriend's work and her normal income (gross and net) and the actual income she received (gross and net) during the period she looked after the Plaintiff.

ANSWER

The Plaintiff's girlfriend is Beverley Belle. She looked after him for 8 months and 5 days. She provided 24-hour-a-day care for him. She previously worked as a section manager. Her net income then was £10,105.26 per annum. She received nothing while off work looking after the Plaintiff.

4 UNDER PARAGRAPH 8 (PARTICULARS OF SPECIAL DAMAGE)

Of: 'Full particulars will be disclosed in the form of a schedule at or after discovery herein . . .'

REQUEST

Please give full particulars of the special damage claimed in accordance with Order 18 Rule 12(1) RSC as amended by the Rules of the Supreme Court (Amendment No 4) 1989.

ANSWER

Schedule herewith.

D. C. FENN

Dated this 22nd day of May 1994 by Greene & Partners of 3 Hiding Place, Whitechaves.

Solicitors for the Plaintiff.

C.18 Reply

IN THE HAROLDWOOD COUNTY COURT Case No 174

BETWEEN:

RICHARD DERMOT Plaintiff

– and –

METALWORKS plc. Defendants

REPLY

1 Save insofar as the same consists of admissions the Plaintiff joins issue with the Defendants on their Defence.

2 The Plaintiff denies that the fact that his cause of action or part thereof arose before 11th December 1988 constitutes a defence to his action herein.

3 The Plaintiff first suffered from a loss of hearing in about 1974 which at that time was slight. In about 1977 he consulted his general practitioner who referred him to Harold Wood Hospital for hearing tests. Following his visit to the said hospital the Plaintiff was given a hearing aid but he was not told that it was connected with his work or that he ought to change his job. In about April 1991 the Plaintiff saw a notice on the board at work to the effect that deafness was an industrial disease for which disablement benefit could be claimed. The Plaintiff then realised that his deafness might have been caused by noise at work as alleged in the Statement of Claim herein and consulted his trade union branch secretary in about May 1991 and made a claim for disablement benefit dated 30th May 1991. Before then the Plaintiff did not appreciate that his deafness was caused by noise at work.

4 In the premises the Plaintiff's date of knowledge within the meaning of section 14 Limitation Act 1980 was a date not earlier than April 1991 and the Plaintiff denies that his cause of action is barred as alleged in paragraph 6 of the Defence or at all.

5 Further and in the alternative if contrary to the Plaintiff's

contention his date of knowledge is held to be prior to 11th December 1988 the Plaintiff will seek the exercise of the Court's discretion pursuant to the provisions of section 33 of the said Act as amended to allow his action to proceed on the grounds that the principal reason for the delay was the Plaintiff's ignorance until April 1991 that his deafness might have been caused by noise at work.

M. T. FENN

Dated etc

C.19 Application for interrogatories

IN THE HIGH COURT OF JUSTICE 1993 A. No. 2937
QUEEN'S BENCH DIVISION

BETWEEN:

TIMOTHY ARNOLD Plaintiff

– and –

MORESBY & SON LTD Defendants

TAKE NOTICE that the above named Plaintiff intends to apply at the hearing of the Summons for Directions herein for an Order:

> That the Plaintiff be at liberty to serve on the Defendants Interrogatories in writing specified in the Schedule hereto and that the said Defendants, through their servant or agent one Jack Moresby, do within 28 days answer the questions in writing by Affidavit.

SCHEDULE OF INTERROGATORIES

1 Are persons employed on the premises in manual labour?
2 If the answer to interrogatory 1 is affirmative, are they employed in manual labour in any process for or incidental to the making of any article?
3 Did F. Bloggs have an accident on the 3rd June 1992?
4 If the answer to interrogatory 3 is in the affirmative, was it a similar accident to the Plaintiff's?
5 If the answer to interrogatory 4 is in the affirmative, was that accident reported in the accident book on the 3rd June 1992?

SERVED this 17th April 1993 by Jones & Co. of 13 High Street, Swansea.

Solicitors for the Plaintiff.

C.20 Interrogatories without an order (re information pursuant to the Management of Health and Safety at Work Regulations 1992)

IN THE MAYOR'S & CITY OF LONDON COURT — Case No. 712

BETWEEN:

TOMMY HANKS — Plaintiff

– and –

ARKLE ENGINEERING LIMITED — Defendants

INTERROGATORIES DELIVERED PURSUANT TO CCR ORDER 14 RULE 11

The Defendants are required to answer the following interrogatories by their Company Secretary or other appropriate Officer upon Affidavit within 28 days.

1 Has the Defendant company carried out a risk assessment of the risks to health and safety of its employees pursuant to the Management of Health and Safety at Work Regulations 1992?

2 If the answer to interrogatory 1 is in the affirmative, when was the assessment and/or the review assessment?

3 Has the work that the Plaintiff was doing at the time of his/her accident been assessed?

4 If the answer to interrogatory 3 is in the affirmative, when was the assessment and/or the review assessment?

5 If the answer to interrogatory 3 is in the affirmative, were any steps taken to improve health and safety as a result of the assessment?

6 If the answer to Interrogatory No 5 is in the affirmative, what steps were taken and when?

7 If the answer to Interrogatory No 3 is in the affirmative, were

any such and if so which steps considered but rejected upon the grounds of reasonable practicability?

8 If the answer to Interrogatory No 7 is in the affirmative, in relation to each step rejected what were the precise factors taken into consideration which led to rejection?

9 Has any assessment taken place since the Plaintiff's accident?

10 If the answer to Interrogatory No 9 is in the affirmative, what steps have been taken to improve health and safety?

11 If the answer to Interrogatory No 9 is in the affirmative, were any such steps considered but rejected upon the grounds of reasonable practicability?

12 If the answer to Interrogatory No 11 is in the affirmative, in relation to each step rejected what were the precise factors taken into consideration which led to rejection?

13 On 19th May 1993, the date of the Plaintiff's accident, did the Defendant Company employ more than 5 employees?

14 Was anyone, prior to the Plaintiff's accident, appointed to provide health and safety assistance by the Defendant Company?

15 If the answer to Interrogatory No 14 is in the affirmative, when was this done and who was so appointed?

16 Was any health surveillance provided by the Defendant Company to its employees?

17 If the answer to Interrogatory No 16 is in the affirmative, what surveillance was provided?

18 If the answer to Interrogatory No 16 is in the affirmative, what were the results of the surveillance with respect to the Plaintiff, his place of work and the work carried out by him?

19 Were any appropriate procedures in the event of serious and imminent danger to persons at work for the Defendants established prior to the Plaintiff's accident?

20 If the answer to Interrogatory No 19 is in the affirmative, were

any competent persons nominated to implement those procedures prior to the Plaintiff's accident?

21 If the answers to either or both interrogatories Nos 19 and 20 are in the affirmative, was any information provided to Plaintiff prior to his accident on:

(a) the risks to his or her health and safety identified by the assessment (if any)?

(b) preventive and protective measures identified by the assessment?

(c) the procedures (if any) identified in the event of serious and imminent danger?

(d) the nominated competent person (if any) to implement these procedures?

(e) other risks to his or her health and safety not dealt with in answer to (a) above?

22 Was any health and safety training provided to the Plaintiff?

23 If the answer to the previous interrogatory is in the affirmative when was this training given?

A party on whom Interrogatories without Order are served may, within 14 days of the service of the Interrogatories, apply to the Court for the Interrogatories to be varied or withdrawn and on any such application the Court may make such Order as it thinks fit (including an Order that the Party who served the Interrogatories shall not serve further Interrgatories without order).

Served the 1st day of May 1994 by Tinker, Taylor Soldier & Co, 55 Middlemarch, Tottenham, Solicitor for the Plaintiff.

C.21 Schedule of damages appended to Particulars of claim

IN THE MAIDSTONE COUNTY COURT — Case No. 765

BETWEEN:

JOHN SMITH	Plaintiff
– and –	
LONG DISTANCE HAULIERS LTD	Defendants

SCHEDULE OF DAMAGES

Medical treatment For 13 wks prior to accident *4.2.90–29.4.90*			£43.10
Gross pay			£6,227.59
Tax @ 25%		£1,387.68	
NIC @ 9%		£323.04	£1,710.72
			£4,516.87
=Ave. wkly net earnings =£4516.87 ÷ 13 =			£347.45
For period *4.5.90–1.6.90 (5 wks)*			
Expected earnings The Plaintiff was off work for 5 weeks 5 × 347.45 =			£1,737.25
Actual earnings			
Gross		£820.68	
Tax	£28.40		
NIC	£60.04		
SSP	£199.50		
Industrial SP	£172.21		
		£460.15	
			£360.53
Net loss of earnings			£1,376.72

(Interest: to be calculated when date of trial known).

Total special damage	£1,419.82

9.1.93

APPENDIX A TO SCHEDULE OF SPECIAL DAMAGE

Pre-accident earnings 4.2.90–29.4.90

	Gross	Tax	NIC
4.2.90	390.80	76.50	26.24
11.2.90	488.49	101.88	26.24
18.2.90	488.49	101.88	26.24
25.2.90	488.49	101.88	26.24
4.3.90	21.25	nil	nil
11.3.90	586.20	140.68	26.24
18.3.90	488.49	101.88	26.24
25.3.90	391.26	76.76	26.24
1.4.90	578.44	137.88	26.24
8.4.90	576.69	137.08	28.28
15.4.90	561.39	131.09	28.28
22.4.90	645.11	164.69	28.28
29.4.90	522.49	115.48	28.28
	6227.59	1387.68	323.04

Gross =	6227.59
Tax =	(1387.68)
NIC =	(323.04)
Net	£4,516.87

= net earnings per week = £347.45

APPENDIX B TO SCHEDULE OF SPECIAL DAMAGE

Post-accident earnings 4.5.90–1.6.90

	Gross	Tax	NIC	ISP	SSP
4.5.90	212.77	(8.11)	15.93	10.13	10.50
11.5.90	126.75	(5.49)	8.19	50.65	52.50
18.5.90	10.50	(30.00)	Nil	Nil	10.50
25.5.90	185.67	23.50	13.49	91.17	94.50
1.6.90	284.99	48.50	22.43	20.26	31.50
Totals	820.68	28.40	60.04	172.71	199.50

Schedules of damages

C.22 Final schedule of damages in serious case

MR PATRICK PYLE

SCHEDULE OF SPECIAL DAMAGE AND FUTURE LOSS

Date of Accident: 1 March 1991

Item number	Head of loss and damage	Sum claimed
1	**Items lost during the accident**	
	(a) The Plaintiff's trousers were damaged beyond repair	40.00
	(b) The Plaintiff's wristwatch was damaged – estimated cost of repair	65.00
		105.00
2	**Prescription charges**	
	(a) As a result of the accident the Plaintiff has had to purchase prescriptions on a regular basis.	
	These are estimated at the sum of £300.00 to date.	300.00
3	**Loss of earnings**	
	Before the accident the Plaintiff was employed as a driver/labourer earning approximately £250 pw gross, £190.94 after deductions for tax and National Insurance. He has not received pay since 10 March 1991. The gross earnings rate has been increased 7% from April 1991 and from April 1992, and 4% from April 1993.	
	Loss of earnings 10/3/91 – 31/3/91 3 weeks at £190.94 pw	£ 572.82
	1/4/91 – 31/3/92 52 weeks at £267.50 gross or £204.30 net	£10,623.60

	1/4/92 – 31/3/93 52 weeks at £286.23 gross or £219.44 net	£11,410.88
	1/4/93 – 13/12/93 36 weeks at £297.67 gross or £227.62 net	£ 8,194.32
	Total	£30,801.62
4	**Total Special Damages** Item 1. £105.00 Item 2. £300.00 Item 3. £30,801.62	
		£31,206.62
5	**Interest on special damages** Interest is claimed at half the special account rate from 1.3.91 to 13.12.93	
	1.3.91–31.3.91 31 days @ 14.25% =	1.21%
	1.4.91–30.9.91 183 days @ 12.00% =	6.02%
	1.10.91–31.1.93 489 days @ 10.25% =	13.72%
	1.2.93–13.12.93 316 days @ 8.00% =	6.93%
	Full rate	27.88%
	Half rate	13.94%
	13.94% × £31,206.62 =	£4,350.97
	Total special damage and interest	£35,557.58

Future loss of earnings

The Plaintiff has not been able to work since the accident.
If he were working in his old job he would be earning £15,478.84 = £11,836.24 net pa

The Plaintiff is now 45 years old. He anticipated working until he was 65. Thus for the remaining 20 years of working life a multiplier of 12 is appropriate[1]

£11,836.24 net pa × 12 = £142,034.88

1 Inclusion of a suggested multiplier is entirely optional, a purely tactical matter (though see *Adamson v Ross* November 1993 Current Law). With the continuing controversy over multipliers inclusion of a multiplier calculated on the higher band is probably useful so as to put the defendants on notice of the existence of yet another factor which puts them at risk. The example given is of a multiplier calculated on the traditional basis.

Because of his injuries the Plaintiff is permanently disabled.		
It is possible that the Plaintiff may be able to work on a part-time basis in light work in the future, following a retraining course.		
The Plaintiff will therefore give credit for the following:		
1 year on government retraining programme at £10 p/w above existing benefits. In the Plaintiff's case there are no existing benefits. Therefore:		
£10 pw for 52 weeks	=	£520.00
Assuming light part-time work after 1 yr's retraining programme based on estimated earning levels of £3.00 – £4.50 per hour. Say 18 hours pw at £3.75 per hour = £67.50 pw or £3,510 pa. Earnings below taxable limit – less NI = £3,398.00 pa.		
The prospects of obtaining such work are not great for a man with the Plaintiff's disadvantages. A multiplier of 9 is appropriate.		
£3,398.00 net pa × 9	=	£ 30,582.00
Total deductions	=	£ 31,102.00
Therefore total future loss	=	£110,932.88
The claim is, therefore:		
Total special damage and interest		£ 35,557.59
Total future loss		£110,932.88
		£146,490.47

(This excludes damages in respect of:

(i) pain, suffering and loss of amenity;
(ii) loss of congenial employment;
(iii) loss of earning capacity;
(iv) interest on the above at 2% p.a.

since the issue of the writ on 14th November 1991.)

DATED etc

C.23 Schedule of damages for interim payment application where child very severely disabled

IN THE HIGH COURT OF JUSTICE
QUEEN'S BENCH DIVISION

BETWEEN:

ALEXANDRA MOORE
(Infant suing by her Mother and Next Friend AVRIL MOORE)
1st Plaintiff

– and –

AVRIL MOORE 2nd Plaintiff

– and –

BRITISH RAIL Defendant

SCHEDULE OF SPECIAL DAMAGE AND FUTURE LOSS SERVED ON BEHALF OF THE PLAINTIFFS' CLAIM FOR AN INTERIM PAYMENT

FIRST PLAINTIFF
(Throughout this Schedule, the First Plaintiff is referred to as 'Alexandra', and her Mother and Next Friend as Mrs Moore).

1 PARENTAL CARE/SUPERVISION
The claim under this head is as follows:

Additional Care:
From 29.4.91 to 31.10.93
(130 wks) @ 45.5 hrs pw @ £3 per hr £17,745.00

Loss of Earnings – Mrs Moore
From 1.5.92 to 31.8.92 – (17½ wks)
Loss of 7 hrs pw @ £4.45 net per hr =
£31.15 net pw £ 545.12

Loss of Earnings – Mr Moore
From 1.9.92 to 31.8.93 – (1 yr)
Difference between salary as a Research
Scientist and grant as a student

	Salary: £16,950 gross pa less tax and NI gives £12,774.00 net pa Less grant of £3,390.00	= £ 9,384.00
	From 1.9.93 to 31.10.93 – (2 mths)	
	Salary as a Researcher (+3%)	
	£17,458 gross pa less tax and NI gives £13,142.00 net pa, ie £1,095.17 net pm	
	2 mths' net loss of earnings	= £ 2,190.34
	Less: *Salary as a Teacher*	
	£13,000 gross pa less tax and NI gives £10,200.00 net pa, ie £850.00 net pm	
	2 mths' net earnings	= £ 1,700.00
	Difference between £2,190.31 and £1,700.00	= £ 490.31
	Plus further 3 yrs' loss of earnings (to likely trial date) on same basis – 3 × annual loss	
	(£13,142,00 – £10,200.00 = £2,942.00)	= £ 8,826.00
		£27,606.43
2	MISCELLANEOUS ADDITIONAL EXPENSES	
	(a) Extra heating costs	
	From 1.9.92 – 31.10.93 (61 wks) @ £7 pw	£ 427.00
	Plus further 3 yrs' costs – 3 × 52 × £7	£ 1,092.00
	(b) Extra washing costs	
	From 1.1.92 to 31.10.93 (93 wks) @ £5 pw	£ 465.00
	Plus further 3 yrs' costs – 3 × 52 × £5	£ 780.00
	Total:	£ 2,764.00

3	TRAVELLING EXPENSES To and from Queen Mary Hospital from house in Peterborough – 1.5.91 to 17.9.92 (72 wks) – average of 3 pw @ 8 miles per trip @ 36p per mile	£ 622.08
4	FUTURE CARE The cost of a nanny would be £11,750.00 pa which for the next 3 yrs would cost	£35,250.00
	The agency costs are: Temporary relief – 6 wks @ £225 pw for 3 yrs	£ 4,050.00
	Cost of taking nanny for 2-wk holiday – £500 for 3 yrs	£ 1,500.00
	Cost of placing Alexandra in care for 2 wks pa £200 for 3 yrs	£ 600.00
		£41,400.00

5 HOUSING AND ASSOCIATED COSTS

(Paragraph 10 of the Affidavit)

The claim is for 2% of £150,000 over the multiplied period of 20 years, being £60,000 together with the expenses of conveyancing and moving, estimated at £5,000

Total: £65,000

6 Aids, Adaptations and Special Equipment

(Reference Report Hart Bellyer of 14.9.93), p&p and VAT not included)

to

Appendix

Page 1	Rifton Adjustable Corner Chair	£ 310.50
Page 2	Spa Controller Chair	£ 480.50
Page 3	Tumbleform Deluxe Floor	£ 104.00
Page 4	Ladderback Chair	£ 85.00
Page 5	Cut Out Table	£ 211.00
Page 6	Computer Work Station	£ 67.50
Page 7	Home Bed Rails	£ 80.00
Page 8	Shelfield Potty Seat	£ 27.20
Page 9	Chailey Toilet Seat	£ 104.24
Page 10	Chiltern 100 Shower Trolley	£1,050.00

Page 11	Alvema Series 8 Pushchair	£ 800.00
Page 12	Physioform Wedge	£ 362.00
Page 13	Prone Standing Frame	£ 262.11
Page 14	Dell Microcomputer etc	£1,500.00
Page 15	Super Pethna	£ 405.80
Page 16	Swing and Seat	£ 115.00
	Boots	£ 420.00
	Physical appliances	£340.00
	Waterproof sheets	£ 5.50
	Computer discs	£ 144.00
	Total . . .	£6,853.55
	+ 25%	£1,713.53
		£8,566.08

7 TRANSPORT

Cost of Nissan Prairie –	£24,215
Less trade-in for present car	£(5,000)
Estimated additional running costs per annum £1,500 × 3	£ 4,500
Total	£23,715

8 TOTAL CLAIM

1	Parental care	£ 27,606.43
2	Additional expenses	£ 2,764.00
3	Travelling expenses	£ 622.08
4	Future Care	£ 41,400.00
5	Housing costs	£ 65,000.00
6	Aids, adaptations etc	£ 8,566.08
7	Transport	£ 23,715.00
	Total	£169,673.59

Dated etc

C.24 Schedule of damages following death of family's breadwinner

IN THE HIGH COURT OF JUSTICE
QUEEN'S BENCH DIVISION

BETWEEN:

LESLEY JOHNSON (Widow and Administratrix of the Estate of WINSTON JOHNSON Deceased)	First Plaintiff
– and –	
NATALIE JOHNSON	Second Plaintiff
– and –	
NORTHERN TRANSPORT	Defendant

SCHEDULE OF DAMAGES

1 Fatal Accidents Act 1976 claim

a) The value of the weekly dependency is put at 75% of an average net weekly wage of £196.80 (during 1990 until the deceased's death on 31st December 1990)

75% of £196.80	£ 147.60
which represents an annual dependency of	£ 7,675.20
To which must be added £300.00 pa loss of the Deceased's services to his family in the form of produce from the family allotment which has now had to be surrendered	£ 7,975.20

Based on the projected increases in the Deceased's rate of earnings (from 1 January 1991) and taking into account the effect of changes in the value of money to the Deceased's projected contribution (including those items which were provided as services by the Deceased), a reasonable percentage increase in the annual dependency would be 5% pa

Pre-trial loss of dependency (calculated to trial on 2nd July 1993)

1991 – 52 wks @ £8,373.96	£ 8,373.96
1992 – 52 wks @ £8,792.66	£ 8,792.66
1993 – 30 wks @ £9,232.96	£ 5,326.32
Total	£22,492.94

Plus interest at half the special account rate over the period ie 15.20%.

applied to £22,492.94 =	£3,418.92
total	£25,911.86

b) Future loss

Based on the age (43 yrs) and future employment prospects of the Deceased an appropriate multiplier would be 12 yrs from date of death, ie 9.5 from date of trial.

The annual value of the dependency in 1993 is £9,232.96 (as before)

9.5 × £9,232.96	£87,713.12

c) Totals

Pre-trial loss	£ 25,911.86
Future loss	£87,713.12
Grand total	£113,624.98

d) Apportionment

i) The dependency of Lesley Johnson the Deceased's widow aged 42 is put at: 33.33% of total — £ 37,871.21

ii) The dependency of Natalie Johnson, aged 12, daughter of the Deceased and the 1st Plaintiff is put at: 29.09% of total — £ 33,053.51

The dependency of Sally Johnson aged 11, daughter of the Deceased and the 1st Plaintiff is put at: 29.09% of total	£ 33,053.51
e) The dependency of Christopher Rose the Deceased's son aged 14, who does not live with the family, is put at: 8.49% of total	£9,646.77
f) Bereavement of the 1st Plaintiff	£ 3,500
Interest thereon at the full Special Account Rate ie 30.4% from 31.12.90 to 21.12.93	£ 1,064.00

2 Law Reform (Miscellaneous Provisions) Act 1934 Claim

i) Special damages

a) Funeral expenses	£1,000.00
Plus interest at the full special investment account rate 30.40%	£ 304.00
totalling	£1,304.00
b) Loss of earnings	
Loss of wages for 4 wks from accident to death 4 × £196.80 = £787.20 Against which credit is given for payment by employer to 1st Plaintiff of £790	£ 0.00

ii) General damages[1]

a) Awareness that his life had been shortened while conscious prior to death say	£1,500.00
Pain and suffering from the date of accident to death say	£1,500.00
TOTAL	£3,000.00

1 It is unusual to quantify the claims for general damages as has been done here under paragraphs 2 and 3. However where counsel feels sure of the valuations and where the figures are needed in what appear to be productive negotiation, it may be sensible to set them out to produce a wholly quantifiable claim.

	Interest at 2% between the date of issue of writ (10th July 1991) until trial, say 2 yrs	£ 120.00
	TOTAL	£3,120.00
iii)	The total sum awardable under the Law Reform (Miscellaneous Provisions) Act 1934 is	
	Special damages	£1,304.0
	General damages	£3,120.00
	TOTAL	£4,424.00

3. Pain and suffering of the 1st and 2nd Plaintiffs in *McLoughlin v O'Brian* claims

First Plaintiff (Widow)	£ 8,000.00
Second Plaintiff (Daughter – Natalie)	£ 2,500.00
TOTAL	£10,500.00
Plus interest at 2% for 2 yrs	£ 420.00
Total general damages	£10,920.00

Dated etc

C.25 Consent of next friend in infant case

[*Heading as in D.1 or D.4 below*]

I of
consent to be next friend to the above-named Plaintiff ,
a minor in this action, and I authorise
Solicitors of to act
on my behalf.

Dated etc Signed......................(Next Friend)

C.26 Certificate of fitness in infant case

[*Heading as in D.1 or D.4 below*]

I of
Solicitor for the Plaintiff certify that I know that the Plaintiff
is an infant and that I believe that the proposed Next
Friend has no interest in this cause adverse
to that of the infant Plaintiff

Dated etc Signed........................(Solicitor)

Jones & Co

D Summonses and applications

D.1 Master's summons (general form)

IN THE HIGH COURT OF JUSTICE 1991 No
QUEEN'S BENCH DIVISION

BETWEEN:

Plaintiff

– and –

Defendant

Master

Let all parties concerned attend the Master in Chambers in Room No , Central Office, Royal Courts of Justice, Strand, London WC2 on day, the day of 19 , at o'clock in the noon, on the hearing of an application on the part of the Plaintiff for an order that

[*body of summons*]

and that the costs of the said application be paid by the Defendant to the Plaintiff.

Dated

To

This Summons was taken out by Wright & Co, 1 Station Road, Harlington, Middx.

Solicitors for the Plaintiff.

D.2 Application for date before a master

Private room application for an appointment before a master

[*Heading as in D.1 above*]

MASTER . . . .

Parties in action . . . .

Type of summons . . . .

Estimated length of hearing . . . .

Dates convenient to all parties . . . .

Dates to be avoided by all parties . . . .

Are counsel attending . . . .

Name of counsel . . . .

Date application made . . . .

Solicitor making application . . . .

D.3 Master's order

[*Heading as in D.1 above*]

Master

Upon hearing

(and upon reading the affidavit of) filed herein,

IT IS ORDERED that

and that the costs of this application be

Dated

D.4 County court application (general form)

IN THE COUNTY COURT Case No

BETWEEN:

Plaintiff

– and –

Defendant

We wish to apply for

[*body of summons*]

Dated

(signed) Grey & Green, 1 Seaview, Bermondsey.

Solicitors for the Plaintiff.

Address for service.

THIS SECTION TO BE COMPLETED BY THE COURT

To the Plaintiff/Defendant

TAKE NOTICE this this application will be heard by the District Judge (Circuit Judge) at
on at o'clock

IF YOU DO NOT ATTEND THE COURT WILL MAKE SUCH ORDER AS IT THINKS FIT

Address all communications to the Chief Clerk AND QUOTE THE ABOVE CASE NUMBER

THE COURT OFFICE AT
is open from 10am to 4pm Monday to Friday.

D.5 Time summons

[*Heading as in D.1 above*]

For an order that:

the Plaintiff have leave to extend the time for service of the Statement of Claim to 14 days from the date hereof.

And that the costs of the application be the Defendant's costs in any event.

D.6 Unless order

[*Heading as in D.1 or D.4 above*]

It is ordered that:

unless the Defendants do serve the Defence within 21 days of the date hereof they be debarred from defending this action with leave to the Plaintiffs to obtain judgment in default damages to be assessed.

And that the costs of the application be the Plaintiff's in any event.

D.7 Summons for interlocutory judgment

[*Heading as in D.1 above*]

For an order that:

1 There be interlocutory judgment in this action;

2 That damages be assessed and costs be taxed.

As above for interlocutory judgment under Order 14 but at the end add:

TAKE NOTICE that a party intending to oppose this application should send to the opposite party or his Solicitor not less than 3 days before the above-mentioned date a copy of any Affidavit intended to be relied upon.

D.8 Application for interlocutory judgment

[*Heading as in D.4 above*]

(The Defendants having failed to comply with the conditions contained in the order in this action made on (*delete if necessary*))

We request you to enter judgment (by default) against

for damages to be assessed and costs and interest.

(We request you to fix a day for the assessment of the damages, the estimated length of hearing is)

Dated

White & Ptners, 1 The Estate, Manor Treeton, Worcs.

Solicitor for the Plaintiff.

Address all correspondence to the Chief Clerk AND QUOTE THE ABOVE CASE NUMBER

The Court Office at

D.9 Consolidation summons and order

Summonses are taken out on both cases with the wording:

FOR an ORDER that actions number 1993 H No 391 and 1993 B No 4061 be consolidated AND that the costs be in the cause.

When consolidation is granted:

[*Title of action on consolidation*]

BETWEEN

ACTION NUMBER 1993 H No 391

JOSEPH HENRY Plaintiff

– and –

MAGNUM plc Defendant

AND

ACTION NUMBER 1993 B No 4061

HUMPHREY GEORGE BLADSTOCK Plaintiff

– and –

MAGNUM plc Defendant

Consolidated by the Order of Master Crump dated the 4th day of December 1993

D.10 Summons or application for split trial

[*Heading as in D.1 or D.4 above*]

For an Order:

1 That the issue of liability in the above matter be tried before the issue of any damages.

2 That there be a trial on damages subject to the Defendant being found liable to the Plaintiff.

3 That the costs of this application be in the cause.

D.11 Summons for directions

Note: only for cases where the automatic directions do not apply.

[Heading as in D.1]

Master in Chambers

Let all parties attend the Master in Chambers in Room No , Royal Courts of Justice, Strand, London WC2 on day the day of 19 at o'clock in the noon on the hearing of an application for directions in this action:

1 Lists of documents be exchanged within 14 days with inspection of the documents within 7 days of the service of the lists.

2 Medical reports as to the Plaintiff's present condition and prognosis be agreed if possible but if not the parties be at liberty to call such medical witnesses limited to two and to those whose reports have been disclosed; disclosure of such reports to be made not later than three months before the date of trial.

3 Other experts' reports be exchanged and be agreed if possible but if not agreed the parties be at liberty to call such expert witnesses limited to two and to those whose reports have been disclosed; disclosure of such reports to be made not later than three months before the date of trial.

4 Mutual and simulataneous exchange of signed statements of witnesses of fact not later than three months before the date of trial. No such witness to be called at trial without leave of the trial judge unless his or her statement has been served in accordance with this direction.

5 The plaintiff do serve an updated schedule of damages not later than two months before the date of trial, the defendant to be at liberty to serve a counter-notice and the plaintiff to be at liberty to serve a supplementary schedule of damages but not later than one month before the trial.

6 Trial. Place – LONDON. Mode – By judge alone. Listing category – B.

7 Estimated length – weeks. To be set down within 56 days.

8 The costs of this application to be costs in the cause.

DATED

TO THE DEFENDANTS

This Summons was issued by Greys & Co, of 14 The Cuttings, East Cheam, Surrey.

Solicitors for the Plaintiff.

D.12 Summons or application to amend terms of automatic directions

[Heading as in D.1 or D.4]

For an order that:

the terms of the automatic directions be varied on the following basis:

1 Experts' reports to be exchanged and agreed within 56 days of the date hereof, each party having leave to call up to three experts providing their reports have been disclosed within the provisions set out herein.

2 Medical experts to be exchanged and agreed within 42 days of the date hereof, each party having leave to call up to four medical experts providing their reports have been disclosed within the provisions set out herein.

3 That the action be set down within 56 days in the judge sitting with a jury list, in London.

And that the costs of the application be costs in the cause.

D.13 Order for inspection

[*Heading as in D.1 or D.4 above*]

It is ordered that:

the Defendants do give the Plaintiffs access to inspect the locus in quo during office hours within 14 days of the date hereof.

And that the costs of the application be the Plaintiff's in any event.

D.14 Application for interim payment

[*Heading as in D.1 or D.4 above*]

We wish to apply for an ORDER THAT:

1 The Defendant do make to the Plaintiff an interim payment in this action.

2 That any such payment be on account of damages which the Defendant may be held to pay to the Plaintiff.

AND that the costs of this application be costs in the cause.

D.15 Summons and affidavit for specific discovery

[*Heading as in D.1 above*]

Let all parties attend the Master in Chambers in Room No 112, Central Office, Royal Courts of Justice, Strand, London on Tuesday 3rd December, 1994 at 11.30 o'clock in the forenoon, on the hearing of an application on the part of the Plaintiff for an order that:

the Defendants do serve upon the Plaintiff a second list of documents containing details of all documents in the following classes:

1 All witness statements made to the Defendants, not in contemplation of these proceedings, following the accident on machine 104 on 13th August 1992.

2 All inspection reports of the machine No 7 for the years 1992 and 1993.

3 All orders, receipts and invoices and correspondence between 1st January 1991 and 17th May 1993 relating to spare parts for or capable of use with the Defendant's machine 7 or similar machines.

4 All notices in writing available to the operators of machine number 7 or machines with similar functions regarding the use of the safety apparatus on the machine.

5 A list of the Plaintiff's gross and net earnings for a 13-week period prior to the Plaintiff's accident on 17th May 1993 and for the period of his absence from work.

And that the documents be served within 14 days and that the costs of the application be the Plaintiff's in any event.

This summons was taken out by Brogan & Co., 286 Long Road, Chatham, Kent.

Solicitors for the Plaintiff.

Paul Smith, 1st, 2 Feb 91, Plt.

IN THE HIGH COURT OF JUSTICE 1993 L No 403
QUEEN'S BENCH DIVISION

Writ issued 14th July 1990

BETWEEN:

J. LIND (male) Plaintiff

and

BOLTCO LIMITED Defendants

AFFIDAVIT OF PAUL SMITH

I Paul Smith of 16 High Street, Chatham, Kent, a Solicitor of the Supreme Court MAKE OATH and state as follows:

1 I am a solicitor in the firm of Brogan and Co of 286 Long Rd, Chatham, Kent and I have the care and conduct of this action on behalf of the Plaintiff. I am authorised by the Plaintiff to make this affidavit in support of the Plaintiff's application for specific discovery of certain documents from the Defendants. All matters set out below are true to the best of my knowledge and belief. Save where I so state I make this Affidavit from matters within my own knowledge.

2 The Plaintiff, Joe Lind, instructs me that he was severely injured at work on the 17th May 1993. It is not in dispute that Mr Lind's employers, the Defendants, operate a factory making plastic bolts at Night Road, Chatham and Mr Lind was a machine operator. At approximately 9.30am Mr Lind tells me he was in the process of opening the machine hood, at the end of a cycle of operation when the flange on the reverberating bolt sheared, causing the retention panel to collapse pouring hot molten plastic onto Mr Lind's lower torso. As a result Mr Lind suffered very serious burn injuries to his legs and feet. He has been unable to return to work since the accident.

3 Proceedings were commenced in the High Court in July 1993 and the Writ and Statement of Claim were served on the Defendants on 21st July 1993. The Defence was served on 3rd October 1993 denying liability.

4 The Plaintiff's List of Documents was served on 5th October 1993 and the Defendants eventually served theirs on 12th December 1993 after I had issued and served a summons to enforce the terms of the Automatic Directions. A copy of the Defendants' List and the summons are now shown and produced to me marked 'PS 1'.

5 On scrutinising the Defendants' List it was apparent that a number of documents were missing. In particular they did not include:

a) Copies of any statements made in the course of a formal investigation which my client tells me took place into a previous similar accident on machine 104 on 13th August 1992.

b) Any of the inspection reports that the Defendants are obliged to keep on the relevant machine, namely No 7. I understand from my client that a six-monthly review of the machine was carried out by the Defendants' engineers.

c) My client tells me that the flange bolt, retention panel and other parts of the machine should be replaced after specified periods regardless of wear and the Defendants' list does not include any orders, receipts, invoices or other correspondence relating to spare parts for this or similar machines since 31st December 1990.

d) Any notices relating to safety apparatus on the machine. My client has discovered that since his accident such a notice has been placed on the wall near the machine.

e) Details of my client's pre-accident earnings and his wage loss since the accident.

6 I verily believe that all the documents referred to are relevant to the issues in this action and that it is likely that the Defendants are in possession of all or some of them. I wrote to the Defendants' solicitors three times asking for them to release these documents to us but have received no response. Copies of my letters are now shown and produced to me marked 'PS 2'.

7 I would therefore ask this Honourable Court to order the Defendants to produce a second list of documents listing the documents in the classes referred to in 5 above.

Sworn by
this day of 19

at

Before me,

A Solicitor

D. 16 Summons and affidavit for pre-action discovery

IN THE HIGH COURT OF JUSTICE 1994 S – No. 5732
QUEEN'S BENCH DIVISION

In the matter of an application under Section 33(2) the Supreme Court Act 1981 and Order 24 rule 7A of the Rules of the Supreme Court

BETWEEN:

YVETTE SMITH Plaintiff

– and –

LIVERPOOL ELECTRICITY plc Defendant

Let Liverpool Electricity plc of Johnson House, 7 High Road, Liverpool attend before Master
In Chambers, Room No , Central Office, Royal Courts of Justice, Strand, London WC2 on day the day of 1994 at o'clock in the forenoon on the hearing of an application by the Plaintiff Yvette Smith of 10 Deans Road, Liverpool for an Order pursuant to s33(1) of the Supreme Court Act 1981 and Order 24 Rule 7A of the Rules of the Supreme Court that the Defendant do make and serve on the Plaintiff a list of documents and file an affidavit certifying such list stating whether any of the following documents:

1 copies of all notes, memoranda, letters, minutes of meetings and discussion papers within Liverpool Electricity plc relating to the discussions prior to the installation of the new Meter System in terms of the dangers of the new Meter system;

2 copies of any internal enquiry report carried out following the accident in question;

3 copies of all records relating to the Plaintiff's account;

are or have been in its possession, custody or power, and if they no longer are, when it parted with the same and what has become of them.

And that the costs of this application may be provided for.

AND let the Defendant within 14 days after service of this summons on him counting the day of service, return the accompanying Acknowledgement of Service to the appropriate court office.

Dated

NOTE: This summons may not be served later than 4 calendar months beginning with the above date unless renewed by order of the court. This summons was taken out by Jones & Co, of 3 Bone Lane, Liverpool.

Solicitors for the Plaintiff.

NOTE: If a Defendant does not attend personally or by his counsel or solicitor at the time and place above-mentioned such order will be made as the Court may think just and expedient.

IMPORTANT

Directions for Acknowledgment of Service are given with the accompanying form.

(*Note: the 'accompanying form' is the standard acknowledgement of service form*).

Jeremy Davis, 1st 3.11.90
On behalf of the Plaintiff

IN THE HIGH COURT OF JUSTICE 1994 S – No. 5732
QUEEN'S BENCH DIVISION

In the matter of an application under Section 33(2) the Supreme Court Act 1981 and Order 24 rule 7A of the Rules of the Supreme Court

BETWEEN:

YVETTE SMITH Plaintiff

– and –

LIVERPOOL ELECTRICITY plc Defendant

AFFIDAVIT OF JEREMY DAVIS

I JEREMY DAVIS of 3 Bone Lane, Liverpool, MAKE OATH and say as follows:

1 I am a solicitor of the Supreme Court and a partner in the firm of Jones & Co. of the above address, who are the solicitors for the Plaintiff. I have the conduct of a claim on behalf of the Plaintiff and am duly authorised to make this affidavit on her behalf.

2 On the grounds hereinafter appearing, the Plaintiff and the Defendant herein are likely to be parties to a subsequent action in the High Court of Justice in which the Plaintiff intends to claim against the Defendant damages in respect of injuries sustained by reason of the negligence and/or breach of statutory duty on the part of the Defendant, his servants or agents.

3 At all material times, the Plaintiff occupied a property at 14 Josling Road, Liverpool. The Plaintiff moved into this property in June 1992. Shortly before this date the Defendant or its servants or agents installed a new electricity meter system into the property. The system required the Plaintiff to attend on one of the Defendants' showrooms where by inserting into a meter a special key together with a sum of money, the key is 'charged'. The key, when inserted into the meter at the Plaintiff's home provides electricity for a period depending upon the amount of money inserted in the meter at the showroom and thus charged upon the key.

4 On the 2nd day of April 1993 at around 4.00 pm the Plaintiff realised that the charge on her meter key was running out. She attended the Defendant's showroom at Bone Lane in Liverpool and charged the key with the sum of £18. On returning to her property she attempted to insert the key into her meter and turn on the electricity. The meter did not register the money charged on the key and the electricity did not come on. The Plaintiff started to walk to a neighbour's flat to attempt to telephone the Defendants' emergency telephone number when she tripped and fell seriously injuring herself.

5 By reason of the matters aforesaid, it is desired and necessary to investigate the circumstances of the said accident to enable me to advise the Plaintiff as to bringing an action against the Defendant for personal injuries and loss and damage and in respect of the injury to the Plaintiff for negligence and/or breach of statutory duty on the part of the Defendant, his servants or agents.

6 It is also desired and necessary to engage a consultant engineer

to inspect the said documents and report on the system the Defendants operated to charge up meter keys and the disclosure of the relevant documents sought herein is likely to be of material importance in preparing the said engineer's report and advising the Plaintiff on bringing the proposed action.

7 I believe that the Defendant has or has at some time had in his possession custody or power the following documents:

a) copies of all notes, memoranda, letters, minutes of meetings and discussion papers within Liverpool Electricity plc relating to the discussions prior to the installation of the new Meter System in terms of the dangers of the new Meter system;

b) copies of any internal enquiry report carried out following the accident in question;

c) copies of all records relating to the Plaintiff's account.

8 The said documents are relevant to the issues likely to arise in the proposed action as to the negligence and or breach of statutory duty on the part of the Defendant, his servant or agents and in particular as to the possibly unsafe system of charging meter keys.

9 Without such documents, the Plaintiff will be seriously prejudiced in preparing her claim in the proposed action in that expert evidence cannot fully or properly be obtained on the negligence and breach of statutory duty on the part of the defendant, his servants or agents and therefore cannot be fully or adequately particularised in her statement of claim.

10 Having regard to all circumstances, I respectfully ask for an order that the Defendant do disclose the said documents in a list of documents (to be verified by Affidavit by the Defendant) as set out in the summons herein.

Sworn

This day of 19

Before me ....
A solicitor

D. 17 Consent order on settlement of action

[Heading as in D. 1 or D. 4 above]

Upon hearing solicitors for both parties and by consent it is hereby agreed that all further proceedings be stayed except to bring the following terms into effect:

1 The Defendants do pay the sum of £10,000 to the Plaintiff in full and final settlement of this claim, such sum to include the interim payment of £3,000 paid by the Defendants to the Plaintiff further to the order dated 16th day of May 1993. The sum of £5,000 paid into court on the 10th day of October 1993 be paid out to the Plaintiff's solicitors forthwith and the balance of £2,000 be paid by the Defendants to the Plaintiff's solicitors within fourteen days of the date hereof.

2 Any interest accrued on the monies in court to be paid out to the Defendants's solicitors forthwith.

3 The Defendants do pay the Plaintiff's costs on the County Court Scale 3 basis, to be taxed if not agreed.

4 That there be leave for the Plaintiff to have his costs taxed under the Legal Aid Acts.

5 That upon payment by the Defendants of the damages and costs set out above they be discharged from any further liability in respect of this action.

E Miscellaneous

E.1 Standard list of documents

[Heading as in D.1 or D.4 above]

The following is a list of the documents relating to the matters in question in this action which are or have been in the possession, custody or power of the above-named Plaintiff and which is served in compliance with Order 24 rule 2.

1 The Plaintiff has in his possession, custody or power the documents relating to the matters in question in this action enumerated in Schedule 1 hereto.

2 The Plaintiff objects to produce the documents enumerated in Part 2 of the said Schedule 1 on the ground that . . . .

3 The Plaintiff has had, but has not now, in his possession, custody or power the documents relating to the matters in question in this action enumerated in Schedule 2 hereto.

4 The documents in the said Schedule 2 were last in the Plaintiff's possession, custody or power on their respective dates of posting.

5 Neither the Plaintiff nor his solicitor nor any other person on his behalf, has now, or ever had, in his possession, custody or power any document of any description whatever relating to any matter in question in this action, other than the documents enumerated in Schedules 1 and 2 hereto.

SCHEDULE 1 – Part 1

Description of document	Date

SCHEDULE 1 – Part 2

Description of document	Date
Statements, notes, letter, memoranda and other communications passing between the Plaintiffs and other witnesses and their solicitors and counsel, brought into existence for the purpose of prosecuting this action. Communications passing between the Plaintiff's solicitors and third parties in relation to the litigation. Communications passing between the client and third parties for the purpose of obtaining legal advice.	

SCHEDULE 2

Dated

NOTICE TO INSPECT

Take notice that the documents in the above list, other than those listed in Part 2 of Schedule 1 (and Schedule 2) may be inspected at
between the hours of 9.30am and 5.00pm by prior appointment.

E.2 Certificate of Readiness

IN THE LAMBETH COUNTY COURT — Case No. 560

EDWARD PETER BOTTOMLEY — Plaintiff

– and –

JOHNSON ENGINEERING MANUFACTURING COMPANY LIMITED — Defendants

CERTIFICATE OF READINESS

As Solicitors for the parties we hereby certify that this case is ready for trial.

1 Liability is not admitted.

2 Medical reports have been exchanged but not agreed. The parties will be calling one medical expert witness each.

3 Experts' reports have been exchanged but not agreed. The parties will be calling one expert engineer each.

4 The Plaintiff's Special Damage Schedule has been served but is not agreed.

5 Estimated length of hearing 1½ days.

Dated this 12th day of June 1992

Edward Smith & Co	Messrs Ford & Michael
10 St David's Square	Haversham Street
London	Southernhay Road
SW3	London, SW3
Solicitors for the Plaintiff	*Solicitors for the Defendants*

Notices

E.3 Notice to admit facts

[*Heading as in D.1 or D.4 above*]

TAKE NOTICE that the Plaintiff in this Action requires the Defendant to admit for the purposes of this Action only the several facts specified below and the Defendant is hereby required to admit the several facts saving all just exceptions as to the admissibility of such facts as evidence in the Action.

Dated

TO: Pink & Co.

Solicitors
for the Defendant

The facts, the admission of which is required, are:

1 Mr James Brown was employed at all material times by the Defendants as their scaffolding foreman at the said premises.

2 Mr James Brown instructed the Plaintiff on or about the morning of 16th July 1993 to climb the scaffolding.

Signed: White, Grey & Partners.
Solicitors for the Plaintiff.

E.4 Notice to admit documents

[*Heading as in D.1 or D.4 above*]

TAKE NOTICE that the Plaintiff in this action proposes to adduce evidence, in addition to the documents contained in his list of documents dated 16th day of May 1993, the several documents hereunder specified and that the same may be inspected by the Defendant, his solicitor or agent at 1 Dartmouth Row London, SE1 on 23rd day of March 1994 between the hours of 9.30am and 5.30pm and that the Defendant is hereby required within 21 days of the service hereof to admit that such of the said documents as are specified to be originals were respectively written, signed or executed as they purport respectively to have been; that such as are specified as copies are true copies; and that such documents as are stated to have been served, sent or delivered were so served, sent or delivered respectively; saving all just exceptions to the admissibility of all such documents as evidence in this cause.

And further take notice that if you do not within the aforementioned 21 days give notice that you do not admit said documents and that you require the same to be proved at the trial you should be deemed to have admitted the said document unless the court or a judge shall otherwise order.

Signed Black & Partners of 1 Dartmouth Row, London, SE1.
Solicitors for the Plaintiff.

To . . . . of . . . . solicitors for the Defendants

The following are the documents above referred to:

Originals

Description of document date

1 Plaintiff's accounts for the financial years 1991/92 and 1992/93.

2 Letter from Inland Revenue to Plaintiff dated 13th July 1990.

E.5 Civil Evidence Act notice

[*Heading as in D.1 or D.4*]

TAKE NOTICE that at the trial of this action the Plaintiff desires to give in evidence the following statement of opinion, namely that the road accident was caused by the negligent driving of the Defendant.

The said statement was recorded in the following document: the police notebook of PC Plod on two pages dated 13th August 1993. A copy of the said document is annexed hereto.

Further take notice that the particulars relating to the said statement are as follows, that it was made:

1) by John Smith orally

2) to PC Peter Plod who recorded it in the said document

3) on the 13th day of August 1993

4) at 13 Dodds Place London E3

5) in the following circumstances: the police officer attended upon Mr Smith at his home at 13 Dodds Place London E3 to obtain a statement from him in pursuance of the investigations into the cause of the accident and wrote down in his notebook what Mr Smith said and, having done so, read it back to Mr Smith who confirmed orally to PC Plod that that which PC Plod had written was accurate and the truth.

And further take notice that the said John Smith cannot be called as a witness at the trial because he died on 30th August 1993.

Dated

E.6 Form PF 200

[*Heading as in D.1 above*]

To all parties

NOTICE OF PROPOSAL TO TRANSFER PROCEEDINGS TO A COUNTY COURT/TO STRIKE OUT PROCEEDINGS

On the day of 19 this action was considered by the judge [master] [district judge].

The judge [master] [district judge] considered that the action falls within the provisions of section 40(1) and (8) of the County Courts Act 1984 and proposes to transfer the action to the County Court/strike out the action unless either you maintain that the case does not fall within those provisions or you object to that particular county court.

If you so maintain and/or object you must file notice of objection in Form No PF201 in the Central Office [or this District Registry]. Notice of objection in Form No PF201 must be filed within 14 days from the date of service of this notice. A copy of the notice of objection should be served on every other party.

If no notice of objection is filed within the time limited this action will be transferred or struck out as proposed.

Dated

E.7 Form PF 201

[*Heading as in D. 1 above*]

To the master [district judge] of [insert Central Office or District Registry as appropriate].

NOTICE OF OBJECTION TO PROPOSED TRANSFER TO A COUNTY COURT/STRIKING OUT

Tick appropriate box

☐ I/we maintain that this action does not fall within the provisions of section 40(1) and (8) of the County Courts Act 1984.

☐ I/we object to the county court proposed in the notice dated (1).

☐ If the action is transferred to a county court, the appropriate court is (2)

County Court.

The reasons why I/we so maintain and/or so object are (*state briefly*)

Dated

Signed

[Solicitor for party objecting/party acting in person]

(1) Insert date of notice

(2) Insert name of county court

E.8 Form PF 202

[*Heading as in D. 1 above*]

To all parties

NOTICE OF PROPOSED TRANSFER TO A COUNTY COURT

On the day of 19 this action was considered by the judge [master] [district judge].

The judge [master] [district judge] proposes pursuant to section 40(2) of the County Courts Act 1984 that this action be transferred to County Court.

If you object to the transfer or transfer to the particular county court proposed above you must file a notice of objection containing reasons in Form No PF203 in the Central Office [or this District Registry]. Notice of objection in Form No PF203 must be filed within 14 days from the date of service of this notice. A copy of the notice of objection must be served on every other party.

If no notice of objection is filed within the time limited this action will be transferred as proposed.

Dated

E.9 Form PF 203

[*Heading as in D. 1 above*]

To the master [district judge] of [insert Central Office or District Registry as appropriate].

NOTICE OF OBJECTION TO PROPOSED TRANSFER TO A COUNTY COURT

Tick appropriate box

☐ I/we object to transfer to a county court.

☐ I/we object to the county court proposed in the notice dated (1)

☐ If the action is transferred to a county court, the appropriate court is (2)

County Court.

The reasons why I/we object are (*state briefly*)

Dated

Signed

[Solicitor for party objecting/party acting in person]

(1) Insert date of notice

(2) Insert name of county court

Witness summonses and subpoenas

E.10 Request for summons in the county court

[*Heading as in D.4 above*]

Date of Hearing: the day of 19

Witness name in full
His or her residence and business or occupation

If documents or books are required to be produced here specify them:

Sum to be paid
or offered to witness £ Fee for summons £

State by whom served: Application made by:

Dated

The certificate overleaf should be completed and signed if service by post is required.

E.11 Summons to witness to attend to give oral evidence and to produce documents

[*Heading as in D.4 above*]

TO

OF

You are summoned to attend at the County Court of on day of at and so from day to day until the hearing of the proceedings is concluded or the court otherwise orders you to give evidence in the above case (and to bring with you and produce the document(s) specified below).

If you fail to attend you will be liable to pay a fine of £400, if at the time this summons was served upon you, you were paid or offered your reasonable expenses of travelling to and from Court together with the prescribed sum as compensation for loss of time.

Sum to be paid to Witness £

Dated

This application was issued on the application of the Plaintiff's solicitor whose name, address and ref number is:

E.12 Subpoena duces tecum at sittings of the High Court

[*Heading as in D.1 above*]

Elizabeth the Second, by the Grace of God, of the United Kingdom of Great Britain and Northern Ireland and of Our other realms and territories Queen, Head of the Commonwealth, Defender of the Faith,

To

WE COMMAND YOU to attend at the Sittings of the Queen's Bench Division of Our High Court of Justice at the Royal Courts of Justice, Strand, London on the day fixed for the trial of the above-named cause, notice of which will be given to you, and from day to day thereafter until the end of the trial, to give evidence on behalf of the Plaintiff.

AND WE ALSO COMMAND YOU to bring with you and produce at the place aforesaid on the day notified to you the following documents

Witness, London High Chancellor of Great Britain

Dated

Issued on the day of 19 by
(Agent for)
Solicitor for the

E.13 Praecipe for subpoena in the High Court

[*Heading as in D.1 above*]

Seal Writ of Subpoena Duces Tecum
for Witnesses
on behalf of the Plaintiff

directed to

returnable

Dated

Signed: White, Grey & Partners

of 3, The Cuttings, East Cheam, Surrey

Solicitors
for the Plaintiff

E.14 Certificate of service of witness summons

[*Heading as in D.4*]]

I CERTIFY THAT the Summons of which this is a true copy was served by me on the within-named personally, at

on the day of 1994 and the sum of £ was at the same time paid (or offered) by me to the said for his expenses and loss of time.

Bailiff/Officer of the Court

Bailiff/Officer at the Court

Case No 94 11761

I CERTIFY THAT the summons of which this is a true copy was served by posting to the witness named
on
at the address stated on the summons in accordance with the certificate of the application or his solicitor, when I enclosed a postal order for £ for his expenses and loss of time.

Officer of the Court

Non-service

I CERTIFY THAT THIS SUMMONS HAS NOT BEEN SERVED FOR THE FOLLOWING REASONS:

Bailiff/Officer of the Court

Judgments

E.15 Standard case

[*Heading as in D.1 above*]

DATED AND ENTERED the 28th day of July 1990.

The ACTION having been tried before the Honourable Mr Justice Harris without a Jury at the Royal Courts of Justice and the said Mr Justice Harris having on the 28th day of March 1994 ordered that judgment as hereinafter provided be entered for the Plaintiff.

IT IS ADJUDGED that the Defendant do pay the Plaintiff £5,611.16 (being as to £1,001.07 for special damages with interest thereon of £510.09 and for General Damages £4,000) with her costs of the action to be taxed if not agreed.

AND IT IS FURTHER DIRECTED that the costs of the Plaintiff be taxed in accordance with the provisions of the Second Schedule to the Legal Aid Act 1974.

The above costs having been taxed and allowed at £ as appears by a Taxing Officer's certificate dated the day of 1994

Signed: Jones & Co. 996 Gray's Inn Road, London WC1.
Solicitors for the Plaintiff.

E.16 Fatal Accidents Act case

[*Heading as in D.1 above*]

DATED AND ENTERED 7th day of April 1994.

This action having been tried before Mr Justice Spleen in London sitting without a jury and the said Mr Justice Spleen having on 7th day of April 1994 ordered judgment as hereinafter provided be entered for the Plaintiff.

It is adjudged that the Defendants do pay to the Plaintiff the sum of £15,000 apportioned in respect of the Law Reform (Miscellaneous Provisions) Act 1934 in the sum of £5,000 and in respect of the Fatal Accidents Act 1976 in the sum of £10,000 such award in respect of the Fatal Accidents Act 1976 to be apportioned on the basis of Joan Smith – £8,000; Thomas Smith (a minor) – £1,000; and Claudia

Smith (a minor) – £1,000 together with the costs of the action to be taxed if not agreed.

The above costs having been taxed and allowed at £ as appears by a Taxing Officer's certificate dated the day of 1994.

Signed: Bloggs & Co of 13 High Street, Dover.
Solicitors for the Plaintiff.

E.17 Notice of appeal – county court

IN THE OXBRIDGE COUNTY COURT Case No. 463

BETWEEN:

JONATHAN SACHS Plaintiff

– and –

FLORABUND LIMITED Defendant

NOTICE OF APPEAL

TAKE NOTICE that the above named plaintiff intends to appeal against the decision of District Judge Strict given on 26th November 1992 ordering that the Plaintiff's application that the Interrogatories served by the Defendant dated 2nd November 1992 be withdrawn or, alternatively, varied, be dismissed and that time for the Plaintiff to reply to Interrogatories be extended to no later than 9th January 1993, Defendant's costs in any event, certificate for Counsel.

AND FURTHER TAKE NOTICE that on the hearing of the said appeal the Plaintiff will seek an Order that:

1 The said decision of District Judge Strict be set aside;

2 The Interrogatories served by the Defendant dated 2nd November 1992 be withdrawn or, alternatively varied;

3 That the costs of and occasioned by the application and appeal be the Plaintiff's in any event.

4 Provision be made for exchange of witness statements.

AND FURTHER TAKE NOTICE that it is the intention of the Plaintiff to attend by Counsel.

Signed Writte & Walters, Solicitors for the Plaintiff
Dated the 10th day of November 1992

Writte & Walters House
High Street
Oxbridge OB1 NN10

THIS SECTION TO BE COMPLETED BY THE COURT

TO THE PLAINTIFF/DEFENDANT

TAKE NOTICE that this application will be heard by the

at

on at o'clock

IF YOU DO NOT ATTEND THE COURT WILL MAKE SUCH ORDER AS IT THINKS FIT

Address all communications to the Chief Clerk AND QUOTE THE ABOVE CASE NUMBER

THE COURT OFFICE AT: The Court House, High Street, Oxbridge OB1 NN9 is open from 10 a.m. to 4 p.m. Monday to Friday.

COUNTY COURT FORM N244

E.18 Notice of appeal – Court of Appeal

In the Court of Appeal on appeal from the High Court of Justice Queen's Bench Division

BETWEEN:

JOHN SMITH Plaintiff

– and –

JOHN DAVIES Defendant

NOTICE OF APPEAL

TAKE NOTICE that the Court of Appeal will be moved as soon as Counsel can be heard on behalf of the above-named Plaintiff on appeal from the judgment hereof of Mr Justice Boon given at the trial of this action on 5th day of March 1994 whereby it was ordered that: judgment be entered for the Plaintiff against the Defendant for the sum of £147,000 with costs

FOR AN ORDER that:

The Plaintiff's said judgment against the Defendant be set aside and that judgment be entered for the Plaintiff against the Defendant in such larger amount that the Court of Appeal thinks fit.

That the Defendant do pay the Plaintiff's costs of the appeal to be taxed if not agreed.

AND FURTHER TAKE NOTICE that the grounds of this appeal are:-

1 The learned judge erred in finding that the Plaintiff was contributorily negligent, in particular in that: the learned judge put undue weight on the Plaintiff's failure to wear a seat belt albeit that this played no part in the injuries sustained.

B Gott
Counsel

Served this 4th day of April 1994.

A B Smith & Co, 7 High Street, London WC1.
Solicitors for the Plaintiff.

To: the Defendant and their solicitors Jones & Co, 7 Low Road, London EC2

No notice as to the date on which this appeal will be in the list for hearing will be given; it is the duty of the solicitors to keep themselves informed as to the state of list. A respondent intending to appear in person should inform the office of the Registrar of Civil Appeals, Royal Courts of Justice, Strand, London WC2 of that fact and give his address; if he does so he will be notified at the address he has given of the date when the appeal is expected to be heard.

Appendix

Addresses

Action for Victims of Medical Negligence (AVMA)
Bank Chambers, 1 London Road, Forest Hill, London SE23 3TP. Telephone 081-291 2793

Association of Personal Injury Lawyers (APIL)
10A Byard Lane, Nottingham NG1 2GJ. Telephone 0602 580585.

Association of Trial Lawyers of America
PO Box 3717, Washington DC 20007, USA. Telephone 0101 202-965 3500.

Compensation Recovery Unit (CRU)
Department of Social Security, Reyrolle Building, Hebburn, Tyne & Wear NE31 1XB. Telephone 091-201 0500.

Criminal Injuries Compensation Authority (CICA)
Tay House, 300 Bath Street, Glasgow G2 4JR. Telephone 041-331 2726; Fax 041-331 2287, 353 3148.

Criminal Injuries Compensation Board (CICB)
Blythwood House, 200 West Regent Street, Glasgow G2 4SW. Telephone 041-221 0945.

General Council of the Bar
3 Bedford Row, London WC1R 4DB. Telephone 071-242 0082; Fax 071-831 9217

Health and Safety Executive (HSE)
HSE Books: PO Box 1999, Sudbury, Suffolk CO10 6FS. Telephone 0787 313995.
HSE Information Centre: Broad Lane, Sheffield S3 7HQ. Telephone 0742 892345; Fax 0742 892333.

Inquest
Ground Floor, Alexandra National House, 330 Seven Sisters Road, London N4 2PJ. Telephone 081–802 7430.

International Paraplegic Claims Service
Robinson's Yard, 7 Cross Lane, Preston, Oakham, Rutland LE15 9NQ. Telephone 0572 85543.

Law Society
113 Chancery Lane, London WC2A 1PL. Telephone 071–242 1222; Fax 071–831 0344.

Motor Insurers Bureau
152 Silbury Boulevard, Central Milton Keynes MK9 1NB. Telephone 0908 240000; Fax 0908 671681.

National Head Injuries Association
7 King Edward Court, King Edward Street, Nottingham NG1 1AW. Telephone 0602 240800.

Spinal Injuries Association
76 St James Lane, London N10 3DF. Telephone 081–444 2121.

Bibliography

Association of Personal Injury Lawyers' Newsletter (see address above)

Bingham and Berrymans, *Motor Claims Cases*, 10th edn, Butterworths, 1993

Deductions from Compensation, DSS, 1990

Duncan and Marsh, *Fatal Accident Claims*, Fourmat, 1993

Goldrein and de Haas, *Butterworth's Personal Injury Litigation Service*, Butterworths (looseleaf)

Gregory (general ed), *The County Court Practice* (Green Book), Butterworths (annual)

Health and Safety Executive, *Watch Your Step: prevention of slipping, tripping and falling accidents at work*, HMSO, 1985

Hendy and Ford (eds), *Redgrave, Fife and Machin's Health and Safety*, Butterworths, 2nd edn 1993

Jacob (general ed), *The Supreme Court Practice* (White Book), Sweet & Maxwell (annual)

Journal of Personal Injury Litigation, Sweet & Maxwell

Judicial Studies Board, *Guidelines for the Assessment of General Damages in Personal Injury Cases*, Blackstone, 1993

Kemp, *Damages for Personal Injury and Death*, Longman, 5th edn 1993

Kemp, *Kemp and Kemp: the quantum of damages*, Sweet & Maxwell (looseleaf)

Legal Aid Board, *Legal Aid Handbook*, Sweet & Maxwell (annual)

Lord Chancellor's Department, *Guide for Use in Group Actions*, LCD, 26–28 Old Queen Street, London SW1H 9HP, 1991

Mullany and Handford, *Tort Liability for Psychiatric Damage*, Law Book Company, 1993

Munkman, *Damages for Personal Injury and Death*, Butterworths, 9th edn 1993

Munkman, *Employers' Liability*, revised by Hendy and Ford, Butterworths, 12th edn 1994

Nelson-Jones and Nuttall, *Tax and Interest Tables*, Fourmat (annual)

Noble, Fanshaw and Hellyer, *Special Damages for Disability*, Sweet & Maxwell, 2nd edn 1988

Personal and Medical Injuries Law Letter, Legal Studies and Services (Publishing), 57–61 Mortimer Street, London W1N 7TD

Personal Injury and Quantum Reports, Sweet & Maxwell

Redmond-Cooper, *Limitation of Actions*, Sweet & Maxwell, 1992

Supreme Court Practice Committee, *Guide for Use in Group Actions*, HMSO, 1991

Index